FROM THE MOST TRUSTED NAME IN TRAVEL

Frommer's®

EASYGUIDE TO AUSTRALIA 2018

5th Edition

Quick to Read · Easy to Carry · For Expert Advice In All Price Ranges

By Lee Mylne

FROMMER'S STAR RATINGS SYSTEM

Every hotel, restaurant, and attraction listed in this guide has been ranked for quality and value. Here's what the stars mean:

★	Recommended
★★	Highly Recommended
★★★	A must! Don't miss!

AN IMPORTANT NOTE

The world is a dynamic place. Hotels change ownership, restaurants hike their prices, museums alter their opening hours, and buses and trains change their routings. And all of this can occur in the several months after our authors have visited, inspected, and written about these hotels, restaurants, museums, and transportation services. Though we have made valiant efforts to keep all our information fresh and up-to-date, some few changes can inevitably occur in the periods before a revised edition of this guidebook is published. So please bear with us if a tiny number of the details in this book have changed. Please also note that we have no responsibility or liability for any inaccuracy or errors or omissions, or for inconvenience, loss, damage, or expenses suffered by anyone as a result of assertions in this guide.

PREVIOUS PAGE: **The Western grey kangaroo, among the largest kangaroo species, can be found across Southern Australian.**
CURRENT PAGE: **A road sign in South Australia warns motorists of camels, wombats, and kangaroos.**

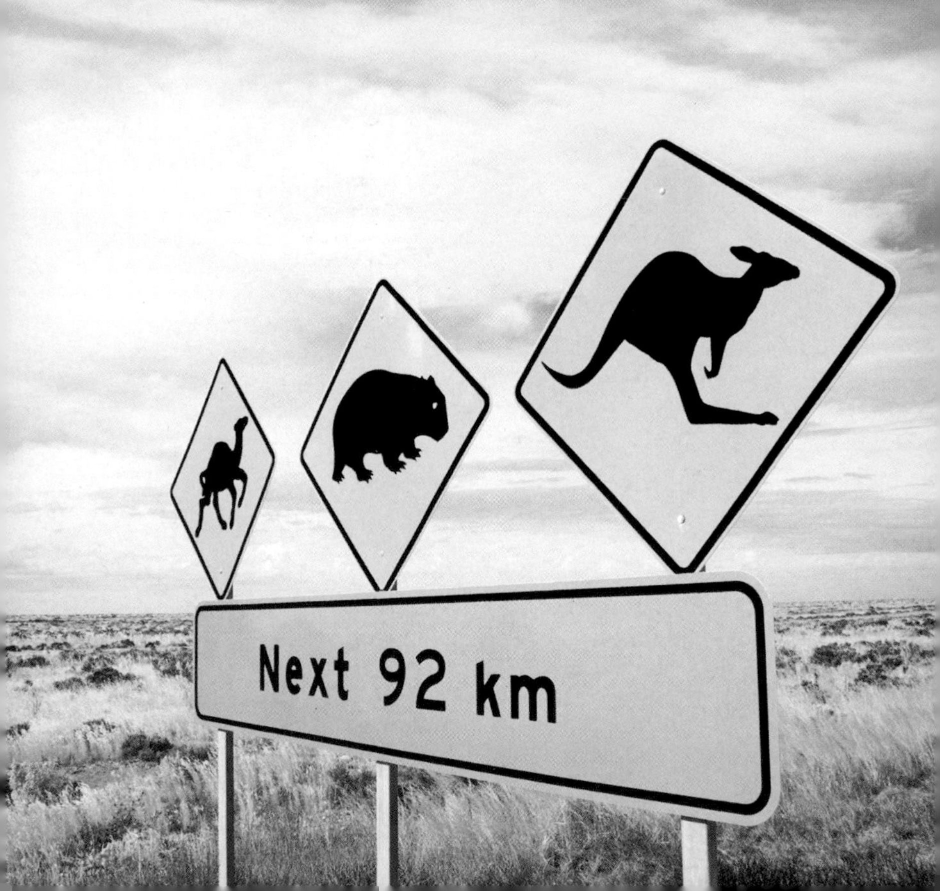

CONTENTS

The Sydney skyline and harbor at night.

A LOOK AT AUSTRALIA

From the rugged Outback with Uluru, the otherworldly monolith sacred to the Aboriginal peoples; to the Great Barrier Reef (the only living structure on earth that can be seen from space); to beaches that extend as far as the eye can see, Australia is custom-made for adventure seekers. But it's also for lovers of innovative cuisine, fine wine, and sophisticated performing arts in Sydney, Melbourne, Brisbane, and beyond. From cuddling koala bears to climbing the Harbour Bridge, educating yourself on the country's fascinating Aboriginal culture, and exploring dynamic, modern cities, our EasyGuide presents the best of a nation of superlatives. So *g'day,* and good journey!

Snorkeling or diving the Great Barrier Reef is tops on the list for many visitors to Australia.

THE BEST OF SYDNEY & MELBOURNE

Completed in 1973, the instantly recognizable Sydney Opera House (p. 85) dominates the harborfront and houses several theaters and concert halls.

Most surf beaches north and south of Sydney Harbour offer shops with board rentals, and group and individual surfing lessons are available. See p. 96.

The monorail glides through downtown, with Sydney Tower, the city's tallest structure, overhead. The tower has a viewing platform, plus a revolving bar and restaurant. See p. 91.

Fresh pasta at Otto Ristorante, Sydney (p. 77).

Several wildlife parks in and near Sydney offer chances to get up close to (and in some cases, even cuddle with) koalas, wombats, and kangaroos. See p. 91.

The Rocks, Sydney's waterfront historic area, is characterized by colonial-era buildings, with boutiques, pubs, restaurants, and exclusive hotels. See p. 78.

On the banks of the Yarra River, Melbourne's Southbank area is known for its restaurants, bars, and public spaces.

Paddy's Markets in Sydney (p. 101) features hundreds of stalls selling everything from cheap clothes to produce to imported gifts.

Melbourne's elaborate, constantly changing graffiti is found on several streets in the city center. Here, an artist tags a wall on Hosier Lane. See p. 132.

Scary and atmospheric Old Melbourne Gaol (p. 134), where the notorious bushranger Ned Kelly was hanged.

Wineries, windswept beaches, gardens, and wildlife make the Mornington Peninsula a popular day trip from Melbourne. See p. 146.

A day trip from Sydney to the Blue Mountains, a UNESCO World Heritage Site, reveals water-falls, spectacular clifftop views, and historic villages. See p. 102.

QUEENSLAND & THE GREAT BARRIER REEF

Much of Brisbane's remaining colonial architecture is centered around Queen Street Mall (p. 172), a shopping and entertainment area known for name-brand and local retailers, plus stylish dining and hotels.

An artificial beach and lagoon, plus shops, cafes, and weekend markets make South Bank Parklands (p. 176) a colorful retreat in Brisbane's city center.

On top of Mount Coot-tha just outside Brisbane, Summit Restaurant focuses on local produce and wines, all served with sweeping views of the city. See p. 171.

A saltwater swimming lagoon, a wide sandy beach, and surrounding parklands make the Esplanade a highlight of a visit to Cairns.

The Tjapukai Culture Park in Kuranda (p. 199) offers a range of immersive Aboriginal experiences, all in a rainforest setting. The Night Fire program features a join-in *corroboree*, or Aboriginal nighttime dance.

The waters off Lady Elliot Island offer snorkeling, diving, and reef walking, as well as the chance to see green and loggerhead turtles, which nest on the beach from November to March. See p. 235.

Though Port Douglas is a stepping-off point for adventures in the rainforest and the Great Barrier Reef, its famous Four Mile Beach (p. 213) tempts visitors to do nothing at all.

During the Australian winter, which runs from June to September, humpback whales pass through the waters of the Great Barrier Reef.

The Whitsundays are a group of more than 70 islands replete with bays, beaches, dazzling coral reefs, fishing spots, and rainforest. Pictured here, Whitehaven Beach (p. 232).

Cinnamon clownfish nest in a section of ribbon reef in the waters north of Cairns.

THE RED CENTRE & ULURU

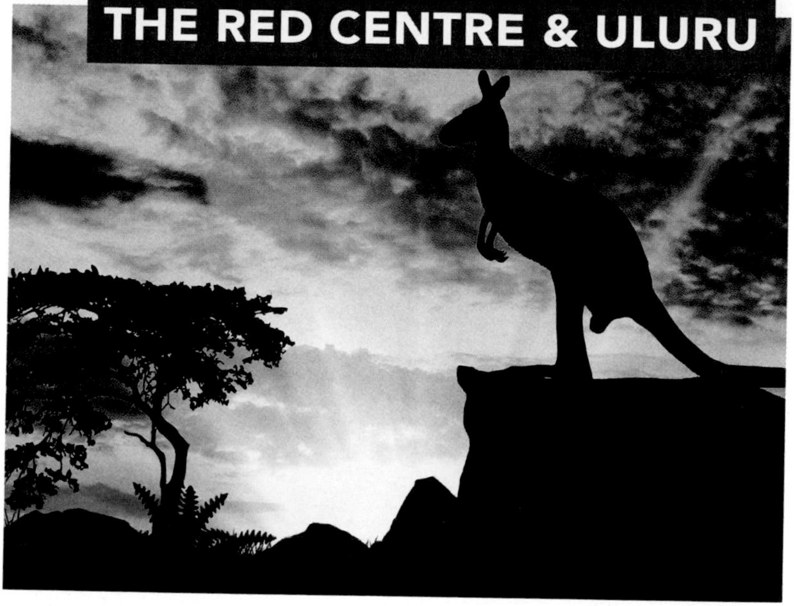

Kangaroo sightings are common in the Outback. The large marsupials are most active at night, early morning, and late afternoon.

Visitors await sunset at Uluru, the red rock monolith that defines the rugged Australian Outback. Though it is not prohibited, climbing the rock, which is sacred to Aborigines, is strongly discouraged.

Originally imported from the Middle East, more than 200,000 wild camels now roam the Outback. A dawn ride on a domestic camel is a memorable way to experience Uluru. See p. 267.

A hike through tall, narrow Standley Chasm is a highlight of a trip to West MacDonnell National Park (p. 255), a region of red gorges, semi-desert, and occasional hidden swimming holes.

A walk along the rim of Kings Canyon offers panoramas of the rugged, seemingly endless Outback.

The Alice Springs Telegraph Station Historical Reserve (p. 250) marks the site of the first European settlement in Alice Springs.

The weekly Sunday market, as well as galleries and shops in Alice Springs, are among the best places to buy authentic Aboriginal paintings, sculpture, and crafts. See p. 254.

TASMANIA

Hobart's picturesque harbor is the focal point of the Tasmanian capital.

Surrounded by ferns, rainforest, and gum trees, Russell Falls is a gem of Mount Field National Park (p. 287).

The Port Arthur Historic Site (p. 286) explores the dark history of the former penal colony, and is the most-visited sight on Tasmania.

WHAT'S GREAT ABOUT AUSTRALIA

1

Australia is like nowhere else you've been. It has truly unique wildlife, some of the world's best natural scenery, the most brilliant scuba diving and snorkeling, the best beaches, the oldest rainforest (110 million years and counting), the oldest human civilization (some archaeologists say 40,000 years, some say 120,000), the best wines, the best weather, and the most innovative East-meets-West-meets-someplace-else cuisine—all bathed in sunlight that brings everything up in Technicolor. Prepare yourself for a lifetime of memories.

Scarcely a visitor lands on these shores without having the **Great Barrier Reef** at the top of their to-do list. And so they should. While parts of the reef are in dire straits from coral bleaching caused by rising water temperatures, those that aren't affected show what a glorious natural masterpiece it is—don't leave it too late to see it! Also high on most lists is **Uluru,** a sacred monolith that (rightly) attracts hundreds of thousands of tourists (including celebrities and royalty, such as Britain's Prince William and his wife Catherine, the Duchess of Cambridge). And it's not just "The Rock" you should see; the vast Australian desert all around it is equally unmissable. The third attraction on most visitors' lists is **Sydney,** Australia's glittering harborside city.

Of course, there is much more to Australia than just these highlights. For those who have more time, Tasmania, South Australia, Western Australia, and the Top End of the Northern Territory have much to offer, too. But I know you can't do everything or go everywhere, so in this book, I'll be introducing you to these three iconic attractions as well as the places that are their gateways—Brisbane, Cairns, the coastal cities of Queensland that give you access to the Reef, and Alice Springs in the Red Centre—as well as Australia's other major city, Melbourne, in Victoria, and the island capital of Hobart, Tasmania.

1 Australia

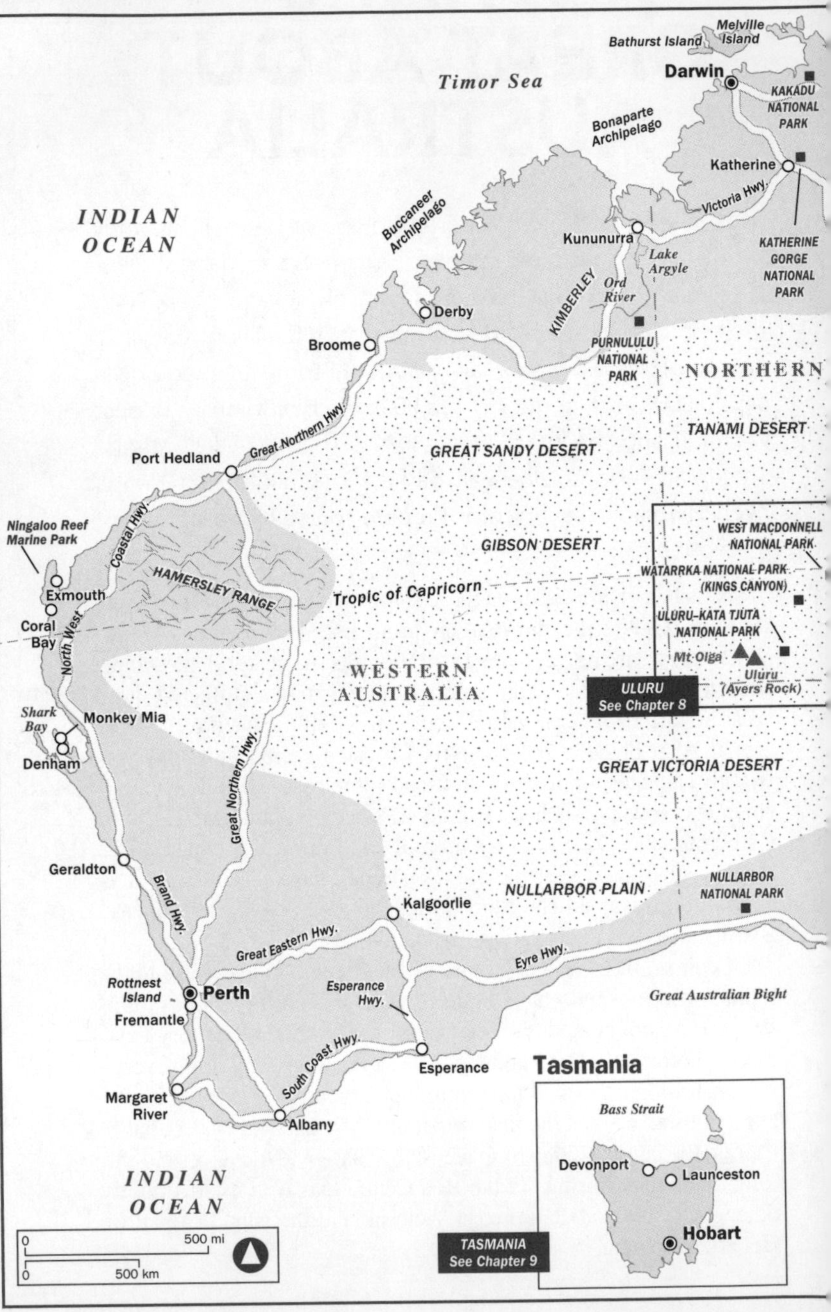
Melville Island
Bathurst Island
Darwin
Timor Sea
KAKADU NATIONAL PARK
Bonaparte Archipelago
Katherine
Victoria Hwy.
KATHERINE GORGE NATIONAL PARK
INDIAN OCEAN
Buccaneer Archipelago
Kununurra
Lake Argyle
Ord River
KIMBERLEY
Derby
Broome
PURNULULU NATIONAL PARK
NORTHERN
TANAMI DESERT
Great Northern Hwy.
GREAT SANDY DESERT
Port Hedland
Coastal Hwy.
Ningaloo Reef Marine Park
WEST MACDONNELL NATIONAL PARK
GIBSON DESERT
WATARRKA NATIONAL PARK (KINGS CANYON)
HAMERSLEY RANGE
Exmouth
Tropic of Capricorn
ULURU-KATA TJUTA NATIONAL PARK
Coral Bay
North West
Mt Olga
Uluru (Ayers Rock)
WESTERN AUSTRALIA
ULURU See Chapter 8
Shark Bay
Monkey Mia
Denham
Great Northern Hwy.
GREAT VICTORIA DESERT
Geraldton
Brand Hwy.
NULLARBOR PLAIN
NULLARBOR NATIONAL PARK
Kalgoorlie
Great Eastern Hwy.
Eyre Hwy.
Rottnest Island
Perth
Esperance Hwy.
Great Australian Bight
Fremantle
South Coast Hwy.
Esperance
Tasmania
Margaret River
Albany
Bass Strait
Devonport
Launceston
INDIAN OCEAN
Hobart
0 500 mi
0 500 km
TASMANIA See Chapter 9

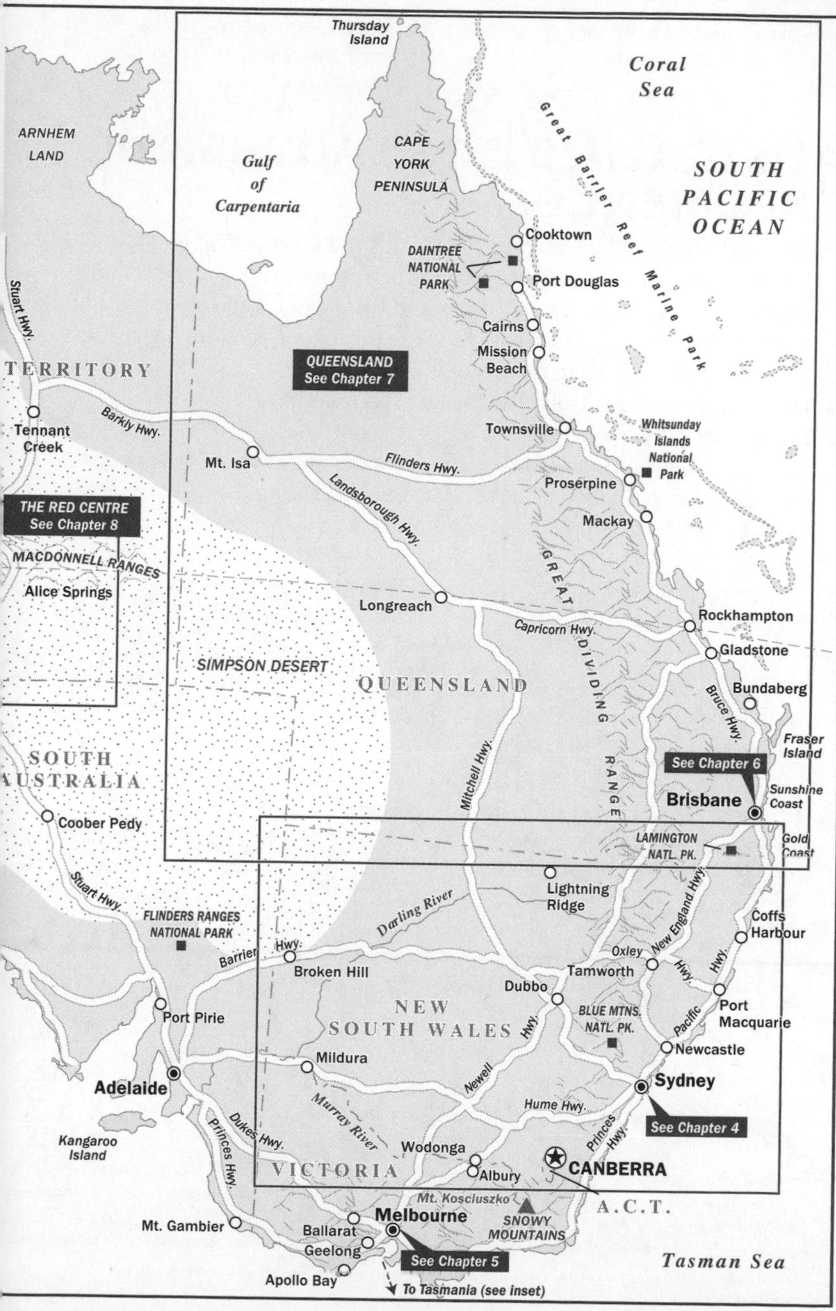
Thursday Island
Coral Sea
Great Barrier Reef Marine Park
SOUTH PACIFIC OCEAN
ARNHEM LAND
Gulf of Carpentaria
CAPE YORK PENINSULA
Cooktown
DAINTREE NATIONAL PARK
Port Douglas
Cairns
Mission Beach
Stuart Hwy.
TERRITORY
QUEENSLAND See Chapter 7
Tennant Creek
Barkly Hwy.
Townsville
Whitsunday Islands National Park
Mt. Isa
Flinders Hwy.
Proserpine
Mackay
Landsborough Hwy.
THE RED CENTRE See Chapter 8
MACDONNELL RANGES
Alice Springs
GREAT DIVIDING RANGE
Longreach
Rockhampton
Capricorn Hwy.
Gladstone
SIMPSON DESERT
QUEENSLAND
Bundaberg
Bruce Hwy.
Fraser Island
Mitchell Hwy.
See Chapter 6
SOUTH AUSTRALIA
Brisbane
Sunshine Coast
Coober Pedy
LAMINGTON NATL. PK.
Gold Coast
Lightning Ridge
Stuart Hwy.
New England Hwy.
Darling River
FLINDERS RANGES NATIONAL PARK
Coffs Harbour
Barrier Hwy.
Broken Hill
Oxley Hwy.
Tamworth
Dubbo
Port Macquarie
Port Pirie
NEW SOUTH WALES
BLUE MTNS. NATL. PK.
Pacific Hwy.
Newell Hwy.
Newcastle
Mildura
Sydney
Adelaide
Murray River
Hume Hwy.
See Chapter 4
Dukes Hwy.
Princes Hwy.
Kangaroo Island
Princes Hwy.
Wodonga
CANBERRA
VICTORIA
Albury
Mt. Kosciuszko
A.C.T.
Mt. Gambier
Melbourne
SNOWY MOUNTAINS
Ballarat
Geelong
See Chapter 5
Tasman Sea
Apollo Bay
To Tasmania (see inset)

A Note on Abbreviations

In the listings below and throughout the book, **NSW** stands for New South Wales, **QLD** for Queensland, **NT** for the Northern Territory, and **VIC** for Victoria.

AUSTRALIA'S best AUTHENTIC EXPERIENCES

- **Seeing the Great Barrier Reef (QLD):** It's a 2,000km-long (1,240-mile) natural wonder of coral, vibrant colors, and bizarre fish life—and it comes complete with warm water and year-round sunshine. When you're not snorkeling over coral and giant clams almost as big as you, scuba diving, calling at tropical towns, or lying on deserted island beaches, you'll be trying out the sun lounges or enjoying the first-rate food. See p. 182.
- **Experiencing Sydney (NSW):** Sydney is more than just the magnificent Harbour Bridge and Opera House. No other city has beaches in such abundance, and few have such a magnificently scenic harbor. Our advice: Try to spend a week here, because you're going to need it. See p. 48.

A scuba diver viewing large orange-colored common gorgonian during a dive at the Great Barrier Reef.

- **Exploring the Wet Tropics Rainforest (QLD):** Folks who come from skyscraper cities such as New York City and London can't get over the moisture-dripping ferns, the neon-blue butterflies, and the primeval peace of this World Heritage rainforest stretching north, south, and west from Cairns. Hike it, four-wheel-drive it, or glide over the treetops in the Skyrail gondola. See p. 198.

The Skyrail Rainforest Cableway near Cairns glides above the canopy of the Wet Tropics Rainforest.

- **Bareboat Sailing (QLD):** "Bareboat" means unskippered—that's right, even if you think port is an after-dinner drink, you can charter a yacht, pay for a day's instruction from a skipper, and then take over the helm yourself and explore the 74 island gems of the Whitsundays. It's easy. Anchor in deserted bays, snorkel over dazzling reefs, fish for coral trout, and feel the wind in your sails. See p. 231.
- **Exploring Kata Tjuta (the Olgas) & Uluru (NT):** This sacred, mysterious, and utterly unforgettable landscape may well be the highlight of your time in Australia. Uluru and Kata Tjuta demand at least 3 days to see everything there is to offer. See p. 240.
- **Taking an Aboriginal Culture Tour:** Seeing the landscape through the eyes of Australia's indigenous people, hearing the creation stories of their ancestors, and learning more about Aboriginal culture will give you a different perspective on Australia, no matter which part of it you are in. See p. 241.

AUSTRALIA'S best RESTAURANTS

- **Donovans** (Melbourne, VIC; © **03/9534 8221**): What better way to end the day than with a glass in hand, watching the sun go down over St Kilda Beach, while you're perched on the veranda at this beachy restaurant in a former 1920s bathing pavilion. See p. 127.
- **e'cco bistro** (Brisbane, QLD; © **07/3831 8344**): Simple food elegantly prepared and accompanied by an extensive wine list has won this small but stylish bistro a stack of awards. Booking ahead is essential. See p. 168.
- **Flower Drum** (Melbourne, VIC; © **03/9662 3655**): Praise pours in for this upscale eatery serving exquisite Cantonese food. Service is impeccable. See p. 121.

The veranda at Donovans offers the perfect view of sunset over St Kilda Beach in Melburnians.

- **Icebergs Dining Room and Bar** (Sydney, NSW; © **02/9365 9000**): Come here for exquisite food and one of the best ocean views in the Southern Hemisphere. Not surprisingly, seafood features highly on the menu. It's our top pick for lunch in Sydney. See p. 78.
- **MoVida** (Melbourne, VIC; © **03/9663 3038**): This little corner of Spain is relaxed and fun, with seriously good food and good wine. Melburnians flock here for the tapas and *raciones.* If it's full, try one of the two sister restaurants, **MoVida Next Door** and **MoVida Aqui.** See p. 124.
- **Quay** (Sydney, NSW; © **02/9251 5600**): Sydney's best seafood restaurant offers perhaps the loveliest view in town. Gaze through the large windows toward the Opera House, the city skyline, the North Shore suburbs, and the Harbour Bridge. See p. 74.
- **Red Ochre Grill** (Alice Springs, NT; © **08/8952 9614**): "Gourmet bush tucker" might sound like a contradiction ("bush tucker," aka bushfood, identifies foods that are native to Australia and were consumed by its original inhabitants), but this restaurant pulls it off. The kitchen combines native ingredients and international techniques to exceptionally good effect. See p. 249.
- **Salsa Bar & Grill** (Port Douglas, QLD; © **07/4099 4922**): The animated atmosphere and attractive surroundings set the scene for an excellent dining experience. Appetizers and main courses run the gamut from simple fare to sophisticated tropical creations; desserts are fantastic. Book as far ahead as possible. See p. 213.
- **Tetsuya's** (Sydney, NSW; © **02/9267 2900**): Chef Tetsuya Wakuda is arguably Sydney's most famous chef, and his nouveau Japanese creations are

imaginative enough to guarantee that this hip eatery is a constant number one in Australia and ranks among the top restaurants in the world. See p. 75.

AUSTRALIA'S best HOTELS

- **Sir Stamford at Circular Quay** (Sydney, NSW; © **02/9252 4600**): Plush and luxurious, with a clubby feel that's relaxed rather than stuffy, Sir Stamford is also perfectly located, a short walk from Circular Quay and the Opera House, and just across the road from the Royal Botanic Gardens. See p. 63.
- **The Reef House** (Palm Cove, QLD; © **07/4080 2000**): Airy rooms look onto tropical gardens, waterfalls cascade into the pools, mosquito nets drape over the beds, and you could swear pith-helmeted colonial officers will be back any minute to finish their gin-and-tonics in the Brigadier Bar. Idyllic Palm Cove Beach is just across the road. See p. 192.
- **qualia** (Hamilton Island, Whitsundays, QLD; © **07/4946 9999**): This is one of Australia's most glamorous island resorts, an exclusive adults-only enclave away from the hurly-burly of the main island accommodations. Each private pavilion has its own plunge pool, and there's a decadent day spa. See p. 227.

Cocktails on the Dunes at Longitude 131°, a luxury safari camp in the Outback.

- **Longitude 131°** (Uluru, Red Centre, NT; ✆ **08/8957 7131**): The luxury option at the Ayers Rock resort scene, Longitude 131° is an African-style safari camp set in the dunes, with great views of Uluru. It's very exclusive and very expensive, but you'll experience the Outback in style. See p. 263.
- **The Russell** (The Rocks, Sydney, NSW; ✆ **02/9241 3543**): This B&B, wonderfully positioned in the city's old quarter, is the coziest place to stay in Sydney. It has creaky floorboards, a ramshackle feel, brightly painted corridors, and rooms with immense character. See p. 64.
- **Marae** (near Port Douglas, QLD; ✆ **07/4098 4900**): Lush bushland full of butterflies and birds is the setting for this gorgeous B&B in a contemporary timber Queenslander house. Owners John and Pam Burden promise a warm welcome and a fine tropical breakfast. See p. 211.
- **The Olsen** (Melbourne, VIC; ✆ **03/9040 1222**): With a giant mural by one of Australia's greatest living artists, John Olsen, and a stunning suspended swimming pool, this flagship of the Art Series Hotels is worth the splurge. Or try one of its sister hotels in Melbourne: The Cullen, The Blackman, or The Larwill Studio. See p. 116.

THE best PLACES TO VIEW WILDLIFE

- **Lone Pine Koala Sanctuary (QLD):** Cuddle a koala (and have your photo taken doing it) at this park in Brisbane, the world's first and largest koala sanctuary. Apart from some 130 koalas, lots of other Aussie wildlife—including wombats, Tasmanian devils, 'roos (which you can hand-feed), and colorful parakeets—are on show. See p. 172.
- **Hartley's Crocodile Adventures (QLD):** Cruise a beautiful lagoon surrounded by paperbark trees to spot crocodiles in their natural setting, and then watch the daily "croc attack" show. There are also snakes, koalas, cassowaries, and other animals to see at this family-run wildlife park just north of Cairns. See p. 200.
- **Australian Butterfly Sanctuary (QLD):** Walk through the biggest butterfly "aviary" in Australia, in Kuranda, near Cairns, and you'll spot some of the most gorgeous butterflies on the continent, including the electric-blue Ulysses. See many species of butterfly feed, lay eggs, and mate; and inspect caterpillars and pupae. Wearing pink, red, or white encourages the butterflies to land on you. See p. 207.

Get up close with colorful residents of the Australian Butterfly Sanctuary in Kuranda.

- **Heron Island (QLD):** You'll spot wonderful wildlife on this "jewel in the reef" off Gladstone any time of year, but the best time to visit is November to March, when the life cycle of giant green loggerhead and hawksbill turtles is in full swing. From November to January, the turtles come ashore to lay their eggs. From late January to March, the hatchlings emerge and head for the water. You can see it all by strolling down to the beach, or join a university researcher to get the full story. See p. 234. **Mon Repos Regional Park,** near Bundaberg in Queensland (p. 263), is another good turtle-watching site.

- **Moonlit Sanctuary (VIC):** For the chance to see many of Australia's nocturnal animals, including some (such as the eastern quoll, the red-bellied pademelon, and the southern bettong) that are now extinct in the wild, take a guided night tour at this sanctuary on the Mornington Peninsula. See p. 147.

THE best DIVING & SNORKELING

- **Port Douglas (QLD):** Among the fabulous dive sites off Port Douglas, north of Cairns, are Split-Bommie, with its delicate fan corals and schools of fusiliers; Barracuda Pass, with its coral gardens and giant clams; and the swim-through coral spires of the Cathedrals. Snorkelers can glide over the coral and reef fish life of Agincourt Reef. See p. 209.
- **Cairns (QLD):** Moore, Norman, Hardy, Saxon, and Arlington reefs and Michaelmas and Upolu cays—all about 90 minutes off Cairns—offer great snorkeling and endless dive sites. Explore on a day trip from Cairns, or join a live-aboard adventure. See p. 189.
- **The Whitsunday Islands (QLD):** These 74 breathtaking islands offer countless dive sites both among the islands and on the Outer Great Barrier Reef,

Whitehaven Beach on uninhabited Whitsunday Island.

90 minutes away. Bait Reef on the Outer Reef is popular for its drop-offs. Snorkelers can explore not just the Outer Reef but also patch reefs among the islands and rarely visited fringing reefs around many islands. See p. 223.

- **Heron Island (QLD):** Easily the number-one snorkel and dive site in Australia—if you stayed in the water for a week, you couldn't snorkel all the acres of coral stretching from shore. Take your pick of 22 dive sites: the Coral Cascades, with football trout and anemones; the Blue Pools, favored by octopus, turtles, and sharks; Heron Bommie, with its rays, eels, and Spanish dancers; and more. Absolute magic. See p. 134.
- **Lady Elliot Island (QLD):** Gorgeous coral lagoons, perfect for snorkeling, line this coral cay island off the town of Bundaberg. Boats take you farther out to snorkel above manta rays, plate coral, and big fish. Divers can swim through the blowhole, 16m (52 ft.) down, and see gorgonian fans, soft and hard corals, sharks, barracudas, and reef fish. See p. 238.

THE best OF THE OUTDOORS

- **Blue Mountains (NSW):** Many bushwalks in the Blue Mountains National Park offer awesome views of valleys, waterfalls, cliffs, and forest. All are easy to reach from Sydney. See p. 102.
- **Four Mile Beach (QLD):** The sea is turquoise, the sun is warm, the palms sway, and the low-rise hotels starting to line this country beach in Port Douglas can't spoil the feeling that it is a million miles from anywhere. But isn't there always a serpent in paradise? In this case, the "serpents" are north Queensland's seasonal and potentially deadly marine stingers. Come

Taking in the sights at Blue Mountains National Park.

The entire continent of Australia is ringed with legendary surfing spots.

from June through September to avoid them, or confine your swimming to the stinger-net enclosures the rest of the year. See p. 213.

- **Larapinta Trail (NT):** You can start from Alice Springs in the Red Centre and walk the entire 223km (138-mile) semi-desert trail, which winds through the stark crimson McDonnell Ranges. You don't have to walk the entire length—plenty of day-length and multi-day sections are possible. This one's for the cooler months only (Apr–Oct). See p. 253.
- **The MacDonnell Ranges (NT):** Aboriginal people say these red rocky hills were formed by the "Caterpillar Dreaming" that wriggled from the earth here. To the east and west of Alice Springs are dramatic gorges, idyllic (and icy cold) water holes, cute wallabies, and ancient Aboriginal rock carvings. See p. 255.
- **Surfing:** No visit to Oz could really be considered complete without checking out one of the iconic Aussie activities—surfing. It's not just the rush of the waves that pulls people in, it's the ethos and everything that goes with surfing. Every state has its special spots where the surf can be especially challenging.
- **Uluru–Kata Tjuta National Park (NT):** Don't go home until you've felt the powerful heartbeat of the desert. Uluru will enthrall you with its eerie beauty. Nearby Kata Tjuta is equally interesting, so make the time to wander through the Valley of the Winds. Hike or cycle around Uluru's base, burn around it on a Harley-Davidson, saunter up to it on a camel . . . but please don't climb it. See p. 258.
- **Whitehaven Beach (QLD):** It's not a surf beach, but this 6km (3¾-mile) stretch of white silica sand on uninhabited Whitsunday Island is pristine and peaceful. Bring a book, curl up under the rainforest lining its edge, and fantasize that the cruise ship is going to leave without you. See p. 232.

AUSTRALIA IN CONTEXT

2

When most people think of Australia, they conjure up images of bounding kangaroos, dusty red deserts, and golden sandy beaches. The Sydney Opera House is right up there, too. They imagine drawling accents and slouch hats, suntanned lifeguards, and men who wrestle crocodiles for the fun of it. Well, it's all that—and more (apart from the crocodile wrestling)! This huge continent is truly remarkable, offering everything from rolling green hills, dense ancient rainforests, and historic towns, to vast areas of sparsely inhabited ochre-red Outback, to giant coral reefs and deserted beaches, unique animals and plants, cosmopolitan modern cities, and intriguing Aboriginal culture.

Most people visiting Australia for the first time head to Sydney or Melbourne. They explore the Red Centre and the giant rock Uluru; or they take to the warm waters of the Great Barrier Reef to dive or snorkel. But it's also often the places that come to visitors by chance, or through deeper research, that remain locked in their memories forever. Who could forget holding a koala in your arms, or feeding a kangaroo from the palm of your hand? Or traveling ochre-red dirt tracks and seeing emus running alongside their 4WD? This book concentrates on the areas that are the most traveled (and on every visitor's wish list) but it also takes you to some of the lesser-known treasures of each city and some of our personal favorite places and experiences. Of course, no travel experience is complete without a little background information, which is where this chapter comes in.

AUSTRALIA TODAY

Perhaps it's to do with the weather, or the wide-open spaces, or the quality of the light, but Australians are generally an optimistic, positive lot—and to me, that's a big part of the country's appeal. Phrases like "It's a lucky country, mate," and "she'll be right" (meaning everything will be okay) may have become clichés, but they sum up the attitude held by most Australians. The food is good and there's plenty of it; the education system is mostly good (and mostly free, unless you choose to pay for a private school or you happen to be saddled with student loans to cover university fees); gun ownership is heavily restricted; the public healthcare system is universal and largely free or inexpensive; and the government—whichever persuasion it is—is generally stable. It's a great place to live—even though it can sometimes feel a long, long way from everywhere else.

Of course, nothing is totally clear-cut. The country has plenty of socially disadvantaged areas, and many of Australia's indigenous people in particular are struggling on the fringes of mainstream society.

As a nation, Australia is also facing tough challenges in balancing the benefits of industry with caring for the environment. Australia makes a massive amount of revenue from mining, supplying China with a significant proportion of its iron and other metals, as well as supplying the rest of the world with everything from uranium and coal to natural gas. This inevitably means the ruin of some once-pristine landscapes. Australia also has one of the world's highest per capita levels of greenhouse gas emissions (nearly twice the OECD average and more than four times the world average) and suffers from severe droughts and dramatic weather events that most experts believe are the result of human-induced climate change.

Australia is also one of the world's fastest-growing industrialized nations. In 2017, the population hit the 24.5-million mark, a figure driven in recent years by immigration, with around 182,000 people settling here in 2015 and 2016.

One thing Australia realized early on was the importance of tourism to its economy. Around 8.3 million people visited in 2016. You'll find Australians

Aboriginal rock art at Nourlangie, Kakadu National Park, Northern Territory, Australia.

THE ancient art OF AUSTRALIA

A history of the Aboriginal people lies partly in the **rock paintings** they have left behind all over Australia. In the tropical north, for example, a wide-ranging body of prehistoric art decorates sandstone gorges near the tiny township of Laura on the rugged Cape York Peninsula. Depictions on rock-shelter sites range from spirit figures of men and women to eels, fish, wide-winged brolga birds, crocodiles, kangaroos, snakes, and stenciled hands. One wall, the "Magnificent Gallery," stretches more than 40m (131 ft.) and is adorned with hundreds of Quinkan figures—Quinkans being the Aboriginal spirits associated with this region.

Much Aboriginal rock art is preserved in national parks. Examples readily accessible on day trips from major Australian cities include Ku-Ring-Gai Chase National Park, and the Royal National Park near Sydney. Then there's the Grampians National Park west of Melbourne, and the fabulous hand stencils at Mutawintji National Park near Broken Hill in New South Wales. There are also ancient paintings near Uluru in Australia's Red Centre. In Queensland, Carnarvon National Park (about 400km/249 miles west of Brisbane) offers a breathtaking display of early indigenous paintings.

helpful and friendly, and services, tours, and food and drink to rival any in the world. Factor in the landscape, the indigenous culture, the sunshine, the unique wildlife, and some of the world's best cities, and, all in all, you've got a fascinating, accessible destination of amazing diversity and variety.

LOOKING BACK AT AUSTRALIA

The Beginning

In the beginning, there was the Dreamtime. Australia's indigenous people have lived on this land for 40,000 years or more. Their "Dreamtime" stories explain how they see the creation story and what followed. In scientific terms, a supercontinent split into two, and over millions of years continental drift carried the great landmasses apart. Australia was part of what we call Gondwanaland, which also divided into South America, Africa, India, Papua New Guinea, and Antarctica. Giant marsupials evolved to roam the continent of Australia. The last of these creatures are believed to have died out around 20,000 years ago, possibly helped toward extinction by drought, or by Aboriginal hunters, who lived alongside them for thousands of years.

Early European Explorers

The existence of a great southern land had been on the minds of Europeans since the Greek astronomer Ptolemy drew a map of the world in A.D. 150 showing a large landmass in the south, which he believed existed to balance out the land in the Northern Hemisphere. He called it Terra Australia Incognita—the "Unknown Southland."

Portuguese ships reached Australia as early as 1536 and charted part of its coastline. In 1606, William Jansz was sent by the Dutch East India Company

The Macquarie Lighthouse on South Head, Sydney Harbour.

to open up a new route to the Spice Islands and to find New Guinea. He landed on the north coast of Queensland instead and fought with local Aborigines. Between 1616 and 1640, many more Dutch ships made contact with Australia as they hugged the west coast of what they called "New Holland," after sailing with the westerly winds from the Cape of Good Hope.

In 1642, the Dutch East India Company, through the governor general of the Indies, Anthony Van Diemen, sent Abel Tasman to search for and map the great Southland. During two voyages, Tasman charted the northern Australian coastline and discovered Tasmania, which he named Van Diemen's Land.

The Arrival of the British

In 1766, the Royal Society hired James Cook to travel to the Pacific Ocean to observe and record the transit of Venus across the sun. In 1770, Cook charted the east coast of Australia in his ship the HMS *Endeavour.* He claimed the land for Britain and named it New South Wales. On April 29, Captain Cook landed at Botany Bay, which he named after the discovery of scores of plants hitherto unknown to science. Turning northward, he passed an entrance to a possible harbor that appeared to offer safe anchorage and named it Port Jackson, after the secretary of the admiralty, George Jackson. Back in Britain, King George III viewed Australia as a potential colony and repository of Britain's overflowing prison population, which could no longer be transported to the United States of America following the War of Independence.

The First Fleet left England in May 1787, made up of 11 store and transport ships (none of them bigger than the passenger ferries that ply modern-day Sydney Harbour from Circular Quay to Manly) led by Arthur Phillip. Aboard were 1,480 people, including 759 convicts. Phillip's flagship, the *Supply,* reached Botany Bay in January 1788, but Phillip decided the soil was poor and the surroundings too swampy. On January 26, now celebrated as Australia Day, he settled for Port Jackson (Sydney Harbour) instead.

THE ABORIGINAL "stolen generations"

When Captain James Cook landed at Botany Bay in 1770 determined to claim the land for the British Empire, at least 300,000 **Aborigines** were living on the continent. Despite varying estimates of how long Aboriginal people have inhabited Australia (some believe it to be since the beginning of time), there is scientific evidence that people were walking the continent at least 60,000 years ago.

At the time of the arrival of Europeans, there were at least 600 different tribal communities, each linked to their ancestral land by **"sacred sites"** (certain features of the land, such as hills or rock formations). They were hunter-gatherers, spending about 20 hours a week harvesting the resources of the land, the rivers, and the ocean. The rest of their time was taken up by complex social and belief systems, as well as by life's practicalities such as making utensils and weapons.

The basis of Aboriginal spirituality rests in the **Dreamtime** stories, which recount how ancient spirits created the universe—earth, stars, moon, sun, water, animals, and humans. Much Aboriginal art is related to their land and the sacred sites that are home to the Dreamtime spirits. Some Aboriginal groups believe these spirits came in giant human form, while others believe they were animals or huge snakes. According to Aboriginal custom, individuals can draw on the power of the Dreamtime spirits by reenacting various stories and practicing certain ceremonies.

When the British came, bringing their unfamiliar diseases along with them, entire coastal communities were virtually wiped out by the onset of smallpox. Even as late as the 1950s, large numbers of Aborigines in remote regions of South Australia and the Northern Territory succumbed to deadly outbreaks of influenza and measles.

Although relationships between the settlers and Aborigines were initially peaceful, conflicts over land and food led to skirmishes in which Aborigines were massacred and settlers and convicts attacked. Within a few years, some 10,000 Aborigines and 1,000 Europeans had been killed in Queensland alone,

The convicts were immediately put to work clearing land, planting crops, and constructing buildings. Phillip decided to give some convicts pardons for good behavior and service, and even granted small land parcels to those who were especially industrious.

When gold was discovered in Victoria in 1852 and in Western Australia 12 years later, hundreds of thousands of immigrants from Europe, America, and China flooded the country in search of fortune. By 1860, more than a million non-Aboriginal people were living in Australia.

The final 10,000 convicts were transported to Western Australia between 1850 and 1868, bringing the total shipped to Australia to 168,000. Some early colonial architecture, built and designed by those convicts, still remains in Sydney. Be on the lookout for buildings designed by the colonial architect Francis Greenway. Between 1816 and 1818, while still a prisoner, Greenway was responsible for the Macquarie Lighthouse on South Head, at the entrance to Sydney Harbour, and also Hyde Park Barracks and St. James Church in the city center.

while in Tasmania, a campaign to rid the island entirely of local Aborigines was ultimately successful, with the last full-blooded Tasmanian Aborigine dying in 1876. By the start of the 20th century, the Aboriginal people were considered a dying race. Most of those who remained lived in government-owned reserves or church-controlled missions.

Massacres of Aborigines continued to go largely or wholly unpunished into the 1920s, by which time it was official government policy to remove light-skinned Aboriginal children from their families. Many children of these "stolen generations" were brought up in white foster homes or church mission stations and never reunited with their biological families. Many children with living parents were told that their parents were dead. This continued into the 1970s.

Today, there are some 517,000 people who claim Aboriginal and Torres Strait Islander descent living in Australia, or 2.5% of the population. Some 32% of these live in the major cities, while 25% live in remote or very remote areas. In general, a great divide still exists between them and the rest of the population. Aboriginal life expectancy is 20 years lower than that of other Australians, with overall death rates between two and four times higher. Aborigines make up the highest percentage of the country's prison population, and reports continue to emerge about Aborigines dying while incarcerated.

It was not until 1962 that Aboriginal people were given the right to hold citizenship or vote in Australia and only in 1992 that the High Court of Australia expunged the concept of *terra nullius* and acknowledged the pre-existing rights of indigenous Australians. Aboriginal people are still not recognized in the Australian Constitution.

In 2007, then-Prime Minister Kevin Rudd made an official apology on behalf of his Labor Government to the "stolen generations." National Sorry Day is held on May 26 each year, when Australians of all backgrounds march in parades and hold other events around the country to honor the Stolen Generations. It is followed by National Reconciliation Week (May 27–June 3).

Federation & the Great Wars

On January 1, 1901, the six states that made up Australia proclaimed themselves to be part of one nation, and the Commonwealth of Australia was formed. In the same ceremony, the first governor-general was sworn in as the representative of the Queen, who remained head of state.

In 1914, Australia joined Britain in World War I. In April of 1915, the Australian and New Zealand Army Corps (ANZAC) formed a beachhead on the peninsula of Gallipoli in Turkey. The Turkish troops had been warned, and 8 months of fighting ended with 8,587 Australian dead and more than 19,000 wounded. That day, April 25, is commemorated each year as Anzac Day.

Australians fought in World War II in North Africa, Greece, and the Middle East. In March 1942, Japanese aircraft bombed Broome in Western Australia and Darwin in the Northern Territory. In May 1942, Japanese midget submarines entered Sydney Harbour and torpedoed a ferry before ultimately being destroyed. Later that year, Australian volunteers fought an incredibly brave retreat through the jungles of Papua New Guinea on the Kokoda Track against superior Japanese forces.

Recent Times

Following World War II, mass immigration to Australia, primarily from Europe, boosted the non-Aboriginal population. "White" Australia was always used to distinguish the Anglo-Saxon population from that of the indigenous people of Australia, and until 1974 there existed a "White Australia Policy"—a result of conflict between European settlers and Chinese immigrants in the gold fields in the 1850s. This policy severely restricted the immigration of people who lacked European ancestry. In 1974, the left-of-Center Whitlam Labor government put an end to the White Australia policy that had largely restricted black and Asian immigration since 1901. In 1986, an act of both British and Australian Parliament once and for all severed any remaining ties to the United Kingdom. Australia had begun the march to complete independence.

> **A Moment in Time**
>
> In 1964, a group of 20 nomadic women and children became the last Aboriginal people to make "first contact" with Europeans. They were living in the Great Sandy Desert, south of Broome, in Western Australia. When they first saw two officers from the Weapons Research Establishment, who were checking land destined for a series of rocket tests, the Aborigines presumed the white-skinned creatures were ghosts.

Waves of immigration have brought in millions of people since the end of World War II. Government statistics show that in 2013, almost 28% of the population was born overseas. Of those, 6% were born in the U.K., 3% from New Zealand, with others from Europe and Asia. New waves of immigration have recently come from countries such as Iraq, Sudan, and Somalia. So what's the typical Australian like? Well, he's hardly Crocodile Dundee.

AUSTRALIA IN POPULAR CULTURE

Movies

Australia has produced its fair share of movies, good and bad. Some of the better ones are listed here.

- ***Walkabout* (1971):** The hauntingly beautiful and disturbing movie set in the Australian desert stars Jenny Agutter and the Aboriginal actor David Gulpilul. A white girl and her brother get hopelessly lost and survive with help from a doomed Aboriginal hero.
- ***Picnic at Hanging Rock* (1974):** This Peter Weir movie is about a group of schoolgirls and a teacher who go missing at an eerie rock formation north of Melbourne. It's set at the beginning of the 20th century, when bonnets and teapots were the norm.

- **Mad Max (1979):** Mel Gibson fights to the death in the Outback, which presents the ideal setting for a post-apocalyptic world. The movie was so popular that it spawned three sequels: *The Road Warrior* (1981), *Mad Max: Beyond Thunderdome* (1985), and *Mad Max: Fury Road* (2015).
- **Gallipoli (1981):** Peter Weir brilliantly captures the World War I military disaster that saw Australian and New Zealand troops fighting against overwhelming odds on the Turkish coastline.
- **The Man from Snowy River (1982):** Kirk Douglas, Tom Burlinson, and Sigrid Thornton star in this startling Australian movie that showcases the mountainous wilderness of Australia, where wild horses roam.
- **Crocodile Dundee (1986):** Paul Hogan shot to worldwide fame as a "typical" crocodile-wrestling Outback hero. He wears the same hat and a few more wrinkles in *Crocodile Dundee II* (1988) and *Crocodile Dundee in L.A.* (2001).
- **Shine (1991):** This portrayal of the real-life classical pianist David Helfgott, who rose to international prominence in the 1950s and '60s before having a nervous breakdown, is remarkable. Oscar-winner Geoffrey Rush gives a powerful performance as Helfgott; Sir John Gielgud plays Helfgott's teacher.
- **Strictly Ballroom (1992):** A boy, played by Paul Mercurio, becomes a champion ballroom dancer in this whimsical, playful movie.
- **Muriel's Wedding (1994):** This classic Australian comedy tells the tale of Muriel Heslop (Toni Collette), a young woman who dreams of getting married and moving far away from her boring life in Porpoise Spit. Fabulous characters, great catchphrases, and Abba music abound.
- **The Adventures of Priscilla, Queen of the Desert (1994):** A trans woman takes to traveling through the desert in a big pink bus with two drag queens. They sing Abba classics and dress the part, kind of. Where else but Australia . . .
- **The Dish (2000):** This comedy about Australia's role in the Apollo 11 mission in 1969 was set around a group of characters operating the Parkes/Canberra radio telescope.
- **Rabbit Proof Fence (2002):** This fictionalized tale addresses the real-life experience of Aboriginal children plucked from their homes in order to put them in white foster families or—as is the case in this true story of three girls—to train them to work as domestic servants.
- **Australia (2008):** An English aristocrat in the 1930s, played by Nicole Kidman, arrives in northern Australia. After an epic journey across the country with a rough-hewn cattle drover played by Hugh Jackman, she is caught in the bombing of Darwin during World War II. Mixed reviews for this one—make up your own mind, if you're inclined!
- **Samson and Delilah (2009):** This challenging movie depicts two indigenous Australian 14-year-olds living in a remote Aboriginal community who steal a car and escape their difficult lives by heading off to Alice Springs.
- **Animal Kingdom (2010):** Jacki Weaver's role as a crime family matriarch in this gripping drama set in Melbourne won her multiple awards, and an Oscar nomination for Best Supporting Actress.

- ***Red Dog* (2011):** A tearjerker family flick about a kelpie looking for his master in a Western Australian Outback mining town, this film was adapted from the novel by Louis de Bernières and based on a true story. A prequel, *Red Dog: True Blue*, was released in 2016.
- ***Last Cab to Darwin* (2014):** A taxi driver from outback Broken Hill discovers he has terminal cancer and decides to drive to Darwin to take advantage of new euthanasia laws. The film is uplifting rather than morbid, with a great performance by Michael Caton in the lead role.
- ***Lion* (2016):** Based on the true story of Saroo Brierley, an Indian orphan adopted by an Australian couple (played by Nicole Kidman and David Wenham), Lion traces Saroo's search for his birth family. Shot in Tasmania and India, it garnered a slew of awards including six Oscar nominations (including one for Best Picture).

Music

Aboriginal music has been around for tens of thousands of years. Best known is the sound of the **didgeridoo,** made from a hollowed-out tree limb. Listen carefully and you might hear animal sounds, including the flapping of wings and the thumping of feet on the ground. You might hear the sounds of wind, or of thunder, or trees creaking, or water running. It just goes to show how connected the Aboriginal people were, and still are in many cases, to the landscape they lived in. For contemporary fusions of indigenous and Western music, look for music by Yothu Yindi, Christine Anu, and Geoffrey Gurrumul Yunupingu (who sings only in his own language).

As far as Australian rock 'n' roll goes, you might know a few of the following names. The big star in the '50s was Johnny O'Keefe, but he soon gave way to the likes of the Easybeats. Running into the 1970s, you find the Bee Gees, AC/DC, Sherbet, John-Paul Young, and the Little River Band. Others who made a name for themselves included the solo stars Helen Reddy, Olivia Newton-John, and Peter Allen. The 1980s saw Men at Work, Crowded House, The Go-Betweens, Hunters and Collectors, Kylie Minogue, and Midnight Oil. INXS, Silverchair, and Savage Garden took us into the 1990s, which Kylie managed to stitch up, too. Jet and the Vines were both Australian rock groups that saw considerable international success in the 21st century, along with, you guessed it, Kylie

The haunting tones of the musical instrument known as the didgeridoo include animal sounds and flapping of wings.

Minogue. For songs with a contemporary Australian voice, go no further than Paul Kelly. In recent years, the best-known Australian singer in the U.S. has probably been Gotye, who won three Grammy awards in 2013.

Australia's Literature

Australian literature has come a long way since the days when the bush poets A. B. "Banjo" Paterson and Henry Lawson penned their odes to a way of life now largely lost. The best known of these is Paterson's epic *The Man from Snowy River,* which first hit the bestseller list in 1895 and was made into a film. But the literary scene has always been lively, and Australia has a wealth of classics, many of them with the Outback at their heart.

Miles Franklin wrote *My Brilliant Career,* the story of a young woman faced with the dilemma of choosing between marriage and a career, in 1901 (made into a film starring Judy Davis in 1979). *We of the Never Never* (1902), by Mrs. Aeneas Gunn, tells the story of a young woman who leaves the comfort of her Melbourne home to live on a cattle station in the Northern Territory. *Walkabout* (1959), by James V. Marshall, explores the relationship between an Aborigine and two lost children in the bush (made into a powerful film by Peter Weir in 1971). Colleen McCullough's *The Thorn Birds* (1977) is a romantic epic about forbidden love between a Catholic priest and a young woman (made into a television miniseries in 1983).

A good historical account of Australia's early days is Geoffrey Blainey's *The Tyranny of Distance,* first published in 1966. Robert Hughes's *The Fatal Shore: The Epic of Australia's Founding* (1987) is a best-selling nonfiction study of the country's European history.

For a contemporary, if somewhat dark, take on the settlement and development of Sydney, delve into John Birmingham's *Leviathan* (1999). From an Aboriginal perspective, *Follow the Rabbit-Proof Fence* (1997), by Doris Pilkington, tells the true story of three young girls from the "stolen generation" who ran away from a mission school to return to their families. (A movie version was released in 2002; see p. 19.)

Modern novelists include David Malouf, Elizabeth Jolley, Helen Garner, Sue Woolfe, and Peter Carey, whose *True History of the Kelly Gang* (2001), a fictionalized autobiography of the outlaw Ned Kelly, won the Booker Prize in 2001. West Australian Tim Winton evokes his part of the continent in stunning prose; his latest work, *Breath* (2008), is no exception. Matthew Condon's *The Trout Opera* (2007) remains one of my all-time favorite Australian novels, covering a century through one man's life. The multi-award-winning *The Light Between Oceans,* by Australian novelist M. L. Stedman, is set in a Western Australian lighthouse. And don't pass up Richard Flanagan's masterpiece *The Narrow Road to the Deep North,* which won the Booker Prize in 2014.

Outsiders who have tackled Australia include Jan Morris and Bill Bryson. Morris's *Sydney* was published in 1992, and Bryson's *In a Sunburned Country* (2001), while not always a favorite with Australians, may appeal to American readers.

EATING & DRINKING IN AUSTRALIA

For a long time, the typical Aussie home-cooked meal consisted of the English-style "meat and three veg" and a Sunday roast. Spaghetti was something foreigners ate, and zucchini and eggplant (aubergine) were considered exotic. Then came mass immigration and all sorts of food that people once only read about in *National Geographic.*

The first big wave of Italian immigrants in the 1950s caused a national scandal. The great Aussie dream was to have a quarter-acre block of land with a hills hoist (a circular revolving clothesline) in the backyard. When Italians started hanging freshly made pasta out to dry on this Aussie icon, it caused an uproar, and some clamored for the new arrivals to be shipped back. As Australia matured, southern European cuisine became increasingly popular, until olive oil was sizzling in frying pans the way only lard had previously done.

In the 1980s, waves of Asian immigrants hit Australia's shores. Suddenly, everyone was cooking with woks. These days, a fusion of spices from the East and ingredients and styles from the Mediterranean make up what's become known as Modern Australian cuisine.

Still, some of the old ways remain. Everyone knows that Aussies like a barbecue, usually referred to as a "barbie." Most Aussies aren't really that adventurous when it comes to throwing things on the hot plate and are usually content with some cheap sausages and a steak washed down by a few beers.

Seafood is popular, as you would expect, and a typical Christmas Day meal usually includes prawns and/or fish.

In the big cities, you'll find every kind of cuisine, including Thai, Vietnamese, Italian, Spanish, Middle Eastern, and Indian. Even the smallest town usually has a Chinese restaurant (of varying quality). Melbourne is proud of its coffee culture, but American readers should note that the bottomless cup of coffee is rare.

Many restaurants allow you to bring your own wine (referred to simply as BYO) but some may charge a corkage fee of a few dollars (even when there's a screw-cap and no cork).

While you might see kangaroo, crocodile, and emu on the menu at some restaurants, Australians tend not to indulge in their local wildlife that much, preferring to stick to introduced species instead.

Beer & Wine

If you order a beer in a pub or bar, you should be aware that the standard glass size differs from state to state. Thus, in Sydney you can order a schooner or a smaller midi. In trendy places, you might be offered an English pint or a half-pint. In Melbourne and Brisbane, a midi is called a pot, while in Darwin it's called a handle, and in Hobart a ten. It can be confusing! You can get smaller glasses, too, though thankfully they're becoming rare. These could either be called a pony, a seven, a butcher, a six, or a bobbie, depending on which city

"Bush tucker," hunter-gatherer foods indigenous to Australia, and increasingly popular on restaurant menus.

you're in. If in doubt, just mime a big one or a small one, and you'll get your meaning across.

As far as wine goes, Australia has come a long way since the first grape vines arrived on the First Fleet in 1788. Today, more than 550 major companies and small winemakers produce wine commercially in Australia. There are dozens of recognized wine-growing regions, but the most well-known include the Hunter Valley in New South Wales; the Barossa Valley, McClaren Vale, Coonawarra, Adelaide Hills, and the Clare Valley in South Australia; the Yarra Valley in Victoria; and Margaret River in Western Australia.

Aboriginal Foods

In the past couple of decades, many Australian chefs have woken to the variety and tastes of "bush tucker," as native Aussie food is tagged. Now it's all the rage in the most fashionable restaurants, where wattleseed, lemon myrtle, and other native tastes have a place in one or two dishes on the menu. Below is a list of some of those foods you may encounter.

- **Bunya nut:** Crunchy nut of the bunya pine, about the size of a macadamia.
- **Bush tomato:** Dry, small, darkish fruit; more like a raisin in look and taste.
- **Native cranberry:** Small berry that tastes a bit like an apple.
- **Illawarra plum:** Dark berry with a strong, rich, tangy taste.
- **Kangaroo:** A strong meat with a gamey flavor. Tender when correctly prepared, tough when not. Excellent smoked.
- **Lemon aspen:** Citrusy, light-yellow fruit with a sharp, tangy flavor.

- **Lemon myrtle:** Gum leaves with a fresh lemon tang; often used to flavor white meat.
- **Lillipilli:** Delicious juicy, sweet pink berry.
- **Quandong:** A tart, tangy native peach.
- **Rosella:** Spiky petals of a red flower with a rich berry flavor.
- **Wattleseed:** Roasted ground acacia seeds that taste a little like bitter coffee. Sometimes used in cakes.
- **Wild lime:** Smaller and more sour than regular lime.

One ingredient you will not see on menus is **witchetty grubs;** most people are too squeamish to eat these fat, juicy, slimy white creatures. They live in the soil or in dead tree trunks and are a common source of protein for some Aborigines. You eat them alive, not cooked. If you are offered one in the Outback, you can either freak out (as most locals would do)—or enjoy its pleasantly nutty taste as a reward for your bravery.

WHEN TO GO

When it is winter in the Northern Hemisphere, Australia is basking in the Southern Hemisphere's summer, and vice versa. Midwinter in Australia is July and August, and the hottest months are November through March. Remember, unlike in the Northern Hemisphere, the farther south you go in Australia, the colder it gets.

The Travel Seasons

Airfares to Australia are lowest from mid-April to late August—the best time to visit the Red Centre and the Great Barrier Reef.

HIGH SEASON The peak travel season in the most popular parts of Australia is the Aussie winter. In much of the country—particularly the northern half—the most pleasant time to travel is April through September, when daytime temperatures are 66°F to 88°F (19°C–31°C) and it rarely rains. June, July, and August are the busiest months in these parts; you'll need to book hotels and tours well in advance, and you will pay higher rates then, too.

On the other hand, Australia's summer is a nice time to visit the southern states, and even in winter temperatures rarely dip below freezing.

Generally, the best months to visit Australia are September and October, when it's often still warm enough to hit the beach in the southern states, it's cool enough to tour Uluru, and the humidity and rains have not come to Cairns (although it will be very hot by Oct).

LOW SEASON October through March (summer) is just too hot, too humid, or too wet—or all three—to tour the Red Centre. North Queensland, including Cairns, suffers an intensely hot, humid wet season from November or December through March or April. So if you decide to travel at this time—and lots of people do—be prepared to take the heat, the inconvenience of potential flooding, and the slight chance of encountering cyclones.

Steer Clear of the Vacation Rush

Try to avoid Australia from Boxing Day (December 26) to the end of January, when Aussies take their summer vacations. In popular seaside holiday spots, hotel rooms and airline seats get as scarce as hen's teeth, and it's a rare airline or hotel that will discount full rates by even a dollar.

Australian National Public Holidays

On national public holidays, services such as banking, postal needs, and purchase of alcohol might be limited or unavailable. There may also be additional holidays as declared by individual states and territories, such as Melbourne Cup Day (1st Tues in November), based on the country's most famous thoroughbred horse race—"the race that stops the nation."

- **New Year's Day,** January 1. Expect the usual fireworks and festivities to begin the night of December 31 to ring in the New Year.
- **Australia Day,** January 26. This national day recognizes the First Fleet's arrival in 1788, when 11 ships made their way from England to establish a colony in Australia.
- **Good Friday,** the Friday before Easter. The Christian commemoration of Jesus' crucifixion and death. In Australia, Good Friday is observed the first Friday after the full moon (on or after Mar 21).
- **Easter Monday,** day after Easter Sunday. The Christian commemoration of Jesus' resurrection from the dead.
- **Anzac Day,** April 25. ANZAC (Australian and New Zealand Army Corps) Day recognizes those who have served the nation in times of war.
- **Christmas Day,** December 25. ***Note:*** If Christmas is on a weekend day, the next Monday is termed a public holiday.
- **Boxing Day,** December 26. Originally a British tradition involving gift-giving, Boxing Day is now an Australian holiday, and some sports kick off their seasons on this date. If Boxing Day falls on a Saturday, the next Monday is deemed a public holiday. If it falls on a Sunday, the next Tuesday is the holiday.

Australia Calendar of Events

For an exhaustive list of events beyond those listed here, check www.frommers.com, where you'll find a searchable, up-to-the-minute roster of what's happening in cities all over the world.

JANUARY

Sydney Festival: Highlights of Sydney's visual and performing-arts festival include 75 free events at indoor and outdoor venues—including the Sydney Opera House, Royal Botanic Gardens, and Barangaroo Reserve—across the city. The festival involves about 154 events featuring 1,330 artists at 49 venues. Call ✆ **02/8248 6500** or go to www.sydneyfestival.org.au. Three weeks from early January.

The Australian Open: The Asia/Pacific Grand Slam is played every year at the Melbourne Park National Tennis Centre. Tickets go on sale in October via Ticketek (www.ticketek.com.au; ✆ **1300/888 104** in Australia or

New Year's fireworks over Sydney Harbour Bridge.

03/9039 9407). For more info check out www.ausopen.com. Last 2 weeks of January.

Australia Day: This national public holiday marks the landing of the First Fleet of convicts at Sydney Cove in 1788. Every town puts on some kind of celebration; in Sydney, there are ferry races and tall ships on the harbor, food and wine stalls in Hyde Park, open days at museums and other attractions, and fireworks in the evening. www.australiaday.com.au. January 26.

FEBRUARY

Sydney Gay & Lesbian Mardi Gras: Two weeks of events, culminating in a spectacular parade of costumed dancers and decorated floats, watched by several hundred thousand onlookers. In 2018 Mardi Gras celebrates its 40th anniversary. Contact Sydney Gay & Lesbian Mardi Gras (www.mardigras.org.au; ✆ **02/9383 0900**). Late February/early March.

MARCH

Formula 1 Australian Grand Prix, Melbourne: The first Grand Prix of the year, on the international FIA Formula 1 World Championship circuit, is battled out on one of its fastest circuits. For tickets, call ✆ **1800/100 030** in Australia, or order online at www.grandprix.com.au. Four days in the second week of March.

Melbourne International Comedy Festival: Venues all over the city participate in this festival of laughs, which attracts top Australian and international talent. For tickets, contact Ticketmaster (www.comedyfestival.com.au; ✆ **1300/660 013**). Late March/mid-April.

APRIL

Anzac Day, nationwide: Australia's national day of mourning for servicemen and women who have died in wars and conflicts. Commemorative services are held even in the smallest towns, some at dawn and some later, with major cities holding street parades for returned servicemen and women. Huge crowds turn out. Visit www.anzacportal.dva.gov.au for details of services throughout Australia. April 25.

JUNE

Sydney Film Festival: Premieres of Aussie and international movies take place in the State Theatre and other venues over 12 days. Contact the Sydney Film Festival (www.sff.org.au; ✆ **1300/733 733** in Australia or 02/8220 6600). Two weeks in June.

AUGUST

Henley-on-Todd Regatta, Alice Springs: Sounds sophisticated, doesn't it? It's actually a harum-scarum race down the dry bed of the Todd River in homemade "boats," made from anything you care to name—an old 4WD chassis, say, or beer cans lashed together. The only rule is the vessel has to look *vaguely* like a boat. Contact the organizers at ✆ **0417/864 085** (mobile phone) or visit www.henleyontodd.com.au. Third Saturday in August.

Melbourne International Film Festival: About 350 films—new releases, shorts, and avant-garde movies—from 50 countries play at venues around the city during this annual festival (www.miff.com.au; ✆ **03/8660 4888**). Three weeks in August.

SEPTEMBER

Melbourne Fringe: During the Fringe festival (www.melbournefringe.com.au; ✆ **03/9660 9600**), the city's streets, pubs, theaters, and restaurants play host to everyone from jugglers and fire-eaters to musicians and indie productions covering all art forms. Three weeks in mid-September/early October.

Brisbane Festival: A highlight of this arts festival is Riverfire, a spectacular pyrotechnics display best seen from the riverbank. The festival program includes music, theatre, dance, comedy, opera, circus, and more. For tickets, contact Qtix (www.brisbanefestival.com.au; ✆ **136 246** in Australia or 07/3846 4444). Three weeks in September.

NOVEMBER

Melbourne Cup, Flemington: They say the entire nation stops to watch this horse race. That's about right. If you're not actually at the A$3.5-million race, you're glued to the TV—or, well, you're probably not an Australian. While it's only a public holiday in Melbourne, all over the country, women wear race-day hats to the office and work is abandoned to make way for a late chicken and champagne lunch while the race is run. And don't even *think* about flagging a cab at the 3pm race time. For tickets, contact Ticketek (www.ticketek.com.au; ✆ **132 849** in Australia); for information, visit www.flemington.com.au. First Tuesday in November.

DECEMBER

Sydney Hobart Yacht Race: Find a cliff-top spot near the Heads to watch the glorious show of spinnakers, as 100 or so yachts leave Sydney Harbour for this grueling world-class event as they head to Hobart, Tasmania. The organizer is the Sydney-based Cruising Yacht Club of Australia (www.cyca.com.au; ✆ **02/8292 7800**). Starts December 26.

New Year's Eve, Sydney: Watching the Sydney Harbour Bridge light up with fireworks is a treat. The main show is at 9pm, not midnight, so young kids don't miss out. Pack a picnic and snag a harborside spot by 4pm, or even earlier at the best vantage point—Mrs. Macquarie's Chair in the Royal Botanic Gardens. December 31.

The Sydney Hobart Yacht Race is a world-class sailing event.

THE LAY OF THE LAND

People who have never visited Australia wonder why such a huge country has a population of just 24.5 million. The truth is, much of Australia is uninhabitable, and about 90% of the population lives on only 2.6% of the continent, mainly clustered around the coast. Climatic and physical land conditions ensure that the only relatively decent rainfall occurs along a thin strip of land around Australia's coast. Compounding that is the fact that Australia falls victim to long droughts. Most of Australia is harsh Outback, characterized by saltbush plains, arid brown crags, shifting sand deserts, and salt-lake country. People survive where they can in this arid land because of one thing—the Great Artesian Basin. This saucer-shaped geological formation comprises about a fifth of Australia's landmass, stretching over much of inland New South Wales, Queensland, South Australia, and the Northern Territory. Beneath it are massive underground water supplies stored during Jurassic and Cretaceous times (some 66–208 million years ago), when the area was much like the Amazon basin is today. Bore holes bring water to the surface and allow sheep, cattle, and humans a respite from the dryness.

As for the climate, as you might expect with a continent the size of Australia, it can differ immensely. The average rainfall in central Australia ranges between just 200 to 250mm (8–10 in.) a year. Summer daytime temperatures range from 90° to 104°F (32°–40°C). In winter, temperatures range from around 64° to 75°F (18°–24°C). Summer in the Southern Hemisphere roughly stretches from early November to the end of February, though it can be hot for a couple of months on either side of these dates, depending where you are.

Parts of the Northern Territory and far northern Queensland are classified as tropical, and as such suffer from very wet summers—often referred to simply as "the Wet." Flooding can be a real fact of life up here. The rest of the year is called "the Dry," for obvious reasons.

Most of Queensland and northern New South Wales are subtropical. This means warm summers and cool winters. Sydney falls into the "temperate" zone, with generally moderate temperatures and no prolonged periods of extreme hot or cold conditions. Parts of central Victoria can get snow in winter, while the Australian Alps, which run through southern central NSW and northeastern Victoria, have good snow cover in winter.

The Queensland coast is blessed with one of the greatest natural attractions in the world. The Great Barrier Reef stretches 2,000km (1,240 miles) from off Gladstone in Queensland to the Gulf of Papua, near Papua New Guinea. It's relatively new, not more than 8,000 years old, although many fear that rising seawater, caused by global warming, will cause its demise. As it is, the invasive Crown of Thorns starfish and a bleaching process believed to be the result of excessive nutrients flowing into the sea from Australia's farming land are already causing significant damage. The Reef is covered in chapter 7.

Australia's other great natural formation is, of course, Uluru—which is sometimes (but not commonly) still called by the name Europeans gave it, Ayers Rock (p. 258).

Australia's Wildlife

Australia's isolation from the rest of the world over millions of years has led to the evolution of forms of life found nowhere else. Probably the strangest of all is the **platypus.** This monotreme, or egg-laying marsupial, has webbed feet, a ducklike bill, and a tail like a beaver's. It lays eggs, and the young suckle from their mother. When a specimen was first brought back to Europe, skeptical scientists insisted it was a fake—a concoction of several different animals sewn together. It is unlikely you will see this shy, nocturnal creature in the wild, but several wildlife parks have them.

Australia is also famous for **kangaroos** and **koalas.** There are 45 kinds of kangaroos and wallabies, ranging in scale from small rat-size kangaroos to the man-size red kangaroos. The koala is a fluffy marsupial (not a bear!) whose nearest relative is the wombat. It eats gum (eucalyptus) leaves and sleeps about 20 hours a day. There's just one koala species, although those found in Victoria are much larger than those in more northern climes.

The animal you're most likely to come across in your trip is the **possum,** named by Captain James Cook after the North American opossum, which he thought they resembled. (In fact, they are from entirely different families of the animal kingdom.) The brush-tailed possum is commonly found in suburban gardens, including those in Sydney.

Then there's the **wombat.** There are four species of this bulky burrower in Australia, but the common wombat is, well, most common.

Hand-feeding kangaroos at Brisbane's Lone Pine Koala Sanctuary.

The **dingo** is a wild dog, varying in color from yellow to a russet red, mainly seen in the Outback. Because dingoes can breed with escaped "pet" dogs, full-blooded dingoes are becoming increasingly rare.

Commonly seen birds in Australia include the fairy penguin or **Little Penguin** along the coast, **black swans, parrots, cockatoos,** and **honeyeaters.**

DANGEROUS NATIVES

Snakes are common in Australia, but you will rarely see one. The most dangerous land snake is the taipan, which hides in the grasslands in northern Australia—one bite contains enough venom to kill up to 200 sheep. If by the remotest chance you are bitten, immediately demobilize the limb, wrapping it tightly (but not tight enough to restrict the blood flow) with a cloth or bandage, and call ✆ **000** for an ambulance. Antivenin should be available at the nearest hospital.

One creature that scares the living daylights out of anyone who visits coastal Australia is the **shark,** particularly the Great White (though these marauders of the sea are mostly only found in colder waters, such as those off South Australia). Unprovoked shark attacks are relatively rare, particularly when you consider how many people go swimming, and vary from year to year. The Australian Shark Attack File kept at Sydney's Taronga Zoo recorded 17 unprovoked attacks in 2016, and two deaths. To put this in perspective, 53 unprovoked attacks (and no fatalities) occurred in U.S. waters (including 10 in Hawaii) that year—the most worldwide—according to the International Shark Attack File maintained by the Florida Museum of Natural History. (More than 60% of these occurred off the coast of Florida.) You are more likely to get hit by a car on your way to the beach than to get taken by a shark. Certainly, more people drown in Australian waters than are victims of shark attack.

There are two types of **crocodile** in Australia: the relatively harmless freshwater croc, which grows to 3m (10 ft.), and the dangerous estuarine (or saltwater) crocodile, which reaches 5 to 7m (16–23 ft.). Freshwater crocs eat fish; estuarine crocs aren't so picky. Never swim in or stand on the bank of any river, swamp, or beach in northern Australia unless you know with certainty that it's croc-free.

Spiders are common all over Australia, with the funnel web spider and the red-back spider being the most aggressive. Funnel webs live in holes in the ground (they spin their webs around a hole's entrance) and stand on their back legs when they're about to attack. Red-backs have a habit of resting under toilet seats and in car trunks, generally outside the main cities. Caution is a good policy.

If you go bushwalking, check your body carefully. **Ticks** are common, especially in eastern Australia, and can cause severe itching and fever. If you find one on you, pull it out with tweezers, taking care not to leave the head behind.

Fish to avoid are **stingrays** (Australian television star Steve Irwin was killed by a stingray barb through the heart), as well as **porcupine fish, stone-fish,** and **lionfish.** Never touch an **octopus** if it has blue rings on it, or a **cone shell,** and be wary of the painful and sometimes deadly tentacles of the **box jellyfish** along the northern Queensland coast in summer. This jellyfish is responsible for more deaths in Australia than snakes, sharks, and saltwater crocodiles.

Closely related to the box jellyfish is the **Irukandji,** which also inhabits northern Australian waters. This deadly jellyfish is only 2.5 centimeters (1 in.) in diameter, which makes it very hard to spot in the water.

If you brush past a jellyfish, or think you have, pour vinegar over the affected site immediately—authorities leave bottles of vinegar on beaches for this purpose. Vinegar deactivates the stinging cells that haven't already affected you, but doesn't affect the venom that has already been injected. If you are in the tropics and you believe you may have been stung by a box jellyfish or an Irukandji, seek medical attention immediately.

In Sydney and north Queensland, you might come across **"stingers,"** also called "blue bottles." These long-tentacled blue jellyfish can inflict a nasty stinging burn that can last for hours. Sometimes you'll see warning signs on patrolled beaches. The best remedy if you are severely stung is to wash the affected area with fresh water and have a very hot bath or shower (preferably with someone else, just for the sympathy).

Threats to the Landscape

Australia is suffering from climate change, water shortages, and serious threats to wildlife and ecosystems. The country is one of the highest per capita polluters in the world, thanks largely to its reliance on mining and coal-fired power generation.

Meanwhile, the Great Barrier Reef is being damaged by coral bleaching, which occurs when water temperatures rise. Corals can recover, but if the heat persists, or if bleaching happens too frequently, they can die. Nutrient-rich sediment washed out to sea from farmland doesn't help matters much, as nutrient-loving algae colonize the already hard-hit corals. The runoff can also contain pesticides and herbicides, which damage the reef further and make it more vulnerable to the introduced crown-of-thorns starfish, which likes snacking on coral.

As for Australia's native animals and birds—well, history hasn't been too kind to them. At least 22 species of birds, 4 frog species, and 27 mammal species have become extinct since European settlement in Australia. Habitat destruction and introduced species have been the main causes of extinctions.

Classified as "critically endangered" or "endangered" today are 24 species of fish, 19 species of frogs, 28 species of reptiles, 65 species of birds, 44 species of mammals, 49 other animals, and 683 species of plants. Many more are classified as vulnerable.

RESPONSIBLE TRAVEL

Sustainable travel—and its close cousin, responsible travel—are important issues in Australia, and you'll find plenty of places that claim to be eco-friendly. So how do you find the places that will truly help you make as little impact as possible on our fragile environment, while still enjoying your holiday? When planning your trip, look for Australian tourism operators who have their tour, attraction, or accommodations accredited under **Ecotourism Australia's** Eco Certification Program (www.ecotourism.org.au). The **Eco Certification** logo is carried by those businesses that are recognized as being tours, attractions, cruises, or accommodations that are environmentally, socially, and economically sustainable. The program assures travelers that these products are backed by a strong commitment to sustainable practices and provide high-quality nature-based tourism experiences. Ecotourism Australia also publishes the online **Green Travel Guide,** which carries a list of its accredited businesses.

Like people in developed nations everywhere, Australians are becoming more aware of their environmental responsibilities. Recycling is common, with local government areas providing bins for general household refuse, paper, and glass, and for vegetative material such as prunings.

Because of frequent and prolonged droughts, Australians have become more aware of where their water supply is coming from. You might be surprised at how water-conscious the average Australian is these days.

That said, what we gain on one hand we often lose on the other. Gas-guzzling four-wheel-drives are popular, four-wheelers zip around the Outback and on some beaches, and air travel within Australia is generally necessary.

If you are keen to offset the large carbon footprint created by your flight to Australia, use public transport where you can, turn electronic gadgets off at the wall when you aren't using them, and recycle batteries if possible. Don't throw cigarette butts on the ground—you risk a possible hefty fine, and your butt might end up polluting Australia's waterways.

There are hundreds of tourism operators and hotels that use the eco-friendly banner when promoting themselves. Choose a hotel designed to reduce its environmental impact with its use of non-toxic cleaners and renewable energy sources. The hotels may be reducing their emissions further by utilizing local food, energy-efficient lighting, and eco-friendly forms of transport. Most hotels now offer you the choice of using the same towels for more than one night—and of course, you should, because laundry makes up around 40% of an average hotel's energy use. Some accommodations offer you the same choice regarding your bed linens if you're staying more than one night.

Choose tours that are eco-friendly, environmentally sustainable, and preferably employ local guides. Opt for a sailing boat rather than a giant motor cruiser to discover the Barrier Reef or the Whitsunday Islands in Queensland, for example, or an Aboriginal guided walking tour over a large coach excursion.

RESOURCES FOR responsible TRAVEL

In addition to the resources for Australia listed above and below, the following websites provide valuable wide-ranging information on sustainable travel.

- Sustainable Travel International (www.sustainabletravel.org) promotes ethical tourism practices.
- Carbonfund (www.carbonfund.org) and **Cool Climate Network** (www.coolclimate.berkeley.edu) provide info on "carbon offsetting," or offsetting the greenhouse gas emitted during flights.

For general info on volunteer travel, visit www.goabroad.com/volunteer-abroad and www.idealist.org.

If you are looking for a way of "giving something back" on your holiday, several organizations offer the opportunity to do some volunteer work in Australia, such as helping to save endangered wildlife. Often there is a fee involved to cover transportation, accommodations, meals, and so on.

Conservation Volunteers (www.conservationvolunteers.com.au; ✆ **1800/032 501** in Australia or 03/5330 2600) offers a range of projects across Australia, including tree planting, wildlife surveys, heritage restoration, and more.

Real Gap Experience (www.realgap.com.au; ✆ **1300/844 270** in Australia) offers you the chance to volunteer in Australia, including in a wildlife sanctuary on Kangaroo Island in South Australia.

Willing Workers on Organic Farms (WWOOF) offers the chance for volunteers to do 4 to 6 hours of work a day in exchange for meals and accommodations, usually in the farmers' family home. WWOOFers (as they are known) have the pick of more than 1,800 host farms around the country. Check out the website (www.wwoof.com.au) or call ✆ **03/5155 0218**.

The official state tourism website for **Victoria** (www.visitvictoria.com/information/volunteer), also recommends volunteering opportunities in that state.

3

SUGGESTED ITINERARIES

Australia's size and its distance from Northern Hemisphere destinations are the two most daunting things about planning a visit here. A week or two is just enough time to scrape the surface of this vast, complex, and fascinating place. It's a long way to come for just a week, but if that's all you can spare, you still want to see as much as possible. While my inclination is to immerse myself in one spot, I know that not everyone can do that. Seeing as much as possible is often a priority, so here are some ideas on how to do just that.

If you're a first-time visitor, with just 1 or 2 weeks, consider **"Australia in 1 Week"** or **"Australia in 2 Weeks."** These itineraries can be adapted to suit your needs; for example, you could replace the Cairns section of "Australia in 1 Week" with the Uluru/ Red Centre suggestions in "Australia in 2 Weeks," flying from Sydney to Uluru.

If you're traveling as a family, the **"Australia for Families"** itinerary is designed to give you some ideas on keeping the young ones occupied (while still being interesting for parents!).

Getting around this continent, where major attractions are thousands of miles apart, can be challenging and time-consuming. Flying is the only way to cover long distances efficiently, but it can also be expensive. Remember to build flying time into your itineraries, and don't try to pack in too much on the days you fly—even domestic flights can be draining, some clocking in at around 3 hours. See "Getting There" and "Getting Around," in chapter 10, for information on air passes and getting the best rates on Australia's domestic carriers.

My best advice: If the pace gets too hectic, just chill out and reorder your sightseeing priorities. Take time to meet the locals and ask their advice on what you should see as well.

AUSTRALIA IN 1 WEEK

Australia is so vast that in 1 week you'll only be able to get to a small corner of it—perhaps one city or a few of its natural wonders. It will be memorable, nevertheless, and careful planning will maximize your time and allow you to see some of the major sights.

Use the following itinerary to make the most of a week in Australia, but make sure you don't exhaust yourself trying to cram everything in. Australians are a laid-back lot, generally, and in some places the pace is relaxed. And that's just the way to enjoy it. One week provides barely enough time to see the best of Sydney, which for most people is the entry point to Australia.

If you have one week and want to head farther afield, there are two main choices, depending on your interests. The **Great Barrier Reef** is a must for divers, but you have to allow time on either side of your reef trip for flying. There are no such problems with Australia's other icon, **Uluru,** in the heart of the **Red Centre.** This triangle of highlights is something of a cliché, but it still gives you a complete Australian experience. Realistically, you will have to choose between the Reef and the Rock, or forego scuba diving while you are in Queensland.

Day 1: Arrive in Sydney ★★★

Check into your hotel and spend whatever time you have upon arrival recovering from the almost-guaranteed jet lag. If you arrive in the morning and have a full day ahead of you, try to stay up. Hit the nearest cafe for a shot of caffeine to keep you going. Head to **Circular Quay,** and from there get a fantastic view of **Sydney Harbour Bridge** ★★★ (p. 83) before strolling to the **Sydney Opera House** ★★★ (p. 85) and soaking up some history at **The Rocks** ★★★. If you have time, take the ferry from Circular Quay to Manly Beach and round off a fairly easy day with fish and chips. Then head to bed for some much-needed sleep.

Sydney's Circular Quay.

Australia in 1 or 2 Weeks

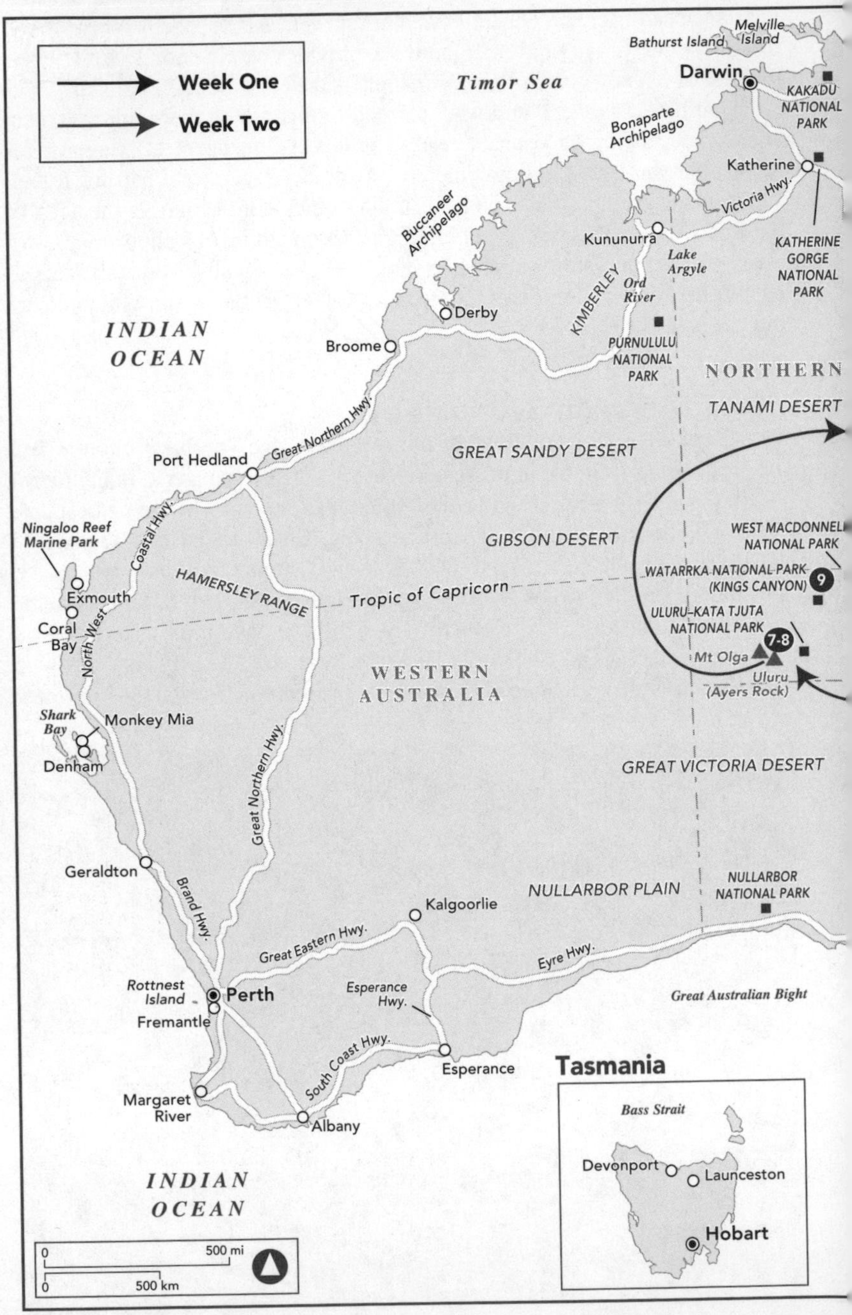

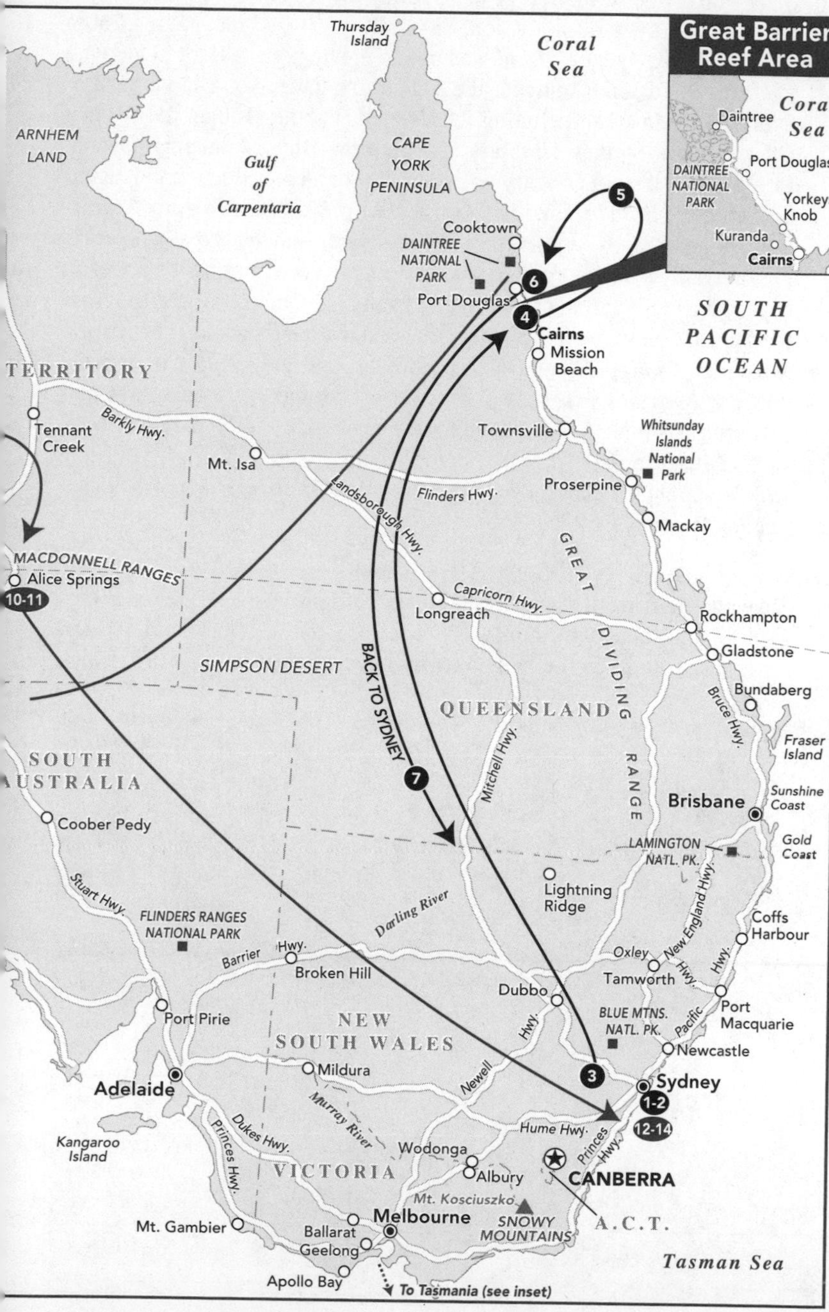

Great Barrier Reef Area
Coral Sea
Daintree
DAINTREE NATIONAL PARK
Port Douglas
Yorkeys Knob
Kuranda
Cairns
Thursday Island
Coral Sea
ARNHEM LAND
Gulf of Carpentaria
CAPE YORK PENINSULA
Cooktown
DAINTREE NATIONAL PARK
Port Douglas
Cairns
Mission Beach
SOUTH PACIFIC OCEAN
TERRITORY
Tennant Creek
Barkly Hwy.
Mt. Isa
Townsville
Whitsunday Islands National Park
Proserpine
Mackay
Landsborough Hwy.
Flinders Hwy.
GREAT DIVIDING RANGE
MACDONNELL RANGES
Alice Springs
Capricorn Hwy.
Longreach
Rockhampton
Gladstone
SIMPSON DESERT
BACK TO SYDNEY
QUEENSLAND
Bruce Hwy.
Bundaberg
Fraser Island
SOUTH AUSTRALIA
Mitchell Hwy.
Brisbane
Sunshine Coast
Gold Coast
Coober Pedy
LAMINGTON NATL. PK.
Lightning Ridge
New England Hwy.
Stuart Hwy.
Darling River
FLINDERS RANGES NATIONAL PARK
Barrier Hwy.
Broken Hill
Oxley Hwy.
Tamworth
Coffs Harbour
Pacific Hwy.
Dubbo
Port Pirie
NEW SOUTH WALES
Newell Hwy.
BLUE MTNS. NATL. PK.
Port Macquarie
Newcastle
Adelaide
Mildura
Sydney
Murray River
Kangaroo Island
Dukes Hwy.
Princes Hwy.
Hume Hwy.
Wodonga
Princes Hwy.
VICTORIA
Albury
CANBERRA
Mt. Kosciuszko
A.C.T.
Mt. Gambier
Ballarat
Melbourne
SNOWY MOUNTAINS
Geelong
Tasman Sea
Apollo Bay
To Tasmania (see inset)

Day 2: Explore Sydney

Start with a ride to the top of the **Sydney Tower** ★ to experience Sydney's highest open-air attraction, **Skywalk** (p. 91), a breathtaking 260m (853 ft.) above Sydney. Harnessed onto a moving, glass-floored viewing platform that extends out over the edge of the tower, you can view all of Sydney's landmarks, including the Sydney Harbour Bridge, the Sydney Opera House, Sydney Harbour, and even the Blue Mountains beyond. Don't worry, it's not as scary as it sounds. For an introduction to Australia's wildlife, head to **Taronga Zoo** ★★★ (p. 92) or the **Sydney Aquarium** ★ (p. 88). If you have time to spare, another great choice is **Featherdale Wildlife Park** ★★★ (p. 91), but keep in mind it's about an hour and a half from the city center. If you enjoy museums, put the **Australian Museum** ★★ (p. 90), the **Australian National Maritime Museum** ★★ (p. 87) at Darling Harbour, and the interactive **Powerhouse Museum** ★★★ (p. 88) on your list for the day. For insight into Sydney's beginnings as a convict settlement, visit the **Hyde Park Barracks Museum** ★★ (p. 90), a convict-built prison. Finish off your day with a twilight (or later on weekends) **BridgeClimb** ★★★ (p. 84) up the Sydney Harbour Bridge.

Day 3: The Blue Mountains ★★★

Take the train from Central Station to **Katoomba** (p. 103) for a day, exploring the beauty of the Blue Mountains—only 2 hours from Sydney. Once there, jump on the **Blue Mountains Explorer** bus (p. 103), which

Wombat cuddling at Featherdale Wildlife Park.

Night Fire by Tjapukai offers enchanting Aboriginal experiences.

allows you to hop on and off wherever you please. There are also many day-tour operators running to the Blue Mountains from Sydney. Whichever mode of transport you use, don't miss the spectacular **Three Sisters** (p. 105) rock formation, best viewed from Echo Point Road at Katoomba. Make sure you also spend some time at **Scenic World** ★ (p. 105), where you can ride the world's steepest railway into a valley full of ancient rainforest, and come back up on a cable car—among other adventures that kids especially will enjoy. At the end of the day, head back to Sydney and have dinner somewhere with a view of the harbor, such as **Waterfront Restaurant** (p. 76), **Sydney Cove Oyster Bar** (p. 75), or **Quay** (p. 74).

Day 4: Cairns, Gateway to the Great Barrier Reef

Take the earliest flight you can from Sydney to Cairns—flight time is 3 hours—and check into a hotel in the city, which on such a tight schedule will make getting to the major attractions quicker and easier than staying out of town on the northern beaches. Explore the city a little and see some wildlife—including a massive saltwater crocodile—in the bizarre setting of the **Cairns ZOOM and Wildlife Dome** ★★ (p. 198), atop the Hotel Sofitel Reef Casino. You will have the rest of the day to head out to visit **Tjapukai** ★★ (p. 199), an Aboriginal cultural park. If you are not going to the Red Centre, this is a great place to learn about Aboriginal culture and life, albeit in a theme-park kind of way. You could spend several hours here, or save the visit for the evening, when **Night Fire by Tjapukai** offers a different look at traditional ceremonies, including dinner and a fire-and-water show.

Day 5: A Day Trip to the Reef ★★★

Day trips to the Great Barrier Reef leave from the **Reef Fleet Terminal.** The trip to the outer reef takes about 2 hours, and once there you will spend your day on a pontoon with about 300 people. Experienced divers may prefer to take a day trip with one of several dive charter companies that take smaller groups and visit two or three reefs. The pontoons of the big operators also offer the chance to take a scenic flight—a truly spectacular experience. Divers must spend another 24 hours in Cairns before flying. If you are content to snorkel, ride the glass-bottom boats, and soak up the sun, you will be able to fly the next day. After returning to Cairns, take a stroll along the **Esplanade** and eat at one of the busy cafes and restaurants that line the strip.

Day 6: Kuranda, a Rainforest Village ★★

Waiting out the day after diving (you can't fly for 24 hr. after you've been on a dive) gives you a chance to discover another aspect of Australia—its rainforests. Take a trip to the mountain village of **Kuranda** aboard the steam train along the **Kuranda Scenic Railway** ★★★ (p. 207), past waterfalls and gorges. In Kuranda, explore the markets and the nature parks and maybe take a **Kuranda Riverboat Tour** ★★ (p. 208), which runs about 45 minutes. Return on the **Skyrail** ★★★ cableway (p. 198), which carries you over the rainforest (you can get to ground level at a couple of stations on the way) to the edge of Cairns. The views are sensational. This is a big day out!

Day 7: Cairns to Sydney

In the morning, head to the airport for your flight to Sydney. Unless you are lucky enough to have an international flight directly out of Cairns, you will spend most of your last day in Australia returning to Sydney. With the time you have left in Sydney, treat yourself to dinner at a restaurant overlooking the harbor, with its bridge and the Opera House illuminated. It's a sight you'll carry home with you.

AUSTRALIA IN 2 WEEKS

With 2 weeks, your visit to Australia will be much more relaxed and you'll get a greater sense of the diversity of Australia's landscape, wildlife, and people. You will be able to explore the country's trio of icons—Sydney, the Great Barrier Reef, and Uluru—in more depth, and maybe even have time to go outside those areas, especially if you limit your icons to two instead of three.

Days 1–6: Sydney to Cairns

Follow the itinerary as outlined in "Australia in 1 Week," above.

Day 7: Cairns to Uluru

Leave Cairns as early as you can. Your flight to Ayers Rock Airport will take around 3 hours. Make sure you book a direct flight, not one that goes

Exploring Uluru–Kata Tjuta National Park on foot.

via Sydney! Try to get a window seat for the spectacular views as you fly over the Outback. If you take the early flight, you can be in **Uluru** by around 10am, which gives you the entire day to take in the enormity of this fabulous monolith. Take the shuttle from **Ayers Rock Resort** (the only place to stay, albeit one with many accommodation choices; p. 262) to the Rock. Spend some time in the impressive and interesting **Uluru–Kata Tjuta Cultural Centre** (p. 260), near the base of Uluru, and explore the area on one of the many walking trails or tours. End the day by watching the sun set over Uluru—an unforgettable sight. After doing all that in a day, you'll be ready for a quiet dinner at whatever hotel you've chosen.

If you decide to **climb Uluru** (remember that the traditional Aboriginal owners would strongly prefer you didn't), make sure you don't do it at the hottest time of day. A climb should take you between 2 and 4 hours, depending on your fitness level.

Day 8: Exploring Uluru ★★★

Sunrise is one of those magic times at Uluru, so make the effort to get up early. This is also a great time to do the 10.6km (6½-mile) **Base Walk** circumnavigating Uluru (p. 265), which takes 2 to 3 hours. There are many ways to experience Uluru, including camel rides, Harley-Davidson tours, and helicopter joy flights, but walking up close to the Rock beats them all.

You will also have time today to head to **Kata Tjuta** (also called "The Olgas"; p. 268), where you'll see there's much more to the Red Centre than just one rock. Kata Tjuta is about 48km (30 miles) west of Uluru, but plenty of tour operators go there if you don't have your own wheels.

End your day in the desert with the **Sounds of Silence** dinner or the slightly more upmarket, more intimate **Tali Wiru ★★★** dinner (p. 263), run by Ayers Rock Resort. Sip champagne as the sun sets over Uluru to the eerie music of the didgeridoo, and then tuck into kangaroo, barramundi, and other native foods. But it's not the food you're here for—it's the silence and the stars. A stargazing session with an astronomer ends a memorable evening.

Day 9: Uluru to Kings Canyon

Hire a four-wheel-drive vehicle and tackle the long Outback drive from Uluru to Alice Springs, stopping for a night at **Kings Canyon Resort** (www.kingscanyonresort.com.au). It is 306km (190 miles) from Uluru to Kings Canyon (also known as **Watarrka National Park**), which offers another unbeatable look at Outback Australia. You can spend the afternoon walking up the side of the canyon and around the rim. Parts of it are very steep, and the whole hike will take you around 4 hours, but the trip is well worth the effort. A gentler walk is the short and shady canyon floor walk.

Day 10: Kings Canyon to Alice Springs

Get an early start for Alice Springs, and take the unpaved but interesting **Mereenie Loop Road,** which threads through the **Glen Helen Gorge** or the historic **Hermannsburg** mission settlement (p. 257). Whichever road you take, the scenery is like nowhere else. You will probably spend most of the day driving to Alice, making a few stops along the way.

On arrival, check into a hotel and head out to one of the local restaurants, several of which offer sophisticated versions of "bush tucker," including kangaroo, emu, and crocodile dishes.

Hiking Kings Canyon/Watarrka National Park.

Day 11: Alice Springs

If you can stand another early start, take a **dawn balloon flight** over the desert (p. 253), usually followed by a champagne breakfast. If you don't head back to bed immediately for a few hours of catch-up sleep, there are plenty of attractions to discover, including the **Alice Springs Desert Park ★★★** (p. 250) for a look at some unusual Australian creatures; the **School of the Air ★★** (p. 252); and the **Royal Flying Doctor Service ★★** base (p. 252). In the afternoon, drop into the **Mbantua Fine Art Gallery and Cultural Museum** (p. 254) to see some of the best Aboriginal art from the outlying communities in the desert region called Utopia, famed for its paintings. Alternatively, visit the **Alice Springs Telegraph Station Historical Reserve ★★** (p. 250), set in an oasis just outside town, for a look at early settler life. Finish the day with a **sunset camel ride** (p. 252) down the dry Todd River bed and have dinner at the camel farm.

Day 12: Alice Springs to Sydney

Direct flights from Alice Springs to Sydney leave in the early afternoon, so you'll have all morning to explore more of the town and perhaps buy some Aboriginal art. (This is one of the best places to get it.)

On arrival in Sydney, after an almost 3-hour flight, check into your hotel and spend the evening discovering the city's nightlife.

Day 13: A Day at Bondi Beach

For sands of a different hue from those you've experienced in recent days, take the bus to Sydney's most famous beach, **Bondi** (p. 95), and spend the day lazing on the sand or—in summer, at least—taking a dip in the surf. Take a public bus or the Bondi Explorer from Circular Quay, which gives you a choice of harborside bays and coastal beaches. The scenic cliff-top walk to **Bronte Beach** is recommended, or you can continue farther to **Coogee.**

Day 14: Sydney

Your final day in Australia can be spent on last-minute shopping and seeing those Sydney sights that you haven't yet had time for. Cap it all off with a seafood dinner somewhere with a fantastic view of the Harbour Bridge.

AUSTRALIA FOR FAMILIES

Australia is a wonderful destination for kids—and not just because of the kangaroos and koalas. Our suggestion is to explore Sydney for 2 days with family in tow, then head up to the beautiful Blue Mountains on a day trip to ride the cable car and the world's steepest railway. The climax comes with a few days of exploring the Barrier Reef and the rainforest around Port Douglas.

Days 1 & 2: Sydney

First off, head to Circular Quay to see the **Sydney Opera House ★★★**. A tour inside might be a bit much for younger kids, but you can walk around a fair bit of it and take the obligatory photos of Australia's most famous landmark. To stretch your legs, head from here into the **Royal Botanic Garden** (p. 97) to spot long-beaked ibises wandering around the grass and hundreds of fruit bats squabbling among the treetops. Walk back past the Opera House and the ferries to **The Rocks,** where you can take a quick stroll through the historic streets, stopping for a look at some of the trendy shops or the market on Saturdays.

There are plenty of places to eat lunch at Circular Quay, where you can sit outside and watch the world go by. After lunch, take a ferry to **Taronga Zoo ★★★**, where a cable car zips you up the hill to the main entrance. All the kids' favorite animals are here, from kangaroos and koalas to platypuses, located in a nocturnal house. A farmyard section edges onto a playground, with lots of water features to give your kids a sprinkle on a hot day.

On **Day 2,** head to the city center for an elevator ride up to the top of **Sydney Tower ★** (p. 91), where you can look right across Sydney as far as the Blue Mountains in the distance. Entry includes admission to the 4D Cinema Experience. It's a short walk from here to Darling Harbour, where you can cap off the morning with a visit to **SEA LIFE Sydney Aquarium ★**. The sharks that swim right above your head are huge, but the penguins are hard to beat for cuteness.

Eat lunch at one of the many cheap eateries at Darling Harbour before taking the ferry from near the Aquarium back to Circular Quay.

Sharks at SEA LIFE Sydney Aquarium.

The Scenic World Railway descends through the ancient tree fern forest.

If it's a hot day, or you simply want to hit the beach, you have two choices: From Circular Quay, you can take a half-hour ferry ride or a 15-minute high-speed JetCat trip to **Manly** (p. 96). Here you can laze the afternoon away and even rent a surfboard or bodyboard. Or hop a bus to **Bondi Beach** (p. 95), where you can reward your efforts with gelato or a late-afternoon pizza from **Pompei's** (p. 78).

Day 3: The Blue Mountains

You could easily spend a couple more days with the kids having fun in Sydney, but you shouldn't miss a trip to the mountains. If you go, prepare for a long day; pack plenty of snacks and a few favorite toys. Several companies run tour buses to the area, stopping off at an animal park along the way. The best one to visit is **Featherdale Wildlife Park ★★★** (p. 91), where you can get up close to more kangaroos, koalas, and Tasmanian devils. The tour also stops at **Scenic World ★** (p. 105), where you can take the short ride on the Scenic Railway. It's very steep, so hold on tight. At the bottom, you'll find yourselves among an ancient tree fern forest—it's truly remarkable. A short walk takes you to the **Skyway,** a cable car that travels 300m (984 ft.) above the Jamison Valley.

Elsewhere in the mountains, there are fabulous views across craggy bluffs and deep bowls of gum trees. See chapter 4 for details.

Days 4, 5 & 6: The Reef & the Rainforest

Now it's time to head north to the Tropics. You'll need to fly, of course; otherwise it would take you several days to drive up the coast. The flight from Sydney to Cairns takes 3 hours. As a family, you might prefer to base yourselves in **Port Douglas** (p. 209) rather than Cairns—the Port Douglas beach is huge and uncrowded, and some of the best Barrier Reef trips originate from here. "Port," as the locals call it, is about an hour's drive from Cairns, so your first day will be largely taken with getting there.

After all that traveling, take the rest of the day to relax on beautiful **Four Mile Beach,** but remember to swim inside the nets off the sand; the "stingers" (box jellyfish) around here can cause life-threatening stings, especially where kids are concerned.

On **Day 5,** it's time to visit the **Reef.** Thankfully, the dangerous jellyfish are very uncommon on the Reef itself. Cruise boats take around 90 minutes to get from Port Douglas to the outer reef; but once there, you are in for some amazing snorkeling. Expect to see numerous species of corals and fish, and even an occasional turtle. A good seafood lunch is generally served on board, so you won't go hungry!

Swimming hole in Mossman Gorge.

Day 6 will be another nature experience, this time meeting some of the giants of the north. In the morning, head out to **Mossman Gorge ★★★** (p. 214), a 15- to 20-minute drive from Port Douglas, for some Aboriginal culture in the rainforest with **Ngadiku Dreamtime Walks,** guided by a member of the local Kuku-Yalanji tribe. On your way back to Cairns, stop off at **Hartley's Crocodile Adventures ★★★** (p. 200) to see crocs in their natural habitat. After the 3pm "croc attack" show, you'll have time for a leisurely drive back to Cairns to get ready for your departure. See chapter 7 for detailed information on these attractions.

Sydney's kid-friendly Luna Park amusement park.

Day 7: Fly Back to Sydney

If you have time to kill before you leave Sydney, take the kids by ferry to **Luna Park ★**, just across from Circular Quay, or walk there across the Harbour Bridge. Although this fun park is small, with few rides suitable for younger kids, it does boast a magnificent view across to the Harbour Bridge and Opera House, which look glorious after the sun's gone down.

SYDNEY

Warm-natured, sun-kissed, and naturally good-looking, Sydney is rather like its lucky, lucky residents. Situated on one of the world's most striking harbors, where the twin icons of the Sydney Opera House and Harbour Bridge steal the limelight, relaxed Sydney is surprisingly close to nature. Within minutes you can be riding the waves on Bondi Beach, bushwalking in Manly, or gazing out across Botany Bay, where the first salt-encrusted Europeans arrived in the 18th century. You can understand why they never wanted to leave.

4

For that "I'm in Sydney!" feeling, nothing beats the first glimpse of the white-sailed Opera House and the iconic Harbour Bridge, which you can climb for a bird's-eye view of the sparkling harbor. Move on to the Royal Botanical Gardens' tropical greenery and the Museum of Contemporary Art's cutting-edge exhibitions. With 70 beaches close by—from the fizzing surf of famous Bondi Beach to Manly's coastal walks and pine-flanked bays—it's no wonder Sydneysiders look so bronzed and relaxed.

Don't let the knockout views of Sydney Harbour distract you from your shopping in The Rocks' specialty shops and galleries, crammed with one-off gifts, quirky fashion, and hand-painted ceramics. Sydneysiders shop for designer styles under the soaring glass arches of the Queen Victoria Building. There's also the city's very own Oxford Street and the fashionable Surry Hills and Paddington suburbs. Combine a morning looking for vintage clothes and swimwear at Bondi Market with time out on the beach.

Dine on a different cuisine every night in multicultural Sydney—whether late-night noodles in Chinatown, tasty tapas in the Spanish Quarter, or authentic Thai curries on bohemian King Street. BYO restaurants and sensible prices make eating out affordable in all but the very top places—French-Japanese Tetsuya's, for instance. Head to Circular Quay's sleek waterfront restaurants for the Opera House view and Australia's distinctive modern cuisine—a fusion of Australian, Mediterranean, and spicy Asian flavors.

There's so much to do in Sydney that you could easily spend a week here and still not see it all.

The iconic Sydney Opera House.

ESSENTIALS

Arriving

BY PLANE

Sydney International Airport (www.sydneyairport.com.au) is 8km (5 miles) from the city center. Shuttle buses and the Airport Link train link the international and domestic terminals. Single tickets on both cost A$6. The journey takes up to 10 minutes by road and 2 minutes by train. The bus operates every 30 minutes from 6am to 9pm (more often in the morning peak period), and the train is more frequent, between 5am and midnight. Bus stops are on arrivals levels, at T1 Bus Bay 1 (near the McDonald's) and at T2 on the first roadway in the center of the terminal. Qantas and Virgin Australia offer seamless transfer services. In both terminals, you'll find luggage carts, wheelchairs, a post office (daily 6am–8:30pm), mailboxes, currency exchange, duty-free shops, restaurants, bars, stores, showers, luggage lockers, a baggage-hold service for larger items, ATMs, and tourist-information desks. You can rent mobile phones in the international terminal. Smarte Carte (at the southern end of the arrivals level) has luggage storage for A$13 a day for a small bag and A$16 for a suitcase or backpack. Luggage trolleys are free to use in the international arrival terminal but cost A$4 outside departure terminals (you'll need coins).

Airport Link (www.airportlink.com.au) trains connect the international and domestic airports to the city stations of Central, Museum, St. James, Circular Quay, Wynyard, and Town Hall. You'll need to change trains for other Sydney stations. Unfortunately, the line has no dedicated luggage areas, and because it's also a commuter train to the city from the suburbs it gets very crowded during rush hours (around 7–9am and 4–6:30pm). If you have lots of luggage, it's probably best to take a taxi. The train takes 10 minutes to reach the Central Railway Station and continues to Circular Quay. Trains leave every 10 minutes and cost A$18 one-way for adults and A$14 for children from the international terminal. Round-trip tickets are available only if you want to return to the airport on the same day.

KST Airporter coaches (www.kst.com.au; ✆ **02/8339 0155**) travel to the city center from bus stops outside the terminals every 15 minutes. This service will drop you off (and pick you up) at hotels in the city, Kings Cross, and Darling Harbour. Pickups from hotels require at least 3 hours' advance notice; you can book online. Tickets cost A$14 adults and A$12 children 4 to 10 one-way; A$26 adults and A$20 children round-trip.

BY TRAIN

Central Station (✆ **131 500** for Sydney Trains, or 132 232 for NSW Train-Link interstate trains) is the main city and interstate train station. It's at the top of George Street in downtown Sydney. All interstate trains depart from here, and it's a major Sydney Trains hub. Many city buses leave from neighboring Railway Square for such places as Town Hall and Circular Quay.

BY BUS

Greyhound coaches (✆ **02/9212 9505**) operate from the Central Station Coach Terminal at the Western Forecourt of the station (Bays 5 and 6, up the escalators from Eddy Ave.).

BY CRUISE SHIP

Ships dock at the **Overseas Passenger Terminal** in The Rocks, opposite the Sydney Opera House, or the White Bay Cruise Terminal in the suburb of Rozelle, about 5km (3 miles) from the city center.

BY CAR

Drivers enter Sydney from the north on the Pacific Highway, from the south on the M5 and Princes Highway, and from the west on the Great Western Highway.

Taxi Savvy

Taxi queues can be long, and drivers may try to cash in by insisting you share a cab with other passengers in line at the airport. Here's the scam: After dropping off the other passengers, the cab-driver will attempt to charge you the full price of the journey, despite the fact that the other passengers paid for their sections. You certainly won't save any money sharing a cab if this happens, and your journey will be a long one. If you are first in line in the taxi stand, the law states that you can refuse to share the cab. Taxi drivers appreciate a tip, but there is no compulsion to do so. If you've had good service, a 10% tip is enough.

A taxi from the airport to the city center costs about A$55. An expressway, the Eastern Distributor, is the fastest way to reach the city from the airport. There's a A$5 toll (the taxi driver pays the toll and adds the cost to your fare), but there is no toll to the airport. A 10% credit-card charge applies, and the Sydney airport charges a A$4.25 fee to catch a taxi from there. An Uber ride will cost around A$30 from the international terminal to the city center.

Visitor Information

The Sydney Visitor Centre, corner of Argyle and Playfair streets, The Rocks (www.bestof.com.au; © **02/8273 0000**), is a good place to pick up maps, brochures, Youth Hostel Association (YHA) cards, and general tourist information. A second outpost is at the **Sydney Visitor Centre Darling Harbour,** at 33 Wheat Rd. (behind the IMAX), Darling Harbour. Both are open from 9:30am to 5:30pm daily (closed Good Friday and Christmas Day). In Manly, find the **Hello Manly Booking and Information Centre** (www.hellomanly.com.au; © **02/9976 1430**) at Manly Wharf (where the ferries come in). It's open Monday to Friday from 9am to 5pm and on weekends and public holidays (closed Christmas Day) between 10am and 4pm.

Elsewhere, **City of Sydney information kiosks,** at Circular Quay (corner of Pitt and Alfred sts.) and at Kings Cross (corner of Darlinghurst Rd. and Springfield Ave.) provide maps, brochures, and advice and are open daily (except Christmas Day) from 9am to 5pm. Another kiosk at Dixon Street (near Goulburn St.) is open from 11am to 5pm.

A good website for events, entertainment, dining, and shopping is **www.sydney.com**.

City Layout

Sydney is one of the largest cities in the world, covering more than 1,730 sq. km (675 sq. miles) from the sea to the foothills of the Blue Mountains. Thankfully, the city center, or Central Business District (CBD), is compact. The jewel in Sydney's crown is its magnificent harbor, which empties into the South Pacific Ocean through headlands known as North Head and South Head. On the southern side of the harbor are the high-rises of the city center; the Sydney Opera House; a string of beaches, including Bondi; and the inner suburbs. The Sydney Harbour Bridge and a tunnel connect the city center to the high-rises of the North Sydney business district and the affluent suburbs and beaches beyond.

MAIN ARTERIES & STREETS

The city's main thoroughfare, George Street, runs up from **Circular Quay,** past Wynyard train station and Town Hall, to Central Station. At the time of this writing, George Street was still a mass of construction work as a new light rail system, due to be completed in 2019, is being built. Other main streets running parallel to George include Pitt, Elizabeth, and Macquarie streets. **Macquarie Street** runs up from the Sydney Opera House, past

Sydney Tower is the city's tallest structure and an easy-to-spot landmark.

the Royal Botanic Garden and Hyde Park. **Martin Place** is a pedestrian thoroughfare between Macquarie and George streets. It's about halfway between Circular Quay and Town Hall—in the heart of the city center. The easy-to-spot Sydney Tower, facing onto pedestrian-only **Pitt Street Mall** on Pitt Street, is the main city-center landmark. Next to Circular Quay and across from the Opera House is **The Rocks,** a cluster of small streets that was once part of a historic larger slum and is now a tourist attraction. Roads meet at **Town Hall** from Kings Cross in one direction and Darling Harbour in the other. From Circular Quay to The Rocks, it's a 5- to 10-minute stroll; to Wynyard a 10-minute walk; and to Town Hall a 20-minute stroll. From Town Hall to the near side of Darling Harbour it's about a 10-minute walk.

Neighborhoods in Brief

SOUTH OF SYDNEY HARBOUR

Circular Quay This transport hub for ferries, buses, and trains is tucked between the Harbour Bridge and the Sydney Opera House. The Quay, as it's called, is a good spot for a stroll, and its outdoor restaurants and street performers are popular. The Rocks, the Royal Botanic Garden, the Contemporary Art Museum, and the start of the main shopping area (centered on Pitt and George sts.) are a short walk. To get there by public transport, take a train, ferry, or city bus to Circular Quay.

The Rocks This small historic area, a short stroll west of Circular Quay, is packed with colonial stone buildings, intriguing back streets, boutiques, pubs, tourist stores, restaurants, and hotels. It's the most exclusive place to stay in the city because of its beauty and its proximity to the Opera House and harbor. Shops are geared toward Sydney's yuppies and wealthy tourists—don't expect bargains. On weekends, a portion of George Street is blocked off for The Rocks Market, with stalls selling souvenirs and crafts. A foodies' market operates on Fridays. To reach the area by public transport, take any bus for Circular Quay or The Rocks or a train or ferry to Circular Quay. Check out www.therocks.com for event info.

Town Hall In the heart of the city, this area is home to the main department stores and two Sydney landmarks, the Town Hall and a historic shopping mall called the Queen Victoria Building (QVB). Also in this area are Sydney Tower and the boutique-style chain stores of Pitt Street Mall. Farther up George Street are movie houses, the entrance to Sydney's Spanish district (around Liverpool St.), and Chinatown. Take any bus from Circular Quay or a train to the Town Hall stop.

Darling Harbour Designed as a tourist precinct, Darling Harbour features Sydney's main convention, exhibition, and entertainment centers; a waterfront promenade; the Sydney Aquarium; an IMAX theater; the Australian Maritime Museum; the Powerhouse Museum; The Star casino; a food court; and plenty of shops. Nearby are the restaurants of Cockle Bay and King Street Wharf. To reach Darling Harbour by public transport, take a ferry from Circular Quay (Wharf 5) or the light rail from Central Station. It's a short walk from Town Hall. Check out www.darlingharbour.com for what's on.

Kings Cross & the Suburbs Beyond "The Cross," as it's known, is the city's red-light district—and it's also home to some of Sydney's best-known nightclubs and restaurants. The area has plenty of backpacker hostels, a few bars, and some upscale hotels. The main drag, Darlinghurst Road, is short but crammed with strip joints, prostitutes, drunks, and such. It's certainly colorful. There's a heavy police presence and usually plenty of "ordinary" people around, but do take care. Beyond the strip clubs and glitter, the neighborhoods of Elizabeth Bay, Double Bay, and Rose Bay hug the waterfront. To get here, take a train to Kings Cross. From the next stop, Edgecliff, it's a short walk to Double Bay and a longer one to Rose Bay along the coast.

Paddington/Oxford Street This central-city neighborhood, centered on trendy Oxford Street, is known for its terrace

Bronte Beach.

houses, off-the-wall boutiques and bookshops, and restaurants, pubs, and nightclubs. It's also the heart of Sydney's large gay community and has a liberal scattering of gay bars and dance spots. To get there by public transport, take bus nos. 333, 380, or 397 from Circular Quay; no. 440 from Central Station; or nos. 333, 378, or 380 from Bondi Junction. The lower end of Oxford Street is a short walk from Museum Station (take the Liverpool St. exit).

Darlinghurst Between grungy Kings Cross and upscale Oxford Street, this extroverted, grimy, terraced area is home to some of Sydney's best cafes—though it's probably not wise to wander around here at night alone. Take the train to Kings Cross and head right from the exit.

Central The congested, polluted crossroads around Central Station, the city's main train station, has little to recommend it. Buses run from here to Circular Quay, and it's a 20-minute walk to Town Hall. The Sydney Central YHA (youth hostel) is here.

Glebe Young professionals and students come to this central-city neighborhood for the cafes, restaurants, pubs, and shops along the main thoroughfare, Glebe Point Road. All this, plus a location 15 minutes from the city and 30 minutes from Circular Quay, makes it a good place for budget-conscious travelers. To reach Glebe, take the light rail from Central Station or Darling Harbour.

Bondi & the Southern Beaches Some of Sydney's most glamorous surf beaches—Bondi, Bronte, and Coogee—lie along the South Pacific coast, southeast of the city center. Bondi has a wide sweep of beach (crowded in summer), some interesting restaurants and bars, plenty of attitude, and beautiful bodies—but no train station. To reach Bondi, take bus no. 333 to Bondi Beach from Circular Quay—it takes about 40 minutes. You need to buy a ticket at a newsstand or 7-Eleven store beforehand. Bus no. 440 from Railway Square, Central Station, goes to Bronte, and bus no. 373 travels to Coogee from Circular Quay.

Watsons Bay Watsons Bay is known for The Gap—a section of dramatic sea cliffs—as well as several good restaurants and a good beer garden. It's a terrific spot to spend a sunny afternoon. To reach it, take bus no. 324 from Circular Quay. There's limited ferry service daily from Circular Quay (Wharf 4), starting at 10:05am Monday through Friday, 9:35am on weekends and holidays.

NORTH OF SYDNEY HARBOUR

North Sydney You can see the giant smiling clown face of Luna Park from Circular Quay, but North Sydney—across the Harbour Bridge—has little in the way of tourist attractions. It's predominantly a business area. Chatswood (take a train from Central or Wynyard station) has some good suburban-type shopping; Milsons Point has a decent pub, the Kirribilli Hotel.

The North Shore Ferries and buses provide access to these wealthy neighborhoods across the Harbour Bridge. Gorgeous Balmoral Beach, Taronga Zoo, and upscale boutiques are the attractions in Mosman. Take a ferry from Circular Quay (Wharf 2) to Taronga Zoo (10 min.) and a bus to Balmoral Beach (another 10 min.).

Manly Half an hour from Circular Quay by ferry, Manly is famous for its ocean beach—it gives Bondi a run for its money—and scores of cheap food outlets. A privately operated fast-ferry service also runs from Circular Quay to Manly.

WEST OF THE CITY CENTER

Balmain A short ferry ride from Circular Quay, Balmain was once Sydney's main shipbuilding area. In the last few decades, the area has become trendy and expensive. The neighborhood has a village feel to it, abounds with restaurants and pubs, and stages a popular Saturday market at the local church. Take bus nos. 441 or 442 from Town Hall or a ferry from Circular Quay, and then a short bus ride (or walk) up the hill to the main shopping area.

Getting Around

BY PUBLIC TRANSPORTATION

State Transit operates the city's buses and ferry network; **Sydney Trains** runs the urban and suburban trains; and **Sydney Ferries** runs the public passenger ferries. Some private bus lines operate buses in the outer suburbs. In addition, a light rail line runs between Central Station and Wentworth Park in Pyrmont; a 12km (7½-mile) network extension is in the works and slated for completion in 2019. **Infoline** (www.transportnsw.info; ✆ **131 500**) is a one-stop search engine for bus, train, light rail, and ferry timetables. Public transit fares are subject to change, so the prices below should act only as a guide. An electronic ticketing system, the **Opal Card,** is used for trains, buses, ferries, and light rail, or you can buy paper tickets.

BY PUBLIC BUS

Buses are frequent and reliable and cover a wide area of metropolitan Sydney. For regular public buses, the minimum fare (which covers most short hops in the city) with a paper ticket is A$2.60 for a 4km (2½-mile) "section." The farther you go, the cheaper each section is. For example, the 44km (27-mile) trip to Palm Beach, way past Manly, costs A$5.40. Sections are marked on bus-stand signs, but if you're confused or in doubt, ask the bus driver. It is much cheaper to travel with an Opal Card, and on Sundays your card allows all-day travel for a maximum of A$2.50.

Most buses bound for the northern suburbs, including night buses to Manly and the bus to Taronga Zoo, leave from Wynyard Park on Carrington Street, behind the Wynyard train station on George Street. Buses to the southern beaches, such as Bondi and Bronte, and the western and eastern suburbs leave from Circular Quay. Buses to Balmain leave from behind the QVB.

Buses run from 4:30am to around midnight during the week, less frequently on weekends and holidays. Some night buses to outer suburbs run throughout the night. You can buy single tickets onboard.

BY SIGHTSEEING BUS

Bright red open-top **Sydney Explorer** buses operate daily, traveling a circuit that takes in 24 places of interest. These include the Sydney Opera House, the Royal Botanic Garden, the State Library, Mrs. Macquarie's Chair, the Art Gallery of New South Wales, Kings Cross, Elizabeth Bay House, the QVB, Sydney Tower, the Australian Museum, Chinatown, Darling Harbour, and The Rocks. Bus stops are identified by a distinctive red sign. The interval between services is about 15 to 20 minutes, and you can board the bus at any stop on the route. The first departure from Alfred Street (near the corner of Pitt St.) at Circular Quay is at 8:30am, and the last service returns you to Circular Quay at 7:30pm.

The **Bondi Explorer** operates every day, traveling a 30km (19-mile) circuit around the eastern harborside bays and coastal beaches. The 10 stops along the way include Chinatown, Sydney Tower, Double Bay, Rose Bay, Bondi Beach, North Bondi, and Paddington's Oxford Street. The interval between the hop-on-hop-off services is around 30 minutes. The first departure is from Central Station (Stop A on Pitt St., bus bay 18) at 9:30am. Tickets allow you to do both the Sydney and Bondi Explorer tours, and cost A$50 for adults, A$33 for children 5 to 16, and A$130 for a family of four for 24 hours; or A$70 adults, A$46 children, and A$186 families for 48 hours. If you stay on the bus, the full circuit of each tour will take around 90 minutes. When planning your itinerary, remember that some attractions, such as museums, close at 5pm. Buy tickets onboard the bus. Call © **02/9567 8400** for details or check out www.theaustralianexplorer.com.au.

BY FERRY

The best way to get a taste of a city that revolves around its harbor is to jump aboard a ferry. The main ferry terminal is at Circular Quay. For ferry information, call © **131 500,** check out **www.transportnsw.info**, or visit the ferry information office opposite Wharf 4. One-way trips within the inner harbor (virtually everywhere except Manly) cost A$6.90 for adults and A$3.45 for children ages 4 to 15. Kids 3 and under travel free.

The ferry to Manly takes 30 minutes, and one-way tickets cost A$8.70 for adults and A$4.35 for children. It leaves from Wharf 3. Ferries run from 6am to midnight. The privately run **Manly Fast Ferry** (www.manlyfastferry.com.au; © **02/9583 1199**) uses its own ticketing system and turnstiles and departs from Wharf 6 at Circular Quay. Tickets cost around A$17 adults and A$10 kids, round-trip, depending on the time of day. The first ferry leaves Circular Quay at 6:40am and the last at 7:30pm; the last fast ferry departs Manly at 7:50pm. Ferries operate every 25 minutes or so and the journey takes 18 minutes. Fast Ferry also offers a Harbour Beaches sightseeing ferry (Sat and Sun only) that goes from Manly to Watson's Bay and Rose Bay, for A$15 adults, half price for children, and A$38 for a family.

BY TRAIN

Sydney's publicly owned train system is a good news/bad news way to get around. The good news is that it can be a cheap and relatively efficient way to

An open-top Sydney Explorer sightseeing bus on George Street, the city's main drag.

see the city; the bad news is that the system is limited. Many tourist areas—including Manly, Bondi Beach, and Darling Harbour—are not connected to the network. Though trains tend to run regularly, the timetable is unreliable. And many carriages aren't air-conditioned, so it can be really hot in summer.

Single tickets within the city center cost A$4.10 adults and A$2 children. Round-trip tickets cost twice as much. Weekly tickets are also available. Information is available from **Infoline** (www.transportnsw.info; or ✆ **131 500** in Australia).

BY METRO LIGHT RAIL

A system of trams runs on a route that traverses a 3.6km (2¼-mile) track between Central Station and Wentworth Park in Pyrmont. The route is currently being extended to a 12km (7½-mile) network that will have 19 stops, extending from Circular Quay along George Street to Central Station, through Surry Hills to Moore Park, then to Kensington and Kingsford and Randwick. Services are expected to start running in 2019; see www.sydneylightrail.transport.nsw.gov.au for updates. The current light rail line provides good access to Chinatown, Paddy's Markets, Darling Harbour, The Star casino and entertainment complex, and the Sydney Fish Markets; and from Pyrmont to inner-west suburbs such as Glebe and Leichhardt. Trams run every 10 minutes. The one-way fare is A$2.60 to A$4.20 for adults and A$1.30 to A$2.10 for kids 4 to 15, depending on the distance. Round-trip tickets are available. Call ✆ **131 500** or check out www.transportnsw.info for details.

BY TAXI

Several taxi companies serve the city center and suburbs. All journeys are metered. If you cross either way on the Harbour Bridge or through the Harbour Tunnel, it will cost a few extra dollars (depending on the time of day). An extra 10% will be added if you pay by credit card.

In the city, taxis line up at stands such as those opposite Circular Quay and Central Station. They are also frequently found in front of hotels. A yellow light on top of the cab means it's vacant. Cabs can be hard to come by on Friday and Saturday nights and between 2 and 3pm every day, when cabbies are changing shifts after 12 hours on the road. Passengers must wear seatbelts in the front and back seats. The **Taxi Complaints Hotline** (✆ **1800/648 478** in Australia) deals with problem taxi drivers. Taxis are licensed to carry up to four people.

The main taxi companies are **Taxis Combined Services** (www.taxiscombined.com.au; ✆ 133 300), **Silver Service Fleet** (www.silverservice.com.au; ✆ 133 100), **RSL Cabs** (www.rslcabs.com.au; ✆ 02/9581 1111), **Legion Cabs** (www.legioncabs.com.au; ✆ 131 451), **Premier Cabs** (www.premiercabs.com.au; ✆ 131 017), and **St. George Cabs** (www.stgeorgecabs.com.au; ✆ 132 166). **Uber** also operates in Sydney.

BY WATER TAXI

Water taxis operate 24 hours a day and are a quick, convenient way to get to waterfront restaurants, harbor attractions, and some suburbs. They can also be chartered for private cruises. Fares for a direct transfer are based on an initial flag-fall for the hire of the vessel and then a charge per person traveling. A 45-minute jaunt on Sydney Harbour costs A$45 adults, A$30 children, or A$120 for a family of four. On most transfers, the more people traveling, the lower the fare per person. The main operators are **Yellow Water Taxis** (www.yellowwatertaxis.com.au; ✆ **1800/326 822** in Australia) and **Water Taxis Combined** (www.watertaxis.com.au; ✆ **02/9555 8888**).

The best—and cheapest—way to see Sydney Harbour is from the deck of a passenger ferry.

BY CAR

Traffic restrictions, parking, and congestion can make getting around by car frustrating, but if you plan to visit some of the outer suburbs or take excursions elsewhere in New South Wales, renting a car will give you more flexibility. The **National Roads and Motorists' Association (NRMA)** is the New South Wales auto club; for emergency breakdown service call ✆ **131 111.**

Tolls apply for some roads, including the Cross City Tunnel and Sydney Harbour Bridge; increasingly you must go through automatic toll booths using a prepaid electronic tag called an **E-Tag.** If you are renting a car, you may be provided with an E-Tag, but make sure to ask about how you pay. Drivers without E-Tags have 2 days to pay; call the **Roads and Traffic Authority** at ✆ **131 865** within 2 days for details on your payment options.

Car-rental agencies in Sydney include **Avis,** 395 Pitt St. (✆ 136 333 in Australia or 02/8255 1616); **Budget,** 93 William St., Kings Cross (✆ 1300/362 848 in Australia or 02/8255 9600); **Europcar,** 818 George St. (✆ 131 390 in Australia or 02/8255 9050); **Hertz,** corner of William and Riley streets, Kings Cross (✆ 133 039 in Australia or 02/9360 6621); and **Thrifty,** 9A York St. (✆ 136 139 in Australia or 02/9276 7330). All agencies also have desks at the airport. One of the best-value operations is **Bayswater Car Rental,** 180 William St., Kings Cross (www.bayswatercarrental.com.au; ✆ 02/9360 3622), which has small cars from around A$40 a day, sometimes less.

[FastFACTS] SYDNEY

ATMs/Banks Banking hours are Monday through Friday from 9am to 5pm. Many banks, especially in the city center, are also open Saturday from around 9:30am to 12:30pm. Most major bank branches offer currency-exchange services.

Business Hours General office hours are Monday through Friday from 9am to 5pm. Shopping hours are usually from 8:30am to 5:30pm daily (9am–5pm Sat), and most stores stay open until 9pm on Thursday. Most city-center stores are open from around 10am to 4pm on Sunday.

Dentists **CBD Dental Practice,** Level 2, 74 Castlereagh St. (www.cbddental.com.au; ✆ **02/9221 2453**), offers same-day emergency treatment. It's open by appointment Monday through Friday 8am to 6pm. The **Sydney Dental Hospital** is on 2 Chalmers St., Surry Hills (✆ **02/9293 3200).**

Doctors & Hospitals **St. Vincent's Hospital** is at Victoria and Burton streets in Darlinghurst, near Kings Cross (✆ **02/8382 1111**). The **V Health Plus** medical center (✆ **02/8188 2299**), 40 Park St. (corner of Pitt St.), in the city center is open Monday through Friday 8:30am to 6pm. The **Travellers' Medical & Vaccination Centre,** Level 7, the Dymocks Building, 428 George St., in the city center (www.traveldoctor.com.au; ✆ **02/9221 7133**), administers travel-related vaccinations and medications. It's open 9am to 5pm Monday to Friday (until 8pm on Thurs), and 9am to 1pm Saturday. Appointments essential.

Embassies & Consulates All foreign embassies are based in Canberra. The following consulates are in Sydney: **Canada,** Level 5, 111 Harrington St. (✆ **02/9364 3000**); **Britain,** Level 16, 1 Macquarie Place (✆ **02/9247 7521**); and **New Zealand,** Level 10, 55 Hunter St. (✆ **1300/559 535**). The **US Consulate General** is in Melbourne (p. 114).

Emergencies Dial ✆ **000** to call the police, the fire service, or an ambulance. Call the **NRMA** for car breakdowns (✆ **131 111**). Other emergency lines include the **Poisons Information Centre** (✆ **131 126**), the **Rape Crisis Centre** (✆ **1800/424 017** in Australia), and the 24-hour **Lifeline** counseling service (✆ **131 114**).

Internet Access Sydney has many Internet and e-mail centers, particularly in and around Kings Cross, Bondi, and Manly, and a widespread network of free Wi-Fi hot spots around the city center and even onboard Sydney Ferries.

Mail & Postage The **General Post Office (GPO)** is at 1 Martin Place (✆ **131 318** in Australia or 02/9244 3711). It's open Monday through Friday 8:15am to 5:30pm and Saturday 10am to 2pm. For the nearest post office, call ✆ **131 318** or find it online at www.auspost.com.au.

Newspapers & Magazines The ***Sydney Morning Herald*** is available throughout metropolitan Sydney. The equally prestigious daily ***The Australian*** is available nationwide. The metropolitan ***Daily Telegraph*** is a more casual read. A newcomer to the market is ***The Saturday Paper,*** an independent weekend newspaper. The ***International Herald Tribune*** and other U.S. and U.K. newspapers can be found at Circular Quay newspaper stands and most news dealers. ***Time Out Sydney*** is published monthly as a guide to everything that's on in and around the city (find the online version at www.timeout.com/Sydney).

Pharmacies Most suburbs have pharmacies that are open late. For after-hours referral, contact the **Chemist Emergency Prescription Referral Service** (✆ **02/9467 7100**).

Police In an emergency, dial ✆ **000.** Make nonemergency police inquiries through the **City Central** police station (✆ **131 444** or 02/9265 6499).

Safety Sydney is generally a safe city, but as anywhere else, it's good to keep your wits about you and your wallet hidden. Be wary in Kings Cross and Redfern and around Central Station and the cinema strip on George Street near Town Hall station in the evening—the latter is a hangout for local gangs. Other places of concern are the back lanes of Darlinghurst, around the naval base at Woolloomooloo, and along the Bondi restaurant strip when sunburned drunken tourists spill out after midnight. If traveling by train at night, ride in the carriages next to the guard's van, marked with a blue light on the outside.

WHERE TO STAY

DECIDING WHERE TO STAY The best location for lodging in Sydney is in The Rocks and around Circular Quay—a short stroll from the Sydney Opera House, the Harbour Bridge, the Royal Botanic Garden, and the ferry terminals.

Hotels around Darling Harbour offer good access to museums, the Sydney Aquarium, and The Star casino. Most Darling Harbour hotels are a 10- to 15-minute walk, or a short light rail trip, from Town Hall and the central shopping district in and around Sydney Tower and Pitt Street Mall.

More hotels are grouped around Kings Cross, Sydney's red-light district. Some of the hotels here are among the city's best, and it's also where you'll find a range of cheaper lodgings and hostels. Kings Cross can sometimes be unnerving (and noisy), especially on Friday and Saturday nights when the area's strip joints and nightclubs are jumping, but it's close to excellent restaurants and cafes around the Kings Cross, Darlinghurst, and Oxford Street areas.

If you want to stay near the beach, check out the options in Manly and Bondi, though you should consider their distance from the city center and the

Central Sydney Hotels

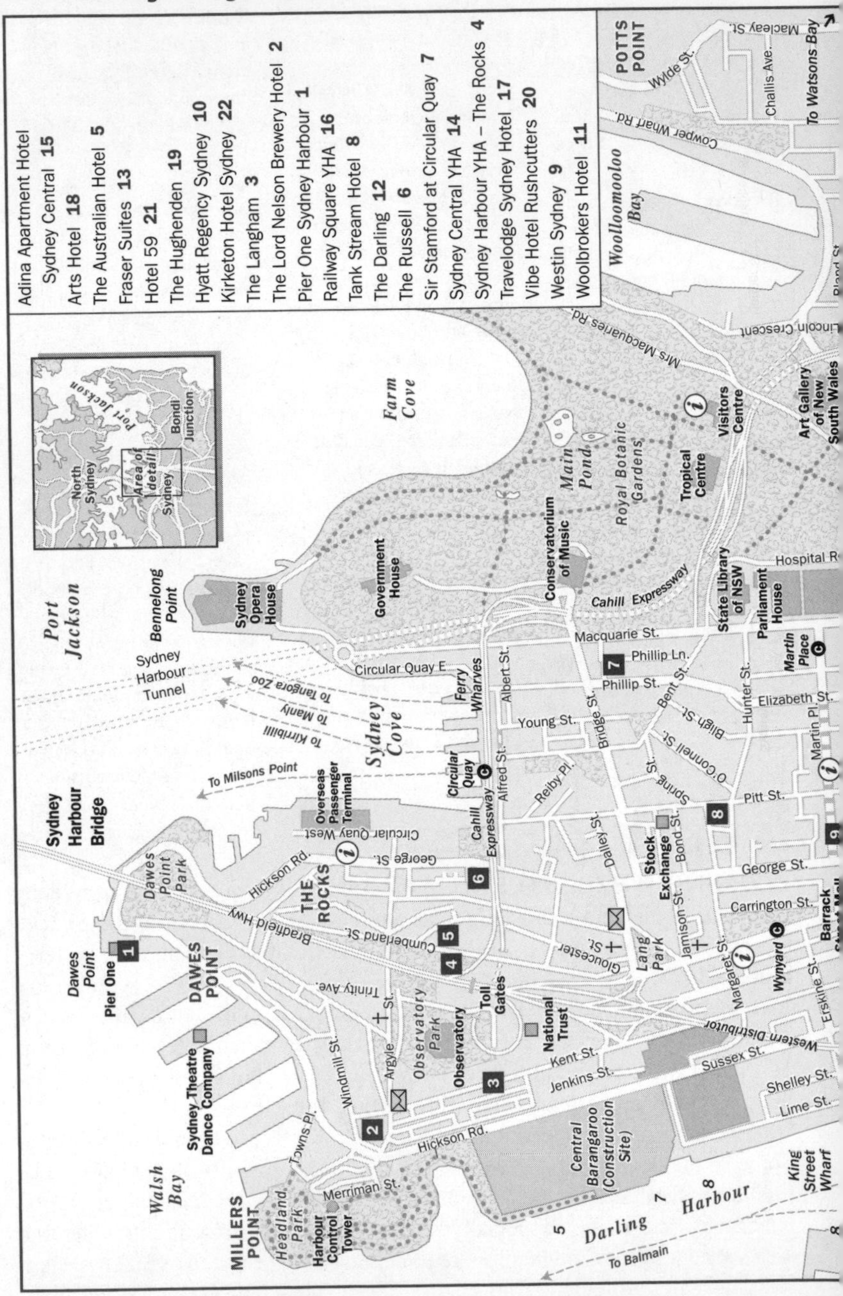

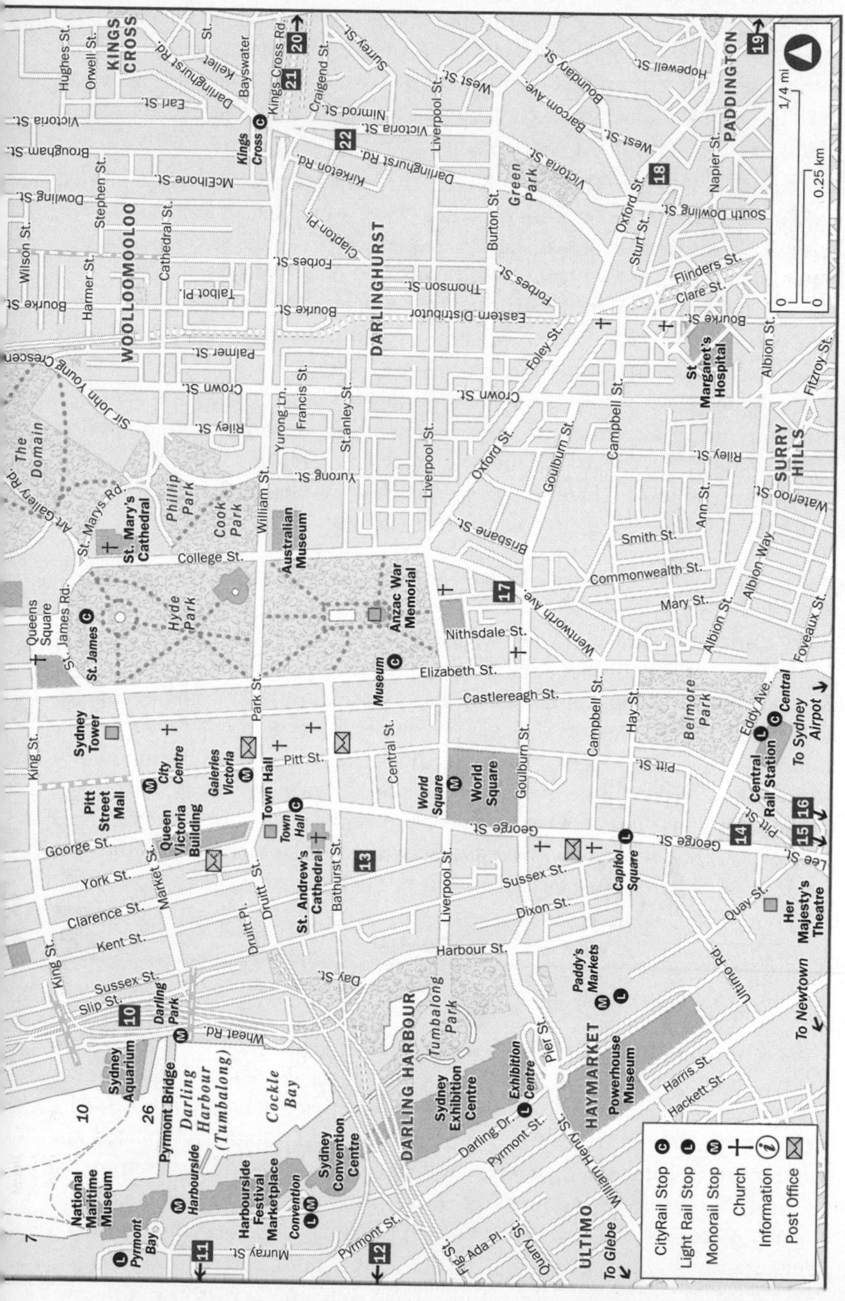
KINGS CROSS
WOOLLOOMOOLOO
DARLINGHURST
PADDINGTON
SURRY HILLS
DARLING HARBOUR
HAYMARKET
ULTIMO
The Domain
Hyde Park
Cook Park
Phillip Park
Green Park
Belmore Park
Tumbalong Park
Cockle Bay
Darling Harbour (Tumbalong)
St. Mary's Cathedral
Australian Museum
Anzac War Memorial
St. James
Queens Square
Sydney Tower
Pitt Street Mall
City Centre
Queen Victoria Building
Galeries Victoria
Town Hall
St. Andrew's Cathedral
World Square
Museum
Capitol Square
Central Rail Station
Central
To Sydney Airport
Her Majesty's Theatre
Paddy's Markets
Powerhouse Museum
Sydney Exhibition Centre
Exhibition Centre
Sydney Convention Centre
Convention
Harbourside Festival Marketplace
Harbourside
National Maritime Museum
Pyrmont Bay
Pyrmont Bridge
Sydney Aquarium
Darling Park
St Margaret's Hospital
Kings Cross
To Newtown
To Glebe
0 1/4 mi
0 0.25 km
CityRail Stop
Light Rail Stop
Monorail Stop
Church
Information
Post Office
10
11
12
13
14
15
16
17
18
19
20
21
22
26
7

lack of trains to these areas. A taxi to Manly from the city will cost around A$55 and to Bondi around A$35.

Almost all hotels offer nonsmoking rooms. Most moderately priced to expensive rooms will have tea- and coffee-making facilities and an iron and ironing board. Coffeemakers are rare in Australian hotels, which instead offer tea bags, instant coffee, small plastic milk cartons, and a kettle. Some smarter hotels have an in-room espresso machine.

MAKING A DEAL The prices given below for expensive hotels are mostly the **rack rates,** the recommended retail price, which guests can pay at the busiest periods if they book at short notice or walk in off the street. Check out **www.lastminute.com.au**, **www.wotif.com**, or a hotel's own website, for discounted rates. **Apartment hotels** may be worth considering, because you can save a bundle by cooking at least some of your own meals, and many also have free laundry facilities.

Most Australian hostels go beyond dorm-type accommodations and also offer private double rooms (some with en suite bathrooms) and a limited number of family rooms (sleeping four or five), making hostels a viable option for families and older travelers. Check **www.yha.com.au** for a full list of its eight Sydney hostels (some are listed in this section).

Around the Rocks & Circular Quay

EXPENSIVE

The Langham ★★★ This exclusive property, a 10-minute walk uphill from The Rocks and 15 minutes from Circular Quay (or a stroll down to Wynyard train station), is a turn-of-the-20th-century beauty competing for top-hotel-in-Sydney honors. It is also renowned for its personalized service. A multi-million-dollar refurbishment in 2014 created a more contemporary style, with a grand marble lobby and quiet guestrooms with huge bathrooms. Some rooms have city views; others look out over the harbor. The pool here is one of the best in Sydney. (Note the Southern Hemisphere constellations on the roof.) The Langham's day spa is one of the most exclusive in the city.

89–113 Kent St. www.langhamhotels.com. ✆ **02/9256 2222.** 98 units. A$398–A$668 double; A$798–A$1,898 suite. Parking A$50. Bus: nos. 339, 431, or 433. **Amenities:** Restaurant; bar; concierge; health club; chemical-free heated indoor pool; 24-hr. room service; sauna; lighted tennis court; free Wi-Fi.

Pier One Sydney Harbour ★★ Tucked just around the corner from Circular Quay, almost under the Harbour Bridge, Pier One is right on the waterfront (you can even arrive by boat at the private pontoon, if you wish). Some rooms offer harbor views, in both directions. Rooms are updated and contemporary, but may add interesting features, such as old timbers from the original Pier One Wharf, built in 1912. It's just far enough from the bustle of the city center to be in a world of its own but with all the benefits of being 5 minutes away.

11 Hickson Rd. www.pieronesydneyharbour.com.au. ✆ **02/8298 9999.** 189 units. A$299–A$419 double; A$674–A$1,499 suite. Valet parking A$50. Train, bus, or ferry:

The wonderfully located Pier One Sydney Harbour.

Circular Quay. **Amenities:** Restaurant; bar; babysitting; concierge; exercise room; room service; free Wi-Fi.

Sir Stamford at Circular Quay ★★★ This is one of my favorite Sydney hotels. It's plush and luxurious, but like all really great hotels the staff is friendly and the atmosphere relaxed rather than stuffy. It has a clubby European atmosphere, with gorgeous antique furniture, but the vibe is warm and welcoming. There's even a large mascot wombat (of the toy variety) called Morris who pops up in the most unexpected places (and can be with you for company, on request). The location is perfect, a short walk from Circular Quay and the Opera House, and just across the road from the Royal Botanic Garden. Rooms are large and luxurious, with good-size marble bathrooms. Most rooms have a small balcony. The rooms on the east side of the hotel have the best views across the Botanic Garden. Most rooms are accessible to wheelchairs.

93 Macquarie St. www.stamford.com.au/sscq. ✆ **02/9252 4600.** 120 units. A$299–A$349 double; A$449–A$1,500 suite. Parking A$40. Train, bus, or ferry: Circular Quay. **Amenities:** Restaurant; bar; babysitting; concierge; exercise room; outdoor heated pool; room service; sauna; Wi-Fi free in-room (only if you book direct), in the business center, or for 30 min. in the lobby.

MODERATE

The Lord Nelson Brewery Hotel ★★★ Book a room upstairs in one of Sydney's oldest pubs (established in 1841) to be part of the city's living history. This attractive, three-story sandstone building is a busy pub on the ground floor, with hotel rooms on the second and third floors. The simple but stylishly outfitted rooms are compact, and some have walls made from convict-hewn sandstone blocks. The creaky floorboards, narrow corridors, wood fire, and boutique brewery in the bar add to Lord Nelson's colonial atmosphere without detracting from its essentially modern style. The smallest (and cheapest) of the rooms has a bathroom across the corridor; all the others have en suites.

19 Kent St. (at Argyle St.), The Rocks. www.lordnelsonbrewery.com. ✆ **02/9251 4044.** 8 units. A$210 double with external bathroom; A$250 double with en suite bathroom. Rates include continental breakfast. No parking. Train or ferry: Circular Quay. **Amenities:** 2 restaurants; bar; free Wi-Fi.

The Russell ★★★ This is the coziest place to stay in The Rocks and perhaps in all of Sydney. It's more than 120 years old, and it shows its age wonderfully in the creaks of the floorboards. There are no harbor views, but all rooms provide immense character and are furnished in period style. Some have shared bathrooms (and all rooms have bathrobes in them). Single rooms are available for solo travelers. Guests have access to a sitting room with a small library and a balcony overlooking Circular Quay. The rooftop garden is another perfect spot for wonderful views of the harbor, with tables and chairs and sun umbrellas. A real find.

143A George St., The Rocks. www.therussell.com.au. ✆ **02/9241 3543.** 29 units, 19 with bathroom. A$165–A$189 double with shared bathroom; A$269–A$325 double with bathroom. Rates include continental breakfast. Parking nearby (A$25 for 24 hr. single entry). Train or ferry: Circular Quay. **Amenities:** Restaurant; lounge; free Wi-Fi.

INEXPENSIVE

The Australian Hotel ★ Rooms here are above one of Sydney's most historic pubs, but despite that, they are not noisy. Carry your bags up the narrow stairs and you'll find a charming—if somewhat frayed around the edges—little haven overlooking the action on the street. Each room has a double or queen bed, or twin beds, and the nine rooms share five bathrooms. The guest lounge, overlooking the street, has a TV, books and magazines, and nice little touches like free tea and coffee available all day, bowls of fruit, and a decanter of port. A second, quieter lounge is down another hallway. The Australian is clean, comfortable, and a bargain.

100 Cumberland St. (entry off Gloucester St.), The Rocks. www.australianheritagehotel.com. ✆ **02/9247 2229.** 9 units. A$149–A$159 double; A$299 family suite. Rates include continental breakfast. Train or ferry: Circular Quay. No parking. **Amenities:** Restaurant; bar; free Wi-Fi.

Sydney Harbour YHA–The Rocks ★★ The Sydney Harbour YHA offers basic, clean rooms at a very reasonable price for this sought-after part of the city. Some rooms have harbor views (if you crane your neck). All are air-conditioned, and even the dorms have private bathrooms. There are also some thoughtful design features, including an electric socket in each of the lockers, so you can securely charge your iPod/laptop/camera. It has a very large common area, and the roof terrace is an excellent place to hang out, particularly because of the fabulous views of the Opera House and the Sydney Harbour Bridge. *Note:* You do have to lug your luggage up a lot of steps to get to the building. There are also a couple of other YHA hostels worth considering (p. 66).

110 Cumberland St., The Rocks. www.yha.com.au. ✆ **02/8272 0900.** A$48–A$56 dorm; A$168–A$198 double; A$210–A$235 family room (sleeps 5). Train or ferry: Circular Quay. **Amenities:** Self-catering kitchen and dining area; Internet cafe; coffee bar; lounge; convenience store; free Wi-Fi.

In the City Center

EXPENSIVE

Adina Apartment Hotel Sydney Central ★★ Built in 1821 and once the parcels post office for Central Station next door, this Heritage-listed property now offers elegant and roomy studios and apartments. My pick is the one-bedroom Premier apartments, which are on the higher levels of the hotel; some are corner rooms, which have wonderful round windows with views of the Central Station clock tower. There's no restaurant, but meals are available in the great, atmospheric cafe **Mezbah Central** (www.mezbah.com.au; ✆ **02/8059 7141**) at the back of the hotel, with a charge-back to your room; you can also order room service from Mezbah.

2 Lee St., Haymarket. www.tfehotels.com. ✆ **02/8396 9800.** 98 units. A$168–A$272 studio; A$200–A$636 1-bedroom apt; A$330–A$571 2-bedroom apt. Parking A$39. Train: Central. **Amenities:** Gym; Jacuzzi; outdoor heated pool; free Wi-Fi.

Fraser Suites Sydney ★★★ One of Sydney's most luxurious apartment hotels, Fraser Suites is just a few minutes' walk from the Queen Victoria Building and Darling Harbour. Choose from studios, one- and two-bedroom suites, or two- and three-bedroom penthouse suites. There are only seven apartments on each floor, and the views are to die for. Studios offer kitchenettes, while larger apartments have separate bedrooms, lounges, and full kitchen and laundry facilities. All rooms have Nespresso coffee machines, iPod docking stations, and a small study area. A buffet breakfast (A$32; A$14 kids) is available daily on the mezzanine floor, and room service is available for breakfast (6:30–10:30am) and dinner (6–11pm).

488 Kent St. www.sydney.frasershospitality.com. ✆ **02/8823 8888.** 201 units. A$225 studio; A$280 1-bedroom suite; A$505 2-bedroom suite; A$999 penthouse. Self-parking A$42, valet parking A$52. Train: Town Hall. **Amenities:** Concierge; indoor heated pool, Jacuzzi; sauna; health club; free Wi-Fi.

Hyatt Regency Sydney ★★★ Opened in early 2017 after a A$250-million redevelopment, this super-swanky hotel is positioned between the city heart and Darling Harbour, across the street from the Sydney Aquarium and a short walk from Cockle Bay. It's one of the largest five-star properties in all of Australia, with 222 new rooms created, including suites and club rooms. Some rooms have views of Darling Harbour, and some have balconies. A highlight is the rooftop bar with harbor views.

161 Sussex St. www.sydney.regency.hyatt.com. ✆ **02/8099 1234.** 892 units. A$269–A$479 double; A$609–A$639 suite. Parking A$70. Bus: no. 441. Train: Town Hall. **Amenities:** Restaurant; bar; concierge; 24-hr. gym; free Wi-Fi.

Westin Sydney ★★★ One of Sydney's most celebrated five-star hotels, the Westin is located in the center of the city, in the Martin Place pedestrian mall. Integrated into Sydney's original 19th-century General Post Office, the Westin has a charm that's modern and classic all at once. The large rooms have wonderfully comfortable beds and floor-to-ceiling windows. The hotel is home to several bars, restaurants, and clothing shops. Just steps from the central shopping streets and the Queen Victoria Building, and a 10- to 15-minute walk from both the Sydney Opera House and Darling Harbour, the hotel features an impressive seven-story atrium, a fabulous two-level health club, and an exclusive day spa.

1 Martin Place. www.starwoodhotels.com. © **02/8223 1111.** 416 units. A$250–A$468 double. Parking A$68. Train: Martin Place. **Amenities:** Cafe; bar; babysitting; health club; day spa; free Wi-Fi.

MODERATE

The Tank Stream Hotel ★★ One of Sydney's newest hotels is situated on one of its most historic sites. Just a few minutes' walk from Circular Quay, the Sydney Opera House, Hyde Park, and Barangaroo, this modest but stylish hotel tells a terrific Sydney story. The Tank Stream is named for the freshwater stream that was the water source for Australia's first European colony in 1788. The hotel is built over the tank stream, and the hotel's wavelike forms reflect its position. Rooms are simply furnished and some are compact, but they are all you need and the location is hard to beat. The complimentary (non-alcoholic) minibar is a nice touch. Ask about underground tours of the original tank stream.

97–99 Pitt St. www.tankstreamhotel.com. © **02/8222 1211.** 280 units. A$249–A$349 double. Train: Wynyard. **Amenities:** Restaurant; bar; free Wi-Fi.

Travelodge Hotel Sydney ★ This business-oriented hotel is cheap for Sydney, comfortable, and reasonably well located, making it a good option for travelers who just want to unpack and explore. The Ikea-style rooms include a kitchenette with a microwave and a queen bed or two twin-size beds. From here it's a short walk to Oxford Street, Town Hall, and Hyde Park.

27–33 Wentworth Ave. www.tfehotels.com. © **1300/886 886** in Australia or 02/8267 1700. 406 units. A$160–A$385 double. Parking (around corner) A$25. Train: Museum. **Amenities:** Restaurant; babysitting; health club; free Wi-Fi.

INEXPENSIVE

Sydney Central YHA ★★ This multiple-award-winning hostel is one of the biggest and busiest in the world, so book as far ahead as possible. The rooms are clean and basic, and come dorm-style for four, six, or eight people or as doubles (with private bathrooms). Family rooms (for up to 5 people) are also available. In the basement is a bar with pool tables and occasional entertainment. There's also an entertainment room with more pool tables and e-mail facilities, TV rooms on every floor, and a cinema. The YHA is accessible to travelers with disabilities.

The **Railway Square YHA** is at the corner of Upper Carriage Lane and Lee Street, or enter via the Henry Dean Plaza (✆ **02/9281 9666**). The historic 1904 building adjoining "Platform Zero" at Central Railway Station has 64 beds in four- to eight-bed dorm rooms and 10 double rooms. Some dorm rooms are in old railway carriages. The facility has a sauna, pool, Internet cafe, tour desk, indoor and outdoor communal areas, and a self-catering kitchen. Rates here are slightly cheaper than at Sydney Central.

11 Rawson Place (at Pitt St., outside Central Station). www.yha.com.au. ✆ **02/9281 9000.** 150 units. A$35–A$46 dorm bed; A$109–A$139 double/twin per room; A$154–A$172 family room (sleeps 5). Parking A$25. Train: Central. **Amenities:** Restaurant; bar; small heated outdoor pool; sauna; free Wi-Fi.

In Darling Harbour

The Darling ★★★ Part of The Star casino complex, this chic hotel stands out from the crowd with splashes of color—purple sheets, even!—and luxurious amenities. All rooms have floor-to-ceiling windows, but some boast views of the Sydney Harbour Bridge. The marble bathrooms have rain showers, bathtubs, and gorgeous Molton Brown products. Touch-controls from the bedside allow you to operate the window blinds, air-conditioning, and television (although sometimes these prove challenging!). It's an easy walk to anywhere in Darling Harbour, or across the Pyrmont Bridge to the city center.

80 Pyrmont St., Pyrmont. www.thedarling.com.au. ✆ **1800/800 830** in Australia or 02/9777 9000**.** 171 units. A$368–A$498 double; A$658–A$1,888 suite. Valet parking A$45–A$55. Bus: no. 389. Light rail: The Star. **Amenities:** 5 restaurants; 3 bars; outdoor heated pool; gym; spa; free Wi-Fi.

Woolbrokers Hotel ★ You'll find this friendly, circa-1886 Heritage building on the far side of Darling Harbour, next to the prominent Novotel hotel and hidden behind a monstrous parking garage. It's on a noisy road, so unless you're used to traffic avoid the rooms at the front. Rooms are simply furnished and come with a fridge and TV. Room no. 3 is one of the nicer choices. Family rooms are outfitted with a king-size bed and a pair of bunk beds. The hotel has 19 shared bathrooms, though some rooms have private bathrooms. Check the website for discounts. This is a good budget option, but note that there is no elevator or air-conditioning.

22 Allen St., Pyrmont. www.woolbrokershotel.com.au. ✆ **02/9552 4773.** 27 units. A$89 double with shared bathroom; A$130 double with bathroom. Continental breakfast A$7.50. Parking A$16 (across the street). Bus: no. 501. Light rail: Convention Centre. **Amenities:** Guest laundry; free Wi-Fi.

In Kings Cross & Suburbs Nearby

Hotel 59 ★ This popular, well-priced, friendly B&B is well worth considering if you want to be near the Kings Cross action but far enough away to get some peace and quiet. It has two rooms for single travelers and three family rooms that can sleep two adults and two children. Rooms are well kept and comfortable, with private bathrooms and TVs. A flight of stairs and the lack of an elevator might make Hotel 59 unsuitable for travelers with disabilities.

59 Bayswater Rd., Kings Cross. www.hotel59.com.au. © **02/9360 5900.** 9 units. A$135 double. Rates include breakfast. No parking. Train: Kings Cross. **Amenities:** Cafe; TV lounge; free Wi-Fi with most rates.

Kirketon Hotel Sydney ★ Popular among hip, fashionable types, this slightly offbeat boutique hotel in Darlinghurst offers rooms with modernist furniture and custom-made fittings, including mirrored headboards and sleek bathrooms hidden away behind mirrored doors. Standard rooms are quite compact and come with a double bed. Premium rooms have a queen-size bed. Superior and Executive rooms are quite large, with a king-size bed, and some have a small balcony overlooking the main road. For a quiet night, ask for a room away from the main road.

229 Darlinghurst Rd., Darlinghurst. www.kirketon.com.au. © **1800/332 920** in Australia or 02/9332 2011. 40 rooms. A$119–A$169 double. Parking A$25. **Amenities:** Restaurant; bar; gym; free Wi-Fi.

Vibe Hotel Rushcutters Bay Sydney ★★ Compared with other hotels in its price bracket, this flagship Vibe Hotel on the far side of Kings Cross really is a bargain, especially when you book online. Standard rooms are a reasonable size, and I love the rooms' brightly accented and colorful—well, yes—vibe. All rooms have king-size beds (which split into twins if necessary), and families can get connecting rooms. The whole place underwent a major refurbishment in 2016, including the heated rooftop swimming pool and gym. The hotel has a good cafe, called **Curve.**

100 Bayswater Rd., Rushcutters Bay. www.tfehotels.com.au. © **02/8353 8988.** 258 units. A$135–A$180 double, A$299–A$349 suite. Parking A$25. Train: Kings Cross. **Amenities:** Restaurant; bar; concierge; gym; heated outdoor pool; free Wi-Fi.

Around Oxford Street & Darlinghurst

Arts Hotel ★ This family-run hotel is right in the heart of the action in one of Sydney's most popular shopping, entertainment, restaurant, and gay pub and club areas. About half of the hotel's guests come from overseas, and it's popular with Americans during Mardi Gras. Rooms are simple, compact, and motel-like, but are fine for a few nights. Standard rooms and garden rooms (which are quieter) have two single beds or a queen-size bed. Art rooms are more up-market, with rainfall showerheads, hypoallergenic bedding, art on the walls, and other little luxury touches—and are offered as upgrades for bookings of 4 nights or more.

21 Oxford St., Paddington. www.artshotel.com.au. © **02/9361 0211.** 64 units. A$148–A$185 double. Limited free parking. Bus: no. 378 from Central Station or no. 380 from Circular Quay. **Amenities:** Breakfast cafe; bikes; gym; small heated outdoor pool; free Wi-Fi.

The Hughenden ★★ I love this boutique hotel, part of which is set in an 1870s mansion and full of antique furnishings. It's warm and comfortable with lots of sitting areas—including a den packed with books—and a permanent exhibition of illustrations from children's books. Hardly surprising given that one of the owners is children's book author Susanne Gervay. Guests are often writers and artists too, though you might run into cricket buffs, given the proximity to the Sydney Cricket Ground. Wander through to enjoy the artwork as well as the architecture, including lovely black marble fireplaces. It's in a great location, at the top end of Oxford Street and just across the road from Centennial Park. Another eight suites are located in a house across the street.

14 Queen St., Woollahra. www.thehughenden.com.au. ✆ **02/9363 4863.** 45 units. A$168–A$308 double; A$275–A$414 suite. Rates include breakfast. Limited secured parking ($33 per night). Bus: no. 440. **Amenities:** Restaurant; bar; guest lounge; free Wi-Fi.

In Bondi

Bondi Beach is a good place to stay if you want to be close to the surf and sand. Two recommended backpacker hostels are good for budget-conscious travelers: **Surfside Backpackers,** 35a Hall St. (www.surfsidebackpackers.com.au; ✆ **02/9365 4900**), offers four- to eight-person dorm rooms from A$25 in winter and A$40 in summer. Single, double, and family rooms are in a separate building (at higher rates). **Noah's Bondi,** 2 Campbell Parade (www.noahsbondibeach.com; ✆ **02/9365 7544**), has a great ambience and modern four- to eight-person dorm rooms for A$25 to A$29 (doubles are A$70–A$75). Rates are higher in the summer peak season (Dec–Jan). Ask about weekly rates.

Hotel Ravesis ★★ Right on Australia's most famous golden sands, this boutique property offers chic and modern minimalist rooms with white marble bathrooms and Juliet balconies. At the time of writing the rooms were undergoing a renovation, due for completion in late 2017. Side View doubles are spacious and modern, but the Beach Front king rooms have the best ocean views. Four split-level suites have a bathroom downstairs, and a bedroom, lounge area, and private outdoor terrace on the second level. There is a lively bar downstairs, which can mean noise until late, especially on weekends, and a good restaurant.

Corner of Hall St. and Campbell Parade. www.hotelravesis.com. ✆ **02/9365 4422.** 12 units. A$175–A$369 double; A$219–A$455 suite. Valet parking A$20. Bus: no. 333. **Amenities:** Restaurant; bar; room service; free Wi-Fi.

In Manly

If you decide to stay in Manly for a few days, consider buying a multiple-ride ferry ticket, which will save you a bit of money. But be warned that ferries from Sydney stop running at midnight. If you get stranded, you'll be facing an expensive taxi ride back.

Manly has several backpacker hostels that are worth checking out; the best of the bunch is **Manly Backpackers Beachside,** 28 Raglan St. (www.manlybackpackers.com.au; ✆ **1800/662 500** in Australia or 02/9977 3411), which offers dorm beds from A$29 to A$50 and doubles from A$71 to A$159, depending on the time of year (pricier during peak summer period).

Manly Paradise Beachfront Motel and Apartments ★ The refurbished rooms are spacious, and some offers glimpses of the sea. The traffic can make it a little noisy in your room during the day, but you'll probably be on the beach anyway. Motel rooms come with queen, double, or twin beds and the magnificently roomy apartments have everything you need, including a full kitchen with dishwasher, a washing machine and dryer, and two bathrooms (one with a tub). Sea views from the main front balcony are heartstopping, and there's a pool on the rooftop.

54 N. Steyne, Manly. www.manlyparadise.com.au. ✆ **1800/815 789** in Australia or 02/9977 5799. 40 units. A$170–A$300 double (motel); A$330–A$495 2-bedroom apt; A$415–A$595 3-bedroom apt. Higher rates in summer (roughly Dec 8–Jan 31). Parking A$18 for motel; free for apts. Ferry: Manly. **Amenities:** Outdoor rooftop pool; free Wi-Fi.

At the Airport

Ibis Budget Sydney Airport ★ If all you want is a clean place to crash before an early flight, this no-frills hotel will do the job. This Ibis has almost no facilities, but it's next to a couple of fast-food joints and has an all-you-can-eat breakfast. Rooms are air-conditioned and have TVs. You can reach the airport via the Airport Shuttle, which costs A$7 one way (or walk there in 10 min.).

5 Ross Smith Ave., Mascot. www.accorhotels.com. ✆ **02/8339 1840.** 200 units. A$119–A$149 double/triple. Parking A$25 per day. **Amenities:** Breakfast room; Wi-Fi (fee).

Stamford Plaza Sydney Airport ★★ At the other end of the scale, this is Sydney's best airport hotel (just 7 min. from the terminals via the A$7 airport shuttle). It has the largest rooms, each with a king or two double beds, access to airport information, and a good-size bathroom with tub. Suites and deluxe rooms have airport views but all windows have been reinforced to keep out the aircraft noise!

Corner of O'Riordan and Robey sts., Mascot. www.stamford.com.au/ssa. ✆ **02/9317 2200.** 315 units. A$239–A$289 double; A$339–A$839 suite. Parking A$30. **Amenities:** 2 restaurants; bar; babysitting; concierge; gym; Jacuzzi; outdoor rooftop pool; room service; sauna; free Wi-Fi (if booking direct).

WHERE TO EAT

Sydney is a gourmet paradise, boasting some of the world's best chefs. Asian and Mediterranean cooking have had a major influence on Australian cuisine, with spices and herbs finding their way into most dishes. Immigration has brought with it almost every type of cuisine, from African to Tibetan, Russian to Vietnamese.

Sydney is a great place to try the Australian style of contemporary cuisine, which emphasizes fresh ingredients and a creative blend of European styles

What to Know About Dining in Sydney

Most moderate and inexpensive restaurants in Sydney are **BYO,** as in "bring your own" bottle (wine only), though some places also have extensive wine and beer lists. More moderately priced restaurants are also introducing corkage fees, which mean you pay anywhere from A$2 to A$8 per person for the privilege of having the waiter open your bottle of wine. Very expensive restaurants are usually fully licensed and don't allow you to BYO.

Sydney's **cheap eats** congregate in center-city areas such as Crown Street in Darlinghurst, and Glebe Point Road in Glebe. There are also inexpensive joints scattered among the more upscale restaurants in Kings Cross and along trendy Oxford Street.

Some restaurants add a surcharge on public holidays and Sundays, usually around 5% or 10% per person. Restaurants argue that it's difficult to get staff to work on these days, so they need to provide a cash incentive. In Australia, waiters rely on their wages rather than tips.

Smoking is banned in all Sydney restaurants, except at some with sidewalk tables or courtyards. Always ask before lighting up.

with Asian influences. And because a really great meal will stay in your mind long after your visit to Australia is over, I've included some of Australia's very top restaurants here. The prices may be high but are almost always well worth it, especially if you are looking for an experience rather than just a meal.

Breakfast is big in Australia, a favorite time of day to meet friends and linger over a hearty repast (albeit often a late one). As for coffee, Australians favor a range of Italian-style creations. Ask for a latte if you just want coffee with milk.

And remember that in Australia, the first course is called the entree and the second course the main.

Circular Quay, City Center & The Rocks

EXPENSIVE

Aria ★★★ CONTEMPORARY With front-row views of the Harbour Bridge and the Sydney Opera House, Aria stands in one of the most enviable spots in the city. The windows overlooking the water are huge, the atmosphere is elegant and buzzy, and many of the intimate tables have a stunning view. The food, created by one of Australia's great chefs, Matt Moran, is imaginative and mouthwatering. Some examples: roasted lamb loin with Jerusalem artichoke, white anchovy, and elephant garlic; or steamed blue-eye trevalla (fish) with buttered carrots and carotene dressing. For lunch on weekdays, a set menu offers one, two, or three courses (A$55, A$90, or A$110). Pre- and post-theater menus are available from 5:30 to 7pm and from 10pm respectively. Reservations are essential.

1 Macquarie St. www.ariarestaurant.com. ✆ **02/9240 2255.** A$115 for 2 courses, A$145 for 3 courses, A$170 for 4 courses. Seasonal 7-course tasting menu A$205, or A$320 with wine pairings. Mon–Fri noon–2:15pm and 5:30–10:30pm; Sat 5–11pm; Sun 5:30–10pm. Train, bus, or ferry: Circular Quay.

Central Sydney Restaurants

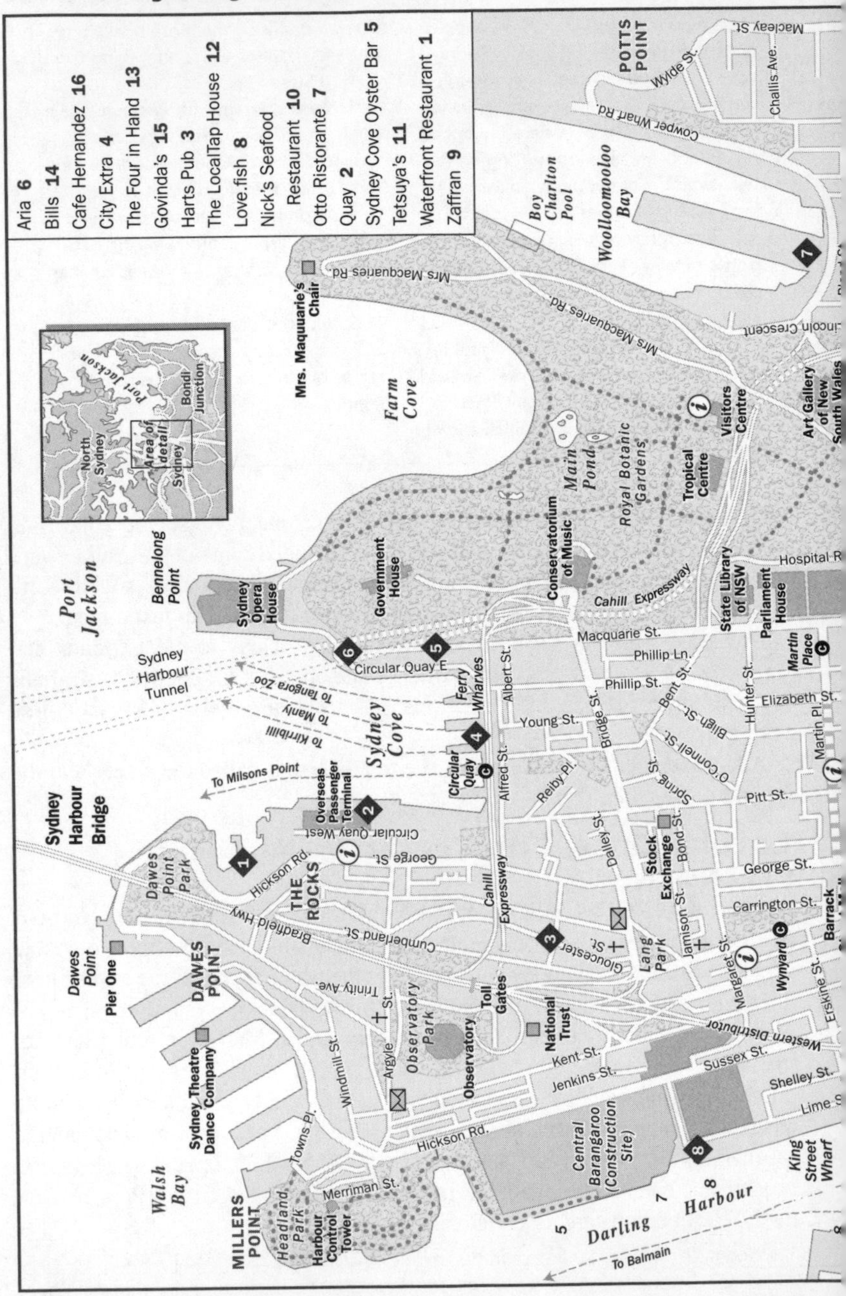

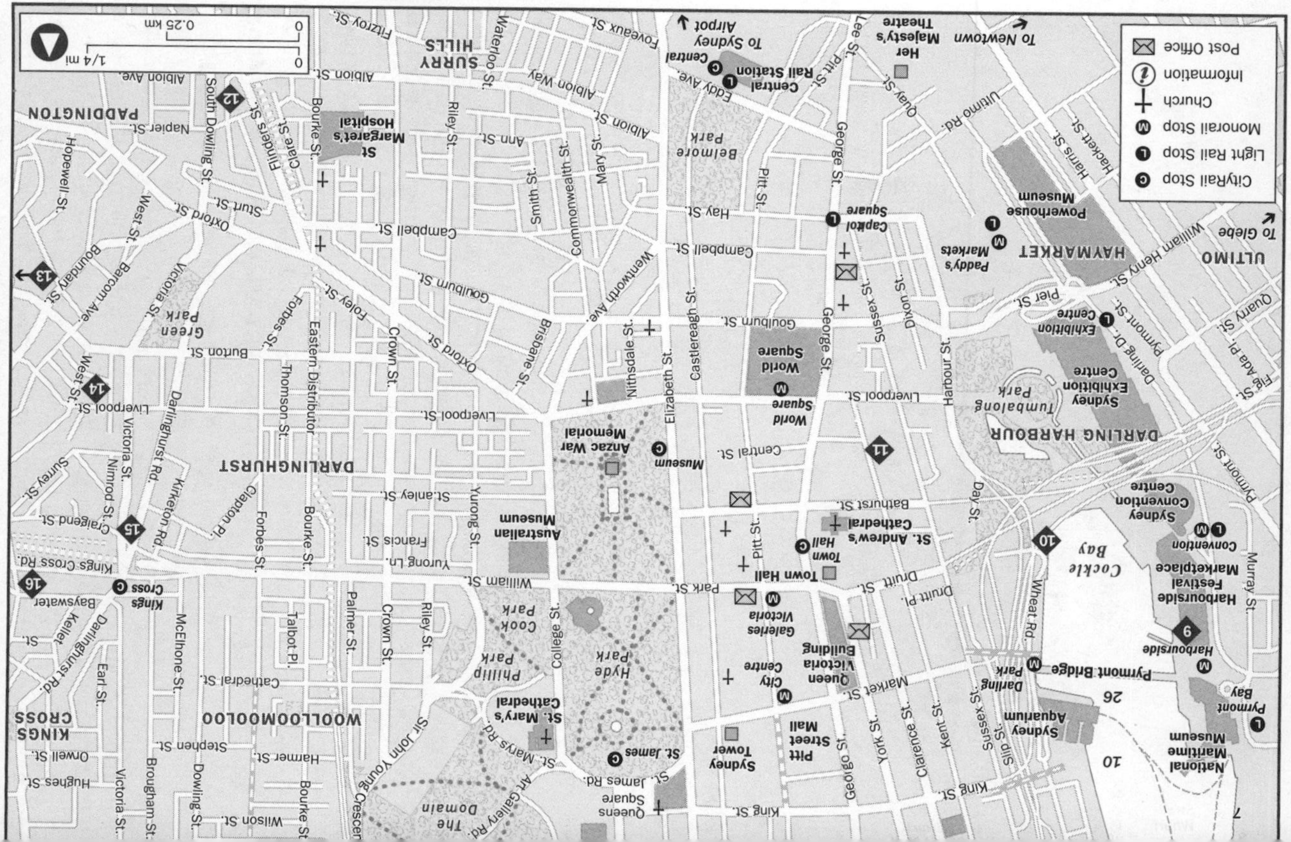
CityRail Stop
Light Rail Stop
Monorail Stop
Church
Information
Post Office
0 1/4 mi
0 0.25 km
KINGS CROSS
WOOLLOOMOOLOO
DARLINGHURST
PADDINGTON
SURRY HILLS
DARLING HARBOUR
HAYMARKET
ULTIMO
The Domain
Hyde Park
Cook Park
Phillip Park
Green Park
Belmore Park
Tumbalong Park
Cockle Bay
St. Mary's Cathedral
Australian Museum
Anzac War Memorial
St Margaret's Hospital
Sydney Tower
Pitt Street Mall
Queen Victoria Building
Galeries Victoria
City Centre
Town Hall
St. Andrew's Cathedral
World Square
Capitol Square
Central Rail Station
Her Majesty's Theatre
Paddy's Markets
Powerhouse Museum
Sydney Exhibition Centre
Exhibition Centre
Sydney Convention Centre
Convention
Harbourside Festival Marketplace
Harbourside
National Maritime Museum
Pyrmont Bay
Pyrmont Bridge
Sydney Aquarium
Darling Park
St. James
Museum
Kings Cross
Queens Square
To Glebe
To Newtown
To Sydney Airport
College St.
William St.
Oxford St.
Elizabeth St.
Castlereagh St.
Pitt St.
George St.
Liverpool St.
Goulburn St.
Campbell St.
Darlinghurst Rd.
Victoria St.
Bourke St.
Crown St.
Riley St.
Park St.
Market St.
King St.
Harbour St.
Wentworth Ave.
Eastern Distributor
South Dowling St.
Flinders St.
Albion St.
Sussex St.
Kent St.
Clarence St.
York St.
Pyrmont St.
William Henry St.
Ultimo Rd.
Sir John Young Crescent
Art Gallery Rd.
9
10
11
12
13
14
15
16

Love.fish Barangaroo ★★★ SEAFOOD One of the exciting dining options in Sydney's new Streets of Barangaroo precinct (p. 98), this indoor/outdoor waterside eatery combines great cocktails with delicious food (and a focus on sustainable seafood) and a helpful staff that can get you in and out quickly for a pre-theater meal. With seating for 160, it's a bustling place offering beautifully presented dishes—anything from oysters and champagne to an impressive seafood platter (A$160) to share.

Wulugul Walk, 23 Barangaroo Ave., Barangaroo. www.lovefishbarangaroo.com.au. ✆ **02/8077 3700.** Main courses A$42–A$72. Daily 11:30am–11pm.

Quay ★★★ CONTEMPORARY You need to book as far in advance as possible for this wonderful, award-winning experience. Quay is nearly always booked out 6 months in advance for Friday and Saturday, but it's hardly surprising. With its enviable location on top of the cruise-ship terminal, Quay offers another of the loveliest views in the city, and Chef Peter Gilmore's menu is a revelation of French, Italian, and Australian ideas. Selections from the four-course dinner might include raw-smoked Wagyu beef with horseradish sour cream, fermented rye crisps, and raw fungi; or Murray River cod with squid, sea cucumber crackling, sake, and lemon. A worthy splurge.

Upper level, Overseas Passenger Terminal, Circular Quay West, The Rocks. www.quay.com.au. ✆ **02/9251 5600.** Lunch: 3 courses A$155, 4 courses A$180. Dinner: 4-course menu A$180. Tasting menu with 6 tasting plates from A$245. Fri–Sun noon–2pm; daily 6–10pm. Train, bus, or ferry: Circular Quay.

Vic's rosé veal T-bone salad at Otto Ristorante.

Best Pub Grub

You can get some really good food with a glass of wine or a schooner of beer on the side in several city pubs. Among the best is **The Four in Hand,** 105 Sutherland St., Paddington (www.fourinhand.com.au; ✆ **02/9326 2254**), which has a great restaurant and also does good bar meals, including hearty sandwiches and grilled steaks, with all main courses under A$30. **Harts Pub,** corner of Essex and Gloucester streets, The Rocks (www.hartspub.com; ✆ **02/9251 6030**), has a great range of craft beers, with gourmet and pub-grub offerings for A$14 to A$42. In Darlinghurst (Kings Cross), delve into the massive beer list at **The Local Taphouse,** 122 Flinders St. (www.thelocal.com.au; ✆ **02/9360 0088**), and graze from the extensive menu; on Sundays, a roast's on offer from noon.

Sydney Cove Oyster Bar ★★ SEAFOOD Just before you reach the Sydney Opera House, you'll notice a couple of small shedlike buildings with tables and chairs set up to take in the stunning views of the harbor and bridge. This is where you'll find some of the best oysters in town. Oysters are A$48 for a dozen (A$24 for a half-dozen), but reliable mains, such as grilled barramundi or Atlantic salmon, tiger prawn linguini, or pasture-fed eye fillet steak, are also on the menu. Share a dozen oysters and follow up with more shellfish or tapas-style bites plus a bottle of crisp white wine or sparkling champagne. It's a perfect lunchtime spot on a sunny day.

Eastern Esplanade, Circular Quay East. www.sydneycoveoysterbar.com. ✆ **02/9247 2937.** Main courses A$35–A$77. Daily 11am–late. Train, bus, or ferry: Circular Quay.

Tetsuya's ★★★ JAPANESE/FRENCH FUSION This is one of the world's best restaurants—it's that simple. To have a chance of getting a table, you need to book as early as possible, and you may be asked to reconfirm a few days before. Request a table next to the floor-to-ceiling windows with intimate views across a Japanese-inspired courtyard of maples and waterfalls. The service is impeccable and the food truly inspired—many diners consider this a once-in-a-lifetime experience. Chef Tetsuya Wakuda's signature dish is a confit of ocean trout served with a salad of celery, endive, apple, and ocean-trout roe.

529 Kent St., Sydney. www.tetsuyas.com. ✆ **02/9267 2900.** 9-course tasting menu A$230 per person. Tues–Fri 5:30–10pm; Sat noon–3pm and 6:30–10pm. Train: Town Hall.

MODERATE

City Extra ★ ITALIAN/AUSTRALIAN Because this place stays open around-the-clock, it's convenient if you get hungry at a ridiculous hour. It's also nicely situated, right next to the ferry terminals. The food varies in quality; if in doubt, stick to the burgers. It's always busy, and service can be a mixed bag too, but the plastic chairs and outdoor tables make it a pleasant enough spot for a quick bite at any time of the day or night. It has a kids' menu and free Wi-Fi.

Shop E4, Circular Quay. www.cityextra.com.au. ✆ **02/9241 1422.** Main courses A$19–A$36. Open 24 hrs. Train, bus, or ferry: Circular Quay.

Waterfront Restaurant ★ CONTEMPORARY You can't help but notice the mast, rigging, and sails that mark this restaurant in a converted stone warehouse. It's one of four in a row next to the water below the main spread of The Rocks, and it's popular at lunchtime, when businesspeople snap up the best seats outside in the sunshine. At night, with the colors of the city washing over the harbor, it can be magical. You get a choice of mains such as steaks, mud crab, fish filets, and prawns. The seafood platter, at A$170 for two, includes Moreton Bay bugs (small, odd-looking crayfish), prawns, blue swimmer crab, oysters, mussels, scallops, and fish. The food is simple and fresh, at prices that reflect the glorious location and views.

In Campbell's Storehouse, 27 Circular Quay West, The Rocks. www.waterfrontrestaurant.com.au. ✆ **02/9247 3666.** Main courses A$27–A$52. Daily noon–3pm and 5–10:30pm. Train, bus, or ferry: Circular Quay.

Darling Harbour

MODERATE

Nick's Seafood Restaurant ★ SEAFOOD This nice indoor and alfresco eatery overlooking the water on the same side as Darling Harbour (to the left of Sydney Aquarium if you're looking at the boats) offers good cocktails and plenty of seafood. The best seats are outside in the sunshine, where you can watch the world go by over a bottle of wine. A seafood platter for two (A$175) arrives piled with crab, prawns, mussels, fish, oysters, and lobster. A kids' menu for under 12s offers pasta, chicken, calamari, or fish with French fries and a soft drink, followed by ice cream for A$16. Nick's has another equally pleasant eatery on the other side of the Aquarium called **Nick's Bar & Grill,** and a sister establishment, **I'm Angus Steakhouse**—also at Cockle Bay Wharf—does good steaks, a great Guinness pie, and some seafood. The food and prices at all three places are similar, and they share the same phone number for bookings.

The Promenade, Cockle Bay Wharf (on the city side of Darling Harbour). www.nicks-seafood.com.au. ✆ **1300/989 989.** Main courses A$32–A$68. Mon–Sat 11:30am–3pm and 5:30–10pm (11pm on Sat); Sun 11:30am–10pm. Ferry: Darling Harbour.

Zaaffran ★★ INDIAN Forget the dark interiors and exotic murals you usually find in an Indian restaurant; here are white surfaces, a glass-fronted wine cellar, and magnificent views of the water and the Sydney skyline from the far side of Darling Harbour. An outdoor terrace provides the best views. Chef Vikrant Kapoor, formerly the chef de cuisine at Raffles in Singapore, has revolutionized classic Indian cuisine on the menu here. Expect such delights as chicken *biryani,* baked in a pastry case and served with mint yogurt, or tiger prawns in coconut cream and turmeric broth, not to mention many interesting vegetarian options.

Level 2, Harbourside Centre, 10 Darling Drive. www.zaaffran.com. ✆ **02/9211 8900.** Main courses A$20–A$30. Daily noon–2:30pm; Mon–Thurs 6–9:30pm; Fri–Sat 5:30–10:15pm; Sun 5:30–9:30pm. Ferry: Darling Harbour.

Woolloomooloo Wharf

Otto Ristorante ★★ ITALIAN Recognized as one of Sydney's premier restaurants, Otto is all lush designer appointments and dim lighting, making it popular with local celebrities and socialites. Hence the price of the food, perhaps. Outside it's light and breezy, with nice views of a boardwalk and some harbor water. Menu possibilities include hand-rolled orecchiette pasta with house-made Italian pork sausage, broccolini, chili, and garlic; or a pork cutlet with parsnip puree, apple, walnuts, and prune salsa.

6 Cowper Wharf Rd. www.ottoristorante.com.au/sydney. ✆ **02/9368 7488.** Main courses A$39–A$59. Daily noon–10pm. Bus: no. 311 from Circular Quay (or take a water taxi).

Kings Cross & Darlinghurst

INEXPENSIVE

Bills ★★★ CAFE Strewn with flowers and magazines, this bright and airy place serves nouveau cafe–style food. It's so popular you might have trouble finding a seat. The signature breakfast dishes—including ricotta hotcakes with honeycomb butter and banana, and sweet corn fritters with roasted tomatoes, spinach, and bacon—are the stuff of legend. In fact, some of my friends think Bills serves the best breakfast in Sydney. Find other Bills cafes in Surry Hills (359 Crown St.; ✆ **02/9360 4762**) and Bondi Beach (79 Hall St.; ✆ **02/8412 0700**).

433 Liverpool St., Darlinghurst. www.bills.com.au. ✆ **02/9360 9631.** Main courses A$22–A$32. Mon–Sat 7:30am–3pm; Sun and public holidays 8am–3pm. Reservations Mon–Fri only. Train: Kings Cross.

Café Hernandez ★★ CAFE The walls of this tiny, cluttered cafe are crammed with eccentric fake masterpieces, and the aroma of 20 types of coffee roasted and ground on the premises permeates the air. It's almost a religious experience for discerning central-city coffee addicts—and even better, it never closes! The Spanish espresso is a treat. Light meals are served: sandwiches, wraps, focaccias, and tortillas, as well as some sweet treats such as churros, Portuguese custard tarts, and Spanish rice pudding.

60 Kings Cross Rd., Potts Point. www.cafehernandez.com.au. ✆ **02/9331 2343.** Main courses A$3–A$10. Open 24 hr. Train: Kings Cross.

Govinda's ★★ VEGETARIAN Simple vegetarian food—usually curries of some kind—coupled with a happy vibe and very cheap prices make this place a winner. Based in the Hare Krishna center, Govinda's serves buffet-style meals in a basic room of black-lacquer tables. The menu changes nightly but always includes a delicious Indian dahl soup, vegetable curry, penne pasta, lentil pie or potato au gratin, cauliflower pakoras, potato wedges, rice, poppadums, and salads. It's BYO, doctrine-free, and very bohemian. After the meal, there's a recent-release movie (albeit on a different floor), which you watch prostrate on large futon-style chairs. It's hugely popular, so make a booking.

112 Darlinghurst Rd., Darlinghurst. www.govindas.com.au. ✆ **02/9380 5155.** Dinner A$23. Movie A$12 (if dining) or A$18. Wed–Sun 5:45–11pm. Train: Kings Cross.

In Bondi Beach

EXPENSIVE

Icebergs Dining Room & Bar ★★★ MEDITERRANEAN Overlooking Bondi Beach and the sea baths at the Bondi Icebergs Club (famed for its year-round swimming), this is a truly fabulous place to dine. From its corner position on the cliffs, the Icebergs Bar looks directly across the beach and water, with floor-to-roof windows offering what is probably the best view in Sydney. The bar features lots of cushions and has a casual bar menu. The dining-room menu is Italian, with seafood featuring as well, and the service is faultless. Go for brunch on Sunday (10–11:30am); you won't be disappointed. A tasting menu (A$140 per person) offers seven courses that will have you swooning.

1 Notts Ave. www.idrb.com. ✆ **02/9365 9000.** Reservations essential. Main courses A$42–A$76. Tues–Sun noon–3pm and 6:30pm–midnight; Sun brunch 10–11:30am. Bus: no. 333.

INEXPENSIVE

Pompei's ★ ITALIAN The formula is simple: Use good ingredients, like an organic tomato sauce, and you'll get good pizzas. In fact, some people think these are the best pizzas in Sydney. The pizzas have a huge range of interesting toppings, but Pompei's also offers a variety of other fare, including salads, antipasto, focaccia, and steaks. Don't miss the homemade gelato, the best in Sydney by far—try chocolate, tiramisu, or pistachio. The water views and outside tables are another plus. When it's busy, it can get cramped inside, and service can vary.

126–130 Roscoe St., at Gould St. www.pompeis.com.au. ✆ **02/9365 1233.** Reservations recommended. Pizza A$18–A$25. Main courses A$24–A$34. Tues–Fri noon–11pm; Sat–Sun 11:30am–11pm. Bus: nos. 380 or 333 from the city.

EXPLORING SYDNEY

The only problem with visiting Sydney is fitting in everything you want to do and see. Of course, you won't want to miss the iconic attractions: the **Opera House** and the **Harbour Bridge.**

You should also check out the native wildlife in **Taronga Zoo,** stroll around the tourist precinct of **Darling Harbour,** and get a dose of Down Under culture at the **Australian Museum.** If it's hot, take your "cozzie" (swimsuit) and towel to **Bondi Beach** or **Manly.**

Sydney Harbour & The Rocks

Officially called Port Jackson, **Sydney Harbour** is the focal point of Sydney and one of the features—along with the beaches and easy access to surrounding national parks—that makes this city so special. It's entered through the **Heads,** two bush-topped outcrops (you'll see them if you take a ferry to Manly), beyond which the harbor laps at some 240km (149 miles) of shoreline before stretching out into the Parramatta River. Visitors are often awestruck by the harbor's beauty, especially at night, when the sails of the Opera

A classic view of Sydney, with the Opera House and the Harbour Bridge.

House and the girders of the Harbour Bridge are lit up, and the waters are swirling with the reflection of lights from the abutting high-rises—reds, greens, blues, yellows, and oranges. During the day, it buzzes with green-and-yellow ferries pulling in and out of busy Circular Quay, sleek tourist craft, fully rigged tall ships, giant container vessels making their way to and from the wharves of Darling Harbour, and hundreds of white-sailed yachts.

The greenery along the harbor's edges is a surprising feature, thanks to the **Sydney Harbour National Park,** a haven for native trees and plants, and a feeding and breeding ground for lorikeets and other nectar-eating bird life. In the center of the harbor is a series of islands; the most impressive is the tiny isle supporting **Fort Denison,** which once housed convicts and acted as part of the city's defense.

The Rocks neighborhood is compact and close to the ferry terminals at Circular Quay. Sydney's historic district is hilly and crosscut with alleyways. Some of Australia's oldest pubs are here, as well as boutique restaurants, stores, and hotels. Pick up a walking map from the visitor center and make sure to get off the main streets to see the original working-class houses that survived development. Today, there are 96 heritage buildings in The Rocks. The oldest house is Cadmans Cottage, built in 1815, while the Dawes Point Battery, built in 1791, is the oldest remaining European structure. On Observatory Hill, you'll find the three remaining walls of Fort Phillip, built in 1804.

Central Sydney Attractions

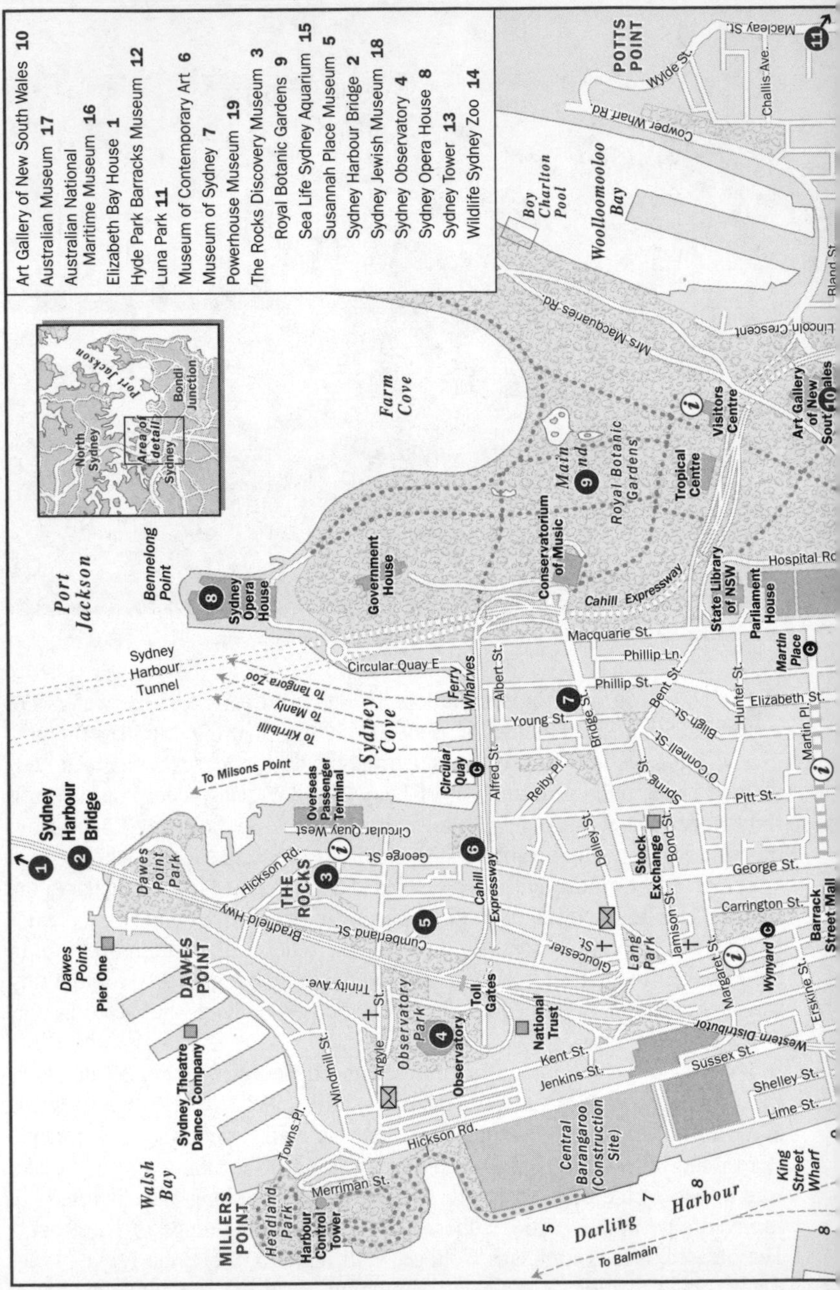

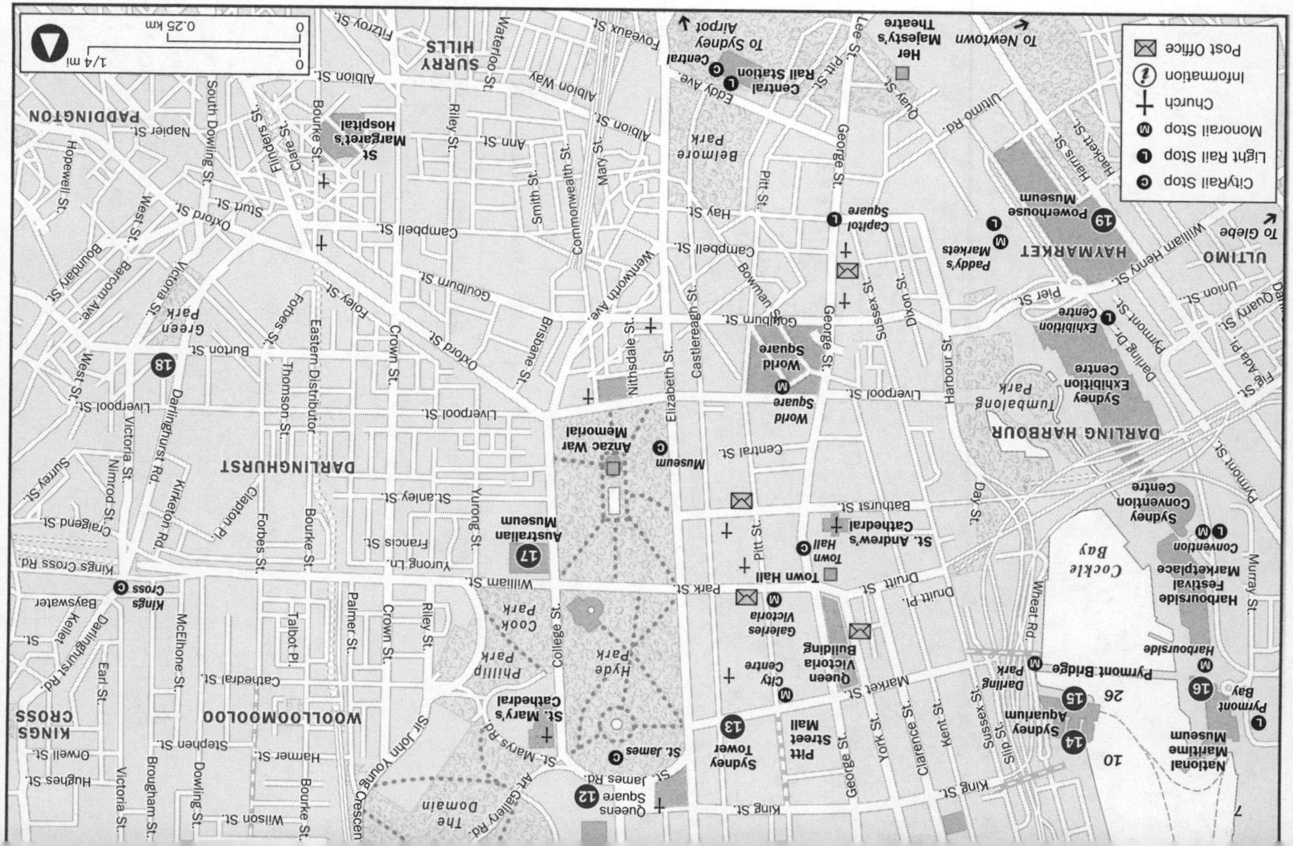
CityRail Stop
Light Rail Stop
Monorail Stop
Church
Information
Post Office
0 1/4 mi
0 0.25 km
KINGS CROSS
WOOLLOOMOOLOO
DARLINGHURST
PADDINGTON
SURRY HILLS
DARLING HARBOUR
HAYMARKET
ULTIMO
The Domain
Hyde Park
Cook Park
Phillip Park
Green Park
Belmore Park
Tumbalong Park
Cockle Bay
Queens Square
St. James
St. Mary's Cathedral
Australian Museum
Anzac War Memorial
Museum
Sydney Tower
Pitt Street Mall
City Centre
Queen Victoria Building
Galeries Victoria
Town Hall
St. Andrew's Cathedral
World Square
Capitol Square
Central Rail Station
Central
Her Majesty's Theatre
St Margaret's Hospital
Paddy's Markets
Powerhouse Museum
Sydney Exhibition Centre
Exhibition Centre
Sydney Convention Centre
Convention
Harbourside Festival Marketplace
Harbourside
Pymont Bridge
Darling Park
Sydney Aquarium
National Maritime Museum
Pyrmont Bay
Kings Cross
To Sydney Airport
To Newtown
To Glebe
10
26
7
12
13
14
15
16
17
18
19

Luna Park ★ The huge smiling clown face and the fairground attractions, which are visible from Circular Quay, make up one of Australia's most iconic attractions. It's fun for kids, with traditional theme-park amusements rather than high-tech rides. It has a carousel, bumper cars, a Ferris wheel, and the like. Many rides are suitable for small children, too. You buy tickets at booths inside the park. The best way to get here is either to walk over the Sydney Harbour Bridge from The Rocks or to catch a train from the city center to Milsons Point. Leave some time for a walk along the foreshore of Sydney Harbour, right beneath the bridge. Hours vary, so check online before setting out.

1 Olympic Dr., Milsons Point. www.lunaparksydney.com.au. ✆ **02/9922 6644** or 02/9033 7676 for information. Free admission. Ride passes based on height: unlimited ride pass A$22 small child; A$38 big kids; A$48 adults. Other prices and deals available. Expect higher prices during school holidays, but better rates if booked online. Mon 11am–4pm; Fri–Sat 11am–10pm; Sun 10am–6pm. During school holidays: Sun–Thurs 10am–6pm; Fri–Sat 10am–10pm. Ferry or train: Milsons Point.

Museum of Contemporary Art (MCA) ★★★ Two MCA Collection Galleries (Level 2 and Level 1 South) feature the works of more than 150 Australian artists acquired since the founding of the MCA in 1989. This imposing sandstone museum, set back from the water on The Rocks side of Circular Quay, also offers a changing program of exhibitions by Australian

An installation at the Museum of Contemporary Art.

and international artists and is worth at least an hour (probably more!) of your time. Free guided tours are conducted at 11am and 1pm daily (and at 7pm Wed and 3pm Sat–Sun), and there's also a program of free talks (check the website for details). The **MCA Café** (✆ **02/9250 8443**) has good views of the harbor and Opera House and has the same hours as the museum.

140 George St., The Rocks. www.mca.com.au. ✆ **02/9245 2400.** Free. Daily 10am–5pm (to 9pm on Wed). Train, bus, or ferry: Circular Quay.

The Rocks Discovery Museum ★★ Drop into this small but interesting museum at lunchtime on Fridays for free half-hour talks on a range of topics—mostly about arts and culture—by guest speakers. Housed in a restored 1850s sandstone warehouse, this museum is dedicated to telling the story of The Rocks from pre-European days to the present. Learn about the area's traditional landowners; the establishment of the English colony; the sailors, whalers, and traders who called the area home; and the 1970s union-led protests that preserved this unique part of Sydney.

Kendall Lane (off Argyle St.), The Rocks. www.therocks.com. ✆ **02/9240 8680.** Free. Daily 10am–5pm. Closed Good Friday and Christmas Day. Train: Circular Quay or Wynyard.

Susannah Place Museum ★★ Entry to this small museum is by guided tour only, but don't let that put you off—it may enhance your visit. Contained in a terrace of four houses built in 1844, this museum is a real highlight of The Rocks area. It provides visitors with the opportunity to explore domestic working-class life from 1844 to 1990. The modest interiors and rear yards illustrate the restrictions of 19th-century inner-city life. The layers of paint, wallpapers, and floor coverings that have survived provide a valuable insight into the tastes of the working class. There's also a delightful little shop selling cordials, postcards, old-fashioned candies, and knickknacks.

58–64 Gloucester St., The Rocks. www.sydneylivingmuseums.com.au. ✆ **02/9241 1893.** Entry by guided tour only, A$12 adults, A$8 children, A$30 family of 4. Daily 2–5pm (last tour at 4pm). Closed Good Friday and Christmas Day. Bus, ferry, or train: Circular Quay.

Sydney Harbour Bridge ★★★ One thing few tourists do—which is a shame—is to walk across the Harbour Bridge. The bridge, completed in 1932, is 1,150m (3,772 ft.) long and spans 503m (1,650 ft.) from the south shore to the north. It has pedestrian walkways, two railway lines, and an eight-lane road. The 30-minute walk from one end to the other offers excellent harbor views. From the other side, you can take a train from Milsons Point back to the city.

As you walk across, stop off at the **Pylon Lookout** (www.pylonlookout.com.au; ✆ **02/9240 1100**) at the southeastern pylon. Admission is A$15 for adults, A$8.50 for children ages 5 to 12. There are four levels inside the pylon, with displays about the bridge's history. On level two, there are observation balconies on both sides, and when you get to the top, 89m (292 ft.) above the water, you get panoramic views of Sydney Harbour, the ferry terminals of

The Sydney BridgeClimb takes you along catwalks and ladders to the top of the bridge.

Circular Quay, and beyond. The Pylon Lookout is open daily from 10am to 5pm (closed Christmas Day).

Another very popular way of enjoying the wonderful views from the Bridge is to climb to the top. The Sydney BridgeClimb is an exhilarating achievement, and one you won't forget. **BridgeClimb,** 3 Cumberland St., The Rocks (www.bridgeclimb.com; ✆ **02/8274 7777**), offers three climbs. The **BridgeClimb** takes you along the outer arch of the bridge on catwalks and ladders all the way to the summit. The **Discovery Climb** takes climbers into the heart of the bridge. You traverse the suspension arch and then wind your way through a tangle of hatchways and girders suspended above the traffic. You also climb between the arches to the summit. Both experiences take 3½ hours from check-in to completion. For those with limited time, the **BridgeClimb Sampler** (A$158 adults, A$133 children Mon–Fri; A$178 adults, A$148 children Sat–Sun) will take you to the halfway point of the climb, and takes only 90 minutes. Climbers wear "Bridge Suits" and are harnessed to a safety line. You will also be given an alcohol breathalyzer test and are not allowed to carry anything, including cameras (the guide will take photos of you at a couple of stops along the way and at the summit). Daytime climbs cost A$293 for adults and A$193 for children ages 10 to 15. Twilight climbs cost A$358 for adults and A$248 for kids. Night climbs cost A$253 for adults and A$173 for kids (rug up, it can be cold up there!). Most climbs cost A$15 more per person on weekends, except the dawn climb costs A$378 for adults and

A$268 for kids no matter when you do it. Prices are slightly higher in the peak time between Christmas and early January. Children 7 and under are not allowed to climb. The **Sydney Harbour Bridge Visitor Centre,** where you set out from, has good displays featuring Sydney's famous icon. It's open daily 8am to 6pm.

Sydney Observatory ★★ The city's only major observatory offers visitors a chance to see the southern skies through modern and historic telescopes. The best time to visit is during the night on a guided tour, when you can take a close-up look at the stars and planets. During the day, 30-minute tours run every hour from 10:15am, including a planetarium show and a telescope viewing (afternoon tours are best, as the mornings are usually reserved for school groups). Two-hour night tours start at 6:30 and 8:15pm and must be booked in advance. There is also a special family tour at 6:30pm. Schedules are subject to change, so check the times when you book. The planetarium and hands-on exhibits are also interesting. Daytime admission to the gardens and the exhibitions is free, but doesn't include the telescope towers, telescope viewings, and 3D theater. For A$300 you can also name a star after yourself or someone you love!

Observatory Hill, 1003 Upper Fort St., Millers Point. www.maas.museum/sydney-observatory. ✆ **02/9217 0111.** Daytime A$10 adults, A$8 children 4–15, A$26 family of 4. Guided night tours (reservations required) A$20–A$22 adults, A$16–A$17 children, A$60–A$65 families. Daily 10am–5pm (until 2pm on Dec 31). Closed Good Friday, Christmas Day, and Boxing Day (Dec 26). Train, bus, or ferry: Circular Quay.

Sydney Opera House ★★★ Only a handful of buildings around the world are as architecturally and culturally significant as the Sydney Opera House. But what sets it apart from some other famous buildings is that this white-sailed construction caught mid-billow over the waters of Sydney Cove is a working building housing a full-scale performing-arts complex with four major performance spaces. The biggest and grandest is the 2,690-seat **Concert Hall.** Come here to experience chamber music, symphonies, dance,

Vivid Sydney

Sydney's spectacular light festival **Vivid** (www.vividsydney.com) runs every winter (late May to mid-June) for three weeks. Rain or shine, from 6 to 11pm, the city lights up at locations all over the city, including the Sydney Opera House, The Rocks, the Royal Botanic Garden, Sydney Town Hall, Circular Quay, Taronga Zoo, Darling Harbour, and Barangaroo. The website has a full list of the events that take place, which includes music and talks. Most events are free, and many are interactive, encouraging Sydneysiders and visitors alike to get involved in the light shows. One of the most popular (and photographically attractive) is the lighting up of the Sydney Opera House sails. Some of the best vantage points are The Rocks, Hickson Road Reserve, Sydney Opera House, Walsh Bay, Darling Harbour, Pyrmont Park, Bradfield Park (under the Harbour Bridge at North Sydney), Luna Park, Lavender Bay, or on the harbour itself.

choral performances, and even rock 'n' roll. The **Joan Sutherland Theatre** is smaller, seats 1,547, and books opera, ballet, and dance. The **Drama Theatre,** seating 544, and the **Playhouse,** seating 398, specialize in plays and smaller-scale performances.

The history of the building is as intriguing as the design. The New South Wales Government raised the construction money with a lottery. Danish architect Jørn Utzon won an international competition to design it. Following a disagreement, Utzon returned home without ever seeing his finished project. The project was budgeted at A$7 million, but by its completion in 1973 it had cost a staggering A$102 million, most raised through a series of lotteries. After a A$152-million upgrade over the past couple of years, the Opera House has never looked better.

Guided tours of the Opera House last about an hour and are conducted daily from 9am to 5pm, except on Good Friday and Christmas Day. If you don't get to see everything, it's because the Opera House is a working venue. There's almost always some performance, practice, or setting up to be done. Tour sizes are limited, so reservations are essential. Backstage tours include up to 300 stairs, and are not open for children 9 and under; the tours include breakfast in the Green Room and are limited to 12 people.

The Tourism Services Department at the Sydney Opera House can book **combination packages,** including dinner and a show; a tour, dinner, and a show; or a champagne-interval performance. Prices vary depending on shows and dining venues. Visitors from overseas can buy tickets by credit card and pick them up at the box office on arrival, or contact a local tour company specializing in Australia. Advance purchases are a good idea, because performances are very popular and it's worth doing to ensure a good seat.

The Opera House is where you will see performances by the Melbourne-based **Australian Ballet** during its Sydney season (www.australianballet.com.au). **Opera Australia** (www.opera.org.au; © **02/9318 8200** for bookings) performs at the Joan Sutherland Theatre. The **Sydney Symphony Orchestra** (www.sydneysymphony.com; © **02/8215 4600** box office) performs throughout the year in the Opera House's Concert Hall. The main symphony season runs March through November, and there's a summer season in February.

Free performances take place outside on the Opera House boardwalks on Sunday afternoons and during festival times. The artists range from musicians and performance artists to school groups.

Bennelong Point. www.sydneyoperahouse.com. © **02/9250 7250** for guided tours and information, or 02/9250 7777 box office. Box office Mon–Sat 9am–8:30pm; Sun 9am–5pm. Tours A$37 for adults, A$20 for kids, and A$95 for a family of 4 (extra child A$12). Book online for discounts. Tours daily 9am–5pm (every 30 min.), subject to theater availability. Backstage tour A$165 starts daily at 7am, for 2 hr., with breakfast. Train, bus, or ferry: Circular Quay.

SYDNEY HARBOUR ON THE CHEAP

The best way to see Sydney Harbour is from the water. Several companies operate tourist craft (see "Harbor Cruises," later in this chapter), but it's easy enough just to hop on a regular passenger ferry (see "Getting Around," earlier in this chapter). The best ferry excursions are to the beachside suburb of **Manly** (return after dusk to see the lights ablaze around The Rocks and Circular Quay); to **Watsons Bay,** where you can have lunch and wander along the cliffs; to **Darling Harbour,** for all the area's entertainment and the fact that you travel right under the Harbour Bridge; and to **Mosman Bay,** just for the ride and to see the grand houses that overlook exclusive harbor inlets.

FAST ACTION ON SYDNEY HARBOUR

For a thrill ride, you can board a 420-horsepower jet boat, which zooms about on three high-speed waterway tours at speeds of up to 40 knots (about 80kmph/50 mph), with huge 240-degree turns and instant stops. **Harbour Jet** (www.harbourjet.com; ✆ **1300/887 373** in Australia or 02/9566 1066) offers a 35-minute Jet Blast ride costing A$80 for adults, A$50 for kids 14 and under, and A$195 for a family (book online for discounts). It leaves at 1, 2, and 3pm on weekends and 1pm Monday through Friday. Rides are fast and furious and pump with rock music. The boat leaves from the King Street Jetty 9 (near the Sydney SEA LIFE Aquarium) at Darling Harbour.

Another option is **Oz Jet Boat** (www.ozjetboating.com; ✆ **02/9808 3700**), with departures every hour from the Eastern Pontoon at Circular Quay (on the walkway to the Opera House). These large red boats are a bit more powerful than the blue Harbour Jet ones, but you might not notice the difference. This company offers a 30-minute Shark Attack Thrill Ride for A$85 for adults, A$49 for kids 15 and under, and A$219 for a family of four. It leaves every hour from 11am to 4pm daily (5pm in summer). Kids must be at least 1.2 meters (3 ft., 11 inches) tall.

Darling Harbour

Many tourists head to Darling Harbour for the cheap eateries and a few interesting shops, but Sydney's dedicated tourist precinct has much more to offer. See **www.darlingharbour.com** for current events.

Australian National Maritime Museum ★★ Australia owes almost everything to the sea, so it's not surprising that there's a museum dedicated to seafarers and ships, from Aboriginal vessels to submarines. Twice a year more names are added to the museum's migrant Welcome Wall, which celebrates the arrival of waves of migrants as part of Australia's maritime history. There are now more than 29,000 names from more than 200 countries on the wall. The museum's "Big Ticket" gives access to everything, including the Australian navy destroyer *Vampire,* an Oberon Class submarine, and a replica of the *Endeavour,* the ship Captain James Cook commanded when he laid claim to Australia, and the tall ship *James Craig,* as well as all the galleries, exhibitions, and the Cape Bowling Green lighthouse, and the Kids on Deck program (Sundays and school holidays). You'll find ships' logs and things to pull and tug at and clamber over—kids love it! Allow 2 hours.

2 Murray St., Darling Harbour. www.anmm.gov.au. ✆ **02/9298 3777.** Free admission to permanent galleries; "Big Ticket" admission to galleries, exhibitions, ships and Kids on Deck A$32 adults, A$20 children 4–15, A$79 families of 5. Additional fees for special

SEEING SYDNEY HARBOUR THROUGH aboriginal EYES

Every visitor to Sydney should get out on the harbor with descendants of the original inhabitants of this most famous waterway. The **Tribal Warrior Association** is an Aboriginal-operated nonprofit organization that provides maritime training programs for Aboriginal youths, and also offers an Aboriginal perspective of Sydney Harbour. Aboard the ketch *Mari Nawi* you will sail past the Royal Botanic Garden as your indigenous guide tells stories of the early Europeans and their hopeless farms, and the smallpox epidemic of 1789. Mixed in with the observations of the landscape are tales of the first Aboriginal tour guides, who took early settlers inland from the harbor, stories of soldiers, statesmen, and farmers who came into contact with the Aborigines, and much more. The cruise stops at Clark Island, where visitors will see cave shelters with roofs stained black from ancient fireplaces, convict engravings, and a natural fish trap. Two Aboriginal guides, their bodies plastered in ghostly white ochre, beat a rhythm with hardwood sticks and growl through a didgeridoo as they beckon tourists to the Welcoming Ceremony. Then comes a repertoire of haunting songs, music, and dance. **Aboriginal Cultural Cruises ★★★** run for 2 hours and cost A$60 adults and A$40 children 4 to 14, A$180 for a family of four. Bookings are essential, and tours run subject to minimum numbers and availability. Cruises generally operate at 1pm from April through October and at 3pm November through March. For more information or to book, call ✆ **02/9699 3491** or visit www.tribalwarrior.org.

exhibitions. Daily 9:30am–5pm (until 6pm in Jan). Closed Christmas Day. Ferry: Darling Harbour. Bus: nos. 389 or 443.

Powerhouse Museum ★★★ Sydney's most interactive museum is also one of the largest in the Southern Hemisphere. Inside, you'll find displays, sound effects, and gadgets relating to the sciences, transportation, human achievement, decorative art, fashion, and social history, much of it with relevance or connections to Sydney and Australian exploration. There's also an Art Deco–style cinema, and exhibitions about global warming, steam trains and steam engines, and even about advertising. You could easily spend 2 or 3 hours discovering everything here. There's plenty to keep kids interested as well.

500 Harris St., Ultimo (near Darling Harbour). www.maas.museum/powerhouse-museum. ✆ **02/9217 0111.** A$15 adults, free for children 15 and under. Daily 10am–5pm. Closed Christmas Day. Ferry: Darling Harbour.

SEA LIFE Sydney Aquarium ★ Sharks, crocodiles, penguins, *dugongs* (sea cows), and platypuses are just some of the marine life you will encounter at this aquarium. The main attractions are the underwater walkways through two enormous tanks—one full of giant rays and gray nurse sharks and the other where you can see the seals. The sharks are fed at 11am and the Fairy Penguins at 3pm daily. The newest exhibit from late 2016 is Penguin Island, where you can raft though a sub-Antarctic environment populated with King and Gentoo penguins. Other exhibits include a section on the Great Barrier Reef, where thousands of colorful fish school around coral outcrops. A touch pool allows you to stroke baby sharks. Among many experiences and animal encounters on offer, you can take a 20-minute behind-the-scenes tour of the Great Barrier Reef oceanarium in a glass-bottom boat, which leaves every 30 minutes from noon to 4pm and costs A$57 adults, A$45 kids 4 to 15 (no children 3 and under). You can also take the boat at shark-feeding time (11am) for about 30 minutes; the cost is slightly higher. Tour prices include general admission. Try to visit during the week, when it's less crowded. Allow around 2 hours.

Aquarium Pier, Darling Harbour. www.sydneyaquarium.com.au. ✆ **02/8251 7800.** A$42 adults, A$30 children 4–15, A$136 families of 4; cheaper if booked online. Mon–Thurs 9:30am–6pm; Fri–Sun 9:30am–7pm; last entry 1 hour before closing. Train: Town Hall. Ferry: Darling Harbour.

Other Top Attractions

Art Gallery of New South Wales ★★★ This beautiful gallery, established in 1871, has a fine collection of international and Australian art that you should take time to see. Contemporary works are displayed in light-filled galleries with views of Sydney and the harbor, while colonial and 19th-century Australian art and European Old Masters are housed in the Grand Courts. There are also dedicated galleries for Asian and Aboriginal and Torres Strait Islander art. The gallery hosts more than 30 temporary exhibitions each year, including the annual Archibald Prize for portraiture (late Mar to early June), in which you'll see plenty of famous Australian faces. Enter from the Domain parklands (across the road from the Royal Botanic Garden) onto the third floor (ground level) of the museum. Allow at least 1 hour, probably more if you are interested in any of the many free tours on offer.

Art Gallery Rd., The Domain. www.artgallery.nsw.gov.au. ✆ **1800/679 278** in Australia or 02/9225 1744. Free admission; prices vary for special exhibitions. Daily 10am–5pm; Wed until 10pm. Closed Good Friday and Christmas Day. Tours of collection highlights daily 2pm. Tours of Aboriginal galleries daily 10:30am. Bus: no. 441. Train: St. James.

Deals on Sightseeing

Several major Sydney attractions offer discounts if you buy passes for entry to more than one of them. If you plan to visit the Sydney Tower, SEA LIFE Sydney Aquarium, Manly SEA LIFE Sanctuary, Wildlife Sydney Zoo, or Madame Tussaud's Wax Museum, it's worth checking their websites for information on **Sydney Attraction Passes.** Passes can be used for two, three, four, or five of the listed attractions. Once you visit your first attraction, you've got 3 months to visit the remaining attraction(s) on the pass. Prices start from A$51 adults and A$36 children for two attractions and go up to A$72 for five attractions (which works out to A$14.40 per attraction for adults, instead of the hefty A$42 that you'd pay at the gate for just the aquarium, for example). So if you're planning to see more than one of these, the pass is a good deal. Buying tickets online also gives good savings (around A$13 for the aquarium).

Australian Museum ★★ This is Sydney's premier natural-history museum. Displays are presented thematically; the Aboriginal section, with traditional clothing, weapons, and everyday implements, is among the best. There are plenty of stuffed Australian mammals and birds, an insect display, and a mineral collection. Children are well catered to, and there are plenty of dinosaurs, mummies, and other wonderful things to observe.

6 College St. www.australianmuseum.net.au. ✆ **02/9320 6000.** A$15 adults, A$8 children 5–15, A$30 families of 4. Special exhibits extra. Daily 9:30am–5pm. Closed Christmas Day. Train: Museum, St. James, or Town Hall.

Elizabeth Bay House ★ Perched on a headland with some of the best harbor views in Sydney, this colonial mansion was built in 1835 and was considered "the finest house in the colony." You can tour the house and get a feeling for the history of that fledgling settlement.

7 Onslow Ave., Elizabeth Bay. www.sydneylivingmuseums.com.au. ✆ **02/9356 3022.** A$12 adults, A$8 children, A$30 families. Fri–Sun 10am–4pm. Closed Good Friday and Christmas Day. Bus: no. 311 from Circular Quay. Train: Kings Cross.

Hyde Park Barracks Museum ★★ If you don't know the terms "Lags and Swells," you will after meeting some convict characters at this museum, where a touchscreen interactive program brings to life some of the 50,000 convicts who passed through the Hyde Park Barracks between 1819 and 1848. These Georgian-style barracks, designed by the convict Francis Greenway (an architect), were built by convicts and inhabited by prisoners. They are among 11 convict sites in Australia that are World Heritage listed. These days they house relics from those days, including log books, settlement artifacts, and a room full of ships' hammocks in which you can lie and listen to fragments of prisoner conversation. If you are interested in Sydney's early beginnings, I highly recommend a visit. There are free audio tours available. Allow at least 1 hour.

Queens Sq., 10 Macquarie St. www.sydneylivingmuseums.com.au. ✆ **02/8239 2311.** A$12 adults, A$8 children, A$30 families. Daily 10am–5pm. Train: St. James or Martin Place.

Museum of Sydney ★ Free 30-minute tours, at 11am and 3pm daily, give a good introduction to this interesting museum. A visit to the Museum of Sydney will make you think! In a postmodern building near Circular Quay, encompassing the remnants of Sydney's first Government House, the museum is certainly not what you might expect. No conventional showcase of history, this museum houses a collection of first-settler and Aboriginal objects and multimedia displays that invite you to discover Sydney's past. Some of it is underfoot, in the archaeological digs exposed through "windows" in the paths. A forest of poles filled with hair, oyster shells, and crab claws in the courtyard, called *Edge of Trees,* represents first contact between Aborigines and the British. Modern . . . yes. And very interesting. There are plenty of reasons to linger, for a game of outdoor chess, perhaps, or just to lounge on the grassy areas.

37 Phillip St., (at Bridge St.). www.sydneylivingmuseums.com.au. ✆ **02/9251 5988.** A$12 adults, A$8 children 14 and under, A$30 families. Daily 10am–5pm. Closed Good Friday and Christmas Day. Train, bus, or ferry: Circular Quay.

Sydney Jewish Museum ★★★ A major new Holocaust exhibition has been developed at this important museum, building on the former 25-year-old exhibition. Developed in consultation with Holocaust survivors, many of whom are volunteer guides at the museum, it aims to give new voice to their history. More than 100 new objects and many new images form part of the display. One of the most moving aspects of any visit to this museum has always been the chance to talk to Holocaust survivors. Another permanent exhibition here is *Serving Australia,* which showcases the contribution that Jewish servicemen and women have made to the Australian armed forces. The museum also has a shop, a resource center, a small theater, and a kosher cafe. Allow 1 to 2 hours. Plan to visit in the afternoon to avoid large school groups.

148 Darlinghurst Rd. (at Burton St.), Darlinghurst. www.sydneyjewishmuseum.com.au. ✆ **02/9360 7999.** A$15 adults, A$9 children, A$32 families of 4. Free 45-min. guided tours Mon, Tues, Thurs at 1pm and Sun at noon. Mon–Thurs and Sun 10am–4pm; Fri 10am–2pm. Closed Sat and Jewish holy days. Train: Kings Cross.

Sydney Tower ★ The Sydney Tower is hard to miss—it resembles a giant steel pole skewering a golden marshmallow. Standing 309m (984 ft.) tall, the tower offers stupendous 360-degree views across Sydney and as far as the Blue Mountains. At the top is a revolving restaurant and bar. The indoor viewing platform on the top floor is called the Sydney Tower Eye. Don't be too concerned if you feel the building tremble slightly, especially in a strong wind—apparently it's built to do that! The ticket price includes admission to a 4D cinema, where you can watch a film about Sydney with footage of the harbor, coastline, famous landmarks, and events. The **Sydney Tower Skywalk** is a heart-stopping experience and definitely not for those who are afraid of heights. You don a special suit, walk out onto a glass-floored platform 260m (853 ft.) above the city floor and walk around the building. The views are breathtaking (even between your feet!). You are harnessed to a safety rail, so there's no chance of falling off, and well-informed guides offer a helping hand to the nervous. Each Skywalk lasts about 90 minutes. Cameras aren't allowed for safety reasons, but the guide will take group or individual shots that you can buy. Children 7 and under aren't allowed on the Skywalk.

100 Market St. (another entrance on Pitt St. Mall). www.sydneytowereye.com.au. ✆ **1800/258 693** in Australia or 02/9333 9222. A$28 adults, A$19 children 4–15. Daily 9am–9:30pm (last entry 8:30pm) mid-Apr to early Oct; 9am–10pm (last entry 9pm) Oct–Apr. Closed Christmas Day. Skywalk A$70 for adults, A$49 for kids 8–15. Train: St. James or Town Hall.

Kangaroos, Koalas & Other Aussie Wildlife

See p. 88 for SEA LIFE Sydney Aquarium.

Featherdale Wildlife Park ★★★ If you have time to visit only one wildlife park in Sydney, make it this one. The selection of Australian animals is excellent, and, most important, the animals are very well cared for. You could easily spend a couple of hours here, despite the park's compact size. You'll have the chance to hand-feed friendly kangaroos and wallabies and get a photo taken next to a koala. The **Reptilian Pavilion** houses 30 native species of reptiles in 26 realistic exhibits. If you are heading to the Blue Mountains (p. 102) on a bus tour, choose one that stops off here. Allow 1½ hours to get here by public transport or 45 minutes by car from the city center.

217 Kildare Rd., Doonside. www.featherdale.com.au. ✆ **02/9622 1644.** A$31 adults, A$17 children 3–15, A$59–A$85 families. Daily 9am–5pm. Closed Christmas Day. Train: Blacktown station; then bus no. 729.

Koala Park Sanctuary ★ In all, around 55 koalas roam within the park's leafy boundaries (it's set in 4 hectares/10 acres of rainforest). Free koala feeding sessions take place at 10:20 and 11:45am, and 2 and 3pm daily (and you can have your photo taken with them too!). There are wombats, dingoes, kangaroos, wallabies, emus, and native birds here as well. Live sheep shearing takes place at 10:30am and 2:30pm daily. Allow 1½ hours to get here by public transport from the city center or about 30 minutes to drive.

84 Castle Hill Rd., West Pennant Hills. www.koalapark.com. ✆ **02/9484 3141.** A$27 adults, A$15 children 4–14. Daily 9am–5pm. Closed Christmas Day. Train: Pennant Hills station via North Strathfield (45 min.). Cross over railway line and join Glenorie Bus routes 651 to 655. The bus takes about 10 min. to Koala Park.

Manly SEA LIFE Sanctuary ★★★ Penguin Cove is the newest attraction at this marine sanctuary (a sister attraction to Sydney Aquarium), showing off a colony of Little Penguins and explaining their importance to the shores of Manly. Talks and feeding demonstrations are offered daily, and you can get "hands-on" in the interactive rock pool, which kids love. There's a good display of Barrier Reef fish, as well as giant sharks. If you're braver than me, you can take the plunge with **Shark Dive Xtreme,** diving into the tank to swim with large grey nurse sharks, turtles, and stingrays. It costs A$299 for all divers, and if you are not a qualified diver, includes an Introduction to Scuba Diving lesson. A **Shark Feed Xtreme** experience—limited to only two divers at a time—is available three times a week and costs A$395 per person. Bookings are essential, and you'll save by booking online. You'll find the aquarium right next to Manly Wharf.

West Esplanade, Manly. www.manlysealifesanctuary.com.au. ✆ **1800/199 742** in Australia or 02/8251 7878. A$25 adults, A$17 children 4–15, A$53–A$75 families (cheaper online). Daily 10am–4:30pm (last entry 4pm). Closed Christmas Day. Ferry: Manly.

Taronga Zoo ★★★ Taronga has the best views of any zoo in the world. Set on a hill, it looks out over Sydney Harbour, the Opera House, and the Harbour Bridge. It's easiest on the legs to explore the zoo from the top down (admission includes a trip on the cable car from the ferry pier to the main entrance). The big attractions are the fabulous chimpanzee exhibit, the gorilla enclosure, and the Nocturnal Houses, where you can see some of Australia's unique marsupials, including the platypus and the cute bilby, out and about. There's an interesting reptile display, a couple of impressive Komodo dragons, a scattering of indigenous beasties—including a few koalas, echidnas, kangaroos, dingoes, and wombats—and lots more. Animals are fed at various times during the day. An "Aboriginal Discovery Tour" is offered Monday, Wednesday, and Friday at 9:45am; it takes around 2 hours and costs A$99 adults and A$69 children and includes zoo entry (advance bookings essential). Despite the quite steep entry price, the zoo can get crowded on weekends, so it's a good idea to plan your visit for a weekday or early in the morning on weekends. Allow around 3 hours.

Bradley's Head Rd., Mosman. www.taronga.org.au. ✆ **02/9969 2777.** A$46 adults, A$26 children 4–15, A$130 family of 4. Daily 9:30am–5pm (until 4:30pm in winter, May–Aug). Ferry: Taronga Zoo. Lower zoo entrance is at ferry terminal.

Wildlife Sydney Zoo ★★ Not to be confused with Taronga Zoo (Sydney's premier outdoor zoo; see above), this inner-city attraction has a big collection of Australian creatures, including kangaroos, a cassowary, snakes, wallabies, Tasmanian devils, birds, butterflies, and a large saltwater crocodile. You'll find koalas lazing around in the rooftop garden. The Wild Discovery Zone was designed especially for kids, with hands-on animal encounters. You walk through eight themed Australian habitats. No elephants or giraffes here, but it might not matter! Behind-the-scenes tours run daily at 10am and 3pm. You can also take a "Wild Flight" across the aviary in a harness, looking down on kangaroos and crocodiles. It costs A$10 (ages 10 and up only).

Aquarium Pier, Darling Harbour. www.wildlifesydney.com.au. ✆ **1800/206 158** in Australia or 02/8251 7800. A$42 adults, A$30 kids 3–15 (cheaper online); Behind the Scenes tours, A$65 adults, A$43 kids (includes zoo entry). Mid-Apr to early Oct daily 9:30am–5pm (last entry 4pm); early Oct to mid-Apr daily 9:30am–7pm (last entry 6pm). Ferry: Darling Harbour.

ORGANIZED TOURS

For details on the **Sydney Explorer** and **Bondi Explorer** sightseeing buses, see "Getting Around," p. 54.

Harbor Cruises

The best thing about Sydney is the harbor, and you shouldn't leave without taking a cruise. **Captain Cook Cruises,** departing Jetty 6, Circular Quay (www.captaincook.com.au; ✆ **02/9206 1111**), offers several harbor excursions on its sleek vessels, with commentary along the way. One-hour afternoon "High Tea Cruises" cost A$59, and there's a range of breakfast and dining cruises as well. The popular 1-hour, 15-minute "Harbour Highlights Cruise" costs A$35 for adults and A$19 for children 4 to 15 and runs daily at 2:30pm from Circular Quay. Whale-watching cruises run from mid-May to early November and cost A$79 adults, A$45 children ages 4 to 15. Check the website for special deals. Captain Cook Cruises has ticket booths at Jetty 6, Circular Quay (open 8:30am–7pm daily), at King Street Wharf 1 (9am–7:30pm Mon–Fri, 5:30–7:30pm Sat–Sun) and at Pier 26, Aquarium Wharf, Darling Harbour (8:30am–5pm daily). A "Zoo Express" cruise includes entry to Taronga Zoo and departs fromDarling Harbour, Circular Quay, or Manly. It costs A$69 for adults and A$39 for kids.

Yellow Water Taxis (www.yellowwatertaxis.com; ✆ **1300/326 822** in Australia or 02/9556 9200) offers a 15-minute mini-tour by small water taxi from its bases at King Street Wharf in Darling Harbour and Circular Quay Jetty 1. This tour is good for a quick look at Sydney's famous harbor and a great way to travel to or from Darling Harbour and Circular Quay. These "snapshot" tours depart every 30 minutes and cost A$20 for adults, A$15 for children (4–12 years of age), and A$55 for a family of four. A 45-minute Harbour Highlights Tour includes Darling Harbour, the Sydney Opera House, Royal Botanic Garden and harbor-front mansions, with a commentary. This tour costs A$45 for adults, A$30 for kids, and A$120 for a family of four.

It's a good idea to check websites or pop into a ticket office at Darling Harbour or Circular Quay, because cruise options, departure times, and prices change frequently.

Walking Tours

If you want to learn more about Sydney's early history, book an excellent guided tour with **The Rocks Walking Tours,** based at Clocktower Square, corner of Argyle and Harrington streets (www.rockswalkingtours.com.au; ✆ **02/9247 6678**). Walks leave daily at 10:30am and 1:30pm. The 1½-hour tour costs A$28 for adults, A$12 for children ages 5 to 16, and A$68 for families of four.

Another good walking tour company is **Two Feet & A Heartbeat Walking Tours** (www.twofeet.com.au; ✆ **1800/459 388** in Australia), which runs seven fascinating small-group tours that take in Sydney's quirky stories and characters in the city center, The Rocks, and King's Cross/Darlinghurst. Most 2-hour tours cost A$45. There's also a 3-hour tour of Sydney's bar scene, for A$55. Or you can spend 2 hours and A$69 for a guided walk around some of The Rocks' historic pubs.

Culture Scouts (www.culturescouts.com.au; ✆ **02/9016 5531**) runs interesting walking tours that focus on art, food, and conversation (think galleries, cafes, bars, street art, and boutiques) in the creative inner suburbs of Chippendale, Glebe, Redfern, Surry Hills, and Newtown. Tours last 2 to 3 hours, go at a gentle pace, and can be tailor made if you wish. All tours cost A$95 per person and are not recommended for kids 14 and under. Two-hour street art tours (A$59 per person) run twice a month on Saturday mornings.

Motorcycle Tours

Wild Ride Australia (www.wildride.com.au; ✆ **1300/738 338** in Australia or 02/9623 8338) runs Harley-Davidson tours of Sydney, the Blue Mountains, and beyond. A 1-hour ride (you sit on the back of the bike) around the city or Bondi costs A$130. A 1½-hour ride through the city and out to Bondi costs A$160. A 3-hour trip to the northern beaches costs A$250. Full-day trips cover the Blue Mountains and the Hawkesbury region. If you love motorcycles and want to rent one for a self-guided or guided tour, contact **Bikescape** (www.bikescape.com.au; ✆ **1300/736 869** in Australia or 02/9569 4111).

OUTDOOR ACTIVITIES

Hitting the Beach

One of the big bonuses of visiting Sydney in the summer (Dec–Feb) is that you get to experience the beaches in their full glory. Most major city beaches, such as Manly and Bondi, have lifeguards on patrol, especially during the summer. They check the water conditions and are on the lookout for **"rips"**—strong currents that can pull a swimmer far out. Always swim in the area between the red and yellow flags that mark the patrolled area. Fiberglass surfboards must be used outside the flags. (Expect a warning from the loudspeakers and a fine if you fail to do this.)

WHAT ABOUT SHARKS & OTHER NASTIES? One of the first things visitors ask before they hit the water in Australia is: "Are there sharks?" The answer is yes, but fortunately they are rarely spotted inshore—you are far more likely to spy a migrating whale. In reality, the chance of a shark attack is very small. Some beaches—such as the small beach next to the Manly ferry wharf—have permanent shark nets, while others rely on portable nets that are moved from beach to beach. Shark attacks are most likely in early morning and at dusk—avoid swimming at these times!

More common off Sydney's beaches are **"blue bottles"**—small blue jellyfish, often called "stingers" in Australia (and Portuguese man-o'-war elsewhere). You'll often find these creatures (which are not the same as the stingers in north Queensland) washed up on the beach. Be on the lookout for warning signs erected on the shoreline. Minute stinging cells that touch your skin can cause minor itching. You might be hit by the full force of a blue bottle if it wraps its tentacles around you, which causes a severe burning sensation almost immediately. Wearing a T-shirt in the water reduces the risk somewhat. If you are stung, rinse the area liberally with seawater or fresh water to remove any tentacles stuck in your skin. To combat intense pain, take a hot shower. In the unlikely event that you experience breathing difficulties or disorientation, seek medical attention immediately.

SOUTH OF SYDNEY HARBOUR

Sydney's most famous beach is **Bondi ★★★**. The beach, sadly, is cut off from the cafe and restaurant strip that caters to beachgoers by a busy road that pedestrians must cross to reach the sand. On summer weekend evenings, it's popular with young men driving souped-up cars and strutting their stuff. To reach Bondi Beach, take the train to Bondi Junction, and then transfer to bus no. 380 or 333 (a 15-min. bus journey). The no. 333 bus takes about 40 minutes from Circular Quay.

If you're facing the water at Bondi, to your right is a scenic cliff-top trail that takes you to **Bronte Beach ★★★** (a 20-min. walk) via gorgeous little **Tamarama ★★★**, nicknamed "Glamourama" for its trendy sun worshippers. Bronte has better swimming, while Tamarama is known for its dangerous rips and is often closed to swimming. To go straight to Bronte, catch bus no. 378 from Circular Quay or pick up the bus at the Bondi Junction train station.

Escaping a Rip

Plenty of tourists get into real trouble on Sydney's beaches each year by being caught in a rip tide—a fast current that moves away from the shore (but that will not pull you under the water). If this happens, the most important thing to do is not to panic. If you can't stand up and are being pulled out to sea, try to attract attention by raising a hand in the air. Whatever you do, don't try to battle it out with the rip by trying to swim against it back to shore. You will quickly become exhausted; this is how people drown. Keep calm, and swim parallel to the beach. If you run out of energy, float on your back. If you swim parallel to the beach you will be pulled a little farther out to sea—it won't take you far out—but before long you should be out of the rip and able to swim back to the beach. Never swim outside of the area marked by yellow and red flags on a beach patrolled by lifeguards. If there are no lifeguards around, it's safest not to swim.

Clovelly Beach ★★★, farther along the coast, is blessed with a large rock pool carved into a rock platform that's sheltered from the force of the Tasman Sea. This beach is accessible for visitors in wheelchairs on a series of ramps. To reach Clovelly, take bus no. 339 from Circular Quay.

The cliff walk from Bondi will eventually bring you to **Coogee ★★**, which has a pleasant strip of sand with a couple of hostels and hotels nearby. To reach Coogee, take bus no. 373 or 374 from Circular Quay.

NORTH OF SYDNEY HARBOUR

On the North Shore you'll find **Manly ★★★**, a long curve of golden sand edged with Norfolk Island pines. The best way to reach Manly is on a ferry from Circular Quay. Follow the crowds through the pedestrian Corso to the main ocean beach, ignoring the two small beaches on either side of the ferry terminal—this is not your destination!

Facing the ocean, head to your right along the beachfront and follow the coastal path to small and sheltered **Shelly Beach ★★★**, a nice area for snorkeling and swimming. This is one of Sydney's nicest walks. Follow the path up the hill to the car park. Here, a track cuts up into the bush and leads toward a firewall, which marks the entrance to the Sydney Harbour National Park and offers spectacular ocean views across to Manly and the northern beaches.

The best harbor beach is at **Balmoral ★★★**, a wealthy suburb with some good cafes and restaurants. Reach Balmoral on the ferry to Taronga Zoo and then a 10-minute ride on a connecting bus from the ferry wharf, or catch the bus from the stop outside the zoo's top entrance.

Surfing

Bondi Beach and **Tamarama** are the best surf beaches on the south side of Sydney Harbour. **Manly, Narrabeen, Bilgola, Collaroy, Long Reef,** and **Palm** beaches are the most popular on the north side. Most beach suburbs have surf shops where you can rent a board. At Bondi Beach, **Lets Go Surfing,** 128 Ramsgate Ave. (www.letsgosurfing.com.au; ✆ **02/9365 1800**), rents surfboards for A$20 for 1 hour or A$40 all day. There are discounts for all-week hires, and you can also hire wet suits for A$10 to A$15. Lets Go also offers surfing lessons for individuals or groups. A 2-hour session in a small group costs A$85 per person; 1-hour private lessons cost A$140.

In Manly, **Manly Surf Guide** (www.manlysurfguide.com; ✆ **0412/417 431** mobile) rents (and delivers) surfboards. **Manly Surf School** (http://manlysurfschool.com; ✆ **02/9199 8910**) offers 2-hour small-group surf classes for A$70 per person. The more lessons you take, the cheaper it is. For A$120 you get a full day's outing that includes pickup from the city, lessons, and surfing at various places on the northern beaches. If you're already proficient, you might want to consider a 1-day trip with **Waves Surf School** (www.wavessurfschool.com.au; ✆ **1800/616 667** in Australia or 02/9641 2358) to the Royal National Park. Trips cost A$99, and include lunch. Waves also offers a 2-day surfing trip to Seal Rocks, north of Sydney, for A$295, as well as 4- and 5-day trips farther afield.

Parks & Gardens

If you have time to spend in one of Sydney's green spaces, make it the **Royal Botanic Garden ★★★** (www.rbgsyd.nsw.gov.au; ✆ **02/9231 8111**), next to the Sydney Opera House. Open daily (7am–dusk), these lovely informal gardens were laid out in 1816 on the site of a farm that supplied food for the colony. The gardens have a scattering of duck ponds and open spaces, with several areas dedicated to particular plant species. These include the rose garden, the cacti and succulent display, and the central palm and rainforest

Surfing on Bondi Beach.

groves. Try to spot the thousands of large fruit bats, which chatter and bicker among the rainforest trees. Free, 90-minute guided walks are run daily at 10:30am and also at 1pm Monday to Friday (Mar–Nov only). Aboriginal Heritage Tours (A$39 adults) run at 10am Wednesday, Friday, and Saturday. **Mrs. Macquarie's Chair ★★**, along the coast path, offers superb views of the Opera House and the Harbour Bridge. The "chair" bears the name of Elizabeth Macquarie (1788–1835), the wife of Governor Lachlan Macquarie. The sandstone building dominating the gardens nearest the Opera House is **Government House.** The gardens are open most days (times vary), and the house is usually open Friday through Sunday (© **02/9228 4111** to check times and closures). Entrance is free, but you'll need a ticket from the gatehouse to tour the house. Note that the house is sometimes closed for official functions.

In the center of the city is **Hyde Park,** a favorite with lunching businesspeople. Here you will find the **Anzac Memorial** to Australian and New Zealand troops killed in action, and the **Archibald Fountain,** complete with spitting turtles and sculptures of Diana and Apollo.

Another Sydney favorite is the giant **Centennial Park ★★★** (www.centennialparklands.com.au; © **02/9339 6699**). The park has five main entrances, but the easiest one from the city is at the top of Oxford Street. The park opened in 1888 to celebrate the centenary of European settlement and today encompasses huge lawns, several lakes, picnic areas with barbecues, cycling and running paths, and a cafe. It's open from sunrise to sunset. The visitor information desk is open 9am to 4pm Monday through Friday and 9am to 2pm Saturday and Sunday.

New in 2015 the harborside **Barangaroo Reserve ★★★** (www.barangaroo.sydney; © **1300/966 480** in Australia or 02/9255 1700) is a spectacular 6-hectare parkland on the headland opposite Luna Park. Still a work in progress, half of the Barangaroo precinct will be public space with a 2km (1¼-mile) waterfront walkway, lined with restaurants and cafes; the rest of the 22-hectare (54-acre) space comprises retail and apartment development. The parkland was planted with 74,000 native plants and landscaped with sandstone blocks, forming a natural amphitheater to be used for concerts and other events. Barangaroo was a key figure in local Aboriginal culture in early colonial times (and the wife of Bennelong, for whom Bennelong Point, site of the Sydney Opera House is named). Aboriginal Cultural Tours of the site run daily at 10:30am for about 90 minutes and cost A$39 adults, A$24 children. Barangaroo is an easy walk from Circular Quay, either along the harbor-front or along Argyle Street. The closest train station is Wynyard, and there's a ferry terminal at Barangaroo South.

Biking

The best place to cycle in Sydney is Centennial Park. Rent bikes from **Centennial Park Cycles,** 50 Clovelly Rd., Randwick (www.cyclehire.com.au; © **02/9398 5027**), which is 200m (656 ft.) from the Musgrave Avenue entrance. Bikes cost A$15 for the first hour, A$20 for 2 hours, A$30 for 4 hours, and A$50 for a full day. Extra days cost just A$15 each.

Bonza Bike Tours (www.bonzabiketours.com.au; ✆ **02/9247 8800**), at 30 Harrington St., The Rocks, runs regular bike tours of the city, and also hires out bikes. A half-day city tour costs A$119 for adults, A$99 for kids, A$349 for families, including a bike and helmet. It also offers a tour of Manly and another that takes you across Sydney Harbour Bridge. Bike hire alone costs A$10 an hour, A$19 a half-day, or A$29 a day.

Kayaking

Natural Wanders (www.naturalwanders.com.au; ✆ **0427/225 072** mobile) takes paddlers out on Sydney Harbour. Tours start from Lavender Bay, near Luna Park; this is the only kayaking company that takes you under Sydney Harbour Bridge. Group tours run on weekends only, but if you'd like a private tour, owner Patrick Dibben will take you during the week too. There's no minimum number for tours, so you may still be in a group of only two or three. A 3½-hour paddle costs A$120 and takes you from Lavender Bay west, across the Harbour and south to explore Balmain, then north to land at Berry Island before returning to Lavender Bay (about 10–12km/6–7 miles). Private tours cost A$190 for one person or A$160 each if there are two or more people. These tours usually go under Sydney Harbour Bridge and past the Opera House and stop on a beautiful beach in a bushland setting before returning. Check the website for tour options. You must be 15 years or older, have a good level of fitness, and be able to swim!

Swimming

With all that ocean, why bother with a pool? Well, Sydney has some great pools that you might want to try just for their settings. The **Bondi Icebergs Club,** 1 Notts Ave. (www.icebergs.com.au; ✆ **02/9130 4804**), at Bondi Beach, has an Olympic-size ocean tidal pool built into the rocks with the ocean

Bondi Icebergs Club features an ocean-fed public pool.

lapping into it. It also has a children's pool. Entrance costs A$6.50 for adults, A$4.50 for kids, or A$18 for a family of five. Spectators pay A$4.50. Towel hire is A$3.50. The pool is open from 6am (6:30am Sat–Sun) until 6:30pm Friday through Wednesday (it's closed Thurs for cleaning). ***Be warned:*** This is a true ocean pool, so the water is sometimes very cold (hence the name of the club!).

Another good pool with fabulous views across Sydney Harbour is the **Andrew (Boy) Charlton Swimming Pool,** the Domain, Mrs. Macquaries Road, near the Royal Botanical Gardens (www.abcpool.org; ✆ **02/9358 6686**). This is an outdoor pool, and it also has a learner's pool and a toddler's pool. Entry is A$6.40 for adults, A$4.80 for kids, A$18 family of four. It's open 6am to 7pm daily September to April.

Yachting

Sydney by Sail (www.sydneybysail.com.au; ✆ **02/9280 1110**), based at Darling Harbour, offers day sails on Sydney Harbour. A skippered, 3-hour afternoon sail leaving at 1pm costs A$175 for adults and A$85 for kids 13 and under, or A$420 for a family of four. You can help sail, or just relax.

SHOPPING

You'll find plenty of places to keep your credit cards in action in Sydney. Most shops of interest to the visitor are in **The Rocks** and along **George and Pitt streets** (including the shops below the Sydney Tower and along Pitt Street Mall). Other precincts worth checking out are **Mosman,** on the North Shore; **Double Bay,** in the eastern suburbs, for boutique shopping; **Chatswood,** for its shopping centers; and various **weekend markets** (see below).

Don't miss the **Queen Victoria Building (QVB),** on the corner of Market and George streets. This Victorian shopping arcade is one of the most ornate in Australia and has around 200 boutiques—mostly men's and women's fashion—on four levels. Here you'll find fashion-statement stores featuring the best of Australian design, including Oroton, Country Road, and David Lawrence. The arcade is open 24 hours, but the shops do business Monday through Saturday from 9am to 6pm (Thurs to 9pm) and Sunday from 11am to 5pm.

The **Strand Arcade** (btw. Pitt Street Mall and George St.) was built in 1892 and is interesting for its architecture and small boutiques, food stores, and cafes, and the Downtown Duty Free store on the basement level. Labels to look for include Scanlan Theodore, Leona Edmiston, and Megan Park.

On **Pitt Street Mall** you'll find a few shops and a Westfield Shopping Centre full of fashion boutiques. **Oxford Street** runs from the city to Bondi Junction through Paddington and Darlinghurst and is home to countless stylish clothing stores. You could spend anywhere from 2 hours to an entire day making your way from one end to the other. Detour down William Street, once you get to Paddington, to visit the trendy boutiques including the luxury recycled goods of Di Nuovo. You'll find the boutique of celebrated international Australian designer Collette Dinnigan on Caledonia Street.

SYDNEY'S markets

Sydney has many good markets worth a look for quirky gifts or souvenirs and to soak up the local vibe, especially on weekends.

Closest to the city is **The Rocks Market** (www.therocks.com), held every Saturday and Sunday (with a smaller "foodies" market on Fri). This touristy market has more than 100 vendors selling everything from crafts, housewares, and posters to jewelry and curios. George Street in The Rocks is closed to traffic from 10am to 5pm to make it easier to stroll around.

Paddy's Markets (www.paddysmarkets.com.au) are a Sydney institution, with hundreds of stalls selling everything from cheap clothes and plants to chickens. It's open Wednesday to Sunday, 10am to 6pm. Above Paddy's Markets is **Market City,** which has three floors of fashion stalls, food courts, and specialty shops, and a huge Asian-European supermarket. Paddy's is at the corner of Thomas and Hay streets, Haymarket, near Chinatown.

Balmain Market (www.balmainmarket.com.au), held from 8:30am to 4pm every Saturday, has about 140 vendors selling crafts, jewelry, and knickknacks. Take the ferry to Balmain (Darling St.); the market is a 10-minute walk up Darling Street, on the grounds of St. Andrew's Church.

Bondi Markets (www.bondimarkets.com.au) is a nice place to stroll around on Sunday and discover upcoming young Australian designers. This market specializes in clothing and jewelry, new, secondhand, and retro. It's open Sunday from 9am to 4pm at the Bondi Beach Public School, Campbell Parade.

Paddington Markets (www.paddingtonmarkets.com.au) is a Saturday-only market where you'll find 150 stalls offering everything from essential oils and designer clothes to New Age jewelry and Mexican hammocks. Expect things to be busy from 10am to 4pm. Take bus no. 380 or 333 from Circular Quay and follow the crowds. It's held in the grounds of St. John's Church, Oxford Street, on the corner of Newcombe Street.

The two big department store names in Sydney shopping are David Jones and Myer. **David Jones** (www.davidjones.com.au; ✆ **02/9266 5544**) is the city's largest department store, selling everything from fashion to designer furniture. You'll find the women's section on the corner of Elizabeth and Market streets, and the men's section on the corner of Castlereagh and Market streets. The food section offers expensive delicacies. **Myer** (www.myer.com.au; ✆ **02/9238 9111**) is similar, but the building is newer and flashier. It's on the corner of George and Market streets.

Nearer to Circular Quay is **Chifley Plaza,** home to a selection of the world's most famous and stylish international brands. For really trendy clothing, walk up Oxford Street to **Paddington** or head to **Surry Hills,** and for alternative clothes, go to **Newtown.**

If you are looking for trendy surf- and swimwear, the main drags at Bondi Beach and Manly Beach offer plenty of choices.

For gifts and souvenirs, the shops at **Taronga Zoo,** the **SEA LIFE Sydney Aquarium,** and the **Australian Museum** are all good sources for gifts and souvenirs. Many shops around **The Rocks** are worth browsing, too.

A DAY TRIP TO THE BLUE MOUNTAINS ★★★

Katoomba: 114km (71 miles) W of Sydney; Leura: 107km (66 miles) W of Sydney, 3km (2 miles) E of Katoomba; Blackheath: 114km (71 miles) W of Sydney, 14km (8¾ miles) NW of Katoomba; Wentworth Falls: 103km (64 miles) W of Sydney, 7km (4½ miles) E of Katoomba.

The **Blue Mountains** offer breathtaking views, rugged tablelands, sheer cliffs, deep, inaccessible valleys, enormous chasms, colorful parrots, cascading waterfalls, historic villages, and stupendous walking trails. In 2000, UNESCO classified it as a World Heritage Site. Although the Blue Mountains are where Sydneysiders now go to escape the humidity and crowds of the city, in the early days of the colony the mountains kept at bay those who wanted to explore the interior. In 1813, three explorers—Gregory Blaxland, William Charles Wentworth, and William Lawson—managed to conquer the cliffs, valleys, and dense forests and cross the mountains to the plains beyond. There they found land the colony urgently needed for grazing and farming. The **Great Western Highway** and **Bells Line of Road** are the access roads through the region today—winding and steep in places, they are surrounded by the Blue Mountains and Wollemi national parks.

This area is known for its spectacular scenery, particularly the cliff-top views into valleys of gum trees and across to craggy outcrops that tower from the valley floor. It's colder up here than in the city, and clouds can sweep in and fill the canyons with mist in minutes, while waterfalls cascade down sheer drops, spraying the dripping fern trees that cling to the gullies. A day tour may only scratch the surface but should give you a glimpse into why Sydneysiders love it.

There are four main towns in the Blue Mountains. **Katoomba** (pop. 11,200) is the largest and the focal point of the Blue Mountains National Park. It's an easy 1½- to 2-hour trip from Sydney by train, bus, or car.

Leura is known for its gardens, its attractive old buildings (many holiday homes for Sydneysiders), and its cafes and restaurants. Just outside Leura is the **Sublime Point Lookout,** which has spectacular views of the **Three Sisters** (p. 105) in Katoomba. From the southern end of Leura Mall, a cliff drive takes you all the way back to **Echo Point** in Katoomba; along the way you'll enjoy stunning views across the Jamison Valley.

The pretty town of **Wentworth Falls** has numerous crafts and antiques shops, but the area is principally known for its 281m (922-ft.) waterfall, situated in **Falls Reserve.** On the far side of the falls is the **National Pass Walk**—one of the best in the Blue Mountains. It's cut into a cliff face with overhanging rock faces on one side and sheer drops on the other. The views over the Jamison Valley are spectacular. The track takes you down to the base of the falls to the **Valley of the Waters.** Climbing up out of the valley is quite a bit more difficult, but just as rewarding.

Blackheath is the highest town in the Blue Mountains at 1,049m (3,441 ft.). Take the Cliff Walk from **Evans Lookout** to **Govetts Leap,** where there are magnificent views over the **Grose Valley** and **Bridal Veil Falls.** The 1½-hour trek passes through banksia, gum, and wattle forests, with wonderful views of mountain peaks and valleys.

> **Color Me Blue**
>
> The Blue Mountains derive their name from the ever-present blue haze that is caused by light striking the droplets of eucalyptus oil that evaporate from the leaves of the dense surrounding forest.

The Blue Mountains are also one of Australia's best-known adventure playgrounds. Rock climbing, caving, abseiling (rappelling), bushwalking, mountain biking, horseback riding, and canoeing are practiced here year-round.

Essentials

GETTING THERE By car from central Sydney, take Parramatta Road and turn off onto the M4 motorway (around 2 hr. to Katoomba). Another route is via the Harbour Bridge to North Sydney, along the Warringah Freeway (following signs to the M2). Then take the M2 to the end and follow signs to the M4 and the Blue Mountains. This takes around 1½ hours.

Frequent rail service connects Sydney to Katoomba and Blackheath from Central Station; contact **Sydney Trains** (www.sydneytrains.info; ✆ **131 500**) for details. The trip takes around 2 hours. Trains leave almost hourly. An adult same-day round-trip ticket costs around A$15 (A$2.50 on Sun). A child's ticket is about A$7.50.

VISITOR INFORMATION You can pick up maps, walking guides, and other information and book accommodations at **Blue Mountains Tourism,** Echo Point Road, Katoomba (www.visitbluemountains.com.au; ✆ **1300/653 408** in Australia). The information center is an attraction itself, with glass windows overlooking a gum forest, and cockatoos and lorikeets feeding on seed dispensers. It's open 9am to 5pm daily (closed Christmas Day).

The **Blue Mountains Heritage Centre,** end of Govetts Leap Road, Blackheath (www.nationalparks.nsw.gov.au; ✆ **02/4787 8877**), is run by the National Parks and Wildlife Service and offers detailed information about the Blue Mountains National Park. It's open daily from 9am to 4:30pm (closed Christmas Day).

Another good website is **www.bluemts.com.au**.

GETTING AROUND The best way to get around the Blue Mountains without a car is the **Blue Mountains Explorer** bus (www.explorerbus.com.au; ✆ **1300/300 915** in Australia or 02/4782 1866). The double-decker "hop-on, hop-off" bus leaves from outside the Katoomba train station about every 30 minutes between 9:45am and 4:45pm and stops at 29 attractions, resorts, galleries, and tearooms in and around Katoomba and Leura. Tickets cost A$44 for adults, A$22 for children, and A$110 for a family; other passes include rides on the Scenic Railway and the Skyway (see "Exploring the Blue

Mountains," below), and entry to the Waradah Aboriginal Centre.

A similar option is **Trolley Tours** (www.trolleytours.com.au; ✆ **1800/801 577** in Australia or 02/4748 7999), a kind of tram on wheels with commentary. A pass costs A$30 adults for 4 hours or A$69 for an all-day pass and includes stops at 29 various attractions around Katoomba and Leura. The trolley leaves from outside the Carrington Hotel on Katoomba Street once an hour from 9:45am until 4:45pm.

> **Timing Is Everything: When to Visit**
>
> If you can, try to visit the Blue Mountains on **weekdays,** when most Sydneysiders are at work and prices are lower. Note that the colder winter months (June–Aug) are the busiest season.

Tours

Many private bus operators offer day trips from Sydney, but it's important to shop around. Some offer a guided coach tour, during which you just stretch your legs occasionally, while others let you get your circulation going with a couple of longish bushwalks. Remember, this will be a long day, leaving at 7am or 8am and returning to the city about 6pm.

Sydney Tours-R-Us (www.sydneytoursrus.com; ✆ **02/9498 4084**) runs minicoaches to the Blue Mountains, stopping off at Sydney Olympic Park on the way. Then you see all the major sights in the mountains and come home via ferry from Parramatta to Circular Quay. The trip costs A$125 for adults and A$95 for kids ages 4 to 12 (lunch is A$15 extra). The tour includes a stop at Featherdale Wildlife Park (p. 91).

Blue Mountains Walkabout (www.bluemountainswalkabout.com; ✆ **0408/443 822** mobile) is owned and operated by Evan Yanna Muru, an Aboriginal. This guided walk follows a traditional walkabout song line for about 3.5km (2 miles), exploring part of the Blue Mountains wilderness for a full day (about 2 hr. walking and 4 hr. of relaxation and activities). You'll see ancient art, ceremonial sites, and artifacts, and hear Dreamtime stories. Also included is ochre-bark and body painting, bush-tucker tastings, wildlife viewing, sandstone cave exploring, and bathing in a crystal-clear billabong (pool) below a waterfall. You should be reasonably fit. Bring wet-weather gear, good boots or walking shoes, lots of water, and lunch. The trek costs A$95 per person (no kids 6 and under). The walk begins in the Blue Mountains on Faulconbridge Railway Station platform at 10:50am. Take the train from Central Station in Sydney (see "Getting There," above). You can get the 4:30pm train back to the city.

Exploring the Blue Mountains

Almost every other activity in the Blue Mountains costs money, but bushwalking (hiking) is the exception. There are some 50 walking trails, ranging from routes you can cover in 15 minutes to the 3-day **Six Foot Track.** The staff at the national park and tourist offices will be happy to point you in the right direction.

The famous Three Sisters rock formation in Blue Mountains National Park.

The most visited and photographed attractions in the Blue Mountains is the rock formation known as the **Three Sisters.** For the best vantage point, head to **Echo Point Road,** across from the Blue Mountains Tourism office. Or try Evans Lookout, Govetts Leap, and Hargreaves Lookout, all at Blackheath.

Four attractions in one are offered at **Scenic World** (www.scenicworld.com.au; ✆ **1300/759 929** in Australia or 02/4780 0200). The **Scenic Railway,** the world's steepest, consists of a carriage on rails that is lowered 415m (1,361 ft.) into the Jamison Valley at a maximum incline of 52 degrees. It's *very* steep and quite a thrill. The trip takes only a few minutes; at the bottom is the 2.4km (1½-mile) **Scenic Walkway,** a boardwalk through forests of ancient tree ferns. Another way to get down is on the **Scenic Cableway,** not to be confused with the **Scenic Skyway,** a different form of cable car that travels 270m (885 ft.) above—and across—the Jamison Valley, between two cliffs. A ticket that includes all four attractions costs A$39 adults, A$21 children 4 to 13, and A$99 families of up to seven (you can't buy separate tickets for any of the

The Legend of the Three Sisters

The Aboriginal Dreamtime legend has it that three sisters (Meehni, Wimlah, and Gunnedoo) lived in the Jamison Valley as members of the Katoomba tribe. These beautiful young women had fallen in love with three brothers from the Nepean tribe, yet tribal law forbade them to marry. The brothers were not happy with this law and so decided to capture the three sisters, which caused a major tribal battle. As the lives of the three sisters were in danger, a witch doctor from the Katoomba tribe took it upon himself to turn the three sisters into stone to protect them from any harm. He had intended to reverse the spell later, but was killed in the battle and the sisters were doomed to remain in their magnificent rock formation forever.

> **Seeing the Blue Mountains from the Back of a Harley**
>
> A thrilling way to see the Blue Mountains is on the back of a chauffeur-driven Harley-Davidson motorcycle. **Wild Ride Australia** (p. 94) can take you on an exhilarating 1-hour tour around Katoomba.

attractions). Scenic World is open 9am to 5pm daily. You'll find it on Violet Street (corner of Cliff Dr.), Katoomba.

If you are driving back to Sydney, take the Bells Line of Road through Bilpin and stop off at the wonderful **Blue Mountains Botanic Garden** (www.bluemountainsbotanicgarden.com.au; ✆ **02/4567 3000**) at Mount Tomah. (You can't miss the large sign on your right about 10 min. before you get to Bilpin.) It is an adjunct of the Royal Botanic Garden in Sydney and well worth a stop.

Where to Eat

Katoomba Street has many ethnic dining choices, whether you're hungry for Greek, Chinese, or Thai. Restaurants in the Blue Mountains are generally more expensive than equivalent places in Sydney. In addition to the ones below, try the **Elephant Bean,** at 159 Katoomba Rd. (✆ **02/4782 4620**), for hearty soups, burgers, muffins, and good coffee. It's open 7am to 4pm Monday to Saturday, 7am to 3pm Sunday (and sometimes in the evenings).

Conservation Hut Cafe ★ CAFE This pleasant cafe is in the national park on top of a cliff overlooking the Jamison Valley. It's a good place for a bit of lunch on the balcony after the Valley of the Waters walk, which leaves from outside. In addition to lighter meals like soup or a steak sandwich, dishes may include a roast lamb rump or seared tuna with warm potato salad. It has vegetarian and great breakfast/brunch options, too. There's a nice log fire inside in winter. Children are welcome.

Fletcher St., Wentworth Falls. www.conservationhut.com.au. ✆ **02/4757 3827.** Main courses A$16–A$35. Daily 9am–4pm (closed Christmas Day).

Paragon Café ★★ CAFE The Paragon has been a Blue Mountains institution since it opened for business in 1916, and it claims to be Australia's oldest cafe. It's worth stopping here—even if it's just for morning or afternoon tea—to see the wonderful, richly detailed Art Deco interior. But the food is delicious, too—try the homemade soups or light lunches—and you may also come away with Paragon's handmade chocolates! Special dinner and show packages (think Elvis or Piaf style) run regularly, as do film nights.

65 Katoomba St., Katoomba. www.facebook.com/TheParagonCafe. ✆ **02/4782 2928.** Main courses A$10–A$24. Mon–Fri 9am–5pm; Sat 10am–6pm; Sun 10am–3pm.

MELBOURNE

It's rare to find anyone who lives in Melbourne who doesn't adore it. I've lived there, and I love it too, and I hope this chapter illustrates the many reasons why. Victoria's capital, Melbourne (pronounced *Mel*-bun), is a cultural melting pot. For a start, more people of Greek descent live here than in any other city except Athens, Greece. Multitudes of Chinese, Italian, Vietnamese, and Lebanese immigrants have all left their mark. Almost a third of Melburnians were born overseas or have parents who were born overseas. With such a diverse population—and with trams rattling through the streets and stately European-style architecture surrounding you—it is sometimes easy to think you are somewhere else.

Melbourne's roots can be traced back to the 1850s, when gold was discovered in the surrounding hills. British settlers took up residence and prided themselves on coming freely to their city, rather than having been forced here in convict chains. The city grew wealthy and remained a conservative bastion until World War II, when another wave of immigration, mainly from southern Europe, made it a more relaxed place.

With elegant tree-lined boulevards and a raging cafe culture, Victoria's capital maintains a distinctly European feel. Expect wonderful architecture both old and new and green spaces like the Royal Botanic Gardens. Wander down atmospheric laneways, often adorned with street art. This cosmopolitan city is also Australia's culture capital, with vibrant dining, shopping, and nightlife.

In fact, Melbourne, which has a population of more than 4.5 million, is at the head of the pack when it comes to shopping, restaurants, fashion, music, nightlife, and cafe culture. It frequently beats other state capitals in bids for major concerts, plays, exhibitions, and sporting events. Oh, and everyone wears black.

ESSENTIALS

Arriving

BY PLANE

Qantas (www.qantas.com.au; ✆ **131 313** in Australia) and **Virgin Australia** (www.virginaustralia.com.au; ✆ **136 789** in Australia) both fly to Melbourne from all state capitals and some regional centers. Qantas's discount arm, **Jetstar** (www.jetstar.com.au;

© **131 538** in Australia) flies to and from Sydney, Brisbane, Cairns, Townsville, Whitsunday Coast (Proserpine), the Sunshine Coast and Gold Coast, Hobart, and various other cities around the country. Jetstar also flies between Avalon Airport, about a 50-minute drive outside Melbourne's city center, and Sydney, Uluru, Hobart, and the Gold Coast. Low-cost carrier **Scoot** (www.flyscoot.com; © **02/9009 0860** in Australia) has its hub in Melbourne, and from there flies to Sydney, Hobart, Cairns, Townsville, Brisbane, and the Gold Coast in Queensland, as well as several other cities.

Melbourne Airport's international and domestic terminals (www.melbourneairport.com.au) are at Tullamarine, 22km (14 miles) northwest of the city center (often referred to as Tullamarine Airport). There are four passenger terminals. The international terminal (T2) and Qantas (T1) and Virgin Australia (T3) terminals are all under one roof. A separate domestic terminal (T4) is home to Scoot, Jetstar, and Regional Express (REX). The travelers' information service desk, on the ground floor of the international arrivals hall (T2), is open from 7am until midnight daily. The international terminal has snack bars, a restaurant, currency-exchange facilities, and duty-free shops. ATMs are available at both terminals. Showers are on the first floor of the international area. Baggage carts are free in the international baggage claim hall but cost A$4 in the parking lot, departure lounge, or domestic terminal. Baggage storage is available in the international terminal and costs A$13 to A$26 per day, depending on the size of your bag. The storage desk is open from 5am to 12:30am daily, and you need photo ID. There are three airport hotels: **Parkroyal Melbourne Airport** (© **03/8347 2000**), **Holiday Inn Melbourne Airport** (© **03/9933 5111**), and **Ibis Budget Melbourne Airport** (© **03/8336 1811**); all are within a 5 minutes' walk of the terminals. The Parkroyal offers a A$20 3-hour package that gives access to its pool, gym, and sauna, and free Wi-Fi in the bar. Room rates are also available for 3 to 8 hours (7am–7pm only) for transiting passengers, starting at A$85. A little farther away is the **Quest Melbourne Airport** (www.questmelbourneairport.com.au; © **03/8340 8400**), an apartment hotel in the Melbourne Airport Business Park, about 4.8km (3 miles) from the terminal precinct.

Avis (© **136 333** in Australia, or 03/9338 1800), **Budget** (© **132 727** in Australia or 03/9241 6366), **Europcar** (© **1300/131 390** in Australia or 03/9241 6800), **Hertz** (© **133 039** in Australia or 03/9338 4044), **Thrifty** (© **1300/367 227** in Australia or 03/9241 6100) and **Redspot** (© **1300/668 810** in Australia) all have airport rental desks. The Tullamarine freeway to and from the airport joins with the CityLink, an electronic toll-way system. Drivers need a CityLink pass. Check with your car-rental company.

The distinctive red **Skybus** (www.skybus.com.au; © **03/9600 1711**) runs between the airport and Melbourne's Southern Cross station in Spencer Street every 10 minutes, 24 hours a day, every day. Buy tickets from Skybus desks outside the baggage claim areas or at the information desk in the international terminal. A free Skybus hotel shuttle will pick you up at your hotel to connect with the larger airport-bound bus at Southern Cross railway station in the city center, but you must book this. It operates from 6am to 10:30pm weekdays and 7am to 7pm Saturday and Sunday (except Christmas Day). Skybus also operates from the airport to the suburb of St Kilda, 6am to 7pm daily, every 30 minutes weekdays and every hour Saturday and Sunday. One-way tickets cost A$19 for adults to either the city or St Kilda, and A$38 round-trip. Tickets for children aged 4 to 16 cost A$9 one-way or A$18 round-trip, but if you buy online, up to four children travel free on your adult ticket. The trip takes about 30 minutes from the airport to Southern Cross station and about an hour to St Kilda, but allow extra time (at least 15 minutes) for your return journey.

Skybus also operates the **Avalon City Express** transfer service to Avalon Airport for Jetstar flights. One-way fares from Avalon Airport are A$22 for adults and A$10 for children 4 to 14 to Southern Cross station, more to other central business district (CBD) locations and other suburbs.

A **taxi** to the city center takes about 30 minutes and costs around A$55.

BY TRAIN

Interstate trains arrive at **Southern Cross Railway Station,** Spencer and Little Collins streets (5 blocks from Swanston St., in the city center). You may hear locals often refer to it as Spencer Street Station. Taxis and buses are available here and connect with the city.

The **Sydney–Melbourne** ***XPT*** travels between Australia's two largest cities daily; trip time is 11 hours. For more information, contact **NSW Trainlink** (www.nswtrainlink.info; ✆ **132 232** in Australia or 02/4907 7501). **V/Line** (www.vline.com.au; ✆ **1800/800 007** in Australia or 03/8363 4427) services also connect Melbourne with country Victoria destinations and other capital cities.

BY BUS

Several bus companies connect Melbourne with other capitals and regional areas of Victoria. Among the biggest are **Greyhound Australia** (www.greyhound.com.au; ✆ **1300/473 946** in Australia or 03/8667 8701). Coaches serve Melbourne's **Transit Centre,** 58 Franklin St., 2 blocks north of the Southern Cross Railway station on Spencer Street. Trams and taxis serve the station; **V/Line buses** (www.vline.com.au; ✆ **1800/800 007** in Australia), which travel all over Victoria, depart from the Spencer Street Coach Terminal.

BY CAR

You can drive from Sydney to Melbourne along the Hume Highway (a straight trip of about 9½ hr.). Another route is along the coastal Princes Highway, for which you will need a minimum of 2 days, with stops. For information on all aspects of road travel in Victoria, contact the **Royal Automotive Club of Victoria** (www.racv.com.au; ✆ **131 329** in Australia or 03/8792 4006).

Visitor Information

The first stop on any visitor's itinerary should be the **Melbourne Visitor Centre,** Federation Square, Swanston and Flinders streets (www.whatson.melbourne.vic.gov.au; ✆ **03/9658 9658**). The center serves as a one-stop shop for tourism information, accommodations and tour bookings, public transport

Half-Price Tickets

Buy tickets for entertainment events, including opera, dance, and drama, on the day of the performance from **Half-Tix** in the Melbourne Town Hall administration building on Swanston Street (right next to the Town Hall). The booth is open Monday from 10am to 2pm, Tuesday through Thursday 11am to 6pm, Friday 11am to 6:30pm, and Saturday 10am to 4pm (also selling for Sun shows). Tickets must be purchased in person and in cash. Available shows are displayed on the booth door and on the website, www.halftixmelbourne.com.

information, and ticket sales. Also here are an ATM, Internet terminals, and interactive multimedia providing information on Melbourne and Victoria. The center is open daily from 9am to 6pm (10am to 5pm Good Friday; closed Christmas Day). The **Melbourne Greeter Service** also operates from the Melbourne Visitor Centre. This service connects visitors to enthusiastic local volunteers who offer free 2- to 4-hour orientation tours of the city at 9:30am daily. Book at least 24 hours in advance (✆ **03/9658 9658** Mon–Fri, 03/9658 9942 Sat–Sun, or online). The Melbourne Visitor Centre also operates a staffed information booth in Bourke Street Mall, between Swanston and Elizabeth streets, open daily 9am to 5pm (closed Good Friday and Christmas Day). In the central city area (mainly along Swanston St.), also look for **Melbourne's City Ambassadors**—people, usually volunteers, who give tourist information and directions. They'll be wearing bright red shirts.

Good websites about the city include the official tourism site, **www.visitmelbourne.com**, and the locally run **www.onlymelbourne.com.au**. Also worth a look is the official City of Melbourne site, **www.melbourne.vic.gov.au**.

St Kilda Pier.

City Layout

Melbourne is on the Yarra River and stretches inland from Port Philip Bay, which lies to its south. On a map, you'll see a distinct central oblong area surrounded by Flinders Street to the south, Latrobe Street to the north, Spring Street to the east, and Spencer Street to the west. Cutting north to south through its center are the two main shopping thoroughfares, Swanston Street and Elizabeth Street. Cross streets between these major thoroughfares include Bourke Street Mall, a pedestrian-only shopping promenade. If you continue south along Swanston Street and over the river, it turns into St Kilda Road, which runs to the coast. Melbourne's various urban "villages," including South Yarra, Richmond, Carlton, and Fitzroy, surround the city center. The seaside suburb of St Kilda is known for its diverse restaurants.

Neighborhoods in Brief

At more than 7,695 sq. km (2,971 sq. miles), Melbourne is one of the biggest cities in the world by area, with a population of about 3.5 million. Below are the neighborhoods of most interest to visitors.

City Center Made up of a grid of streets north of the Yarra River, the city center is bordered by Flinders, Latrobe, Spring, and Spencer streets. There's good shopping and a charming cafe scene, and in recent years an active nightlife has sprung up with the opening of a swath of funky bars and restaurants playing live and recorded music to suit all ages. The gateway to the city is the Flinders Street Station, with its dome and clock tower, flanked by the Federation Square precinct.

Chinatown This colorful section centers on Little Bourke Street, between Swanston and Exhibition streets. The area marks Australia's oldest permanent Chinese settlement, dating from the 1850s, when a few boardinghouses catered to Chinese prospectors lured by gold rushes. Plenty of cheap restaurants crowd its alleyways. Tram: Any to the city.

Carlton North of the center, Carlton is a rambling suburb famous for Italian restaurants along Lygon Street with outdoor seating—though the quality of the food varies. It's the home of Melbourne University, so there's a healthy student scene. From Bourke Street Mall, it's a 15-minute walk to the restaurants. Tram: 1 or 22 from Swanston Street.

Fitzroy A ruggedly bohemian place 2km (1¼ miles) north of the city center, Fitzroy is raw and funky, filled with students and artists and popular for people-watching and its amazing street art. Fitzroy revolves around Brunswick Street, with its cheap restaurants, busy cafes, late-night bookshops, art galleries, and pubs. Around the corner, on Johnston Street, is a growing Spanish quarter with tapas bars, flamenco restaurants, and Spanish clubs. Tram: 11 from Collins Street.

Richmond One of Melbourne's earliest settlements is a multicultural quarter noted for its historic streets and back lanes. Victoria Street is reminiscent of Ho Chi Minh City, with Vietnamese sights, sounds, aromas, and restaurants everywhere. Bridge Road is a discount-fashion precinct. Tram: 48 or 75 from Flinders Street to Bridge Road; 70 from Batman Avenue at Princes Bridge to Swan Street; 109 from Bourke Street to Victoria Street.

Southgate & Southbank This flashy entertainment district on the banks of the Yarra River opposite Flinders Street station (linked by pedestrian bridges) is home to the Crown Casino, Australia's largest gaming venue. Southbank has a myriad of restaurants, bars, cafes, nightclubs, cinemas, and designer shops. On the city side of the river is the Melbourne Aquarium. All are a 10-minute stroll from Flinders Street Station. Tram: 8 from Swanston Street.

Docklands Near the city center, at the rear of the Spencer Street station, this industrial area has become the biggest development in Melbourne. NewQuay on the waterfront has a diverse range of restaurants, shops, and cinemas. This is also where you'll find Melbourne's celebration of the dominance of Australian Rules football, the 52,000-seat Etihad Stadium. Docklands is accessible by the free City Circle Tram.

St Kilda Hip and bohemian in a shabby-chic sort of way, this bayside suburb (6km/ 3¾ miles south of the city center) has Melbourne's highest concentration of restaurants, ranging from glitzy to cheap, as well as some superb cake shops and delis. Historically it was Melbourne's red-light district. The Esplanade hugs a beach with a vintage pier and a lively arts-and-crafts market on Sundays. Acland Street houses many restaurants. Check out Luna Park, one of the world's oldest fun parks, built in 1912, and ride the wooden roller coaster. Tram: 10 or 12 from Collins Street; 15 or 16 from Swanston Street; 96 from Bourke Street.

South Yarra/Prahran This posh part of town abounds with boutiques, cinemas, nightclubs, and galleries. Chapel Street is known for upscale eateries and designer fashions, while Commercial Road is popular with the gay and lesbian community. Off Chapel Street in Prahran is Greville Street, a bohemian enclave of boutiques and music outlets. Every Sunday from noon to 5pm, the Greville Street Market offers crafts, old clothes, and jewelry. Tram: 8 or 72 from Swanston Street.

South Melbourne One of the city's oldest working-class districts, South Melbourne is known for its historic buildings, old-fashioned pubs and hotels, and markets. Tram: 12 from Collins Street; 1 from Swanston Street.

The River District The muddy-looking Yarra River runs southeast past the Royal Botanic Gardens and near other attractions such as the Arts Centre, the National Gallery of Victoria, the Sidney Myer Music Bowl, the Melbourne Cricket Ground, and Birrarung Marr parkland. It is accessible by the free City Circle Tram.

Williamstown A lack of extensive development has left this waterfront suburb with a rich architectural heritage. It centers on Ferguson Street and Nelson Place—both reminiscent of old England. On the Strand overlooking the sea is a line of bistros and restaurants and a World War II warship museum. Ferry: From Southgate, the World Trade Center, or St Kilda Pier.

Getting Around

BY PUBLIC TRANSPORTATION

Trams are the major form of transport in the city; you will probably only use a train or bus if you are going into the suburbs. Melbourne's transport system uses an electronic ticketing system called **myki,** a reusable smart card to pay for your travel. The card costs A$6, then you put money on it for travel. You "touch on" and "touch off" at an electronic machine on board the tram or bus, or as you enter the train station. When your myki balance gets low, just top up your card. A 2-hour trip in Zones 1 and 2, which will allow you to travel on all trams and trains within the city and close surrounding suburbs mentioned in this chapter from 5:30am to midnight (when transportation stops), costs A$4.10; the daily fare of A$8.20 allows unlimited travel. On weekends and public holidays, pay the off-peak rate of A$6 per day. A **7-day myki pass** will cost A$41 to travel in Zones 1 and 2. You can get cards at Flinders Street or Southern Cross stations, at the MetShop or at most 7-Eleven convenience stores, and top them up through the **Public Transport Victoria** website (www.ptv.vic.gov.au) or at the call center (✆ **1800/800 007**); or top up as little as A$1 at myki machines in train stations and at selected tram platforms and bus interchanges.

Money-Saving Transit Passes

Visitors to Victoria can buy a **myki Explorer** card, which gives one day's unlimited travel as well as discounts on entry to 16 major attractions around the city and region. Buy this at the Melbourne Visitor Centre (p. 109) or Skybus terminal at Melbourne Airport or Southern Cross station. It costs A$15 adults or A$7.50 children, and you can top it up for another day.

You can pick up a free route map from the Melbourne Visitor Centre, Federation Square, or from the **PTV Hub** at Southern Cross station (www.ptv.vic.gov.au; ✆ **1800/800 007** in Australia), open Monday through Friday from 7am to 7pm, and weekends and public holidays (except Christmas Day) 9am to 6pm. There's another hub at 750 Collins St., Docklands, open from 8am to 6pm weekdays only (closed Sat–Sun and public holidays).

BY TRAM

Melbourne has the oldest tram network in the world. Trams are an essential part of the city, a major cultural icon, and a great non-smoggy way of getting around. Several hundred trams run over 325km (202 miles) of track.

Trams stop at numbered tram-stop signs, sometimes in the middle of the road (so beware of oncoming traffic!). To get off the tram, press the button near the handrails or pull the cord above your head.

A **free tram zone** operates in the inner city center, bounded by Spring, Flinders, and La Trobe streets, and running along Victoria, William, and Elizabeth streets (around the Victoria Market) and to Docklands. Drivers announce when you are leaving the free zone. If you are staying in the free zone, you don't need to "touch on" with your myki, but if you are beginning or ending your trip outside the free zone, you must do so.

There is also a free **City Circle Tram** (tram no. 35) that travels a circular route between all the major central attractions and past shopping malls and arcades. The trams run in both directions every 12 minutes between 10am and 6pm (and until 9pm Thurs–Sat), except on Good Friday and Christmas Day. The trams run along all the major corridors including Flinders and Spencer streets.

BY BUS

The **Melbourne Visitor Shuttle** operates buses that pick up and drop off at 13 stops around the city, including Federation Square, the Melbourne Museum, Queen Victoria Market, Immigration Museum, Southbank Arts Precinct, the Shrine of Remembrance and Botanic Gardens, Chinatown, and many other attractions. You can hop on and off during the day. The entire loop takes about 90 minutes nonstop, and there's a commentary. The bus runs every 30 minutes from 9:30am until 4:30pm daily (except Christmas Day, and with limited service on some public holidays and major event days). The cost is A$10 per person for 2 days, free for children 9 and under. Buy from ticket machines at each stop or from the Melbourne Visitor Centre at Federation Square.

BY TAXI

Cabs are plentiful in the city, but it may be difficult to hail one in the city center late on Friday and Saturday night. From 10pm to 5am, anywhere in

Victoria, you must prepay your fare. The driver estimates the fare at the start of the journey, gives you a receipt, and then adjusts it according to the meter reading (plus any fees such as road tolls) at the end of your trip. Taxi companies include **Silver Top** (✆ **131 008** in Australia) and **13CABS** (Yellow) (✆ **132 227** in Australia). **Uber** also operates in Melbourne.

BY CAR

Driving in Melbourne can be challenging. Roads can be confusing, there are trams everywhere, and there is a rule about turning right from the left lane at major intersections in the downtown center and in South Melbourne (which leaves the left lane free for trams and through traffic). Here, you must wait for the lights to turn amber before turning. Also, you must always stop behind a tram if it stops, because passengers usually step directly into the road. Add to this the general lack of parking and expensive hotel valet parking, and you'll know why it's better to avoid driving and get on a tram instead. For road rules, pick up a copy of the Victorian Road Traffic handbook from bookshops or from a **Vic Roads** office (✆ **131 171** in Australia for the nearest office).

Major car-rental companies, all also with offices at Tullamarine Airport, include **Avis,** Shop 2, 8 Franklin St. (✆ **03/9204 3933**); **Budget,** Shop 3, 8 Franklin St. (✆ **03/9203 4844**); **Europcar,** 89 Franklin St. (✆ **03/8633 0000**); **Hertz,** 97 Franklin St. (✆ **133 039** in Australia or 03/9663 6244); and **Thrifty,** 390 Elizabeth St. (✆ **03/8661 6000**).

[Fast FACTS] MELBOURNE

ATMs/Banks Banks are open Monday through Thursday from 9:30am to 4pm, and Friday from 9:30am to 5pm.

Business Hours In general, stores are open Monday through Wednesday and Saturday from 9am to 5:30pm, Thursday from 9am to 6pm, Friday from 9am to 9pm, and Sunday from 10am to 5pm.

Dentists The **Royal Dental Hospital of Melbourne** (✆ **1800/833 039** in Australia or 03/9341 1000), at 720 Swanston St., Carlton, offers emergency services 8am to 8:30pm Monday to Friday and 8:30am to 8pm weekends and public holidays.

Doctors & Hospitals The emergency department at the **Royal Melbourne Hospital,** 300 Grattan St., Parkville (✆ **03/9342 7000**), is open 24 hours. The **Traveller's Medical & Vaccination Centre,** Second Floor, 393 Little Bourke St. (www.traveldoctor.com.au; ✆ **03/9935 8100**), offers full vaccination and travel medical services. It is open 9am to 5pm Monday through Friday (until 8pm on Thurs), and 9am to 1pm on Saturday.

Embassies & Consulates The following English-speaking countries have consulates in Melbourne: **United States,** Level 6, 553 St Kilda Rd. (✆ **03/9526 5900**); and **United Kingdom,** Level 17, 90 Collins St. (✆ **03/9652 1600**).

Emergencies In an emergency, call ✆ **000** for police, ambulance, or the fire department.

Internet Access The **State Library of Victoria,** 328 Swanston St. (www.slv.vic.gov.au; ✆ **03/8864 7000**), has free wireless Internet in all areas of the library and PowerPoint powering stations in all reading rooms. It is open Monday to Thursday 10am to 9pm and Friday to Sunday 10am to 6pm. Free public Wi-Fi is available in the Melbourne CBD at train stations and the Bourke Street Mall, Queen Victoria Market, and South Wharf Promenade at the Melbourne Convention and Exhibition Centre.

Mail & Postage The **General Post Office (GPO)** at 250 Elizabeth St. (✆ **131 318** in Australia) is open Monday through Friday 8:30am to 5:30pm, Saturday 9am to 5pm.

Newspapers & Magazines Melbourne's daily newspapers are ***The Age*** and the ***Herald-Sun.*** Both have Sunday versions as well.

Pharmacies (Chemist Shops) The **Mulqueeny Pharmacy,** 99 Swanston St. (✆ **03/9654 8569**), is open Monday through Friday from 8am to 8pm, Saturday from 9am to 6pm, and Sunday 11am to 6pm. The **Mulqueeny Midnight Pharmacy,** 416 High St., Windsor (✆ **03/9510 3977**), is open every day of the year (9am–midnight).

Safety St Kilda might be coming up in the world, but walking there alone at night still isn't wise. Parks and gardens can also be risky at night, as can the area around the King Street nightclubs in the city center.

WHERE TO STAY

Getting a room is easy enough on weekends, when business travelers are back home. You need to book well in advance, however, during the city's hallmark events (say, the weekend before the Melbourne Cup, and during the Grand Prix and the Australian Open). Hostels in the St Kilda area tend to fill up quickly in December and January.

You'll feel right in the heart of the action if you stay in the city center, which seems to buzz all day (and night). Otherwise, the inner-city suburbs are all exciting satellites, with good street life, restaurants, and pubs—and just a quick tram ride from the city center. Transportation from the airport to the suburbs is a little more expensive and complicated than to the city center, however.

The **Best of Victoria** booking service, Federation Square (www.bestof.com.au; ✆ **03/9928 0000**), open daily 9am to 6pm (except Christmas Day), can help you book accommodations after you arrive in the city. They also have a desk in the Arrivals Hall at Melbourne International Airport.

In the City Center

EXPENSIVE

Hotel Lindrum ★★ This gorgeous hotel has always felt quite "clubby" to me; perhaps the billiard room has something to do with it. In some ways the vibe hasn't changed, but a total renovation of the guest rooms in 2015 has given an already smart hotel a new, stylish, and contemporary look. Studios have queen-size beds or two singles, plenty of hardwood, soft lighting, and neutral tones with red accents. Superior rooms have king-size beds and lovely polished-wood floorboards, and deluxe rooms have wonderful views across to the Botanic Gardens through large bay windows. The hotel also boasts a worthy restaurant and a bar with an open fire.

26 Flinders St. www.hotellindrum.com.au. ✆ **03/9668 1111.** 59 units. A$220–A$300 double; A$340 suite. Public parking next door (discounted for guests). **Amenities:** Restaurant; bar; nearby health club; room service; free Wi-Fi.

The Hotel Windsor ★★ For the moment, at least, it's still business as usual at The Windsor, one of Australia's grandest and most historic hotels. But a controversial A$330-million redevelopment and restoration of the hotel was finally given planning approval in 2016 after a years-long debate and is expected to be completed by 2020. The Windsor opened in 1883, an upper-crust establishment that oozed sophistication and hosted the rich, famous, and glamorous ever since. The hotel holds a special place in Australia's history as the setting for the drafting of the country's Constitution in 1898. The planned redevelopment will add a 26-story tower (and 152 guest rooms) behind the heritage building. But some things won't ever change: The renowned "high tea" will continue to be served each afternoon, as it has been for 130 years. Many guest bedrooms have striking views of Parliament House and the Treasury Gardens. I'd suggest you stay there as soon as you can!

103 Spring St. www.thehotelwindsor.com.au. ✆ **03/9633 6000.** 180 units. A$208–A$298 double; A$348–A$648 suite. Valet parking A$50–A$60 per night. **Amenities:** Restaurant; 2 bars; babysitting; concierge; health club; room service; free Wi-Fi.

Quest Grand Hotel Melbourne ★★ This majestic, Heritage-listed six-story building—originally home to the Victorian railway administration—is striking for its remarkable scale and imposing Italianate facade. Building started in 1887, and it became a hotel in 1997. Studios have plush carpets and full kitchens with dishwashers; one-bedroom loft suites have European-style espresso machines and a second TV in the bedroom, and some have great

MELBOURNE'S art hotels

Melbourne's Deague family has combined a passion for the arts and a desire to join the global boutique hotel trend by dedicating a series of hotels to well-known Australian artists. The flagship of the **Art Series Hotel Group** (www.artseries hotels.com.au) is **The Olsen ★★★,** at Chapel Street and Toorak Road, South Yarra (✆ **03/9040 1222**). Named for the man regarded as Australia's greatest living painter, John Olsen, it has 229 spacious rooms and claims to have the world's largest glass-bottom swimming pool, suspended over the street. Rates start from A$249 double per night for a studio suite. It's a little bit out of the city center, but there's a tram almost on the doorstep, and I vote it one of my favorite hotels. **The Cullen,** a 115-room boutique hotel at 164 Commercial Rd., Prahran (✆ **03/9098 1555**), is named for the controversial artist Adam Cullen and has a rooftop cocktail bar and two restaurants. **The Blackman,** named for Sydney artist John Blackman and housed within the Heritage-listed Airlie House (backed by a modern high-rise annex), is at 452 St Kilda Rd. (✆ **03/9039 1444**) and has 209 rooms. North of Melbourne's city center, **The Larwill Studio,** 48 Flemington Rd., Parkville (✆ **03/9032 9111**), is dedicated to artist David Larwill.

Each hotel features a major artwork commissioned especially for the hotel foyer by the naming artist, including one from Adam Cullen's *Ned Kelly* series and Olsen's 6m (19-ft.) mural *The Yellow Sun and Yarra*, set in the spectacular glass lobby of The Olsen. Prints and a photographic history of each artist's life adorn walls of rooms and public spaces of the hotels while the architecture, interior design, linens, and stationery also reflect the artist's style. If you like the concept, there are Art Series hotels in other Australian cities: **The Schaller** in Bendigo, **The Johnson** in Brisbane, and **The Watson** and in Adelaide, if your travels take you there. Visit the Art Series website for links to all properties.

Melbourne Hotels

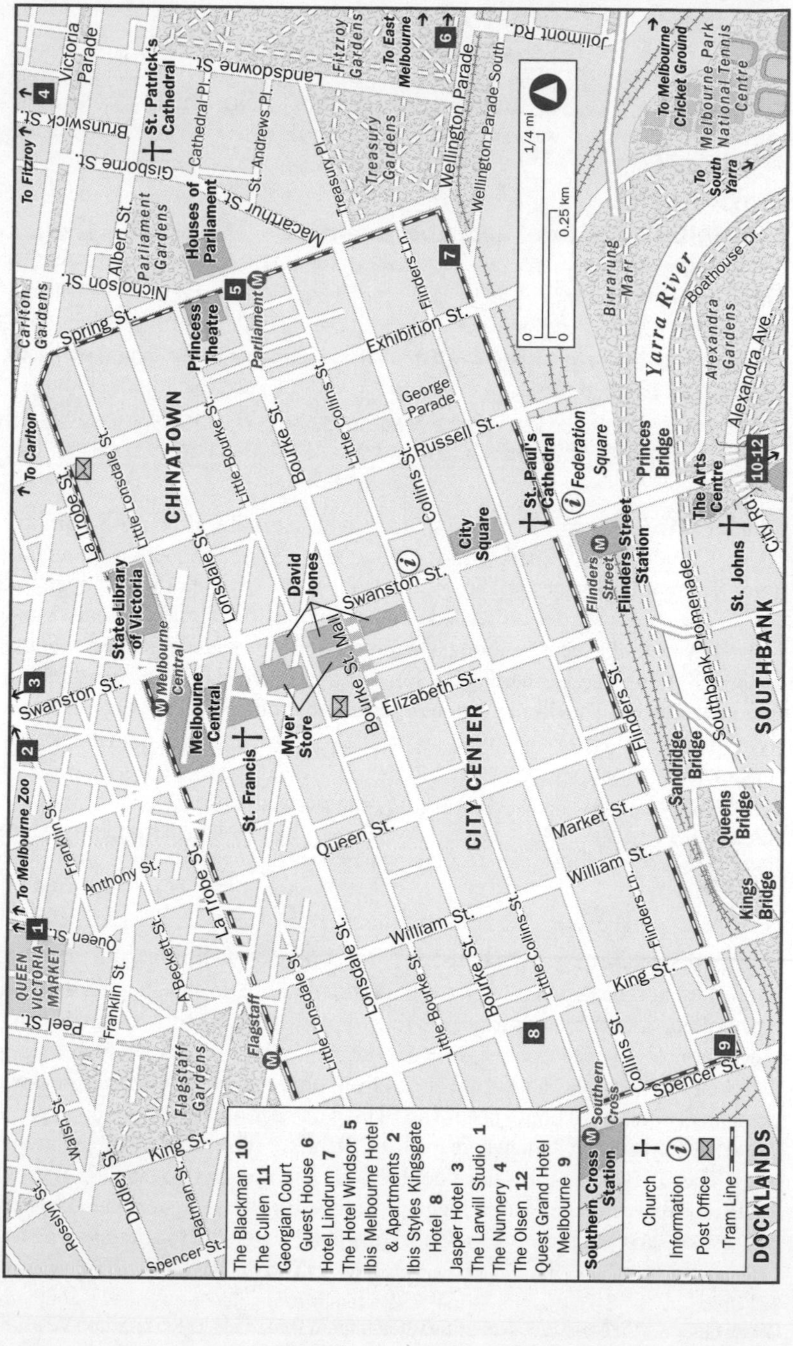

views over the new Docklands area beyond—though rooms are whisper-quiet. All vary in size; some have balconies (mostly on the 6th floor). Many of the suites are split-level, with bedrooms on the second floor.

33 Spencer St. www.grandhotelmelbourne.com.au. ✆ **03/9611 4567.** 94 units. A$539–A$589 studio; A$650 1-bedroom apt. Parking A$45. Tram: 48 or 75 from Flinders St. **Amenities:** Restaurant; bar; babysitting; concierge; golf course nearby; exercise room; Jacuzzi; heated indoor swimming pool (with retractable roof); room service; sauna; Wi-Fi (A$28/24 hr.).

MODERATE

Ibis Melbourne Hotel and Apartments ★ The Ibis Melbourne is a good deal, next door to a tram stop, close to the bus station, *and* a short walk from the central shopping areas and Queen Victoria Market. Rooms in the AAA–rated three-star hotel are spacious, immaculate, and bright, and the whole hotel was refurbished in 2015. All apartments come equipped with kitchenettes and bathtubs.

15–21 Therry St. www.ibis.com. ✆ **03/9666 0000.** 250 units. A$149 double; A$179 1-bedroom apt; A$279 2-bedroom apt. Parking A$25. **Amenities:** Restaurant; bar; Wi-Fi (A$28/24 hr.).

Jasper Hotel ★★ Looking sharp and welcoming after a A$7-million upgrade completed in 2014, this is a good choice for an inner-city boutique hotel. There are 16 suites on the hotel's second level, some of which open out onto a guest courtyard with walled gardens and artificial grass. Levels 2 and 3 also have small executive lounges with free refreshments (and check out the hallways' star-spangled ceilings). Some rooms have balconies overlooking Elizabeth Street. The Jasper Kitchen restaurant sources most of its produce from the Queen Victoria Market, just outside the back door; Oko Oko serves snacks and light meals from 4pm.

489 Elizabeth St. www.jasperhotel.com.au. ✆ **1800/468 359** or 03/8327 2777. 90 units. A$155–A$235 double; A$255–A$305 suite. Parking nearby (around A$35 per day). Tram: 19, 57, 59. Train: Melbourne Central. **Amenities:** 2 restaurants; bar; room service; free Wi-Fi.

INEXPENSIVE

Ibis Styles Kingsgate Hotel ★ A 10-minute walk from the city, this interesting hotel resembles a terrace building from the outside, but inside it's a maze of corridors and rooms. At the time of writing the hotel was undergoing renovation of its guest rooms, due for completion in mid-2018, which means there may be some daytime noise issues from time to time. The least expensive economy rooms have double beds (no twins); these rooms are small but a good value if you just want somewhere to sleep. Standard rooms have double or twin beds. The 21 family rooms have double beds and one or two singles. There's a 24-hour reception desk, free luggage-storage facilities, a guest laundry, and free use of safety deposit boxes. Check the hotel's website for excellent deals.

131 King St. www.kingsgatehotel.com.au. ✆ **1300/734 171** in Australia or 03/9629 4171. 171 units. A$99–A$174 double; A$164–A$244 family room. Parking at nearby Southern Cross Station, A$25 per day. **Amenities:** Restaurant (breakfast only); bar; free Wi-Fi.

In East Melbourne

Georgian Court Guest House ★ The appearance of the comfortable Georgian Court, set on a beautiful tree-lined street, hasn't changed much since it was built in 1910. The sitting and dining rooms have high ceilings and offer old-world atmosphere. The guest rooms are simply furnished, and some are in need of a refurbishment; others have already been refreshed. Some have en suite bathrooms; others have private bathrooms in the hallway. One room comes with a queen-size bed and Jacuzzi. The Georgian Court is a 15-minute stroll through the Fitzroy and Treasury Gardens from the city center and is also close to the fashion shops of Bridge Road.

21 George St., East Melbourne. www.georgiancourt.com.au. © **03/9415 8225.** 31 units. A$95–A$135 double; A$145–A$169 family room. Rates include breakfast. Free parking. Tram: 75 from Flinders St., or 48 from Spencer St. **Amenities:** Free Wi-Fi.

In Fitzroy

The Nunnery ★★ This former convent offers smart budget accommodations—and something a little more upmarket—a short tram ride from the city center, close to the restaurants and nightlife of Brunswick and Lygon streets in nearby Carlton. The informal, friendly 1860s main building has high ceilings, handmade light fittings, polished floorboards, marble fireplaces, and a hand-turned staircase. There's also a clever and rather irreverent play on its past in the decor. It's well suited to couples and families. The Guesthouse next door, built in the early 1900s, is also comfy, stylish, and decorated with tasteful furnishings and artwork. The seven rooms share three bathrooms. The Nunnery, former home of the Daughters of Charity, also houses dorm rooms that have 4, 8, or 12 beds. There are no elevators.

116 Nicholson St., Fitzroy. www.nunnery.com.au. © **1800/032 635** in Australia or 03/9419 8637. 30 units, all with shared bathroom. Guesthouse A$115–A$130 double, A$210–A$225 double family room; A$28–A$30 per person bunk rooms. Rates include breakfast. Free parking (reservation required). Tram: 96. **Amenities:** Kitchen; free Wi-Fi.

In St Kilda

Novotel Melbourne St Kilda ★ Ask for a room with a view at this seaside hotel; the best of them overlook St Kilda beach, the pier, and Port Philip Bay. Standard rooms have a queen or king bed, a small desk, and minibar; some have a Jacuzzi. This well-located property is a 2-minute walk to the beach, Luna Park, and Acland Street shopping—and on Sundays you're right across the street from the St Kilda art and craft markets that line the Esplanade.

16 The Esplanade. www.novotel.com. © **03/9525 5522.** 211 units. A$169–A$269 double, A$419 1-bedroom penthouse, A$269 family room (sleeps 4). Parking A$25. Tram: 16, 96. **Amenities:** Restaurant; bar; outdoor heated pool; fitness center; Wi-Fi (A$10/24hr.).

Tolarno Hotel ★★ Quirky Tolarno is in the middle of St Kilda's cafe and restaurant strip and just a short stroll from the beach. Set in the former private residence and gallery of artist Mirka Mora, the rooms and corridors of this

St Kilda Hotels & Restaurants

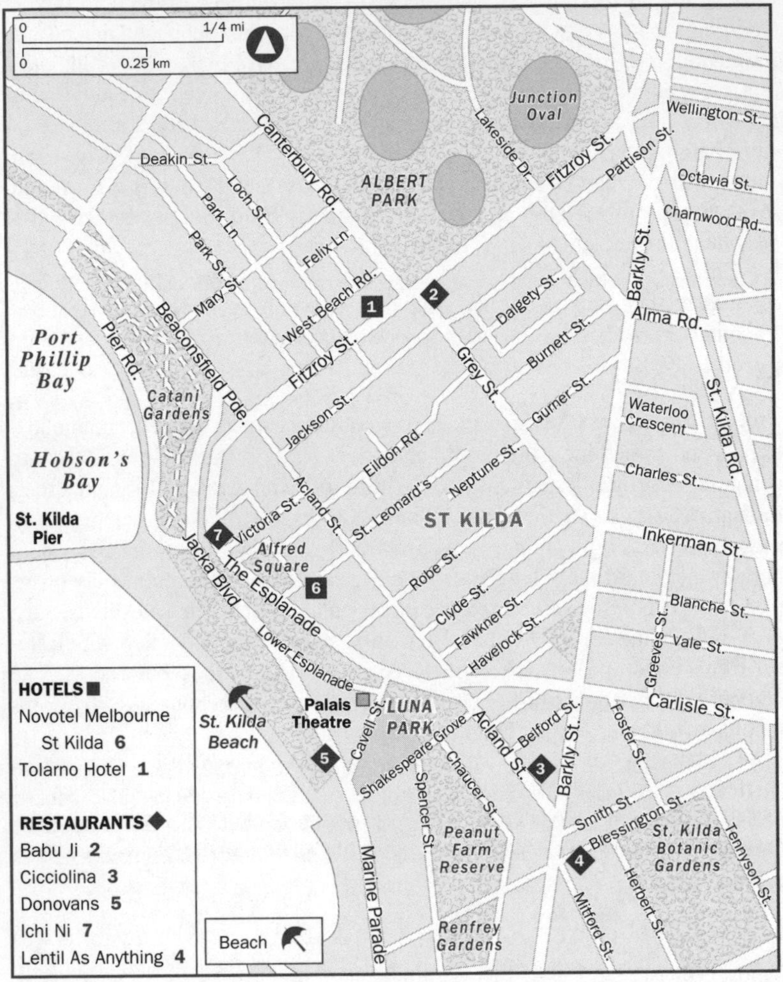

modern, colorful property are adorned with 150 contemporary works by Melbourne artists, many of them by Mora, for whom the hotel's restaurant is named. Rooms vary but the deluxe doubles in the front of the building, with balconies overlooking the main street, are the most popular. These rooms are larger than the standard rooms, but if you are a light sleeper you might prefer something away from the noise of the trams running by. Superior doubles come with microwaves, and two have Japanese baths. Suites have a separate kitchen and lounge, but no balcony. At press time, the hotel restaurant was closed indefinitely; if it has not re-opened by the time you visit, rest assured there are plenty of options right on Fitzroy Street, the heart of St Kilda's restaurant strip.

42 Fitzroy St. www.tolarnohotel.com.au. ✆ **03/9537 0200.** 37 units. A$104–A$154 double; A$215–A$275 suite. Free street parking or A$10 in the building opposite. Tram: 16 from Swanston St., 12 from Collins St., or 96 from Flinders St. **Amenities:** Bar; babysitting; bikes; concierge; room service; free Wi-Fi.

WHERE TO EAT

Melbourne's ethnically diverse population ensures a healthy selection of international cuisines. Chinatown, in the city center, is a fabulous hunting ground for Chinese, Malaysian, Thai, Indonesian, Japanese, and Vietnamese fare, often at bargain prices. Carlton has plenty of Italian restaurants, but some of the outdoor eateries on Lygon Street target unsuspecting tourists with overpriced and disappointing fare; avoid them. Richmond is crammed with Greek and Vietnamese restaurants, and Fitzroy has cheap Asian, Turkish, Mediterranean, and vegetarian food. To see and be seen, head to Chapel Street or Toorak Road in South Yarra, or travel to St Kilda, where you can join the throng of Melburnians dining out along Fitzroy and Acland streets. Most of the cheaper places in Melbourne are strictly BYO (bring your own wine or beer). Smoking is banned in Melbourne cafes and restaurants, so don't even think about lighting up.

In the City Center

EXPENSIVE

Flower Drum ★★★ CANTONESE Praise pours in from all quarters for this upscale restaurant just off Little Bourke Street, Chinatown's main drag. Take a slow elevator up to the restaurant, which has widely spaced tables (perfect for politicians and businesspeople to clinch their deals). Take note of the specials—the chefs are extremely creative and use the best ingredients they find in the markets each day. A smart idea is to put your menu selections into the hands of the waiter. The signature dish is Peking duck, and the seafood dumplings in soup is a great starter. Or, you can order more unusual dishes, such as abalone (at a price: A$1,700 per kilogram) or pearl meat. The atmosphere is clubby and a bit old-fashioned, but the service is impeccable. But be prepared to pay for the privilege.

17 Market Lane. www.flowerdrum.melbourne. ✆ **03/9662 3655.** Main courses A$18–A$48. Mon–Sat noon–3pm and 6–11pm; Sun 6–10:30pm.

Grossi Florentino ★★★ ITALIAN Under the management of the Grossi family, this is probably the best Italian restaurant in Melbourne, with three dining options. The casual bistro, the Grill, is downstairs, right next to the Cellar Bar where a bowl of pasta on the bar menu is less than A$25, but the upstairs, outfitted with chandeliers and murals reflecting the Florentine way of life, is reserved for fine dining. With such innovative dishes as pasta with

Berkshire pork, black pudding, pumpkin, and pine nuts, the food is not traditional Italian, but everything has a distinctive Italian twist to it. Seafood and steak dishes are also on the menu. Save room for dessert: perhaps spiced pear with almond cake and yogurt ice cream, or the cheese plate to share? On weekdays, two-course lunch specials are available in the Grill for A$45 or in the restaurant for A$65.

80 Bourke St. www.grossiflorentino.com. ✆ **03/9662 1811.** Main courses A$26–A$58. Mon–Fri noon–3pm; Mon–Sat 6–11pm (cellar bar opens at 7:30am for breakfast Mon–Sat).

Koko ★★ JAPANESE Though you'll find plenty of sushi and noodle bars around Chinatown, there's nothing quite like raw fish with a bit of panache. Koko's decor is contemporary-traditional, with a goldfish pond in the center of the main dining room and wonderful views over the city. There are separate teppanyaki grills and screened tatami rooms where you sit on the matted floor. Koko has a vast and changing seasonal menu that includes a variety seafood dishes (think grilled crayfish with soy salt), or you can opt for a set menu to take the agony out of choosing. A large selection of sakes aids digestion. The A$50 lunch special includes a selection of hot and cold dishes, including tempura, sashimi, Wagyu beef, and miso soup, and a glass of wine, beer, or soft drink.

Level 3, Crown Towers, Southbank. www.crownmelbourne.com.au/koko. ✆ **03/8582 3079.** Main courses A$35–A$98. Daily noon–2:30pm; Sun–Thurs 6–10pm; Fri–Sat 6–10:30pm.

MODERATE

Bamboo House ★★ CHINESE/CANTONESE If Flower Drum (see above) is full or strains your budget, try this more budget-friendly place, esteemed by both the Chinese community and local business big shots. Service is a pleasure, and the food is worth writing home about. The waiters will help you construct a feast from the myriad Cantonese and northern Chinese dishes. Order ahead to get a taste of the signature dish, Szechuan tea-smoked duck. Other popular dishes include pan-fried beef dumplings and spring-onion pancakes.

47 Little Bourke St. www.bamboohouse.com.au. ✆ **03/9662 1565.** Main courses A$22–A$44. Mon–Fri noon–3pm (except public holidays); Mon–Sat 5:30–11pm; Sun 5:30–10pm.

Becco ★★ ITALIAN Tucked away on a quiet lane, this favorite of Melburnians consistently lives up to its many accolades. Here you find stylish service and stylish customers, all without pretension. The cuisine mixes Italian flavors with Australian flair. Try the slow-cooked oxtail with polenta, one of the tasty pasta dishes, or the specials, which your waiter will fill you in on. If you prefer something lighter, there's a bar menu of equally tempting dishes.

11–25 Crossley St., near Bourke St. www.becco.com.au. ✆ **03/9663 3000.** Main courses A$25–A$39. Mon–Fri noon–3pm; Mon–Sat 6–11pm.

Melbourne Restaurants

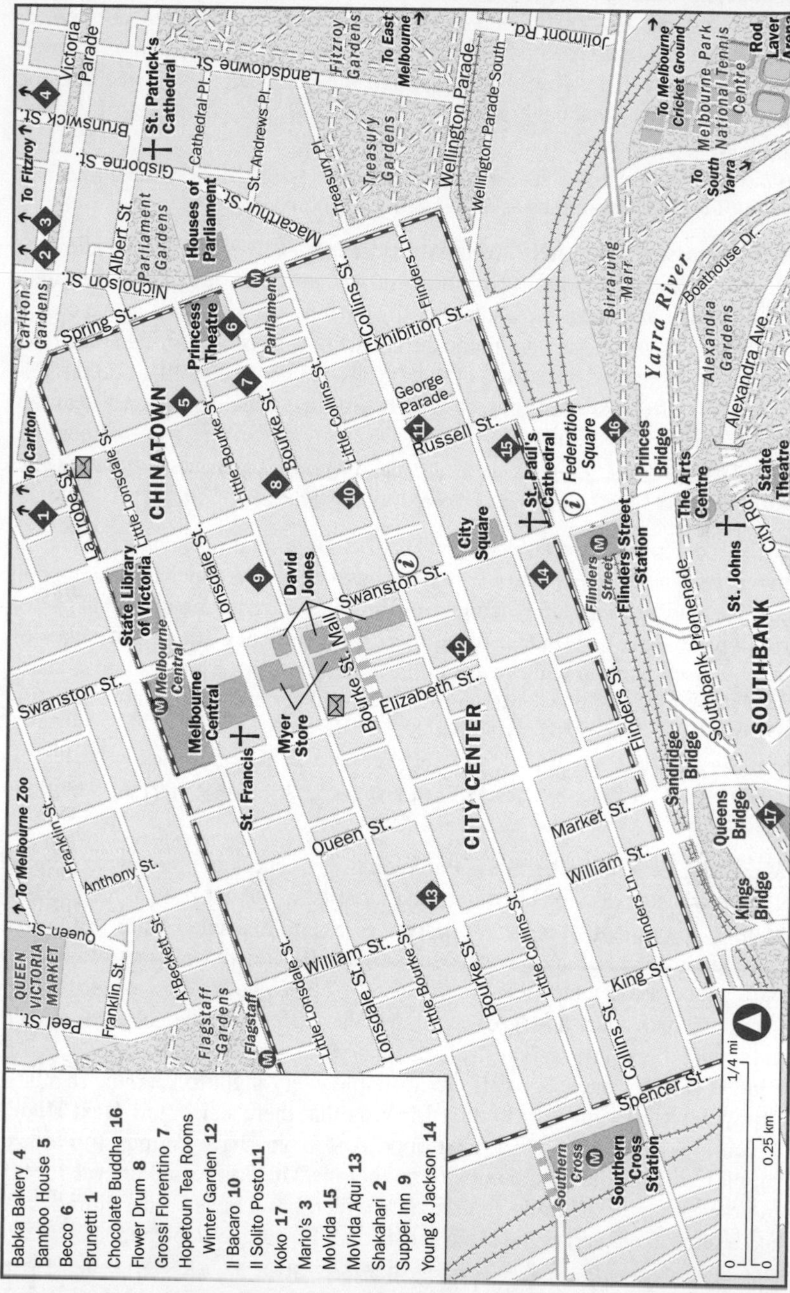

Chocolate Buddha ★★ JAPANESE This place offers mostly organic produce, including some organic wines. Based mostly on Japanese-inspired noodle, ramen, and soba dishes to which the kitchen adds meat, chicken, or seafood, it's casual yet satisfying dining. The best way to eat here is to order dishes to share. The food is creative, and the view across the square to the Yarra River and Southbank is a delight at dusk. It can get very crowded, so book ahead if you can.

Federation Sq., corner of Flinders and Swanson sts. www.chocolatebuddha.com.au. ✆ **03/9654 5688.** Main courses A$15–A$26. Daily noon–11:30pm.

Il Bacaro ★★ ITALIAN Walk into Il Bacaro and you'll experience a little piece of Venice. Dominated by a horseshoe-shaped bar, it's jam-packed with small tables and weaving waiters carrying interesting dishes such as pappardelle with goat ragu, porcini mushrooms, snow peas, and truffled pecorino. The pasta dishes and the risotto of the day always go down well, as do the side salads. It's often crowded at lunch with businesspeople digging into the excellent wine list.

168–170 Little Collins St. www.ilbacaro.com.au. ✆ **03/9654 6778.** Main courses A$27–A$47. Mon–Sat noon–3pm; Mon–Thurs 6–10:30pm; Fri–Sat 6–11pm.

Il Solito Posto ★★ ITALIAN This below-ground restaurant consists of two parts. The casual bistro or *caffeteria* has a blackboard menu offering good pastas, soups, and salads. Then there's the sharper and more upmarket trattoria, with an a la carte menu of northern Italian dishes offering the likes of slow-braised lamb in white wine, chili, garlic, herbs, fresh peas, and tomato; as well as steak, fish, and veal dishes. It's open for breakfast, lunch, and dinner. You'll find the coffee excellent, too.

113 Collins St., basement (enter through George Parade). www.ilsolitoposto.com.au. ✆ **03/9654 4466.** Main courses A$27–A$33 in bistro, A$22–A$46 in trattoria. Mon–Fri 7:30am–1am; Sat 9am–1am.

MoVida ★★★ SPANISH Barcelona-born chef and co-owner Frank Camorra has made MoVida one of the most talked-about restaurants in Melbourne. His restaurant reflects the spirit of Spain, relaxed and fun, with seriously good food and good wine. Melburnians flock here, and it's truly one of those places I was tempted to keep a secret (if that's possible, considering that everyone talks about how great it is). MoVida offers a choice of tapas (small individual dishes) or *raciones* (plates to share among two or more people, or a larger dish for one). Specials are available every night to keep the regulars happy. So successful was the first MoVida that there's also now **Next Door,** which is . . . you guessed it, next door. And if you have a group (up to six people), or you want to dine outdoors, there is **MoVida Aqui,** at level 1, 500 Bourke St. (entry off Little Bourke St.), which has a huge casual dining area and a terrace and serves the same great food. Be sure to book a table.

1 Hosier Lane. www.movida.com.au. ✆ **03/9663 3038** (for all restaurants). Tapas A$3.50–A$8.50; *raciones* (main courses) A$14–A$36; banquet menu (10 dishes) A$80 per person. Daily noon–late.

Spanish tapas and a convivial vibe draw crowds to MoVida.

Young & Jackson ★★ PUB Melbourne's oldest and most famous pub—it's a great place to stop in for a drink at the bar or a meal in the stylish upstairs restaurant or bistro areas. It has fairly standard pub food (burgers, schnitzel, ribs, and so on) in the cafe downstairs and at the rooftop bar, but offerings are more refined in the restaurant. It's a landmark on the corner opposite Federation Square and Flinders Street Station. Head upstairs to see the nude *Chloe,* the famous painting brought to Melbourne from Paris for the Great Exhibition in 1880, which has a special place in the hearts of customers and Melburnians. The pub, which was built in 1853 and started selling beer in 1861, has a few years on *Chloe,* which was painted in Paris in 1875.

At the corner of Flinders and Swanston sts. www.youngandjacksons.com.au. ✆ **03/9650 3884.** Main courses A$26–A$46. Bar meals available 10am–late. Restaurant open daily noon–2:30pm, Sun–Thurs 5:30–9pm, Fri–Sat 5:30–10pm.

INEXPENSIVE

Hopetoun Tea Rooms Winter Garden ★ CAFE The first cup of tea served in this Melbourne institution left the pot in 1892. With its green-and-cream Regency wallpaper and marble tables, the Tea Rooms caters to a loyal clientele of little old ladies and students, with the odd tourist or businessperson thrown into the mix. At times, there are long queues waiting for a table, but most people think it's worth it. There's a full lunch menu, but really you should come for tea or coffee and very good cakes. Try the chocolate strawberry Swiss roll. Scones, croissants, pasta, and grilled food are also available. Traditional "High Tea" at A$55 per person can be taken between 10am and 3pm.

Block Arcade, 280–282 Collins St. www.hopetountearooms.com.au. ✆ **03/9650 2777.** Main courses A$15–A$25; sandwiches A$13–A$19. Mon–Sat 8am–5pm; Sun 9am–5pm.

Supper Inn ★★ CANTONESE Head here if you get the Chinese-food munchies late at night. It's a friendly place with a mixed crowd of locals and tourists chowing down on such dishes as steaming bowls of *congee* (rice-based porridge), barbecued suckling pig, mud crab, or stuffed scallops. Everything here is the real thing.

15 Celestial Ave. ✆ **03/9663 4759.** Main courses A$17–A$40. Daily 5:30pm–2:30am.

In Carlton

Brunetti ★★ ITALIAN Don't be daunted by the crowds around the cake counters—and there *will* be crowds! This is a real Italian/Melbourne experience. If you can get past the mouthwatering array of excellent cakes, the cafe menu offers authentic Italian cuisine, done very well. The open kitchen allows you to watch the chefs in action; there's a wood-fired pizza oven (imported from Italy) and a traditional *gelatieri* (ice-cream maker) at work. Or pop in for breakfast. If you can't get to Carlton, there's the cafe-style **Brunetti City Square** at Swanston Street and Flinders Lane in the city, and another on level three of the city Myer store. Or you can check out their cafe at Terminal 4 at Melbourne Airport before you leave town!

380 Lygon St. www.brunetti.com.au. ✆ **03/9347 2801.** Main courses A$16–A$23. Sun–Thurs 6am–11pm; Fri–Sat 6am–midnight. Tram: 1, 15, 21, or 22 going north on Swanston St.

Shakahari ★ VEGETARIAN Good vegetarian food isn't just a meal without meat; it's a creation in its own right. At Shakahari you're assured a creative meal that's not at all bland. The large restaurant is quite low-key, and there's a lovely courtyard out the back. The signature satay dish—skewered, lightly fried vegetables and tofu pieces with a mildly spicy peanut sauce—is a perennial favorite. Also available are curries, croquettes, green papaya salad, a linguine dish, and a fragrant laksa. A second restaurant, **Shakahari Too,** is located in South Melbourne (✆ **03/9682 2207**).

201–203 Faraday St. www.shakahari.com.au. ✆ **03/9347 3848.** Main courses A$22–A$23. Mon–Sat noon–3pm; Mon–Fri 6–9:30pm; Sat–Sun 6–10:30pm. Tram: 1, 8, 16, or 96 (or any traveling north along Swanston St.).

In Fitzroy

Marios ★★★ ITALIAN Opened in 1986 by two Italian-Australian friends, both named Mario, this place has ambience, groovy decor, and impeccable service. And after 30 years in business, there's little here you can fault, including the food. Offerings include a range of cakes and pastas (like gnocchi with pancetta, peas, basil, tomato, and shaved Parmesan), and breakfast is

> **The Staff of Life**
>
> The aroma of fresh bread will draw you to **Babka Bakery,** a Russian-style cafe-bakery that is nearly always packed. Come for breakfast or a light lunch of eggs on fresh sourdough, or any of the bakery's quiches, tarts, and brioches. Or perhaps try the homemade borscht. It's at 358 Brunswick St., in Fitzroy (© **03/9416 0091**), and is open Tuesday to Sunday 7am to 6pm.

served all day. The art on the walls, all by local artists, is always interesting—and for sale. The coffee is excellent (just don't ask for skim, decaf, or anything other than the real deal). You can also buy a jar of Marios' marmalade to take home for A$8.

303 Brunswick St. www.marioscafe.com.au. © **03/9417 3343.** Main courses A$16–A$32. Mon–Sat 7am–10:30pm; Sun & public holidays 8am–10:30pm. Tram: 112 from Collins St.

Seaside Dining in St Kilda

Babu Ji ★★ INDIAN This very popular Indian eatery is fun and noisy and focuses on good food and good service. The menu offers curries of all kinds and Indian street food. On Sundays, there's a A$28 "thali" all-you-can-eat meal offer, and there are set menus for A$49 (four courses) and A$69 (six courses) per person. Pair your meal with a craft beer (grab your own from the good selection in the fridge) or glass of wine—BYO with A$10 per bottle corkage fee, or buy it there. Takeout service available.

The George Building, 4–6 Grey St. www.babuji.com.au. Reservations for parties of 4 or more only. Main courses A$16–A$25. Fri–Sun 11:30am–2:30pm; Sun–Wed 5:30–9:30pm; Thurs–Sat 5:30–10pm. Closed Christmas Day, Dec 31, and Jan 1. Tram: 16 from Swanston St. or 96 from Bourke St.

Cicciolina ★★★ CONTEMPORARY It's difficult enough to get a table at this wonderful but understated place without encouraging more people to line up, but I'd be depriving you of a terrific night out if I kept quiet. Cicciolina is intimate, crowded, and well run and has superb but simple food. Although you cannot book for dinner (there's a waitlist after 6pm), you may have to wait an hour or so for a table. Have a drink in the Back Bar, and they'll call you when your table is ready; I assure you it will be worth it for delights such as veal saltimbocca with fried saffron risotto, Jerusalem artichokes, peas, and ricotta, or a simple linguine with Atlantic salmon, braised leek, baby spinach, lemon, and olive oil (my eternal favorite). If you're not into the wait, Cicciolina accepts reservations for lunch.

130 Acland St. www.cicciolinastkilda.com.au. © **03/9525 3333.** Main courses A$25–A$44. Mon–Sat noon–11pm; Sun noon–10pm. Reservations for lunch only. Tram: 16 from Swanston St., or 94 or 96 from Bourke St.

Donovans ★★ CONTEMPORARY Watching the sun go down over St Kilda Beach from the veranda at Donovans (with glass in hand) is a perfect way to end the day. Owners Gail and Kevin Donovan's much-loved restaurant—housed in a 1920s bathing pavilion—is a place that many of their loyal customers see as being welcomed into their home (or at least their beach

Pay What You Think

With a novel approach that not surprisingly has become a hit, the vegetarian restaurant **Lentil as Anything** (www.lentilasanything.com) has a menu without prices. Here you eat—then pay "as you feel" for the meal and service (or for some people, what they can afford). The food is organic, with lots of noodles and veggies, plus tofu, curries, and stir-fries. Before you leave, you put your money in a box. The original restaurant is at 41 Blessington St., St Kilda (✆ **0424/345 368** mobile; daily noon–9pm). A second outlet at the Abbotsford Convent, 1 St. Heliers St., Abbotsford (✆ **03/9419 6444**), is open daily from 9am to 11:30am, noon to 3pm, and 5 to 9pm. To avoid long waits, you can now book a table (for a booking fee of A$15 or more per person). Cash only.

house). Lots of comfy cushions, a log fire, coffee-table books, and the sound of jazz and breakers on the beach create a wonderful atmosphere. The menu includes a mind-boggling array of dishes, many big enough for two. Try the seafood linguine or perhaps a slow-cooked pork belly with cauliflower puree, broccolini, Brussels sprouts, a confit of potato and green pepper relish, and mustard seed jus. The bombe Alaska for two is legendary. There's also a children's menu.

40 Jacka Blvd. www.donovanshouse.com.au. ✆ **03/9534 8221.** Main courses A$34–A$65. Daily noon–10:30pm. Tram: 16, 94, or 96.

Ichi Ni ★★ JAPANESE Join Melbourne's beautiful people at one of the city's most popular *izakaya* (Japanese gastropub), a great place for a casual meal with a view of Port Philip Bay. Take a booth inside, or a table on the deck (heated in winter), for the full experience—sharing is best—of yakitori, sashimi, sushi, and Japanese-style tapas dishes. The prices are great, the atmosphere lively, and the service good—a fine combination that keeps me coming back.

12 The Esplanade. www.ichini.com.au. ✆ **03/9534 1212.** Main courses A$10–A$20. Daily noon–10:30pm. Tram: 16, 94, or 96.

EXPLORING MELBOURNE

Visitors to Melbourne come to experience the contrasts of old-world architecture and the exciting feel of a truly multicultural city. This is a wonderfully compact city, with all the major attractions within easy reach of the city heart. Most visitors also venture to the bayside suburb of St Kilda, an easy tram ride away.

The Arts Centre ★★ The spire atop the Theatres Building of the Arts Centre, on the banks of the Yarra River, crowns the city's leading performing arts complex. Beneath it, the State Theatre, the Playhouse, and the Fairfax Studio present performances that are the focal point of culture in Melbourne. The **State Theatre,** seating 2,085 on three levels, can accommodate elaborate stagings of opera, ballet, musicals, and more. The **Playhouse** is a smaller

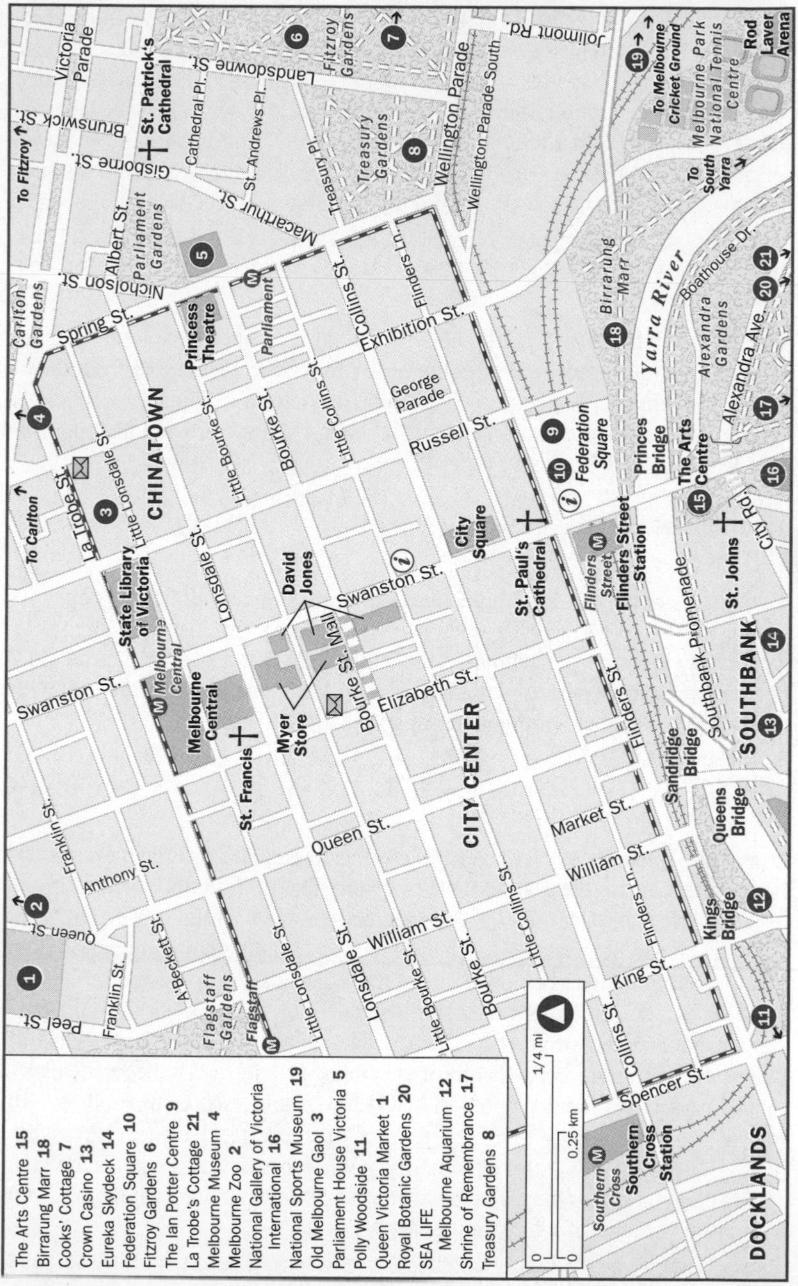
The Arts Centre 15
Birrarung Marr 18
Cooks' Cottage 7
Crown Casino 13
Eureka Skydeck 14
Federation Square 10
Fitzroy Gardens 6
The Ian Potter Centre 9
La Trobe's Cottage 21
Melbourne Museum 4
Melbourne Zoo 2
National Gallery of Victoria International 16
National Sports Museum 19
Old Melbourne Gaol 3
Parliament House Victoria 5
Polly Woodside 11
Queen Victoria Market 1
Royal Botanic Gardens 20
SEA LIFE Melbourne Aquarium 12
Shrine of Remembrance 17
Treasury Gardens 8
0
1/4 mi
0
0.25 km
CHINATOWN
CITY CENTER
SOUTHBANK
DOCKLANDS
Yarra River
To Carlton
To Fitzroy
To Melbourne Cricket Ground
To South Yarra
State Library of Victoria
Melbourne Central
St. Francis
Myer Store
David Jones
Princess Theatre
Parliament
St. Patrick's Cathedral
Parliament Gardens
Carlton Gardens
Fitzroy Gardens
Treasury Gardens
Flagstaff Gardens
Flagstaff
City Square
St. Paul's Cathedral
Federation Square
Flinders Street Station
Southern Cross Station
St. Johns
The Arts Centre
Princes Bridge
Sandridge Bridge
Queens Bridge
Kings Bridge
Birrarung Marr
Alexandra Gardens
Melbourne Park National Tennis Centre
Rod Laver Arena
Swanston St.
Elizabeth St.
Queen St.
William St.
King St.
Spencer St.
Flinders St.
Collins St.
Bourke St.
Lonsdale St.
La Trobe St.
Spring St.
Exhibition St.
Russell St.
Wellington Parade
Southbank Promenade
Alexandra Ave.
Boathouse Dr.
City Rd.

venue that often books the Melbourne Theatre Company. The **Fairfax** is more intimate still and is often used for experimental theater or cabaret. Adjacent to the Theatres Building is **Hamer Hall,** home of the Melbourne Symphony Orchestra and often host to visiting orchestras. Many international stars have graced this stage that's known for excellent acoustics. You can do a guided Theatres and Exhibition Tour daily (except Sun) at 11am. The tour takes an hour, and costs A$20 adults and A$15 children 17 and under, and includes morning tea. On Sundays at 11am, the Backstage Tour takes about 90 minutes and costs A$20 per person (not suitable for children 11 and under).

100 St Kilda Rd. www.artscentremelbourne.com.au. ✆ **1300/182 183** for tickets. Ticket prices vary depending on the event. Box office (in the Theatres Bldg.): Mon–Sat 9am–8:30pm; Sun 10am–5pm.

Cooks' Cottage ★ Built in 1755 by the parents of explorer Captain James Cook, this golden-brick cottage was moved to Melbourne from Great Ayton, in Yorkshire, England, in 1934 to mark Victoria's centenary. Inside, it's spartan and cramped, not unlike a ship's cabin. Displays provide the opportunity to learn about Cook's voyages of discovery around the world.

Fitzroy Gardens, off Wellington Parade. www.melbourne.vic.gov.au/cookscottage. ✆ **03/9658 9658.** A$6.50 adults, A$3.50 children 5–15, A$18 family of 4. Daily 9am–5pm. Closed Christmas Day. Tram: 48, 75, or 35 (City Circle).

Crown Casino ★ Australia's largest casino is a plush affair that's open 24 hours. You'll find all the usual roulette and blackjack tables and so on, as well as an array of gaming machines. This is also a major venue for international headline acts, and some 25 restaurants and 11 bars are on the premises, with more in the extended Southgate complex.

8 Whiteman St. (at Clarendon St.), Southbank. www.crownmelbourne.com.au. ✆ **03/9292 8888.** Daily 24 hr., except on Christmas Day, Good Friday, and Anzac Day (Apr 25) when it is closed 4am–noon.

Eureka Skydeck ★ The vertigo-challenging Skydeck is the highest public vantage point in the Southern Hemisphere. On the 88th floor of the Eureka Tower, a viewing deck gives a 360-degree panorama of the city from 297m (935 ft.) above the ground. But there's more adrenaline-pumping action than just the view: A huge glass cube called the Edge is actually a 6-ton horizontal elevator, which emerges from inside the walls of Skydeck carrying 12 passengers out over the tower's east side. As the opaque glass cube reaches its full extension, the reinforced, 45-millimeter-thick (1¾-in.) glass becomes clear, giving passengers uninterrupted views below, above, and to three sides. All this is accompanied by recorded sounds of creaking chains and breaking glass—just to scare you more! Actually, it's not as scary as it sounds, and the ride is only 4 minutes long. For an extra A$5.50 on your admission price, you can return at night for a look at the city all lit up.

Eureka Tower, Riverside Quay, Southbank. www.eurekaskydeck.com.au. ✆ **03/9693 8888.** A$20 adults, A$11.50 children 4–16, A$34–A$46 families; additional A$12 adults, A$8 children for the Edge. Daily 10am–10pm (last entry 9:30pm); 10am–5:30pm on Christmas Day and New Year's Eve (last entry 5pm).

The Eureka Skydeck offers 360-degree, glassed-in views from high above Melbourne.

Federation Square ★★ You have to get into Federation Square, physically, to appreciate it. The controversial design—Melburnians either love it or hate it (I fall into the former category)—has given the city a gathering place, and you only have to visit on the weekends to see that it works. A conglomerate of attractions is centered on a large open piazza-style area cobbled with misshapen paving. Here you'll find the **Ian Potter Centre** (see below) and the **Australian Centre for the Moving Image (ACMI),** which has two state-of-the-art cinemas and large areas where visitors can view movies, videos, and digital media. It has a one-stop visitor center (see "Visitor Information," earlier in this chapter), and there are many cafes and coffee shops throughout the precinct. It's worth visiting "Fed Square" just to see the architecture, made up of strange geometrical designs, and the glass Atrium. Lots of events happen in the square's 450-seat amphitheater, including theatrical performances and free concerts. Other events take place on the plaza and along the banks of the Yarra River. Melbourne's biggest **book market** is held every Saturday from 11am to 5pm in the Atrium, with 5,000 titles, both new and secondhand. There's free Wi-Fi anywhere in the square. Free 50-minute guided tours are run Monday through Saturday at 11am.

Flinders St. (at St Kilda Rd.). www.fedsquare.com.au. © **03/9655 1900.** Free; charges for some special events and exhibitions. Outdoor spaces open 24 hr. Tram: City Circle.

The Ian Potter Centre ★★★ This fascinating gallery, featuring 20 rooms dedicated to Australian art, is in the heart of Federation Square. Part of the National Gallery of Victoria (NGV), it contains the largest collection of Australian art in the country, including works by Sidney Nolan, Russell Drysdale, and Tom Roberts, as well as Aboriginal and Torres Strait Islanders. Some 20,000 objects are stored here, but only about 800 are on display at any one time. Aboriginal art and colonial art collections are the centerpieces of the gallery, but you will find modern paintings here, too. Temporary exhibitions include anything from ceramics to shoes. Free tours are run daily.

Federation Sq. (corner of Flinders St. and St Kilda Rd.). www.ngv.vic.gov.au. ✆ **03/8620 2222.** Free. Daily 10am–5pm. Closed Good Friday, Christmas Day, and until 1pm on Anzac Day (Apr 25). Tram: City Circle. Bus: City Explorer.

Melbourne Museum ★★★ This museum is Australia's largest and one of its most interesting. For me, the highlight is **Bunjilaka,** the Aboriginal Cultural Centre, which gives an insight into the Victorian Koori people. Other highlights of the museum include a genuine blue-whale skeleton, an indoor rainforest, and a brilliant insect and butterfly collection with lots of real-life exhibits, including revolting cockroaches, ant colonies, and huge spiders (kids love these creepy-crawlies). Apart from that, there are interactive exhibits and science displays and social history, including a stuffed racehorse called Phar Lap. Check out the brightly colored **Children's Museum,** which will bring hours of enjoyment to the little ones. Allow 2 hours, more if you would like to tour the adjacent 19th-century **Royal Exhibition Building.** Tours of this magnificent building run at 2pm daily and cost A$10 adults and A$7 children.

11 Nicholson St., Carlton. www.museumvictoria.com.au. ✆ **131 102** in Victoria or 03/8341 7777. A$14 adults, free for children 15 and under. Daily 10am–5pm. Closed Good Friday and Christmas Day. Tram: 86 or 96 or the free City Circle Tram.

Melbourne Zoo ★★ Built in 1862, this is one of the oldest zoos in the world and makes a great day out with kids. Some 3,000 animals reside here, including kangaroos, wallabies, echidnas, koalas, wombats, and platypuses.

Art in the Streets

Melbourne's street art is some of the best in the world. Often tucked away in laneways or where you'd least expect them, they are among the city's most popular attractions and worth seeking out. Some of the best known in the city center are in **Hosier Lane** (off Flinders Street), **Union Lane** (off the Bourke Street Mall), **Centre Place** (off Degraves St.), and **Croft Alley**—but these spots are being left in the shadow of the suburb of Fitzroy, north of the city. Head there by tram to take a walk around Johnston, Gertrude, and Brunswick streets, remembering to head into the alleys as well. You'll also find some good street art in St Kilda. **Melbourne Street Art Tours** (www.melbournestreettours.com; ✆ **03/9328 5556**), run by street artists, offers 3½-hour walking tours. For A$69 (half price for kids 15 and under), you can see the best of it, meet some of the artists, and see them at work.

Playing with kangaroos at Melbourne Zoo.

Rather than being locked in cages, most animals are in almost natural surroundings or well-tended gardens. Don't miss the butterfly house, with its thousands of colorful occupants flitting around; the free-flight aviary; the lowland gorilla exhibit; and the treetop orangutan exhibit. Allow at least 90 minutes if you just want to see the Australian natives, and around 4 hours for the entire zoo.

Elliott Ave., Parkville. www.zoo.org.au. ✆ **1300/966 784.** A$33 adults, A$16 children 4–15. Entry is free for children on Sat–Sun, public holidays, and school holidays. Daily 9am–5pm. Tram: 55 going north on William St. to stop 25; 19 from Elizabeth St. to stop 16 (then a short walk to your left, following signposts). Train: Royal Park Station.

National Gallery of Victoria International ★★ The NGV International is a showcase for Australia's finest collections of international art. On display are Gainsboroughs and Constables, as well as paintings by Bonnard, Delacroix, Van Dyck, El Greco, Monet, Manet, Magritte, and Rembrandt. Architecturally, the building itself is a masterpiece, with high ceilings, fabulous lighting, and great open spaces. Free tours are run daily.

180 St Kilda Rd. www.ngv.vic.gov.au. ✆ **03/8620 2222.** Free; fees for some temporary exhibitions. Daily 10am–5pm. Closed Good Friday, Christmas Day, and until 1pm on Anzac Day (Apr 25). Tram: Any tram from Swanston St. to Victorian Arts Centre.

National Sports Museum ★★★ In a nation that's quite frankly sports-mad, you really can't miss this outstanding and interesting museum, located within the Melbourne Cricket Ground (MCG). It tells Australia's sporting story from its early beginnings to the present, celebrating memorable moments and achievements in just about every sport you can think of, from basketball and boxing to hockey, rugby, tennis, and everything in between. It also includes the Australian Cricket Hall of Fame, the Sport Australia Hall of Fame, and the Champions Racing Gallery. The huge collection includes Australia's first-ever Olympic gold medal, Ian Thorpe's swimsuit, and the Malvern Star bicycle that Hubert Opperman rode in his record-breaking 24-hour cycling marathon in Sydney in 1940. Recognition has been given to Australia's first Paralympic gold medalist and first female Paralympian in the Paralympic display. There's lots of interactive areas, and even room for kids to bowl a ball or two. Allow 1 hour (more if you are a real sports fanatic).

During MCG major event days, including the AFL Grand Final, Day 1 of the Boxing Day Test, and Anzac Day football, access to the museum (at half-price) is restricted to patrons holding an event ticket. Opening hours on weekends when events are being held within the MCG arena vary, so check the website.

Tours of the MCG run every half-hour daily from 10am to 3pm. Tickets include admission to the museum. Tours leave from Gate 3 in the Olympic Stand on non-event days only.

Melbourne Cricket Ground, Brunton Ave., Richmond. www.nsm.org.au. ✆ **03/9657 8879.** A$24 adults, A$13 children 5–15, or A$57 families of 4 for museum only; A$33 adults, A$17 children, or A$73 families for museum and MCG tour. Daily 10am–5pm (last admission 4:30pm). Closed Good Friday and Christmas Day. Bus: Melbourne City Tourist Shuttle. Tram: 75 or 70 from the city center. Train: Jolimont. Entry is through Gate 3 at the MCG.

Old Melbourne Gaol ★★★

This is number one on my list of favorite Melbourne attractions. Roaming the Old Melbourne Gaol complex is a fascinating way to spend a few hours. Start off at the spooky old prison, with its stone walls, tiny cells, and bizarre collection of death masks and artifacts of 19th-century prison life. Among the 135 hangings that took place here was that of notorious bushranger Ned Kelly, in 1880. The scaffold where he was hanged still stands, and his gun, as well as a replica suit of homemade armor (similar to those used by his gang), is on display. The jail closed in 1924, and profiles of former prisoners give a fascinating insight into what it was like to be imprisoned here.

Old Melbourne Gaol, where bushranger Ned Kelly was hanged.

After exploring the jail move next door for a guided tour of the former City Watch House to find out first-hand what it might have been like to spend time here. The lockup, which operated from 1908 to 1994, is just across the road from the scene of one of Melbourne's most notorious crimes, the 1986 bombing of the Russell Street police station. There's role-playing involved for everyone, but it can be quite challenging for children. During holiday times, you can also visit the adjacent former Magistrate's Court and take part in a reenactment of Ned Kelly's trial.

Three tours give the brave a chance to explore the gaol by night, and they are not for the fainthearted. Ghost tours and equally chilling "hangman" tours run by candlelight and last for an hour. Check the website for session days and times. A Night in the Watch House tours, set in the cellblock, run for 1 hour, are conducted in the dark, and are not for anyone under 16 years. Tickets for all night tours cost A$38 per person. Ghost and hangman's tours are not recommended for children 11 and under.

377 Russell St. www.oldmelbournegaol.com.au. ✆ **03/9663 7228.** A$25 adults, A$14 children, A$55 families of 4. Daily 9:30am–5pm. Closed Good Friday and Christmas Day. Tram: 30 or 35 (City Circle) to corner of Russell and Latrobe sts.

Parliament House Victoria ★ Now the home of the Victorian Parliament, this monument to Victorian (as in Queen Victoria) architecture at the top of a run of sandstone steps was built in 1856. During the Australian Federation (1900–27), it was used as the national parliament. When the state government is in session—generally on Tuesday afternoon and all day Wednesday and Thursday March through July, and again from August through November (there's a break between sessions)—you can view the proceedings from the public gallery. Call ahead or check the website, as sitting times do vary. During non-sitting times, both the opulent Upper House and the less ornate Lower House chambers are open to the public by guided tour. In addition to regular tours, free architecture tours are held at 2pm on the last Friday of the month. Finally, there's a guided tour that finishes with High Tea in the Strangers Corridor, weekdays from 2:30 to 4pm. The cost is A$47 per person.

Spring St. www.parliament.vic.gov.au. ✆ **03/9651 8568.** Mon–Fri 9am–5pm. Free 1-hr. guided tours Mon–Fri at 9:30, 10:30, 11:30am, 1:30, 2:30, and 3:30pm when Parliament is not in session; 20-min. "Express Tours" Mon–Fri at 1 and 4pm. Reservations required for 1-hour tours for groups of 6 or more and for architecture tours.

Polly Woodside ★★ The historic tall ship *Polly Woodside* sits beside the original Dockside sheds, and is beloved by generations of Melburnians for its many fun diversion and hands-on activities for kids. The exhibit includes six zones with interactive displays about life at sea, the crew, navigation, maritime language, and Melbourne's docks (you can even try your hand at loading coal onto a robot ship!). Launched in 1885 in Ireland, the ship sailed to all corners of the globe between 1885 and 1904, rounding the infamous Cape Horn 16 times. After World War II, the ship was towed back to Melbourne and worked as a coal supply ship for the next 20 years. Tours are offered

Kid-friendly tours and hands-on fun aboard the historic tall ship *Polly Woodside*.

throughout the day, and the first Sunday of the month is "Pirate Day" for kids, from 11am to 3pm.

21 South Wharf Promenade, South Wharf. www.pollywoodside.com.au. ✆ **03/9699 9760.** A$16 adults, A$9.50 children, A$30–A$43 families. Sat–Sun 10am–4pm (last entry 3:15pm); daily during Victorian school holidays. Closed Christmas Day, Boxing Day (Dec 26), New Year's Day, and Easter. Tram: 96, 109, or 12.

Queen Victoria Market ★ This Melbourne institution—the "Vic Market"—covers several blocks. Ignore the hundreds of stalls selling everything from live rabbits to bargain clothes. There's a lot of junk here, and the crowds can be awful. The indoor food section, particularly the interesting delicatessen section, is the best part of the markets. The 90-minute **Queen Vic Market Ultimate Foodie Tour** explores the market's food and heritage and is well worth doing. It departs Tuesday, Thursday, and Saturday at 9 and 11am, and costs A$69 adults; the tour includes generous tastings and a A$5 shopping voucher. Bookings (online) are essential. **Night markets** are held every Wednesday from 5 to 10pm in winter (June–Aug) and 5:30 to 10pm in summer (Nov to late Feb, except the last week of Dec).

Btw. Peel, Victoria, Elizabeth, and Therry sts. on the northern edge of the city center. www.qvm.com.au. ✆ **03/9320 5822.** Tues and Thurs 6am–2pm; Fri 6am–5pm; Sat 6am–3pm; Sun 9am–4pm. Closed public holidays. Tram: 35 (City Circle) or any tram traveling north along William or Elizabeth sts.

SEA LIFE Melbourne Aquarium ★ The Melbourne Aquarium's prize exhibit is an Antarctica display featuring King and Gentoo penguins playing in the pool (with underwater viewing) and sliding across the snow-covered

Queen Victoria Market.

ice. These beguiling birds are Australia's only collection of sub-Antarctic penguins. The aquarium also features a reef exhibit, a crocodile exhibit, some jellyfish displays, and a 2.2-million-liter (581,000-gallon) oceanarium walk-through tank with larger fish, sharks, and rays. You can arrange to dive with the sharks (A$299 per person; must be 15 years or older). Bookings are required; call ✆ **03/9923 5911.**

Corner of Flinders and Kings sts. www.melbourneaquarium.com.au. ✆ **03/9923 5999.** A$42 adults, A$28 children 4–15, A$69–A$99 families (cheaper if booked online). Daily 9:30am–6pm (last admission 5pm). Tram: 35.

Outlying Attractions

Healesville Sanctuary ★★★ The sanctuary is a great place to see native animals in almost-natural surroundings. Walk through the peppermint-scented gum forest, which rings with the chiming of bellbirds, and see wedge-tailed eagles, dingoes, koalas, wombats, reptiles, and more. The platypus show at 11:15am daily (and again at 1:30pm Sat–Sun) is a great chance to get up close to these elusive creatures. The sanctuary opened in 1921 to preserve endangered species and educate the public and played a major role in saving and rehabilitating the hundreds of animals injured or displaced by the bushfires that devastated parts of Victoria in 2009. You can visit the Wildlife Health Centre (an animal rescue hospital) to see veterinarians caring for injured or orphaned wildlife. The sanctuary has a gift shop, a cafe, and picnic grounds.

Badger Creek Rd., Healesville. www.zoo.org.au. ✆ **03/5957 2800.** A$33 adults, A$16.30 children ages 4–15, A$82–A$106 families (Mon–Fri only). Children free on weekends,

Fit for a King—Or a Governor

Northwest of the city center, the sprawling parklands called **King's Domain** surround **Government House,** residence of Victoria's governor. Free tours of the Government House gardens run on the third Thursday of every month at 11am. Online registration is essential (www.governor.vic.gov.au/government-house/tours/monthly-garden-tours). Also worth a visit is historic **La Trobe's Cottage** (www.nationaltrust.org.au/places/la-trobes-cottage; ✆ **03/9656 9889**), Victoria's first Government House, which was built in England and transported to Australia brick by brick in 1836. The cottage is open on Sundays from 2 to 4pm, October through April. Admission is A$5 adults, A$4 children, A$12 for a family. Across Birdwood Avenue, stop by the **Shrine of Remembrance,** a memorial to servicemen lost in Australia's wars. It's designed so that at 11am on Remembrance Day (Nov 11), a beam of sunlight hits the Stone of Remembrance in the Inner Shrine. Note the eternal flame in the forecourt.

public holidays, and Victorian school holidays. Daily 9am–5pm (last admission 3:30pm). Train from Flinders St. station to Lilydale; then bus no. 685 to Healesville and bus no. 686 toward Badger Creek, which will stop at the sanctuary.

Puffing Billy Railway ★★★ Generations of Australians have clambered aboard the Puffing Billy steam train to chug over a 13km (8-mile) track from Belgrave to Emerald and Lakeside. Passengers ride on open carriages—often dangling their legs from the "windows"—and enjoy lovely views as the train passes through forests and fern gullies and over a National Trust–classified wooden trestle bridge. Trips take around an hour each way, and there's time to walk around the lake before the return journey. Special "Steam and Cuisine" fares are available daily: choose from a cheese platter and dessert for A$75 adults or A$68 children, or a three-course lunch (and perhaps a glass of wine) in a "first class" enclosed carriage with white tablecloths for A$99 adults, A$89 children (excluding drinks). On Thursday, Friday, and Saturday nights you can take the train to dinner at a historic packing shed for A$93. Other special trains—jazz nights, murder themes, and so on—also run; check the website for details. Trains do not run on days of total fire ban.

Belgrave Station, Belgrave. www.puffingbilly.com.au. ✆ **03/9757 0700.** Round-trip fares A$32–A$72 adults, A$17–A$36 children 4–16, A$108–A$143 families of 6 (depending on how far you travel). Closed Christmas Day. Train from Flinders St. station in Melbourne to Belgrave; Puffing Billy station is a short walk away.

Werribee Mansion ★★★ I never tire of visiting this stately 60-room Italianate mansion, just a 30-minute drive along the Princes Freeway from Melbourne, at Werribee Park. Dubbed "the palace in the paddock," it was built in 1877 and is surrounded by 132 hectares (326 acres) of magnificent formal gardens and bushland. Get the audio tour (A$6.20) for further insight as you wander around the house, or take a guided tour (A$9.80). Be sure to meander

Eternally popular Puffing Billy scenic railway.

through the interesting and extensive contemporary sculpture garden. There's a cafe on-site.

K Rd., Werribee. www.werribeepark.com.au. ✆ **131 963.** A$9.80 adults, A$7.30 children 4–15, A$31 families of 4. Guided tours A$9.80 per person. Nov to mid-Apr: daily 10am–5pm. Mid-Apr to Oct: Mon–Fri 10am–4pm, Sat–Sun and public holidays 10am–5pm. Closed Christmas Day. Train from Flinders St. station to Werribee; then bus no. 439. The **Werribee Park Shuttle** (www.werribeeparkshuttle.com.au; ✆ **03/9748 5094**) leaves the National Gallery of Victoria, 180 St Kilda Rd., daily at 9:30am and costs A$35 adults, A$25 children 10–14, A$20 children 4–9 (reservations essential).

Werribee Open Range Zoo ★ This zoo is part of Zoos Victoria, which also runs the Melbourne Zoo. It has a collection of Aussie animals, but the focus is on the open range section of the zoo, where you will see giraffes, hippos, rhinoceros, lions, zebras, and more. The zoo also has one of the largest gorilla exhibits in the world, home to the silverback Motaba and his two sons. Access to the zoo's open-range area is strictly by a 40-minute guided tour on a safari bus. On busy days, it might pay to spend the extra money to take a small group tour in an open-sided jeep, as you'll get a better view and better photo opportunities. The zoo also has a walk-through section featuring African cats, including cheetahs, and monkeys. If you've been to Africa, you may find little to excite you, but kids love it, and it's crowded with families.

K Rd., Werribee. www.zoo.org.au/werribee. ✆ **1300/966 784** in Australia or 03/9731 9600. A$33 adults, A$16.30 children 4–15, A$82–A$106 families (Mon–Fri only). Children free on weekends, public holidays, and school holidays. Daily 9am–5pm (last entry at 3:30pm). Safari tours run regularly all day. Take train from Flinders St. station to Werribee, then bus no. 439. The **Werribee Park Shuttle** (www.werribeeparkshuttle.com.au;

✆ **03/9748 5094**) leaves the National Gallery of Victoria, 180 St Kilda Rd., daily at 9:30am and costs A$35 adults, A$25 children 10–14, A$20 children 4–9 (bookings essential).

Organized Tours

Melbourne River Cruises (www.melbcruises.com.au; ✆ **03/8610 2600**) offers a range of boat trips up and down the Yarra River, lasting 1 to 2 hours. It's a great way to get a feel for the city, and the tours include commentaries. A 2-hour Melbourne Highlights tour or a tour from the city to Williamstown costs A$29 adults, A$16 kids, or A$75 families. Call ahead to confirm cruise departure times, because they change, and pick up tickets from the blue Melbourne River Cruises kiosks at the Federation Square riverfront (opposite Flinders St. Station) or on the river at Southgate (Berth 5, on the lower promenade at South Bank).

Real Melbourne Bike Tours (www.rentabike.net.au/bike-tours.htm; ✆ **0417/339 203** mobile) can help you find your bearings and discover some of hidden Melbourne—the back streets and bluestone lanes, markets, cafes, arcades, and bike paths. Run by former journalist Murray Johnson, tours are fun and interesting. The cost is A$110 adults and A$79 children ages 12 to 18, or A$299 for a family of 4, and includes bike hire, helmet, and guided tour,

Melbourne River Cruises offers boat tours on the Yarra River.

plus coffee, cake, and lunch along the way. Tours leave at 10am (or other times by arrangement) from Rentabike at Federation Square and return around 2pm. Tours can be customized to suit your needs and interests. Bookings are essential.

Sports Lovers Tours (www.melbournesportstours.com.au; ✆ **03/8802 4547**) are designed for passionate sports fans or just those who want to get into the spirit of some local sporting action. Half- and full-day tours cater to all tastes and include visits to the National Sports Museum (p. 133), behind the scenes at the Melbourne Cricket Ground or Rod Laver Arena, Flemington Racecourse and the Albert Park Formula 1 track. Other options include attending an Aussie Rules football game with a local host who can explain the rules, or a horse-racing themed tour for fans of the Melbourne Cup. Tour prices range from A$115 per person for a 5-hour tour to A$149 for a full day.

Outdoor Activities

Birrarung Marr, along the Yarra River east of Federation Square on Batman Avenue (www.melbourne.vic.gov.au/parks; ✆ **03/9658 9658**), is Melbourne's newest major parkland. *Birrarung* means "river of mists" in the Woiwurrung language of the Wurundjeri people who originally inhabited the area; *marr* relates to the side of the river. The wide-open spaces and large, sculptured terraces were designed to host some of Melbourne's top events and festivals throughout the year, and the terraces provide views of the city, Southbank, King's Domain, and the Yarra River.

The **Royal Botanic Gardens,** 2km (1¼ miles) south of the city on Birdwood Avenue, off St Kilda Road (www.rbg.vic.gov.au; ✆ **03/9252 2429**), are the best gardens in Australia and well worth a few hours of wandering. More than 40 hectares (99 acres) are lush and blooming with some 12,000 plant species from all over the world. Don't miss a visit to the oldest part of the garden, the Tennyson Lawn, with its 120-year-old English elm trees. Other special corners include a fern gully, camellia gardens, an herb garden, rainforests packed with fruit bats, and ponds full of ducks and black swans. A hop-on, hop-off "Garden Explorer" tour operates year-round from 10am to 3pm daily, offering a golf-buggy style transport (with commentary) and stops around the gardens. It costs A$10 adults, A$8 children 15 and under, and A$25 for a family of four. Buy tickets at the visitor center or from the driver. On weekends and public holidays, you can also take a traditional punt cruise (www.punttours.com.au; ✆ **0481/455 410** mobile) on the Ornamental Lake for A$25 adults, A$12 children, or A$65 for a family of 5. The gardens are open daily from 7:30am to sunset. Admission is free. To get there, catch the no. 8 tram and get off at stop 21. Allow at least 2 hours.

Extensive bicycle paths wind through the city and suburbs. **Melbourne Bike Share,** Melbourne's public bike hire (www.melbournebikeshare.com.au; ✆ **1300/711 590**), has 50 bike stations and 600 bikes at locations around the city. You can't miss the racks of bright blue bikes. You can pay for a bike with Visa or MasterCard (limit of two bikes per credit card). Your card swipe will also take a A$50 security deposit, which will be refunded after return of the bikes. You pay a daily hire rate of A$3 (or A$8 for a week) and the first 30 minutes of usage are free; then you pay A$2 for 30 minutes (up to your first hour), A$7 for 90 minutes, and A$10 for every half-hour after that. The daily rate makes the bike-share system one of the cheapest transport options in town, but only if you have the bike for less than about 2 hours. If you need a bike for longer than that, it's probably cheaper to hire a bike elsewhere. Bike helmets are compulsory by law, and come free when you hire a bike. You must be 16 years or older to use the bike-share system.

Melbourne Bike Share has developed a range of suggested bike tours that you can download from the website. You can also buy books and maps from **Bicycle Network Victoria** (www.bicyclenetwork.com.au). This website is a font of useful information about cycling in Victoria and Australia.

SHOPPING

Ask almost any Melburnian to help you plan your time in the city, and he or she will advise you to shop until you drop. All Australia regards Melbourne as a shopping capital—it has everything from fashion houses to major department stores and unusual souvenir shops. So even if you're also visiting Sydney, save your money until you get to Melbourne, and then indulge!

Start at the magnificent city arcades, such as the **Block Arcade** (btw. Collins and Little Collins sts.), which has more than 30 shops, including the historic **Hopetoun Tea Rooms** (p. 125), and the **Royal Arcade** (stretching from Little Collins St. to the Bourke St. Mall). Then hit the courts and lanes around **Swanston Street** and the huge **Melbourne Central shopping complex** between Latrobe and Lonsdale streets.

Department store giants **David Jones** (www.davidjones.com.au; ✆ **03/9643 2222**)—or DJs, as it's affectionately known—and **Myer** (www.myer.com.au;

Shop 'til You Drop

For an easy way to shop—with local guidance—take a tour with Jessica Lothian to either Melbourne's outlet stores or to hunt out designer styles. **Melbourne Outlet Shopping Tours** (www.outletshoppingtours.com.au; ✆ **03/8822 4568**) offers small group tours for some retail therapy. Jess will help you explore back-street warehouses, pop-up sales, and discount shopping streets such as Swan Street and Bridge Road. Tours operate Monday to Saturday, 9am to 5pm, and cost A$89 adults, A$67 children 13 and under. The tour includes lunch and a glass of bubbles, and is adapted to fit the interests of the group. Pickups from city hotels on request.

✆ **03/9661 1111**) both have stores in the city center. DJs spans 2 blocks separated into men's and women's stores and has a vast and tantalizing food hall. Myer is the grand dame of Melbourne's department stores and is in hot competition with David Jones. It has household goods, perfume, jewelry, and fashions, as well as a food section. Both stores are on the Bourke St. Mall.

High-fashion boutiques line the eastern stretch of **Collins Street,** between the Grand Hyatt and the Hotel Sofitel. Collins Street features most international labels, as well as shoe heaven **Miss Louise,** 205 Collins St. (www.misslouise.com.au; ✆ **03/9654 7730**). Nearby Flinders Lane has earned style status with the likes of **Christine,** 181 Flinders Lane (christineaccessories.com; ✆ **03/9654 2011**), where women are reputed to sometimes faint over the accessories. Down the road is **Little Collins Street,** another fashion rat run with lots of local labels.

Next, fan out across the city, taking in **Chapel Street** in South Yarra for its Australian fashions and the **Jam Factory,** 500 Chapel St., South Yarra, a series of buildings with a range of shops and food outlets as well as 16 cinema screens. Get there on tram no. 8 or 72 from Swanston Street.

There's also **Toorak Road** in Toorak, for Gucci and other high-priced, high-fashion names; **Bridge Road** in Richmond, for budget and outlet fashion stores; **Lygon Street** in Carlton, for Italian fashion, footwear, and accessories; and **Brunswick Street** in Fitzroy, for a more alternative scene.

DAY TRIPS FROM MELBOURNE

Phillip Island: Penguins on Parade ★★★

139km (86 miles) S of Melbourne

Phillip Island's **penguin parade,** which happens every evening at dusk, is one of Australia's most popular animal attractions. There are other, less crowded places in Australia where watching homecoming penguins feels less staged, but at least the guides and boardwalks protect the little ones and their nesting holes from the throngs. Nevertheless, the commercialism of the penguin parade puts a lot of people off—busloads of tourists squashed into a sort of amphitheater hardly feels like being one with nature. But Phillip Island also offers nice beaches, good bushwalking, fishing, and Seal Rocks.

ESSENTIALS

GETTING THERE Most visitors come to Phillip Island on a day trip from Melbourne and arrive in time for the penguin parade and dinner. Several tour companies run day trips. Among them are **Gray Line** (www.grayline.com.au; ✆ **1300/858 687** in Australia), which operates a number of different tours, including the daily "penguin express" trips for those who are short of time. The express tour departs Melbourne at 4:30pm and returns around 11:30pm. Tours cost A$140 for adults and A$70 for children, and can be booked online.

Upgrades to premium seating at the penguin parade and various other options are available.

If you're driving yourself, Phillip Island is an easy 2-hour trip from Melbourne along the South Gippsland Highway and then the Bass Highway. A bridge connects the island to the mainland.

V/Line (www.vline.com.au; ✆ **136 196** in Australia) runs a bus from Melbourne to Cowes, but does not take you to any of the attractions on Phillip Island. Once on the island, you need to hire a car, take a tour, or hire a bicycle to get around. The parade is 15km (9½ miles) from the center of Cowes.

VISITOR INFORMATION There are two information centers on the island. The **Phillip Island Information Centre** is at 895 Phillip Island Rd., Newhaven, just a few kilometers onto the island, and is open daily from 9am to 5pm (6pm Dec–Jan) and closed Christmas Day. The **Cowes Visitor Information Centre** is at Thompson Avenue (corner Church St.), Cowes, and is open daily 9am to 5pm (except Christmas Day). The centers share the toll-free number ✆ **1300/366 422** in Australia and the website www.visitphillipisland.com.

EXPLORING PHILLIP ISLAND

Visitors approach the island from the east, passing through the town of **Newhaven.** The main town on the island, **Cowes** (pop. 4,000), is on the north coast. The penguin parade is on the far southwest coast.

A **4 Parks Pass** gives discounted entry to the top attractions, the **Koala Conservation Centre** (see below), the penguin parade, and **Churchill Island Heritage Farm** and the **Antarctic Journey** experience at the Nobbies Centre. The pass costs A$58 adults, A$29 children ages 4 to 15, and A$145 for families of four; it can be purchased online (www.penguins.org.au) or at any of the attractions.

The trip to the west coast of Phillip Island's Summerland Peninsula ends in an interesting rock formation called the **Nobbies.** This strange-looking outcropping can be reached at low tide by a basalt causeway. You'll get some spectacular views of the coastline and two offshore islands from here. On the farthest of these islands is a population of up to **12,000 Australian fur seals,** the largest colony in Australia. Bring your binoculars, or for a closer view take a 1-hr. speedboat ride to the seal colony for A$85 adults, A$65 children, or A$235 for a family of 4 (or combine with a 3 Parks Pass or Penguin Parade ticket). This area is also home to thousands of nesting silver gulls. The three-level **Antarctic Journey** attraction at the Nobbies (www.penguins.org.au; ✆ **03/5951 2800**) is an interactive display that showcases the natural world of Phillip Island and the Antarctic landscape and wildlife to its far south. Entry is A$18 adults, half price for children 4 to 15, and A$45 for a family of four. There is free entry to the boardwalks and cafe. It is open daily from 10am until an hour before sunset, when the area closes to the public to protect the wildlife.

On the north coast of the island, you can explore **Rhyll Inlet,** an intertidal mangrove wetland inhabited by wading birds such as spoonbills, oystercatchers, herons, egrets, cormorants, and the rare bar-tailed godwit and whimbrel. Birders will also love **Swan Lake,** another breeding habitat for wetland birds.

Elsewhere, walking trails lead through heath and pink granite to **Cape Woolamai,** the island's highest point, where there are fabulous coastal views. From September through April, the cape is home to thousands of short-tailed shearwaters (also known as mutton birds).

PHILLIP ISLAND ATTRACTIONS

Koala Conservation Centre ★★ Koalas were introduced to Phillip Island in the 1880s, and at first they thrived in the predator-free environment. However, overpopulation, the introduction of foxes and dogs, and the clearing of land for farmland and roads have taken their toll. Though you can still see a few koalas in the wild, the best place to find them is at this sanctuary, set up for research and breeding purposes. Visitors can get quite close to them, especially on the elevated boardwalk, which lets you peek into their treetop homes. Around 4pm, the ordinarily sleepy koalas are on the move—but this is also the time when tour buses converge on the place, so it can get crowded.

Fiveways, Phillip Island Tourist Rd., Cowes. www.penguins.org.au. ✆ **03/5952 1610.** A$13 adults, A$6.40 children 4–15, A$32 families of four. Daily 10am–5pm, slightly later in summer (2–6pm on Christmas Day).

National Vietnam Veterans Museum ★★ Phillip Island may seem an unusual place to find a national museum, but it's definitely worth a stop. Dedicated to the Australian veterans of the Vietnam War, the collection includes about 6,000 artifacts, including marbles used in Australia's conscription lottery, uniforms, vehicles, and weapons. Four galleries tell the story of Australia's involvement in the war: a Remembrance Gallery and separate Air, Ground, and Naval Operations galleries. There is also a large exhibit telling the Vietnamese story, and by the time you visit there may be a new life-size diorama showing a Viet Cong tunnel system. The big-ticket item is a Bell AH-IG HueyCobra helicopter gunship, one of only three in Australia, and the museum is also restoring a Canberra bomber, the only surviving example of its kind in the world. There's a moving audiovisual on Australia's involvement in the war from 1962 to 1972. You can have a coffee in the **Nui Dat Café** or buy books and memorabilia from the shop.

25 Veterans Dr., Newhaven. www.vietnamvetsmuseum.org. ✆ **03/5956 6400.** A$15 adults, A$12 veterans, A$10 children 5–15, A$40 families of 5. Daily 10am–5pm. Closed Good Friday, Christmas Day, Boxing Day (Dec 26), New Year's Day, and from noon on Christmas Eve.

Phillip Island Penguin Reserve ★★ The penguin parade takes place every night at dusk, when hundreds of Little Penguins appear at the water's edge, gather in the shallows, and waddle up the beach toward their burrows in the dunes. They're the smallest of the world's 17 species of penguins, standing

The Phillip Island penguin parade is a nightly event.

just 33 centimeters (13 in.) high, and the only penguins that breed on the Australian mainland. **Photography is banned,** because it scares the penguins, as are smoking and touching the penguins. Wear a sweater or jacket, because it gets chilly after the sun goes down. A kiosk selling food opens an hour before the penguins turn up. Reservations for the parade are essential during busy holiday periods such as Easter and in summer.

For a better experience, the more exclusive small-group tours give you a better view of the penguins. **Penguins Plus** allows you to watch the parade from a boardwalk in the company of rangers, while an **Underground Viewing** option allows you to watch up-close from indoors. The **Ultimate Adventure Tour** for groups of only 10 people (no children 15 and under) takes you to a secluded beach away from the main viewing area to watch penguins coming ashore. Other options include ranger-guided tours a few hours before the penguins appear, one with a focus on the Aboriginal heritage of the area that ends with front-row seats on the viewing platform.

Summerland Beach, Phillip Island Tourist Rd., Cowes. www.penguins.org.au. ✆ **03/5951 2820.** A$26 adults, A$13 children 4–15, A$64 families of 4. Penguins Plus A$50 adult, A$25 child, A$125 families; Underground Viewing A$65 adults, A$33 children, A$163 families of 4; Aboriginal Heritage Tour A$60 (no children 11 and under); VIP Tour (no children 11 and under) and Guided Ranger Tour (no children 11 and under) A$80; Ultimate Adventure Tour A$90. Visitor center opens daily at 10am (2pm on Christmas Day).

The Mornington Peninsula ★★

80km (50 miles) S of Melbourne

The Mornington Peninsula, a scenic 40km (25-mile) stretch of windswept coastline and hinterland, is one of Melbourne's favorite day-trip and weekend-getaway destinations—and not just because it's a popular wine-producing region. The peninsula's fertile soil, temperate climate, and rolling hills produce excellent wine, particularly pinot noir, shiraz, and chardonnay. Many wineries offer cellar-door tastings; others have excellent restaurants.

ESSENTIALS

GETTING THERE From Melbourne, you can drive to the Mornington Peninsula in about an hour. There are two toll roads, but taking the toll-free Neapean Highway, and then the Point Nepean Road, is just as easy. Getting there by public transport is a time-consuming process, and does not solve the problem of how to get around once you are there.

VISITOR INFORMATION The **Mornington Peninsula Visitor Information Centre,** 359 Point Nepean Rd., Dromana (www.visitmornington peninsula.org; ✆ **1800/804 009** in Australia or 03/5950 1579), has plenty of maps and information on the area and can also help book accommodations. It's open daily from 9am to 5pm (except Christmas Day and Good Friday), and from 1 to 5pm on Anzac Day (Apr 25).

EXPLORING THE MORNINGTON PENINSULA

The coastline of the Mornington Peninsula is lined with good beaches and thick bush. The **Cape Shanck Coastal Park** stretches along the peninsula's Bass Strait foreshore from Portsea to Cape Shanck. It's home to gray kangaroos, southern brown bandicoots, echidnas, native rats, mice, reptiles, bats, and many forest and ocean birds. The park has numerous interconnecting walking tracks providing access to some remote beaches. You can get more information on this and all the other Victorian national parks from www.park web.vic.gov.au or by calling ✆ **131 963.**

Along the route to the south, stop at the **Mornington Peninsula Regional Gallery,** 350 Dunns Rd., Mornington (www.mprg.mornpen.vic.gov.au; ✆ **03/5975 4395**), to check out the work of well-known Australian artists (Tues–Sun 10am–5pm; admission A$4), or visit the summit at **Arthurs Seat State Park** for glorious views of the coastline. At Sorrento, take time out to spot pelicans on the jetty or visit the town's many galleries.

If you are traveling with kids, stop in at Australia's oldest maze, **Ashcombe Maze & Lavender Gardens,** 15 Shoreham Rd., Shoreham (www.ashcombe maze.com.au; ✆ **03/5989 8387**). In addition to the big hedge maze, there is also a rose maze comprised of 1,200 rose bushes, and the gardens are huge. It also has a pleasant cafe with indoor and outdoor dining. The park is open daily from 9am to 5pm, except Christmas Day; admission is A$19 for adults, A$10 for children 4 to 15, and A$52 to A$66 for families.

For fabulous wildlife viewing, take a night tour of **Moonlit Sanctuary,** 550 Tyabb Tooradin Rd., Pearcedale (www.moonlitsanctuary.com.au; ✆ **03/5978 7935**), at the northern end of the peninsula. The sanctuary is open daily from 10am to 5pm (except Christmas Day), but the best way to see Australia's nocturnal animals is on a guided evening tour. The bushland tour will enable you to see animals such as the eastern quoll, the red-bellied pademelon, and the southern bettong, all of which are extinct in the wild on Australia's mainland. Night tours must be booked in advance (at least by 3pm on the day of your visit). I highly recommend this—it's a wonderful way to see and interact with animals and birds you'd never see during daylight hours! Day admission is A$21 adults, A$11 children 4 to 17, and A$56 families of four (extra children A$7). Night-time admission and guided tour is A$44 adults, A$27 children, A$17 children 3 and under, or A$132 for a family of four (extra children A$22). Night tours begin at dusk, with times varying throughout the year; call ahead for current times.

WHERE TO EAT

The Portsea Hotel ★★ The large restaurant at this Tudor-style pub on the seafront is very popular, and the outdoor beer garden overlooking the sea is hard to beat on a sunny day. This lovely sprawling old hotel has a large terrace area at the back so you can enjoy the sea views from a sheltered spot. The bistro "pier to paddock" menu features plenty of choices for steak-lovers, vegetarians, and diners looking for something a bit different—try the miso black barramundi (fish) with black miso broth, sesame ginger–tossed shitake, sautéed Chinese broccoli, and green onion. Daily seafood specials change according to the local catch of the day. There's also a kids' menu. After dining, it's an easy walk down the stairs through the sand dunes to the beach below (keep your eye out for dolphins).

3746 Point Nepean Rd., Portsea. www.portseahotel.com.au. ✆ **03/5984 2213.** Main courses A$17–A$41. Sun–Fri noon–9pm; Sat noon–9:30pm.

The Macedon Ranges ★★

Some of Victoria's finest gardens dot the hills and valleys of the Macedon Ranges, just an hour from Melbourne. In bygone times, the wealthy swapped the city's summer heat for the cooler climes of Macedon. Their legacy of "hill station" private gardens and impressive mansions, along with the region's 40 cool-climate wineries and gourmet foods, are enough reason to visit.

ESSENTIALS

GETTING THERE & GETTING AROUND The Macedon Ranges are less than an hour's drive from Melbourne along the Calder Freeway, which is a continuation of the Tullamarine Freeway. Follow the signs toward Bendigo until you reach Gisborne, and then move off the freeway. **V/Line** (www.vline.com.au; ✆ **136 196** in Australia) trains from Melbourne to Bendigo pass through the Macedon Ranges, stopping at stations including Macedon, Woodend, Kyneton, and Malmsbury.

VISITOR INFORMATION There are two visitor information centers in the region: the **Woodend Visitor Centre,** 711 High St., Woodend (✆ **03/5427 2033**), and the **Kyneton Visitor Information Centre,** 127 High St., Kyneton (✆ **03/5422 6110**). Both share the same telephone information line (✆ **1800/244 711**) and are open daily 9am to 5pm (except Christmas Day and Good Friday). The website **www.visitmacedonranges.com** is also a good source of information.

EXPLORING THE MACEDON RANGES

The best times to visit the Macedon Ranges for the gardens are April (autumn) and November (spring). Some private homestead gardens are open to the public, including **Duneira** (www.duneira.com.au; ✆ **03/5426 1490**) and **Tieve Tara** (www.gardensoftievetara.com.au; ✆ **0418/337 813** mobile phone) at Mount Macedon; and **Bringalbit,** near Kyneton (www.bringalbit.com.au; ✆ **03/5423 7223**). It pays to call ahead to check times and access (the gardens are often closed in winter). Entry fees apply.

At **Hanging Rock Recreation Reserve,** South Rock Road, Woodend (✆ **1800/244 711** in Australia or 0418/373 032 [mobile] for the ranger), the ghost of Miranda, the fictional schoolgirl who vanished at Hanging Rock in author Joan Lindsay's 1967 novel *Picnic at Hanging Rock,* is never far away. Peter Weir's 1975 film of the novel cemented its fame, but the natural beauty of the area overshadows its slightly spooky reputation. You can climb the rock, walk the tracks, and explore caves like the Black Hole of Calcutta and the Cathedral. You can take a guided tour (night tours are offered in summer). The Hanging Rock Discovery Centre explains the geology and history of the area and revisits the book and movie. The reserve is also home to lots of wildlife including koalas, kangaroos, sugar gliders, echidnas, and wallabies. It's open daily 9am to 5pm (except Christmas Day). Admission is A$10 per car or A$4 per pedestrian.

After the gold rush of the 1850s, Woodend became a resort town with guesthouses, gardens, a racecourse, a golf club, and hotels. Reminders of those days are found in the historical buildings and clock tower on High Street. Cafes, boutiques, and galleries abound. Stop in for a beer at the family-run **Holgate Brewhouse,** in the historic Keatings Hotel on High Street (www.holgatebrewhouse.com; ✆ **03/5427 2510**). They produce a range of draught beers, and you can buy "tastings" until you decide on your favorite. The beer is brewed using just four ingredients—malt, hops, yeast, and pure Macedon Ranges water. It's open daily noon 'til late (except Christmas Day).

The hamlet of **Malmsbury** offers two main reasons to stop along the Calder Highway. First, the **Malmsbury Botanic Gardens,** next to the Town Hall, were designed to take advantage of the Coliban River valley and a billabong that was transformed into a group of ornamental lakes. The 5-hectare (12-acre) gardens have a superb collection of mature trees; it's also a popular spot for barbecues, and at Apple Hole you'll find kids leaping into the river from a rope swing. At quiet times, you may even spot a platypus. But Malmsbury's most famous landmark may be the **bluestone railway viaduct** built by 4,000 men in 1859. At 25m (82 ft.) high, with five 18m (59-ft.) spans, it is one of Australia's longest stone bridges and is best viewed from the gardens. I also like to pop in to **Tin Shed Arts** (✆ **03/5423 2144**), a spacious gallery on the highway that always has something interesting and unexpected. It hangs contemporary and traditional art from both local artists and well-known names from around Australia. You'll find paintings, mixed media, sculpture, and craftwork. It's open Friday to Monday 10am to 5pm. The gallery is next door to the **Malmsbury Bakery** (✆ **03/5423 2369**), a local institution where you'll find plenty of tempting hot pies, bread, and pastries. The gallery and bakery share a website: www.malmsburybakeryandgallery.com.au.

In **Kyneton,** turn down **Piper Street** for antiques, homewares, cafes, a heritage pub, and more. The **Kyneton Farmers' Market** is held at Saint Paul's Park in Piper Street on the second Saturday of the month from 8:30am to 1pm.

With more than 40 vineyards and 20 cellar doors in the region, wine buffs who want to sample the product should consider a tour. **Victoria Winery**

Tours (www.winetours.com.au; ✆ **1800/946 386** in Australia or 03/5428 8500) runs small-group (minimum 2 people) day tours from Melbourne, visiting four or five wineries. Pickup in Melbourne is at 9am, returning by about 5:30pm. The A$180 cost per person includes morning tea and lunch.

WHERE TO EAT

Pizza Verde Woodfire Kitchen ★★ PIZZA If you like your pizza thin and crisp, made from organic or gluten-free flour, and adorned with tasty organic toppings, then this 1950s-style diner is the place for you. Some unlikely combinations include the "green" pizza—topped with zucchini, ricotta, mint, garlic, and lemon (with optional chili)—or the potato-topped pizza with caramelized onion jam and pancetta. Some have the traditional tomato base, others an olive-oil base. There are also meatballs, chicken wings, and other wood-fired dishes for those who don't want pizza.

62 Piper St., Kyneton. www.pizzaverde.com.au. ✆ **03/5422 7400.** Main courses A$18–A$26. Kids' pizzas (until 5pm) A$9. Wed–Fri 5pm–late; Sat–Sun noon–3pm and 5pm–late.

Daylesford ★★★

108km (67 miles) NW of Melbourne

Daylesford can be a terrific day trip from Melbourne or can easily be combined with a trip to the Macedon Ranges (see above). Part of "spa country," this village is a bit of a trendy getaway for Melburnians. Along the main street, you'll find small galleries, homewares shops, and some smart foodie outlets.

ESSENTIALS

GETTING THERE From Melbourne, take the CityLink toll road (the M2) north toward Melbourne Airport. Take the Calder Highway turnoff toward Bendigo (M79) and continue until you see the turnoff to Daylesford (C792); then follow the signs. The road will take you through Woodend, Tylden, and Trentham. At Trentham take the C317 to Daylesford. When you arrive in Daylesford, turn right at the roundabout as signposted to get to Hepburn Springs.

VISITOR INFORMATION The **Daylesford Regional Visitor Information Centre,** 98 Vincent St. (www.visitdaylesford.com.au; ✆ **1800/454 891** in Australia or 03/5321 6123), features an interpretive display about the area's mineral waters. It's open daily from 9am to 5pm, except Christmas Day.

EXPLORING DAYLESFORD

Australians have been heading to Hepburn Springs, on the edge of Daylesford, to "take the waters" since 1895, and the region now has about a dozen or so day spas. The original, and most famous, is **Hepburn Bathhouse & Spa** (www.hepburnbathhouse.com; ✆ **03/5321 6000**). Not everyone likes the slick, modern, and rather cold new extension that has replaced the elegant old wooden building, but sink into the hot pools and it's easy to forget what the exterior looks like. There's traditional communal bathing in the Bathhouse and the Sanctuary, or you can book in to the Spa (in the original bathhouse building; reservations essential) for the usual range of therapies and treatments. The complex includes an aroma steam room, salt therapy pool, relaxation pool, and "spa couches" submerged in mineral water (which I didn't find very comfortable). The complex is on Mineral Springs Reserve Road and is open Monday to Thursday 9am to 6:30pm, Friday 9am to 8pm, Saturday 8am to 8pm, and Sunday 8am to 6:30pm (or 8pm on long weekends). Closed Christmas Day. Tuesday to Thursday Bathhouse entry for 2 hours costs A$34 adults, A$20 children 2 to 16, and A$90 for a family of four; Friday to Monday and on public holidays it's A$44 adults, A$25 children, and A$138 families. Towel rental is A$5. Entry to the Bathhouse and Sanctuary is A$74 Tuesday to Thursday and A$94 Friday to Monday and public holidays, including towel and robe rental. A 30-minute private mineral bath at The Spa costs from A$89 to A$99 depending on the day of the week.

On the hill behind Daylesford's main street is **The Convent** (www.conventgallery.com.au; ✆ **03/5348 3211**), a historic 19th-century mansion, complete with twisting staircases. The Convent comprises a restaurant, a gallery, gardens, a chapel, and shops, as well as a small museum that speaks to its origins as a private home, which later became the Holy Cross Convent and Boarding School for Girls. After years of dereliction, it reopened as a gallery in 1991, but the nuns' infirmary and one of the "cells," or bedrooms, were left unrestored. You'll find it on the corner of Hill and Daly streets. It's open daily 10am to 4pm (3pm on New Year's Eve), closed Good Friday, Christmas Day, Boxing Day (Dec 26), and New Year's Day. Admission is A$5 per person. Take time to wander through the lovely gardens, with their sculptures and bench seats.

Just outside Daylesford is **Lavandula** (www.lavandula.com.au; ✆ **03/5476 4393**), a Swiss-Italian lavender farm that has a rustic trattoria-style cafe and a cobblestone courtyard with a cluster of farmhouse buildings. Swiss immigrants ran a dairy farm here in the 1860s, but today you can see the process of lavender farming and buy lavender products. The restored stone farmhouse is a picturesque backdrop to gardens where you can picnic, play *boules* (similar to bocce), or just relax and admire the scenery. The lavender is in full bloom in December, with harvesting in January. Lavandula is at 350 Hepburn-Newstead Rd., Shepherds Flat, about 10 minutes' drive north of Daylesford. It is open Friday to Tuesday from 10:30am to 5:30pm September to May (except Dec 23–26) and only on Saturday, Sunday, public holidays, and school holidays in June, July, and August. Admission is A$4 adults, A$1 school-age children.

WHERE TO EAT

The Lake House ★★★ Treat yourself to one of Australia's best restaurants while you're in Daylesford. Set on the edge of Lake Daylesford, on 2.4 hectares (6 acres) of beautiful gardens, the Lake House is the creation of Alla and Allan Wolf-Tasker. Alla is the executive chef, and Allan's vibrant artworks adorn the walls of the light-filled restaurant overlooking the lake (and adjoining the accommodation, if you can't tear yourself away). The restaurant is renowned for its commitment to local and seasonal produce, and the menu changes daily. If—like me—you are tempted by tastes not often on offer at city restaurants, you will relish the offerings on the lunch menu: for example, a shared plate of Murray River cod, trout, eel, yabbies garnished with watercress and wild fennel; or roasted free-range duck with coffee-roasted carrots, black barley, almonds, and carrot-top pesto. Walk it off on the track around the lake!

King St., Daylesford, VIC 3460. www.lakehouse.com.au. © **03/5348 3329.** Lunch and dinner A$95–A$120 for 2 to 4 courses; 8-course tasting menu A$155. Daily noon–2:30pm and 6–9pm.

Ballarat ★★★

113km (70 miles) W of Melbourne

History buffs will love Ballarat. Victoria's largest inland city (pop. 90,000) is synonymous with two major events in Australia's past: the gold rush of the 1850s and the birth of Australian democracy in the early–20th century. It all started with gold; in 1851 two prospectors found gold nuggets scattered on the ground at a place known as, ironically, Poverty Point. Within a year, 20,000 people had drifted into the area, and Australia's El Dorado gold rush had begun.

In 1858, the second-largest chunk of gold discovered in Australia (the Welcome Nugget) was found, but by the early 1860s, most of the easy diggings were gone. Larger operators continued digging until 1918, but by then

A eureka MOMENT

The story that is central to Ballarat's history, and many of its attractions, is that of the **Eureka Uprising** in 1854. The story goes like this: After gold was discovered, the government introduced gold licenses, charging miners even if they came up empty-handed. The miners had to buy a license every month, and corrupt gold-field police (many of whom were former convicts) instituted a vicious campaign to extract the money. When license checks intensified in 1854, resentment flared. Prospectors began demanding political reforms, such as the right to vote, parliamentary elections, and secret ballots. The situation exploded when the Eureka Hotel's owner murdered a miner but was set free by the government. The hotel was burned down in revenge, and more than 20,000 prospectors joined together, burned their licenses in a huge bonfire, and built a stockade over which they raised a flag. Troops arrived at the "Eureka Stockade" the next month, but only 150 miners remained. The stockade was attacked at dawn, with 24 miners killed and 30 wounded. The uprising forced the government to act: The licenses were replaced with "miners' rights" and cheaper fees, and the vote was introduced to Victoria. It was a definitive moment in Australia's history, and the Eureka flag (p. 154) is still a potent (and often controversial) symbol of nationalism.

Ballarat had developed enough industry to survive without mining. Today, you can still see the gold rush's effects in the impressive buildings, built from the miners' fortunes, lining Ballarat's streets.

ESSENTIALS

GETTING THERE From Melbourne, Ballarat is a 1½-hour drive on the Great Western Highway. **V/Line** (www.vline.com.au; ✆ **136 196** in Victoria, or 03/8608 5011) runs trains between the cities every day; the trip takes about 90 minutes.

Several companies offer day trips from Melbourne. They include **AAT Kings** (www.aatkings.com; ✆ **1300/228 546** in Australia). A full-day tour costs A$165 for adults and A$83 for children ages 2 to 15.

VISITOR INFORMATION The **Ballarat Visitor Information Centre** is at 225 Sturt St., in the Ballarat Town Hall (www.visitballarat.com.au; ✆ **1800/446 633** in Australia or 03/5337 4337). It is open daily from 9am to 5pm (except Christmas Day).

EXPLORING BALLARAT

Art Gallery of Ballarat ★★★ This excellent gallery, founded in 1884, is Australia's oldest regional gallery and houses a fine collection of Australian art, including paintings from the Heidelberg School and a stunning collection of 20th-century modernists. It also hosts interesting contemporary exhibitions on popular themes (there is usually a fee for these). Free guided tours at 2pm daily.

40 Lydiard St. N. www.artgalleryofballarat.com.au. ✆ **03/5320 5858.** Free. Daily 10am–5pm. Closed Christmas Day and Boxing Day (Dec 26).

Ballarat Botanical Gardens ★★★ These delightful gardens are well worth visiting. The gold-rich citizens of Ballarat bestowed magnificent gifts on the gardens from its early days, including the collection of 12 marble statues that now stand in the conservatory, the elegant Statuary Pavilion and its contents—including the wonderful *Flight from Pompeii*—and a statue of William Wallace near the gardens' entrance. Other highlights include Prime Ministers Avenue, lined with bronze busts of Australia's 28 former PMs, and the striking Australian Ex-Prisoners of War Memorial at the southwestern end of the gardens. One of the greatest attractions is an avenue of 70 giant redwoods, planted about 130 years ago. Free guided tours run every Sunday at 11am and on request by advance booking. The gardens' cafe overlooks Lake Wendouree.

Wendouree Parade. www.ballaratbotanicalgardens.com.au. ✆ **03/5320 5135.** Free. Daily 7:30am–9pm (Oct–Apr) and 7:30am–6pm (May–Sept). Conservatory daily 9am–4:30pm. Bus: 16.

Blood on the Southern Cross ★★★ This breathtaking sound-and-light show re-creates the Eureka Uprising, one of the most important events in Australia's history (see box, above). You will be outdoors, so bring something warm to wear because it can get chilly at night. It's stirring stuff, and the reenactment does the story justice. The 90-minute show is full of surprises.

Sovereign Hill, Bradshaw St. www.sovereignhill.com.au. ✆ **03/5337 1199.** Reservations required. A$60 adults, A$32 children 5–15, A$162 families of 4. Package with daytime entry to Sovereign Hill and dinner (see below), A$150 adults, A$76 children, A$400 families. Ask about packages with overnight accommodations. 2 shows nightly (times vary seasonally).

The Gold Museum ★ A 4.4kg (nearly 10 lb.) gold nugget—known as "Goldasaurus"—is the latest highlight in this surprisingly interesting small museum. Found by a local prospector, it is one of the things you will discover here, as well as a large collection of gold nuggets found at Ballarat, displays of alluvial deposits, gold ornaments, coins, and the history of gold mining in the area.

Bradshaw St. (opposite Sovereign Hill). ✆ **03/5337 1107.** A$15 adults, A$8 children 5–15, A$37 family of 6. Free with entry to Sovereign Hill (see below). Daily 9:30am–5:30pm. Closed Christmas Day.

Museum of Australian Democracy at Eureka ★★ The highlight of a visit to Australia's newest museum—especially after you've learned the story of the Eureka Uprising (see "A Eureka Moment," p. 152)—is the sight of the original Eureka flag, made from petticoat fabric by the women of the

The Sovereign Hill living history museum illuminates Victoria's 1850s gold-rush era.

uprising and now enshrined here. The museum features an evocative, purpose-built display gallery for the beautiful, fragile blue-and-white Eureka Flag. Interactive exhibitions look at the evolution and future of democracy and associated issues such as culture, civics, history, and citizenship. It also has a cafe, gift shop, and gardens. Guided tours run daily at 11am.

102 Stawell St. S. (at Eureka St.). www.made.org. ✆ **1800/287 113** in Australia. A$12 adults, A$8 children 6–15, A$34 families. Daily 10am–5pm. Closed Christmas Day.

Sovereign Hill ★★★ Living in the gold-rush times wasn't all beer and skittles, and the latest multimillion-dollar underground exhibit at this colonial-era "living museum" tells the story of a mining disaster that struck in 1882. "Trapped" is a multisensory experience that tells a story of bravery, love, and loss. Ballarat's history comes to life at Sovereign Hill, long described as Australia's best outdoor museum, which transports you back to the 1850s and the heady days of the gold rush. More than 40 reproduction buildings, including shops and businesses on Main Street, sit on the 25-hectare (62-acre) former gold-mining site. There are also tent camps around the diggings on what would have been the outskirts of town. Sovereign Hill has a lot to see and do, so expect to spend at least 4 hours here. The township bustles with actors in period costumes going about their daily business. You can pan for real gold, ride in horse-drawn carriages, and watch potters, blacksmiths, and tanners make their wares. Don't miss the gold pour at the smelting works, or the redcoats as they parade through the streets. On top of Sovereign Hill are the mineshafts and pithead equipment. The guided tour of a typical underground gold mine takes around 45 minutes and costs A$7.50 for adults, A$4 for children, and A$20 for a family of six. A restaurant and several cafes and souvenir stores are scattered around the site.

Bradshaw St. www.sovereignhill.com.au. ✆ **03/5337 1199.** A$56 adults, A$25 children 5–15, A$100–A$140 families. **VIP Gold Pass** (including Gold Museum, unlimited coach rides, mine tour, and 1 souvenir costume photograph, Devonshire tea, and more) A$102 adults, A$46 children, A$204–A$246 family. Daily 10am–5pm. Closed Christmas Day. Bus: no. 9 from Curtis St. or the railway station. A free bus meets the weekday 9:17am (9:14am on Sat, 9:34am on Sun) train (the "Goldrush Special" from Melbourne's Southern Cross railway station) when it arrives at Ballarat Station and takes visitors direct to Sovereign Hill. Return service connects with the 3:52pm (4:16pm on Sat–Sun) train back to Melbourne.

WHERE TO EAT

Eclectic Tastes ★★ CAFE After a renovation in 2016, this unusual cafe, spread out over five rooms, serves up all-day breakfast, lunch, coffee, and snack. Take up the crayons and doodle on the paper tablecloth as you ponder the menu offerings, which may include simple sweet corn fritters, a roast beetroot salad, or Eclectic's own take on *yum cha* (similar to dim sum), with pork dumplings, chicken, and bokchoy gyozas, prawn toast, and an Asian-style salad. You'll find this smart little cafe opposite the Ballarat Cemetery near the shores of Lake Wendouree (a bit off the beaten track but worth the effort).

2 Burnbank St. www.eclectictastes.com.au. ✆ **03/5339 3391.** Main courses A$18–A$24. Mon–Fri 7am–4:30pm; Sat–Sun 8am–4pm.

Oscar's ★ CONTEMPORARY This cafe and bar inside one of Ballarat's historic old pubs is in the heart of the town, walking distance from shopping, the art gallery, and many other attractions. The former gold rush–era hotel has an appealing open-plan restaurant, with a courtyard and bar. It's open for breakfast, lunch, and dinner, and you can get snacks all day. Meals include Asian specialties, pizzas, pasta, steaks, and gluten-free dishes.

18 Doveton St. S. www.oscarshotel.com.au. ✆ **03/5331 1451.** Main courses A$21–A$37. Daily 7am–10pm.

BRISBANE

Brisbane is one of those cities that seems always to be changing, without ever losing its essential heart and character. It's that most Australian of cities—big-hearted, blue-skied, and with a down-to-earth attitude that soon rubs off on you. Brisbane will most likely be your first port of call in Queensland, and you can even reach the southernmost part of the Great Barrier Reef on a day trip from here.

Brisbane (pronounced *Briz*-bun), "Brizzie" to locals, functions on a very human scale. It's a place where you can cuddle koalas, join bronzed urbanites on the beaches on the weekend, and sunbathe by the Brisbane River while gazing up at gleaming skyscrapers. Beyond landmarks such as the 1920s **City Hall** and the **Treasury Building's** graceful colonnades, Brisbane's major attractions are outdoors. Cool down under a canopy of subtropical foliage at the **Brisbane Botanic Gardens.** Gaze at contemporary art at the **Gallery of Modern Art (GOMA),** dinosaurs at the **Queensland Museum,** and the city skyline from the gently revolving **Wheel of Brisbane.** Koalas—more than 130 of them—beg a cuddle at the **Lone Pine Koala Sanctuary.**

The **city center** and surrounding suburbs represent fusion cuisine at its finest. Party and dining hotspot **Fortitude Valley** serves the world on a plate—everything from Spanish tapas to Thai—in chic lounge-style restaurants. **South Bank** goes alfresco in casual eateries dishing up fresh seafood and modern Australian fare, with glittering Brisbane River views.

On the city river bank, opposite South Bank and adjacent to the Treasury Casino and Hotel, a major redevelopment to be called **Queen's Wharf** is taking shape and will transform the city over the next 5 years. It will include five new hotels, three residential towers, around 50 new restaurants, cafes, and bars, and a riverfront outdoor cinema. A pedestrian bridge will link the precinct to South Bank.

ESSENTIALS

Arriving

BY PLANE About 30 international airlines serve Brisbane from Europe, North America, Asia, and New Zealand. From North America, you can fly direct from Los Angeles to Brisbane on

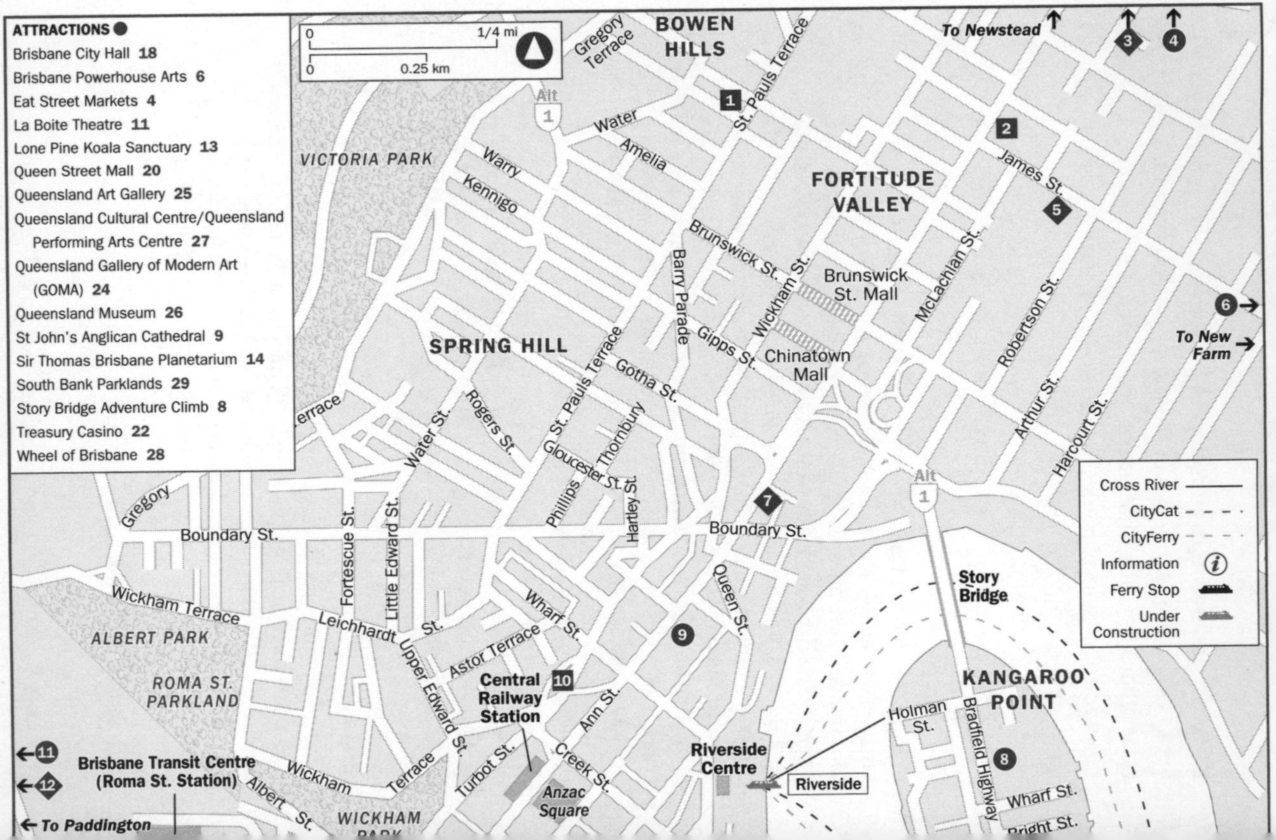
ATTRACTIONS
Brisbane City Hall 18
Brisbane Powerhouse Arts 6
Eat Street Markets 4
La Boite Theatre 11
Lone Pine Koala Sanctuary 13
Queen Street Mall 20
Queensland Art Gallery 25
Queensland Cultural Centre/Queensland Performing Arts Centre 27
Queensland Gallery of Modern Art (GOMA) 24
Queensland Museum 26
St John's Anglican Cathedral 9
Sir Thomas Brisbane Planetarium 14
South Bank Parklands 29
Story Bridge Adventure Climb 8
Treasury Casino 22
Wheel of Brisbane 28
0 1/4 mi
0 0.25 km
Cross River
CityCat
CityFerry
Information
Ferry Stop
Under Construction
To Newstead
To New Farm
To Paddington
BOWEN HILLS
FORTITUDE VALLEY
SPRING HILL
VICTORIA PARK
ALBERT PARK
ROMA ST. PARKLAND
KANGAROO POINT
WICKHAM PARK
Brunswick St. Mall
Chinatown Mall
Story Bridge
Central Railway Station
Riverside Centre
Riverside
Anzac Square
Brisbane Transit Centre (Roma St. Station)
Gregory Terrace
St. Pauls Terrace
Water
Amelia
Warry
Kennigo
James St.
Brunswick St.
Wickham St.
McLachlan St.
Robertson St.
Arthur St.
Harcourt St.
Barry Parade
Gipps St.
Gotha St.
Rogers St.
Water St.
Thornbury
Gloucester St.
Phillips
Hartley St.
Boundary St.
Gregory
Fortescue St.
Little Edward St.
Leichhardt St.
Upper Edward St.
Wickham Terrace
Astor Terrace
Wharf St.
Queen St.
Ann St.
Creek St.
Turbot St.
Albert St.
Holman St.
Bradfield Highway
Bright St.
Alt 1

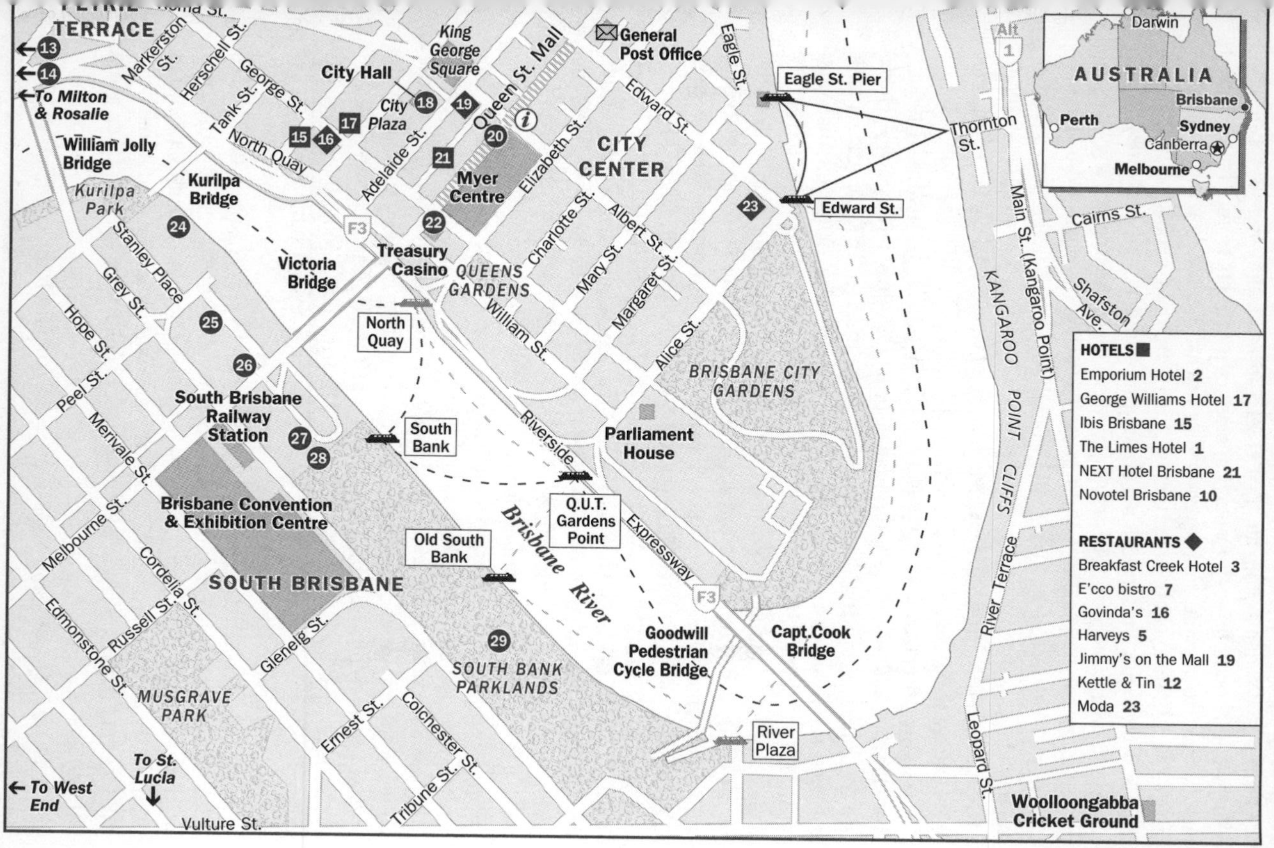
AUSTRALIA
Darwin
Brisbane
Perth
Sydney
Canberra
Melbourne
HOTELS
Emporium Hotel 2
George Williams Hotel 17
Ibis Brisbane 15
The Limes Hotel 1
NEXT Hotel Brisbane 21
Novotel Brisbane 10
RESTAURANTS
Breakfast Creek Hotel 3
E'cco bistro 7
Govinda's 16
Harveys 5
Jimmy's on the Mall 19
Kettle & Tin 12
Moda 23
TERRACE
To Milton & Rosalie
Markerston St.
Herschell St.
George St.
Tank St.
North Quay
King George Square
City Hall
City Plaza
Queen St. Mall
Adelaide St.
Myer Centre
Elizabeth St.
General Post Office
Eagle St.
Edward St.
CITY CENTER
Eagle St. Pier
Edward St.
Thornton St.
Alt 1
Main St. (Kangaroo Point)
Cairns St.
Shafston Ave.
KANGAROO POINT CLIFFS
River Terrace
Leopard St.
Woolloongabba Cricket Ground
William Jolly Bridge
Kurilpa Bridge
Kurilpa Park
Stanley Place
Grey St.
Hope St.
Peel St.
Merivale St.
Melbourne St.
Cordelia St.
Russell St.
Edmonstone St.
MUSGRAVE PARK
To St. Lucia
To West End
Vulture St.
F3
Treasury Casino
Victoria Bridge
QUEENS GARDENS
Charlotte St.
Albert St.
Mary St.
Margaret St.
William St.
Alice St.
BRISBANE CITY GARDENS
Parliament House
Riverside
Expressway
North Quay
South Bank
South Brisbane Railway Station
Brisbane Convention & Exhibition Centre
SOUTH BRISBANE
Glenelg St.
Q.U.T. Gardens Point
Old South Bank
Brisbane River
Goodwill Pedestrian Cycle Bridge
Capt.Cook Bridge
River Plaza
SOUTH BANK PARKLANDS
Ernest St.
Colchester St.
Tribune St.

Qantas, but from other places you will likely fly to Sydney first, then take a connecting flight to Brisbane, or come via Auckland, New Zealand.

Qantas (www.qantas.com.au; ✆ **131 313** in Australia) and its subsidiary **QantasLink** (book through Qantas) operate daily flights from all state capitals, Cairns, Townsville, and several other towns. **Jetstar** (www.jetstar.com.au; ✆ **131 538** in Australia) has daily service from the Queensland centers of Cairns, Townsville, Proserpine, and Hamilton Island, as well as Sydney, Melbourne, Hobart, and other Australian cities. **Virgin Australia** (www.virginaustralia.com.au; ✆ **136 789** in Australia) offers direct services from all capital cities as well as Cairns, Townsville, Hamilton Island, and Proserpine in the Whitsundays, and other centers. **Scoot** (www.flyscoot.com; ✆ **02/9009 0860** in Australia) flies from Sydney, Melbourne, Darwin, Adelaide, Perth, the Whitsunday Coast, and Cairns.

Brisbane International Airport (www.bne.com.au) is 16km (10 miles) from the city, and the domestic terminal is 2km (1¼ miles) farther away. There is a free inter-terminal bus, or you can catch the train (p. 163) for A$5. A taxi between terminals costs about A$15. The arrivals floor of the international terminal, on Level 2, has a check-in counter for passengers transferring to domestic flights and an information desk to meet all flights, help with flight inquiries, dispense tourist information, and make hotel bookings. **Travelex** currency-exchange bureaus are on the departures and arrivals floors. **Avis** (✆ **07/3633 8666**), **Budget** (✆ **1300/362 848** in Australia or 07/3000 1030), **Europcar** (✆ **131 390** in Australia or 07/3874 8150), **Hertz** (✆ **07/3860 4580**) **Thrifty** (✆ **07/3000 8600**), and local company **Red Spot Rentals** (✆ **1300/668 810** in Australia or 07/3860 6274) have desks on Level 2. On levels 2, 3, and 4 you will find ATMs, free showers, and baby-changing rooms. The domestic terminal has a Travelex currency-exchange bureau, ATMs, showers, and the big four car-rental desks. For security reasons, luggage lockers are not available at either terminal.

Con-x-ion (www.cxn.com.au; ✆ **1300/918 923** in Australia) runs a shuttle between the airport and city hotels and the Brisbane Transit Centre every 30 minutes from 5am to 11pm. The one-way cost is A$15 per person (or A$25 for two; cheaper the more in your group). The trip takes about 40 minutes. No public buses serve the airport. A **taxi** to the city costs around A$40, plus a A$3.40 airport fee for departing taxis.

Airtrain (www.airtrain.com.au; ✆ **1800/119 091** in Australia or 07/3216 3308), a rail link between the city and Brisbane's domestic and international airport terminals, runs every 15 minutes from around 5am (6am Sat–Sun) to 10pm daily. Fares from the airport to city stations are A$18 per adult one way, A$34 round trip; children ages 14 and under travel free. The trip takes about 20 minutes.

BY TRAIN **Queensland Rail** (www.queenslandrailtravel.com.au; ✆ **1300/131 722** in Australia or 07/3606 6630) operates long-distance trains north from Brisbane along the coast. The swish Spirit of Queensland takes about 24 hours between Brisbane and Cairns and costs A$390 for an airline-style "rail bed" seat, and includes meals. The high-speed Tilt Train takes about 4½ hours from Brisbane to Bundaberg or 7½ hours to Rockhampton. NSW Trainlink (www.nswtrainlink.info; ✆ **132 232** in Australia) runs daily train services to Brisbane from Sydney. The trip takes around 14½ hours, with the final 3½ hours (from the town of Casino, south of the Queensland border) by bus. Fares vary but cost around A$91 for an adult economy seat or A$130 for a first-class seat. A sleeper costs around A$210.

All intercity and interstate trains pull into the city center's **Brisbane Transit Centre at Roma Street,** often called the Roma Street Transit Centre. From here, most city and Spring Hill hotels are a few blocks' walk or a quick cab ride away. The station has food outlets, showers, tourist information, and lockers.

Queensland Rail CityTrain (✆ **131 230** in Queensland) provides daily train service from the Sunshine Coast and plentiful service from the Gold Coast.

BY BUS All intercity and interstate coaches pull into the Brisbane Transit Centre (see "By Train," above). **Greyhound Australia** (www.greyhound.com.au; ✆ **1300/473 946** in Australia or 07/3336 5591 for the Brisbane terminal) serves the city several times daily. A one-way Cairns-Brisbane ticket costs around A$320; the trip takes nearly 30 hours. The Sydney-Brisbane trip takes about 17 hours and costs around A$190 one way.

BY CAR The Bruce Highway from Cairns enters the city from the north. The Pacific Highway enters Brisbane from the south.

Visitor Information

The **Brisbane Visitor Information Centre** (www.visitbrisbane.com.au; ✆ **07/3006 6290**) is in the Regent Theatre building in the Queen Street Mall, between Edward and Albert streets. It's open Monday through Thursday from 9am to 5:30pm, Friday 9am to 7pm, Saturday 9am to 5pm, Sunday 10am to 5pm, public holidays 9:30am to 4:30pm, and from 1pm on Anzac Day (Apr 25). It's closed Christmas Day and Good Friday. There are also visitor information centers at the airport, and at South Bank Parklands (p. 176).

City Layout

The city center's office towers shimmer in the sun on the north bank of a curve of the Brisbane River. At the tip of the curve are the lush Brisbane City Gardens (sometimes called the City Botanic Gardens). The 30m (98-ft.) sandstone cliffs of Kangaroo Point rise on the eastern side of the south bank; to the west are the South Bank Parklands and the Queensland Cultural Centre, known as South Bank. Two pedestrian bridges link South Bank with the city: The **Goodwill Bridge** links South Bank with the City Gardens, while the **Kurilpa Bridge** links Tank Street, in the city center, with the Gallery of Modern Art at South Bank. To the west 5km (3 miles), Mount Coot-tha (pronounced *Coo*-tha) looms out of the flat plain.

Post Office Square, a shopping and leisure area in downtown Brisbane.

MAIN ARTERIES & STREETS It's easy to find your way around central Brisbane once you know that the east-west streets are named after female British royalty, and the north-south streets are named after their male counterparts. The northernmost is Ann, followed by Adelaide, Queen, Elizabeth, Charlotte, Mary, Margaret, and Alice. From east to west, the streets are Edward, Albert, George, and William, which becomes North Quay, flanking the river's northeast bank.

Queen Street, the main thoroughfare, becomes a pedestrian mall between Edward and George streets. Roma Street exits the city diagonally to the northwest. Ann Street leads all the way east into Fortitude Valley. The main street in Fortitude Valley is Brunswick Street, which runs into New Farm.

Neighborhoods in Brief

City Center The vibrant city center is where Brisbane residents eat, shop, and socialize. Queen Street Mall, in the heart of town, is popular with shoppers and moviegoers, especially on weekends and Friday night (when stores stay open until 9pm). The Eagle Street financial and legal precinct has great restaurants with views of the river and Story Bridge. Much of the city's surviving colonial architecture is here, too. Strollers, bike riders, and in-line skaters shake the summer heat in the green haven of the Brisbane City Gardens at the business district's southern end.

Fortitude Valley "The Valley," as locals call it, was once one of the sleazier parts of town. Today, it is a stamping ground for street-smart young folk who meet in restored pubs and eat in cool cafes. The lanterns, food stores, and shopping mall of Chinatown are here, too. On weekends, you'll find Brisbane's only alternative market, Valley Markets in the Brunswick Street and Chinatown malls (take Turbot Street from the city center). Venture a little farther to the trendy boutiques and cafes of James Street.

New Farm Always an appealing suburb, New Farm is an in-spot for cafe-hopping. Merthyr Street is where the action is, especially on Friday and Saturday nights. From the intersection of Wickham and Brunswick streets, follow Brunswick southeast for 13 blocks to Merthyr.

Paddington This hilltop suburb, a couple of miles northwest of the city, is one of Brisbane's most attractive. Brightly painted Queenslander cottages line the main street, Latrobe Terrace, as it winds west along a ridge top. Many of the houses have been turned into shops and cafes, where you can browse, enjoy coffee and cake, or just admire the charming architecture.

Milton & Rosalie Park Road, in Milton, is not quite a little bit of Europe, but it tries hard—right down to a replica Eiffel Tower above the cafes and shops. Italian restaurants line the street, buzzing with office workers who down espressos at alfresco restaurants, scout interior-design stores for a new objet d'art, and stock up on European designer rags.

West End This small inner-city enclave is alive with ethnic restaurants, cafes, and the odd, interesting housewares or fashion store. Most action centers on the intersection of Vulture and Boundary streets, where Asian grocers and delis abound.

Getting Around

BY PUBLIC TRANSPORTATION

TransLink operates a single network of buses, trains, and ferries. For timetables and route inquiries, call **TransInfo** (www.translink.com.au; ✆ **131 230**). It uses an integrated ticket system, and the easiest place to buy your tickets is on the buses and ferries or at the train stations. You can also buy tickets and pick up maps and timetables at the Queen Street bus station information center (in the Myer Centre, off Queen Street Mall) and the Brisbane Visitor Information Centre in the Queen Street Mall. Tickets and electronic go cards are also sold at some inner-city newsdealers and convenience stores.

A trip in a single sector or zone on the bus, train, or ferry costs A$4.60. A single ticket is good for up to 2 hours on a one-way journey on any combination of bus, train, or ferry. When traveling with a parent, kids under 5 travel free and kids 5 to 14 and students pay half fare. If you plan on using public transport a lot, it is worth investing in a **go card,** which gives discounted rates (you can also buy online and just top up the card balance as you need it). This reduces the price of a one-zone one-way trip to A$3.20 or less, depending on the time of day. You will probably not need to travel farther than four zones on the transport system. This will cost you the princely sum of A$11. On weekends and public holidays, it's cheaper to buy an **off-peak ticket.** The off-peak ticket is also available on weekdays, but you must plan your sightseeing around the fact that it cannot be used before 8:30am or between 3:30 and 7pm. You might also like to buy a **SEEQ card,** specially designed for visitors, which offers 3 or 5 consecutive days' travel on all public transport services (including to the Gold Coast), including two Airtrain trips. SEEQ cards cost A$79 adults and A$40 children for 3 days or A$129 adults and A$65 children for 5 days.

BY PUBLIC BUS

Buses operate from around 5am to 11pm Monday through Friday, with less service on weekends. On Sunday, many routes stop around 5pm. Most buses depart from City Hall at King George Square, Adelaide, or Ann Street. The Loop is a free bus service that circles the city center. The Loop's distinctive red buses run on two routes, stopping at convenient places including Central Station, Queen Street Mall, City Botanic Gardens, Riverside Centre, and King George Square. Look for the red bus stops. They run every 15 minutes Monday through Friday, from 7am to 6pm.

BY FERRY

The fast **CityCat** ferries run to many places of interest, including South Bank and the Queensland Cultural Centre; the restaurants and Sunday markets at the Riverside Centre; and New Farm Park, not far from the cafes of Merthyr Street. They run every half-hour between the University of Queensland to the south of the city center, and Hamilton to the north (a route of around 20km/ 12 miles). Slower but more frequent CityFerry service (the **Inner City** and

One of Brisbane's speedy CityCat ferries.

Cross River ferries) has stops at points including the south end of South Bank Parklands, Kangaroo Point, and Edward Street right outside the Brisbane City Gardens. Ferries run from around 6am to 10:30pm daily. Two hours on the CityCat takes you the entire length of the run (and there's free Wi-Fi on board too!).

BY TRAIN

Brisbane's suburban rail network is fast, quiet, safe, and clean. Trains run from around 5am to midnight (until about 11pm on Sun). All trains leave Central Station, between Turbot and Ann streets at Edward Street.

BY BICYCLE

CityCycle (www.citycycle.com.au; ✆ **1300/229 253**) has 150 bike parking stations across inner city Brisbane, with bright yellow bikes and helmets (compulsory by law) to hire. You can hire a bike between 5am and 10pm daily and return it to the station at any time. You can buy a casual subscription for A$2 a day, and the first 30 minutes of hire is free. After that, usage charges start from A$2 for 30 minutes and then A$5 for every 30 minutes, to a maximum of A$97—so unless you are only planning a short ride, it's cheaper to hire a bike elsewhere.

BY CAR OR TAXI

Brisbane's grid of one-way streets can be confusing, so plan your route before setting out. Brisbane's biggest parking lot is at the Myer Centre (86 Elizabeth St.), open 24 hours (✆ **07/3229 1699**). Most hotels and motels have free parking for guests.

Avis (✆ **136 333** or 07/3247 0577), **Budget** (✆ **1300/362 848** in Australia or 07/3247 0599), **Europcar** (✆ **131 390** in Australia or 07/3006 7440), **Hertz** (✆ **133 039** or 07/3221 6166) and **Thrifty** (✆ **07/3006 3255** in Australia) all have outlets in the city center.

For a taxi, call **Yellow Cabs** (✆ **131 924** in Australia) or **Black and White Taxis** (✆ **133 222** in Australia). There are taxi stands at each end of Queen Street Mall, on Edward Street and on George Street (outside the Treasury Casino).

[Fast FACTS] BRISBANE

ATMs/Banks Banks are open Monday through Thursday 9:30am to 4pm, until 5pm on Friday.

Business Hours Brisbane shops are open Monday through Thursday 9am to 6pm, Friday 9am to 9pm, Saturday 9am to 5:30pm, and Sunday 10am to 6pm. On Friday evening in the city, the Queen Street Mall is abuzz with cinemagoers and revelers; the late (until 9pm) shopping night in Paddington is Thursday. Some restaurants close Monday night, Tuesday night, or both; bars are generally open from 10 or 11am until midnight.

Dentists **Maven Dental,** 171 Moray St., New Farm (✆ **07/3358 1333**), is open 8am to 7pm Monday through Thursday, and 9am to 5pm Friday and Saturday.

For after-hours emergencies, call for recorded info on whom to contact.

Doctors & Hospitals The **Royal Brisbane Hospital** is about a 15-minute drive from the city at Herston Road, Herston (✆ **07/3636 8111**). The **Travel Doctor** (www.thetraveldoctor.com.au; ✆ **07/3221 9066**) is on Level 5, 247 Adelaide St., between Creek and Edward streets. It's open Monday, Tuesday, Thursday, and Friday 8am to 4:30pm; Wednesday 10am to 6:30pm; and Saturday 8:30am to 2pm.

Embassies & Consulates The United States, Canada, and New Zealand have no representation in Brisbane; see chapter 4, "Sydney," for those countries' nearest offices. The **British Consulate** is at Level 9, 100 Eagle St. (✆ **07/3223 3200**); it's open 9am to 5pm on weekdays.

Emergencies Dial ✆ **000** for fire, ambulance, or police help in an emergency. This is a free call from a private or public telephone. **Lifeline** (✆ **131 114**) is a 24-hour emotional crisis counseling service.

Internet Access The **State Library of Queensland,** Stanley Place, South Bank (www.slq.qld.gov.au; ✆ **07/3840 7666**), has free Internet and computer access, as well as wireless, on levels 1 to 4. The library is open Monday through Thursday 10am to 8pm and Friday through Sunday 10am to 5pm.

Mail & Postage The General Post Office is at 261 Queen St., opposite Post Office Square. It is open Monday through Friday 7am to 6pm and Saturday 9am to 12:30pm.

Newspapers & Magazines The ***Courier-Mail*** (Mon–Sat) and the ***Sunday Mail*** are Brisbane's daily newspapers. Another good news source is the online newspaper ***Brisbane Times*** (www.brisbanetimes.com.au). The free weekly ***Brisbane News*** magazine is a good guide to dining, entertainment, and shopping.

Pharmacies (Chemist Shops) The **Queen Street Pharmacy,** 141 Queen St. (on the mall) (✆ **07/3221 4585**), is open Monday through Thursday 7am to 9pm, Friday 7am to 9:30pm, Saturday 8am to 9pm, Sunday 8:30am to 7pm, and public holidays 9am to 7:30pm.

Police Dial ✆ **000** in an emergency, or ✆ **131 444** for police headquarters. Police are stationed 24 hours a day at 67 Adelaide St. (✆ **07/3224 4444**).

Safety Brisbane is relatively crime free, but as in any large city, be aware of your personal safety, especially when you're out at night. Stick to well-lit streets and busy precincts.

WHERE TO STAY

Expensive

Emporium Hotel ★★★ With its zebra-skin chairs, frangipani motifs, rich fabrics and colors, huge antique chandelier, and French stained-glass window in the cocktail bar, this is Brisbane's grooviest and most eclectic hotel. It has luxury touches such as bathrobes and slippers, a pillow menu, and a pampering menu. The whole place oozes modern elegance. Kitchens—cunningly hidden from view—are standard in all rooms and have a small dishwasher as well as a microwave. One suite is designed for guests with disabilities.

1000 Ann St. www.emporiumhotels.com.au. ✆ **1300/883 611** in Australia, or 07/3253 6999. 102 units, 42 with spa baths. A$199–A$229 double; A$259–A$459 suite. Valet parking A$35 per day. Train: Fortitude Valley. **Amenities:** Restaurant; bar; concierge; exercise room; outdoor heated lap pool; room service; sauna; free Wi-Fi.

The Limes Hotel ★ The first Australian hotel to be part of Design Hotels, the Limes considers itself "backstreet boutique." There are no frills or frippery, but that doesn't mean it's not stylish, interesting, and functional, designed with an eye to what travelers want. Three rooms on the ground floor have courtyards with hammocks and a table and chairs; all are practical in design, with a kitchen area that doubles as a work station. The hotel bar is also home to a popular 30-seat rooftop cinema (run on Wed and Thurs nights), two Jacuzzis, and an area for smokers on the mezzanine. A guest swipe card for lift access ensures security. Breakfast is provided by adjacent restaurant Alfred and Constance and is included in the room rate.

142 Constance St., Fortitude Valley. www.limeshotel.com.au. © **07/3852 9000.** 21 units. A$139–A$359 double. Rates include breakfast. Parking A$20 per day (nearby). Train: Brunswick St. **Amenities:** Bar; free access to nearby health club; free Wi-Fi.

NEXT Hotel Brisbane ★★★ This is one of my favorite Brisbane hotels. Not just for the location—up an escalator at the top of the Queen Street Mall—and fabulous city and river views, but for service that is casual, friendly, and efficient. NEXT opened in 2015 after a major redevelopment transformed one of the city's old hotels into one of its smartest. And I don't just mean the look of it: This is Australia's first hotel to use smart technology that allows guests to control just about everything. You can even use your smartphone as your room "key." Don't have a smartphone? That's okay, there's one in the room for you to use. Add to this an outdoor terrace bar overlooking the 20m lap pool, and "sleep pods" if you're in transit. Don't forget to take advantage of the four free items each day from the mini-bar. Seems they've thought of everything.

72 Queen St. www.silverneedlehotels.com/next. © **1800/303 186** in Australia, or 07/3222 3222. 304 units. A$159–A$209 double. Valet parking A$45. Train: Central. **Amenities:** Restaurant; bar; babysitting; concierge; gym; outdoor pool; room service; free Wi-Fi.

Novotel Brisbane ★★ This well-appointed contemporary hotel, a short walk from Brisbane's main shopping areas, is popular among families and business travelers. Rooms and suites are modern, stylish, and spacious. The lap pool is very inviting and offers terrific city views. For dining, you can choose among **The Restaurant,** the more casual **Plan B** bistro, or an all-day menu in **The Bar.** All rooms are nonsmoking.

200 Creek St. www.novotelbrisbane.com.au. © **1300/656 565** in Australia, or 07/3309 3309. 296 units. A$189–A$329 double. Parking A$25–A$40. Train: Central. **Amenities:** 2 restaurants; bar; babysitting; concierge; gym; outdoor pool; room service; sauna; Wi-Fi (A$28/24 hr.).

Moderate

George Williams Hotel ★★ This smart, great-value hotel had a A$2.5-million refurbishment in 2016 and is a good budget choice for inner-city stays. Rooms are small, but some manage to sleep up to four adults. Queen terrace rooms have a small, sheltered balcony with table and chairs. Among the useful facilities are a 24-hour front desk, a business center, and safe-deposit boxes. Several rooms are designed for guests with disabilities (inquire when booking).

317–325 George St. (btw. Turbot and Ann sts.). www.georgewilliamshotel.com.au. ✆ **1800/064 858** in Australia, or 07/3308 0700. 106 units. A$135–A$450 double. Limited parking, A$24 per night. Train: Roma St. Bus: Downtown Loop. Ferry: North Quay (CityCat or CityFerry). **Amenities:** Restaurant; bar; free Wi-Fi.

Ibis Brisbane ★★ You get what you pay for at this AAA three-and-a-half-star sister property to the Novotel Brisbane (see above). In this case, what you get is a comfortable room—with all new beds in 2015—and the standard amenities you might expect in a large hotel. But the Isis Brisbane has much larger rooms than those in most hotels of this standard, furnished in contemporary style, with sizeable work desks and small but smart bathrooms. If you don't mind doing without river views, porters, a pool, or other small luxuries, this could be the place for you. Guests can also use the restaurant and bar at the adjoining Mercure Brisbane.

27–35 Turbot St. (btw. North Quay and George St.). www.ibishotels.com.au. ✆ **1300/656 565** in Australia or 07/3237 2333. 218 units. A$119–A$139 double. Parking (at the Mercure Brisbane) A$36. Train: Roma St. Bus: Downtown Loop. Ferry: North Quay (CityCat or CityFerry). **Amenities:** Restaurant; bar; babysitting; Wi-Fi (A$28/24 hr.).

WHERE TO EAT

Brisbane has a sophisticated dining scene. Stylish bistros and cafes line the riverfront at South Bank; cute cafes are plentiful in Paddington; Asian eateries are a good choice in West End; and in Fortitude Valley, you'll find Chinatown. A street lined with upscale but laid-back restaurants, many with a Mediterranean flavor, sits under the kitschy replica Eiffel Tower on Park Road in Milton, and in the city center you can find slick waterfront restaurants at Eagle Street Pier and Riverside. The intersection of Albert and Charlotte streets buzzes with inexpensive, good-quality cafes.

Expensive

e'cco bistro ★★★ CONTEMPORARY *E'cco* means "here it is" in Italian, and that's the philosophy behind the food at this award-winning bistro. It serves simple food, done exceptionally well and with passion. In a former tea warehouse on the city fringe, it's one of Australia's best. Dishes include such delights as organic chicken with Jerusalem artichokes, hazelnut, smoked celeriac, and lemon; or free-range suckling pig, with apple, potato foam, and black lime ash. The bistro is enormously popular, so bookings are advisable (although less imperative at lunch). Large windows, bold colors, and modern furniture make it a pleasant setting. There's an extensive wine list—many by the glass.

100 Boundary St. (at Adelaide St.). www.eccobistro.com. ✆ **07/3831 8344.** Reservations required. Main courses A$37–A$41. 5-course tasting menu A$89 (or A$154 with wine pairings). Thurs–Fri noon–2:30pm; Tues–Sat 5:30–10pm. Closed Christmas Day–Jan 2.

Moda ★★★ CONTEMPORARY Whether you choose the more formal and private mezzanine floor or the relaxed courtyard dining area (my pick), you're sure to enjoy this Spanish-flavored restaurant. Owner-chef Javier Codina has combined his Catalan, French, and Italian influences with fresh (often organic) Queensland produce to make some marvelous dishes. The menu changes often, but you might find something like traditional Catalan zarzuela made with Queensland seafood, or a lamb shoulder (for two) with capsicum chutney and Catalan potato. If you're there for Friday lunch (or order ahead), you can sample Javier's wonderful paella (A$39). The share plates for two or four are a good choice, for A$46 or A$78, or Javier's three-course "table experience" for A$89 per person. ***Fair warning:*** The wine list is expensive.

12 Edward St. www.modarestaurant.com.au. ✆ **07/3221 7655.** Main courses A$29–A$45. Thurs–Fri noon–late; Mon–Wed and Sat 6pm–late.

Moderate

Breakfast Creek Hotel ★★ STEAKHOUSE Built in 1889 and listed by the National Trust, this Renaissance-style pub is fondly known as the Brekky Creek—or simply the Creek—and is considered a Brisbane icon. The quintessentially Queensland establishment is famed for its gigantic steaks (choose your own), served with baked potato (or chips), coleslaw, salad, and a choice of mushroom, pepper, or chili sauce, and for serving beer "off the wood" (from the keg). The pub's **Spanish Garden Steakhouse** and the **Staghorn beer garden** are always popular, and an outdoor dining area overlooks Breakfast Creek. The **Substation No. 41** bar, created in the shell of a derelict electricity substation next to the hotel, makes the most of its exposed brick walls and soaring ceilings. The 4.5m-long (15-ft.) wooden bar is just the place to sip the latest cocktail.

2 Kingsford Smith Dr. (at Breakfast Creek Rd.), Albion. www.breakfastcreekhotel.com. ✆ **07/3262 5988.** Main courses A$33–A$59. Daily 10am–late. Substation No. 41 daily

Eat Street

Brisbane foodies love this vibrant outdoor market designed to emulate the street food stalls of Asia. **Eat Street Northshore** (www.eatstreetmarkets.com; ✆ **0411/884 499** mobile) unleashes the aromas of exotic foods every Friday and Saturday from 4 to 10pm and Sunday from 11am to 7pm, at Hamilton Wharf on Brisbane's North Shore. Around 180 shipping containers have been transformed into kitchens and cafes, and it's all very industrial chic. There's also live music and other entertainment and design galleries. Bars serve craft beers, cocktails and other cool drinks, and there's every type of cuisine from Thai to Turkish, noodles and dumplings to tacos, seafood or salads, or even a good old Aussie (gourmet) pie. You'll find it by heading to Macarthur Avenue, Hamilton, where there's parking for 1,200 cars, but a better way to get there is by CityCat to North Shore Hamilton, or take bus no. 305 from George Street, in the city, or no. 300 from Adelaide Street, outside City Hall. There's an entry fee of A$2.50 per person (over 12 years old).

noon–late. Bus: 300 or 322. Wickham St. becomes Breakfast Creek Rd.; the hotel is just off the route to the airport.

Harveys ★★ CONTEMPORARY In the heart of trendy James Street, take a table in this modern, light-filled restaurant and prepare for something wonderful. Chef/owner PJ McMillan has a strong local following for his deceptively simple dishes. Personally, I can never go past the Asian chicken salad, with coriander, mint, peanuts, coconut, and tamarind dressing—and it always seems that half the other patrons are having it, too! Service is friendly and attentive, and the coffee's good, too!

31 James St., Fortitude Valley (next to the Centro Cinemas). www.harveys.net.au. ✆ **07/3852 3700.** Main courses A$28–A$44. Mon–Fri 7am–3pm; Sat–Sun 7:30am–3pm; Tues–Sat 5:30pm–late. Closed public holidays. Train: Brunswick St.

Jimmy's on the Mall ★★ INTERNATIONAL/CAFE FARE Jimmy's is a Brisbane institution, at the heart of the city's shopping precinct and open around-the-clock. The food here is consistently good, which is why the place is always busy and takes no reservations. The vertical gardens that decorate the eatery's walls open up to the passing shopping trade on the lower level, while upstairs you can take a bar-style table overlooking the mall, or a booth. The downstairs menu focuses on Asian fusion and includes wok dishes such as pad Thai noodles or satay chicken; the upstairs menu adds pizzas (try the pescatore). An open kitchen adds to the lively atmosphere.

Queen Street Mall, at Albert St. www.jimmysonthemall.com.au. ✆ **07/3077 7126.** Main courses A$20–A$44. Daily 24 hrs. Train: Central.

Inexpensive

Govinda's ★★ VEGETARIAN Tasty, cheap vegetarian food is served up at this Hare Krishna restaurant. That means a buffet of vegetable curry, *dahl* (lentil) soup, poppadum, koftas, and other tasty stuff with a north-Indian influence. And it's a stimulant-free zone, so don't come expecting alcohol, tea, or coffee—you're likely to get something like homemade ginger-and-mint lemonade instead. Check the website for details about Govinda's other locations, in Fortitude Valley and the inner suburb of West End.

358 George St. www.brisbanegovindas.com.au. ✆ **07/3210 0255.** A$13 all-you-can-eat; A$10 students. No credit cards. Mon–Fri 7am–8pm; Sat 11am–8pm.

Kettle & Tin ★★ CAFE I've been a fan of this cute cafe, with its picket fence outside, since my daughter took me here for lunch. In the Paddington cafe strip, it's a converted cottage, opened up for tables on the verandah or tucked away in its few rooms. My favorite time to come now—along with lots of locals—is for weekend brunch. I love the Vietnamese crepe with pork and prawns but there's more traditional fare if you prefer. At night, shared plates are on offer—and if you go on Tuesday night you might get involved in the trivia quiz.

215 Given Terrace, Paddington. www.kettleandtin.com.au. ✆ **07/3369 3778.** Main courses A$14–A$25. Mon 7am–4pm; Tues–Sun 7am–11pm.

Sup at the Summit

A teahouse of some kind has been on top of Mount Coot-tha for more than a century. Part 19th-century Queenslander house and part modern extension, the **Summit** restaurant (www.brisbanelookout.com; ✆ **07/3369 9922**) has wraparound covered decks with views of the city and Moreton Bay. A changing menu features local produce and wines. The sunset dinner menu—A$40 for three courses if you finish by 7pm—is available starting at 5pm. After your meal, enjoy the observation deck—the city lights provide a glittering panorama. On Sundays, high tea is served from 3 to 5pm (A$35 per person or A$45 with a glass of champagne). Reservations are recommended for Friday, Saturday, and Sunday evenings. The Summit is open daily 11:30am to midnight (closed for lunch New Year's Day, Good Friday, and Boxing Day [Dec 26]; closed for dinner Christmas Day). For breakfast (starting at 8am Mon–Fri and 7am Sat–Sun) or lighter fare (served from 11am daily) there's also the casual **Kuta Café** (no bookings taken). To get to the summit, take bus no. 471 from Adelaide Street, in the city; if you're driving, take Upper Roma Street from the city center, then Milton Road 3.5km (2¼ miles) west to the Western Freeway roundabout at Toowong Cemetery. Veer right into Sir Samuel Griffith Drive, and follow the road about 3km (2 miles) up the mountain. A taxi from the city will cost about A$30.

EXPLORING BRISBANE

Brisbane City Hall ★★★ The imposing Brisbane City Hall was built in the 1920s and was once the city's tallest building, standing at the heart of the city center. Free 45-minute guided tours are offered daily at 10:30 and 11:30am, 12:30, 1:30, 2:30, and 3:30pm. Tours are hugely popular and numbers are limited, so it's essential to book your spot, except for the 12:30pm tours, which can't be booked in advance. This is still a working civic building, so at times some of the rooms and features are not open. Separate free tours are run to the top of the **Clock Tower** every 15 minutes daily from 10:15am to 4:45pm. You cannot book ahead for these tours, and it pays to arrive early, because the heritage elevator only holds seven passengers. You'll need to get a ticket from the **Museum of Brisbane** reception counter on Level 3, and then wait your turn. The museum is also well worth spending time in; it provides an insight into the history and essence of Brisbane. Changing exhibitions relate the stories, events, and ideas that have shaped the city. This is a beautiful building—don't miss it!

City Hall, King George Sq. www.museumofbrisbane.com.au. ✆ **07/3339 0845.** Free. Daily 10am–5pm. Closed New Year's Day, Good Friday, Christmas Day, and Boxing Day (Dec 26), and until 1pm Anzac Day (Apr 25). Train: Roma St. or Central. Bus: The Loop.

Brisbane Powerhouse Arts ★★ A former electricity powerhouse, this massive brick factory is now a dynamic art space for exhibitions, contemporary performance, and live art. The building retains its character, an industrial mix of metal, glass, and stark surfaces etched with 20 years of graffiti. It's a short walk from the New Farm ferry terminal along the riverfront through New Farm Park. **Farmers markets** operate every Saturday morning, and there's a restaurant/cafe/bar overlooking the river.

119 Lamington St., New Farm. www.brisbanepowerhouse.org. ✆ **07/3358 8600.** CityCat to New Farm Park.

La Boite Theatre ★★ This is a well-established innovative company that performs contemporary Australian plays and some classics in the 400-seat Roundhouse Theatre, ensuring an intimate theatre experience. Tickets typically cost A$30 to A$60.

6 Musk Ave., Kelvin Grove. www.laboite.com.au. ✆ **07/3007 8600.** Take bus no. 390 from the city to Kelvin Grove Rd., and get off at stop 12.

Lone Pine Koala Sanctuary ★★ This is the best place in Australia to cuddle a koala—and one of the few places where koala cuddling is still allowed. Banned in New South Wales and Victoria, holding a koala is legal in Queensland under strict conditions that ensure that each animal is handled for less than 30 minutes a day—and gets every third day off! When it opened in 1927, Lone Pine had just two koalas, Jack and Jill; it is now home to more than 130. You can cuddle them anytime and have a photo taken holding one (for an extra A$18); once you've paid, you can have some photos taken using your own camera, too. Lone Pine isn't just koalas—you can also hand-feed kangaroos and wallabies and get up close with emus, snakes, baby crocs, parrots, wombats, Tasmanian devils, skinks, lace monitors, frogs, bats, turtles, possums, and other native wildlife. There is a currency exchange, a gift shop, a restaurant, and a cafe. Picnic and barbecue facilities are also available.

The nicest way to get to Lone Pine is a cruise down the Brisbane River aboard the **MV *Mirimar*** (www.mirimar.com; ✆ **0412/749 426**), which leaves the Cultural Centre at South Bank Parklands at 10am. The 19km (12-mile) trip to Lone Pine takes 75 minutes and includes commentary. You have 2½ hours to explore before returning, arriving in the city at 3pm. The round-trip fare is A$75 for adults, A$45 for children ages 3 to 13, and A$210 for families of five, and includes entry to Lone Pine. Cruises run daily except Anzac Day (Apr 25) and Christmas Day.

Jesmond Rd., Fig Tree Pocket. www.koala.net. ✆ **07/3378 1366.** A$36 adults, A$22 children 3–13, A$60–A$85 families. Daily 9am–5pm; Anzac Day (Apr 25) 1:30–5pm; Christmas Day 9am–4pm. By car (20 min. from city center), take Milton Rd. to the roundabout at Toowong Cemetery, and then Western Fwy. toward Ipswich. Signs point to Fig Tree Pocket and Lone Pine. Bus: nos. 430 or 445 from the city center. A taxi from the city center will cost about A$40.

Queen Street Mall ★ Brisbane's inner-city shopping centers on **Queen Street Mall,** which has around 500 stores. Fronting the mall at 171–209 Queen St. is the three-level **Wintergarden** shopping complex (www.wgarden.com.au; ✆ **07/3229 9755**), housing upscale jewelers and Aussie fashion designers. Farther up the mall at 91 Queen St. (at Albert St.) is the **Myer Centre**

(www.themyercentre.com.au; ✆ **07/3223 6900**), which has Brisbane's biggest department store and five levels of moderately priced stores, mostly fashion. The gorgeous **Brisbane Arcade,** 160 Queen St. (www.brisbanearcade.com.au; ✆ **07/3231 9777**), runs through to Adelaide Street, and abounds with jewelers and the boutiques of local Queensland designers. Across from the Edward Street end of the mall, at 255 Queen St., is a smart fashion and lifestyle shopping precinct, **MacArthur Central** (www.macarthurcentral.com; ✆ **07/3007 2300**), right next door to the General Post Office on the block between Queen and Elizabeth streets. This is where you'll find top designer labels, Swiss watches, galleries, and accessory shops. On Edward and Adelaide streets, you'll find more chic shopping at **QueensPlaza** (www.queensplaza.com.au; ✆ **07/3234 3900**). There are also weekly **farmers markets** in the Queen Street Mall (at the Victoria Bridge/George Street end) on Wednesdays from 8am to 6pm.

Queen St. www.queenstreetmall.com.au.

Queensland Cultural Centre ★★★ This modern complex stretching along the south bank of the Brisbane River houses many of the city's performing-arts venues as well as the state art galleries, museum, and library. With plenty of open plazas and fountains, it is a pleasing place to wander or just sit and watch the river and the city skyline. It's a 7-minute walk from town, across the Victoria Bridge from the Queen Street Mall.

The **Queensland Performing Arts Centre** (www.qpac.com.au; ✆ **136 246** for bookings Mon–Sat 9am–8:30pm) houses the 2,000-seat Lyric Theatre for musicals, ballet, and opera; the 1,800-seat Concert Hall for orchestral performances; the 850-seat Playhouse theater for plays; and the 315-seat Cremorne Theatre for theater-in-the-round, cabaret, and experimental works. The complex has a restaurant and a cafe.

This is where you will come for performances by the **Queensland Theatre Company** (www.queenslandtheatre.com.au), which offers eight or nine productions a year, from the classics to new Australian works; **Opera Queensland** (www.operaq.com.au), which performs a lively repertoire of traditional as well as modern works, musicals, and choral concerts; and the **Queensland Symphony Orchestra** (www.qso.com.au), which provides classical music lovers with a diverse mix of orchestral and chamber music, with the odd foray into fun material, such as movie themes, pop, and gospel music. It schedules about 30 concerts a year.

The **Queensland Art Gallery ★★★** (www.qagoma.qld.gov.au; ✆ **07/3840 7303**) is one of Australia's most attractive galleries, with vast light-filled spaces and interesting water features inside and out. It is a major player in the Australian art world, attracting blockbuster exhibitions of works by the likes of Renoir, Picasso, and van Gogh, and showcasing diverse modern Australian painters, sculptors, and other artists. It also has an impressive collection of Aboriginal art. The adjacent **Queensland Gallery of Modern Art (GOMA) ★★★** houses collections of modern and contemporary Australian, Indigenous Australian, Asian, and Pacific art, and also gives a stunning sense of light and space. Admission is free to both galleries, and both run regular free tours that take around 30 to 40 minutes. Tours of each gallery's collection highlights are held daily at 11am and 2pm. The galleries are open daily 10am to 5pm; closed Good Friday, Christmas Day, Boxing Day (Dec 26) and until noon on Anzac Day (Apr 25).

Stanley Place, South Brisbane.

Queensland Museum ★★★ Fossils that are 50 million years old—including a frog, snail, crocodile, and fish—are just some of the many fascinating "lost creatures" on show at this interesting and eclectic museum. Displays here range from natural history specimens to insects, dinosaurs—including Queensland's own *Muttaburrasaurus*—and more. Children will love the blue whale model that greets you at the entrance and the interactive Sciencentre on Level 1. The museum also has a cafe and gift shop. Admission is free, except to the Sciencentre and to any special exhibitions.

Grey St., (at Melbourne St.), next to the Queensland Art Gallery. www.qm.qld.gov.au. ✆ **07/3840 7555.** Daily 9:30am–5pm; closed Good Friday, Christmas Day, and Boxing Day (Dec 26), and until 1:30pm on Anzac Day (Apr 25). Museum free. Sciencentre A$15

Queensland's own *Muttaburrasaurus* is on display at the Queensland Museum.

The manmade beach at South Bank Parklands.

adults, A$12 children 3–15, A$45 family of 6. Ferry: South Bank (CityCat) or Old South Bank (Inner City Ferry). Bus: Numerous buses from Adelaide St. (near Albert St.). Train: South Brisbane.

St. John's Anglican Cathedral ★★ Brisbane's stunning neo-Gothic Anglican cathedral took more than a century to complete, but the result has been worth the wait. Plagued by lack of funding throughout its history, the building was finally completed in 2009, making it one of the last Gothic-style cathedrals to be completed anywhere in the world, with stonemasons using traditional medieval building techniques. Volunteer guides are on hand to point out some of the details that make this cathedral uniquely Queensland—such as the carved possums on the organ screen and the hand-stitched cushions.

373 Ann St. (btw. Wharf and Queen sts.). www.stjohnscathedral.com.au. ✆ **07/3835 2222.** Daily 9:30am–4:30pm. Closed to visitors, except for services, Apr 25 (Anzac Day), Christmas Day, and some other public holidays. Train: Central Station.

Sir Thomas Brisbane Planetarium & Cosmic Skydome ★★ Digital multimedia systems that present real-time digital star shows and computer-generated images in the Cosmic Skydome theater are a popular feature here for all ages. The fascinating 40-minute astronomical show includes a re-creation of the Brisbane night sky using a Zeiss star projector. Show times vary, and there are also special shows designed for kids ages 6 and under. Check the website for details.

Brisbane Botanic Gardens, Mt. Coot-tha Rd., Toowong. www.brisbane.qld.gov.au/planetarium. ✆ **07/3403 2578.** A$16 adults, A$9.60 children 14 and under, A$43 families of 4. Tues–Fri 10am–4pm; Sat 11am–8:15pm (last entry at 7:30pm); Sun 11am–4pm. Closed Mon (except school holidays) and public holidays. Bus: nos. 471, 598, or 599.

South Bank Parklands ★★★ Follow the locals' lead and spend some time at this delightful 16-hectare (40-acre) complex of parks, restaurants, cafes, shops, playgrounds, street theater, and weekend markets. There's a manmade beach lined with palm trees, with waves and sand, where you can swim, stroll, and cycle the meandering pathways. From the parklands it's an easy walk to the museum, art gallery, and other parts of the adjacent **Queensland Cultural Centre** (p. 173). Hop on the **Wheel of Brisbane** (www.thewheelofbrisbane.com.au; ✆ **07/3844 3464**) for a 13-minute ride in an air-conditioned enclosed gondola, where you get a 360-degree bird's-eye view of Brisbane from 60m (197 ft.) up; it costs A$20 for adults, A$14 for children 4 to 12, and A$57 for a family of four. The buzzing outdoor **Collective Markets** (www.collectivemarkets.com.au) is illuminated by fairy lights at night. The market is open Friday 5 to 9pm, Saturday 10am to 9pm, and Sunday 9am to 4pm. The South Bank Parklands are a 7-minute walk from town.

South Bank. www.visitsouthbank.com.au. ✆ **07/3156 6366** for Visitor Centre. Free. Park daily 24 hr.; Visitor Centre daily 9am–5pm (closed Good Friday and Christmas Day, open from 1pm on Anzac Day [Apr 25] and 10am on other public holidays). From the Queen Street Mall, cross the Victoria Bridge to South Bank or walk across the Goodwill Bridge from Gardens Point Rd. entrance to Brisbane City Gardens. Train: South Brisbane. Ferry: South Bank (CityCat or Cross River Ferry). Bus: Numerous routes from Adelaide St. (near Albert St.), including nos. 100, 111, 115, and 120, stop at the Queensland Cultural Centre; walk through the Centre to South Bank Parklands.

Story Bridge Adventure Climb ★★★ Brisbane seems to have a fascination with building bridges across its wide river. There are 15 (at last count), but the most interesting is the Story Bridge, built in 1940. If you are over 10 years old and at least 130 centimeters (just over 4 ft., 3 in.) tall, you can "climb" this overgrown Meccano set. The Story Bridge Adventure Climb peaks at a viewing platform on top of the bridge, 44m (143 ft.) above the roadway and 80m (262 ft.) above the Brisbane River. On Sunday mornings, you can also rappel down to the park below from the top of the bridge. This is only the third "bridge climb" in the world (after Sydney's and Auckland's), so make the most of the chance. You'll be rewarded with magnificent 360-degree views of the city, river, and Moreton Bay and its islands, not to mention interesting stories from your guide. Children must be accompanied by an adult. Go ahead—you'll love it!

170 Main St. (at Wharf St.), Kangaroo Point. www.sbac.net.au. ✆ **1300/254 627** in Australia or 07/3514 6900. Day climbs A$119 adults, A$101 children (or A$79 per

person mid-week); night climbs A$129 adults, A$109 children; twilight climbs and abseil climbs (Sun only) A$139 adults, A$118 children; dawn climbs (first Sat of month only) A$159 adults, A$135 children. Ferry: Holman St.

Treasury Casino ★ This lovely heritage building—built in 1886 as, ironically enough, the state's Treasury offices—houses a modern casino. Three levels of 100 gaming tables offer roulette, blackjack, baccarat, craps, sic bo, and traditional Aussie two-up. Open 24 hours, the casino has more than 1,600 gaming machines, six restaurants, and six bars. DJs bring music to **The Kitty** bar on Friday and Saturday nights, or you can relax in the clubby atmosphere of **Ryan's on the Park.** A massive 10-block redevelopment of the George Street precinct around the casino is currently taking place, while the Queen's Wharf project is slated for completion in 2024.

Queen St. (btw. George and William sts.). www.treasurybrisbane.com.au. ✆ **07/3306 8888.** Must be 18 years old to enter; neat, casual attire required (no beachwear or flip-flops). Closed from 3am Good Friday, Christmas Day, and from 3am until 1pm Apr 25 (Anzac Day). Train: Central or South Brisbane, and then walk across the Victoria Bridge.

ORGANIZED TOURS

RIVER CRUISES The best way to cruise the river, in my view, is aboard the fast **CityCat ferries** ★★★. Board at Riverside and head downstream

The *Kookaburra River Queen* paddlewheeler.

Whale-Watching in Moreton Bay

Gasps of delight and wonder are the norm aboard Captain Kerry Lopez's whale-watching boat, and Australia's only female whale-watching captain never tires of hearing them. Lopez's purpose-built vessel, the MV *Eye-Spy,* carries up to 320 passengers out into Moreton Bay between June and November for one of the most awesome sights you may ever see. When I traveled with them, we witnessed the antics of 17 humpback whales as they breached and displayed in the waters around the boat. It was an amazing, unforgettable experience.

Brisbane Whale Watching ★★★ (www.brisbanewhalewatching.com.au; ✆ **07/3880 0477**) will organize your 30-minute transfers from city hotels to the departure point in the northern suburb of Redcliffe. If you choose to drive yourself, there's free all-day parking near the jetty. Tours depart daily at 10am, returning around 2:30 to 3pm. The trip onto the bay features excellent educational commentary about the whales while Kerry and her crew keep a lookout for these gentle giants of the deep. Prices are A$135 adults, A$125 seniors and students, A$95 children 4 to 14, or A$365 for a family of four, including lunch and morning and afternoon tea. Transfers from Brisbane hotels are an extra A$30 per person.

The best part? There's a guarantee you'll see a whale—or you can take another cruise for free.

Brisbane Whale Watching offers tours in Moreton Bay.

under the Story Bridge to New Farm Park, past Newstead House to the restaurant row at Brett's Wharf, or cruise upriver past the city and South Bank for only a few dollars. For more information, see "Getting Around," earlier in this chapter.

For those who'd like to dine as they cruise, the **Kookaburra River Queen** paddlewheelers (www.kookaburrariverqueens.com; ✆ **07/3221 1300**) are a good option. Lunch cruises, for around 90 minutes, cost A$49 adults and A$29 kids 4 to 12 on Thursday and Friday, or A$59 adults and A$39 children on Saturday and Sunday. Dinner cruises run on Thursday, Friday, and Saturday for A$79 adults and A$59 children. The boat departs from the Eagle Street Pier (parking is available under the City Rowers tavern on Eagle St.) at 7pm. On weekend lunch cruises there's live jazz. Or you can take a High Tea cruise on Saturdays at 3:30pm, for A$58 adults and A$25 children.

WALKING TOURS The best walking tours in town are run by the **Brisbane Greeters** (www.visitbrisbane.com.au)—and even better, they're free. You get your own personal tour guide (or you can join a group), often a local with a particular area of expertise or interest in some aspect of the city. You can choose from tours that look at architecture, arts and culture, history, and more, or at a particular neighborhood or precinct. Guides are volunteers with a passion and enthusiasm for the city, and you'll learn a lot along the way. Some tours combine bicycling using the CityCycle bikes (p. 165). But really, it's up to you to decide what to do and how long the walk will be. You'll likely see the Greeters in their bright red shirts out and about in the city. Tours start from the Visitor Information Centre in the Queen Street Mall, and last anywhere from 1 to 4 hours. Try to book at least 48 hours ahead. Book online or at the Visitor Information Centre.

Free guided walks of the **City Botanic Gardens** at Alice Street leave from the rotunda at the Albert Street entrance Monday through Saturday at 11am (except public holidays and mid-Dec to mid-Jan). They take about 1 hour. Bookings are not necessary.

Playabout Productions leads 1-hour theatrical walking tours every Wednesday at 10am (Mar–Aug) from the Brisbane Powerhouse (p. 171), in which actors Therese Collie and Tim Mullooly tell **The Story of Brisbane** in the words of its best writers, set against the backdrop of the Brisbane River. Therese and Tim veer off into subjects that can't be found in tourist brochures, giving a fabulous insight into Brisbane life, from its Indigenous inhabitants to the European convicts and free settlers, through wars and depression to the present day. Tours cost A$30 per person.

Prepare for shivers up your spine when you take one of Jack Sim's **Ghost Tours** ★ (www.brisbaneghosttours.com.au; ✆ **07/3344 7265**), which relive Brisbane's gruesome past. His 90-minute "Haunted Brisbane" walking tours depart from the Queen Street Mall at 7:30pm Thursday and Sunday (A$26 for adults, A$15 for kids 5–17, or A$65 for a family of four). On Friday and Saturday nights, you can take a 2-hour tour of the historic and haunted Toowong cemetery (A$45 for adults, A$30 for children 12–17). Or choose from a range of other spooky tours. Reservations are essential; some tours are not suitable for children 11 and under.

A DAY TRIP TO THE GREAT BARRIER REEF ★★★

Brisbane is south of the most southern parts of the Great Barrier Reef (see chapter 7), but it is still possible to experience the Reef in a day trip to **Lady Elliot Island,** off the coast near Bundaberg (384km/238 miles north of Brisbane). If you are pressed for time before heading south or to Central Australia and Uluru, this is an excellent option.

Lady Elliot (www.ladyelliot.com.au) is a small coral cay ringed by a lagoon filled with coral and marine life. Reef walking, snorkeling, and diving are the main reasons people come to this coral cay, but you can snorkel and reef walk only for the 2 to 3 hours before and after high tide, so your day-trip activities will be reliant on nature to some extent.

Keep in mind that you will not be able to dive and fly on the same day. But the snorkeling on Lady Elliot is a wonderful experience (and the island has accommodations if you wish to stay longer or do some diving; see p. 238). You will see beautiful corals, brightly colored fish, clams, sponges, urchins, and anemones, and with luck, green and loggerhead turtles (which nest on the beach Nov–Mar) and manta rays. Whales migrate through these waters from June through September.

Be aware that Lady Elliot is a sparse, grassy island rookery, not a sandy tropical paradise. Some find it too spartan; others relish chilling out in a beautiful, peaceful spot with reef all around. Just be prepared for the smell and constant noise of the birds.

Lady Elliot's own airline, **Seair,** offers a day-trip package from Brisbane for A$849 adults and A$449 children ages 3 to 12. In addition to the flights, the price includes snorkel gear, a glass-bottom-boat ride, lunch, and guided activities (and the Reef tax).

Your day trip begins with an early pickup (around 6:30am) from your Brisbane hotel to drive to the northern Brisbane suburb of Redcliffe for the coastal scenic flight. The flight takes about 80 minutes. Seair operates a fleet of 9- and 13-seat aircraft. All you need to take is a daypack with swimwear, camera, sunscreen, and footwear suitable for getting wet (no more than 10kg in luggage). Take some cash too, in case you decide to buy an underwater camera or a small souvenir from the resort gift shop.

You'll have around 5 hours to explore the island and Reef. You can take an island orientation tour, a guided reef walk at low tide (if possible), a snorkeling lesson in the resort pool (if you need it), and a glass-bottom-boat or guided snorkel tour, and even feed the fish in the lagoon fish pool.

All snorkel equipment (mask, snorkel, fins, and wetsuit) is provided, along with towels and reef-walking shoes. Storage lockers are available, as are resort shower facilities. A hot and cold buffet lunch includes fresh prawns, champagne, wine, beer, and soft drinks.

You'll be boarding your light plane for the return trip at 2:30pm, arriving back at your Brisbane hotel at around 4:45pm—but you'll feel like you've been gone much longer. Such is the magic of a day on the Great Barrier Reef!

7

CAIRNS & THE GREAT BARRIER REEF

Fish out your flippers and prepare to dive! Or snorkel. Beneath the aqua blue waters off Queensland's northern coast lie the jewels of the deep—gardens of coral, inhabited by colorful reef fish. Welcome to Australia's most famous natural attraction, the Great Barrier Reef. And while the Reef is by no means the only thing worth seeing in a state that's two and a half times the size of Texas, it is the focus of this chapter. There are many gateways to the Reef along the Queensland coast, but Cairns is the major center and where most commercial boat tours depart from. I've also included some of the smaller towns that offer easy access to this natural wonder.

White sandy beaches grace nearly every inch of coastline in Queensland, and a string of islands and coral reefs dangles just offshore. Cairns, set between rainforest hills, sugarcane fields, and the Coral Sea, still has fewer options for direct arrivals; for most people, Brisbane or Sydney will be their first stop before heading to the far north of Australia's east coast. In Cairns, a harbor full of boats awaits to take you to the Reef. An hour north, the village of **Port Douglas** provides another for point of departure for the Reef.

Departing from Airlie Beach on the Whitsunday Coast, you'll be tempted by one tropical island after another; a cluster of 74 makes up the **Whitsunday** and **Cumberland** groups. These idyllic islands are laced by coral reefs rising out of calm, blue waters teeming with colorful fish—warm enough for swimming year-round.

Townsville boasts 320 days of sunshine a year and marks the start of the Great Green Way—an area of lush natural beauty on the way to Cairns—for those who choose to drive. Townsville is also the home to the Great Barrier Reef Marine Park Authority.

ESSENTIALS

Visitor Information

The **Tourism & Events Queensland** website at **www.queensland.com** is a great resource on traveling and touring the state, including the Great Barrier Reef, and on this site you can select your own country for information specifically designed for travelers from your country. In Australia, call **Go Queensland** (www.goqueensland.com.au; ✆ **138 833** in Australia) to book online or speak to a Queensland travel specialist.

When to Go

Winter (June–Aug) is high season in Queensland; the water can be chilly—at least to Australians—but its temperature rarely drops below 72°F (22°C). April through November is the best time to visit the Great Barrier Reef, because although southeast trade winds can sometimes make it a tad choppy at sea, this is peak visibility time for divers. December through March can be uncomfortably hot and humid, particularly as far north as the Whitsundays, Cairns, and Port Douglas.

Getting Around

BY CAR

The Bruce Highway travels along the coast from Brisbane to Cairns. It is mostly a narrow, two-lane highway, with the scenery varying from eucalyptus bushland to sugarcane fields.

Tourism Queensland (see "Visitor Information," above) publishes regional motoring guides but all you are likely to need, however, is a state map from the **Royal Automobile Club of Queensland (RACQ)** (www.racq.com.au; ✆ **131 905** in Australia). A large range of touring maps is available online, and the website is brimming with advice about driving in Australia. For recorded road-condition reports, call ✆ **131 940.** Brisbane-based online specialist map shop **World Wide Maps & Guides** (www.worldwidemaps.com.au) offers a wide range of Australia maps, atlases, and street directories.

See It Now

In recent years, parts of the Great Barrier Reef have been affected by changing environmental factors that cause coral to degrade and, in some cases, die. One of the major problems on the reef is coral bleaching, caused by heat stress resulting from rising sea temperatures. Other stressors can also cause bleaching, including freshwater inundation (low salinity) and poor water quality from sediment or pollutant run-off from agriculture, mining, and other coastal development. Tour operators are well aware of the best places to see healthy coral, so you can still have the experience you expect—but of course, things can change in a relatively short time. Get there while you can still see some of the glory of the Reef.

BY TRAIN

Queensland Rail (www.queenslandrailtravel.com.au; ✆ **1300/131 722** in Australia) operates two long-distance trains along the coast north from Brisbane, a 24-hour trip aboard the **Spirit of Queensland** to Cairns or about five hours less on the **Tilt Train** to Bundaberg and Rockhampton. See the "Getting Around" section in chapter 10 for more details.

BY PLANE

This is the fastest way to cover the most ground in such a big state. **Qantas** (www.qantas.com.au; ✆ **131 313** in Australia) and its subsidiaries **QantasLink** and **Jetstar** (www.jetstar.com.au; ✆ **131 538** in Australia) serve most coastal towns from Brisbane, and a few from Cairns. **Virgin Australia** (www.virginaustralia.com; ✆ **136 789** in Australia) services Brisbane, Cairns, Townsville, Gladstone, Bundaberg, and Proserpine and Hamilton Island in the Whitsundays, as well as other centers.

Exploring the Great Barrier Reef

First, a few facts: The Great Barrier Reef is the only living thing on earth that's visible from the moon; at 348,700 sq. km (135,993 sq. miles), it's bigger than the United Kingdom and more than 2,000km (1,240 miles) long,

Cairns is the stepping-off point for exploring the Great Barrier Reef.

The Great Barrier Reef

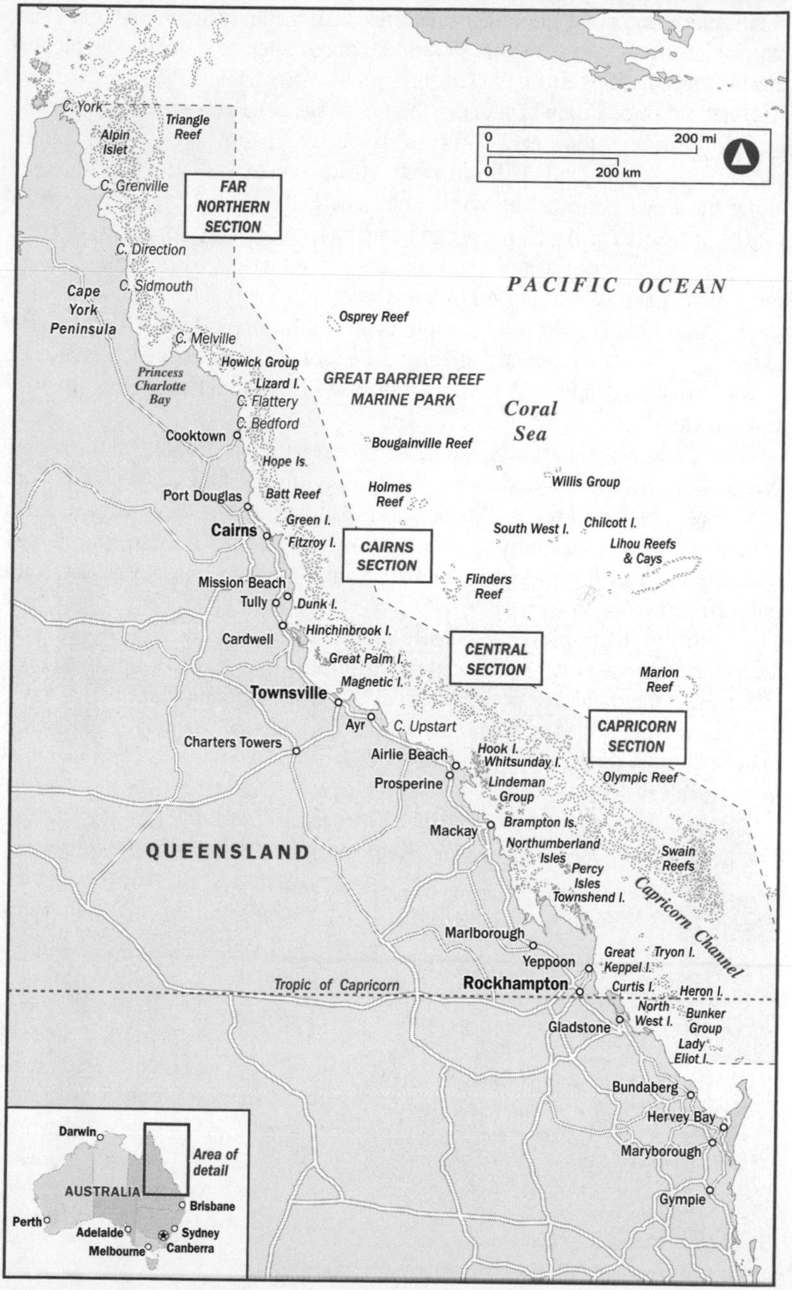

stretching from Lady Elliot Island off Bundaberg to Papua New Guinea. It's home to 1,500 kinds of fish, 400 species of corals, 4,000 kinds of clams and snails, and who knows how many sponges, starfish, and sea urchins; the Great Barrier Reef region is listed as a World Heritage Site and contains the biggest marine park in the world.

There are three kinds of reef on the Great Barrier Reef—*fringing, ribbon,* and *platform.* **Fringing reef** is the stuff you see just off the shore of islands and along the mainland. **Ribbon reefs** create "streamers" of long, thin reef along the outer edge of the continental shelf and are only found north of Cairns. **Platform** or **patch reefs** can be up to 16 sq. km (10 sq. miles) of coral emerging off the continental shelf all the way along the Reef's length. Platform reefs, the most common kind, are what most people think of when they refer to the Great Barrier Reef. Island resorts in the Great Barrier Reef Marine Park are either "continental," meaning part of the Australian landmass, or "cays," crushed dead coral and sand amassed on the reef tops over time by water action.

The rich colors of the coral can be seen best with lots of light, so the nearer the surface, the brighter and richer the marine life. That means snorkelers are in a prime position to see it at its best. Snorkeling the Reef can be a wondrous experience. Green and purple clams, pink sponges, red starfish, purple sea urchins, and fish from electric blue to neon yellow to lime green are truly magical sights.

Apart from the impressive fish life around the corals, the Reef is home to large numbers of green and loggerhead turtles, one of the biggest dugong (relative of the manatee) populations in the world, sharks, giant manta rays, and sea snakes. In winter (June–Aug), humpback whales gather in the warm waters south of the Reef around Hervey Bay and as far north as Cairns to give birth to calves. This is what you've come to see!

You can snorkel the Reef, dive, ride a semisubmersible, or fly over it. For most people, the Great Barrier Reef means the Outer Reef, the network of reefs that are an average of 65km (40 miles) off the coast (about 60–90 min. by boat from the mainland).

If your Reef cruise offers a guided snorkel tour or "snorkel safari," take it. Some include it as part of the price, but even if you pay an extra A$30 or so, it is worth it. Most safaris are suitable for beginners and advanced snorkelers and are led by guides trained by

The Reef Tax

Every passenger over 4 years old must pay a A$6 daily **Environmental Management Charge (EMC),** commonly called the "reef tax," every time they visit the Great Barrier Reef. This money goes toward the management and conservation of the Reef. Your tour operator will collect it from you when you pay for your trip (or it may be included in the tour price).

> **Reef Health & Safety Warnings**
>
> Coral is very sharp, and coral cuts get infected quickly and badly. If you cut yourself, ask the staff on your cruise boat for immediate first aid as soon as you come out of the water.
>
> The sun and reflected sunlight off the water can burn you fast. Remember to put sunscreen on your back and the back of your legs, especially around your knees and the back of your neck, and even behind your ears—all places that rarely get exposed to the sun but will be exposed as you swim facedown. Apply more when you leave the water. If you can, use a sunscreen that does not contain Oxybenzone (also known as BP-3 or Benzophenone-3), a chemical that scientists believe causes damage to coral reefs. However, labels don't always list all ingredients in these products so the safest way to be sure is to cover up wearing a wetsuit or sunsuit (known in Australia as a "rashie").

marine biologists. Snorkeling is easy to master, and crews on cruise boats are always happy to tutor you.

A day trip to the Reef also offers a great opportunity to go scuba diving—even if you have never dived before. Every major cruise boat listed in this book and many dedicated dive boats offer introductory dives ("resort dives") that allow you to dive without certification to a depth of 6m (20 ft.) with an instructor. You will need to complete a medical questionnaire and undergo a 30-minute briefing on the boat.

Find out more about the Reef from the **Great Barrier Reef Marine Park Authority** (www.gbrmpa.gov.au; ✆ **07/4750 0700**).

Choosing a Gateway to the Reef

Cairns and **Port Douglas** are good places from which to visit the Reef—but the quality of the coral is just as good off any town along the coast between **Bundaberg** and Cairns. The Reef is about 90 minutes away by high-speed catamaran. From **Townsville,** it is farther, about 2½ hours away.

Think carefully about where to base yourself. The main gateways, north to south, are **Port Douglas, Cairns, Townsville,** the **Whitsunday Islands, Gladstone** (for Heron Island), and **Bundaberg** (for Lady Elliot Island). The Whitsundays have the added attractions of dazzling islands to sail among; beautiful island resorts offering a wealth of watersports and other activities; and a large array of diving, fishing, and day cruises. You can snorkel every day off your island or join a sailing or cruise day trip to a number of

> **Safe Swimming**
>
> All the northern beaches have small, netted enclosures for safe swimming from October through May, when deadly stingers (box jellyfish) render all mainland beaches in north Queensland off-limits.

DIVING the reef

Divers have a lot to choose from: dive boats that make 1-day runs to the Outer Reef, boats that offer overnight stays, live-aboard dive boats that make excursions that last up to a week, or staying on an island. As a general rule, on a typical 5-hour day trip to the Reef, you will fit in about two dives. The companies listed in this book give you an idea of the kinds of trips available and how much they cost. Prices quoted include full gear rental; knock off about A$20 if you have your own gear. It is recommended that you only dive with members of **Dive Queensland.** The website, **www.dive-queensland.com.au**, has more information on diving in Queensland.

Many dive companies in Queensland offer instruction, from initial open-water certification all the way to dive-master level, rescue-diver, and instructor level. To take a course, you will need to have a medical exam done by a Queensland doctor. (Your dive school will arrange it; it usually costs between A$45 and A$70.) You can find out more about dive medicals on **www.divemedicals.com.au**. You will also need two passport photos for your certificate, and you must be able to swim! Courses usually begin every day or every week. Some courses take as little as 3 days, but 5 days is regarded as the best. Open-water certification usually requires 2 days of theory in a pool, followed by 2 or 3 days on the Reef, where you make four to nine dives. Prices vary but are generally around A$600 for a 4-day open-water certification course, or A$700 for the same course as a live-aboard.

Deep Sea Divers Den (www.diversden.com.au; ✆ **07/4046 7333**) has been in operation since 1974 and claims to have certified more than 55,000 divers. Courses range from 4-day open-water courses (from A$665 per person) to 6-day courses on a live-aboard boat, which cost from A$1,345 per person, and include all meals on the boat, all gear, a wetsuit, and transfers from your city hotel. Prices include reef tax, port and administration charges, and fuel levy. New courses begin every day of the week.

Virtually every Great Barrier Reef dive operator offers dive courses. Most island resorts offer them, too. You will find dive schools in Cairns, Port Douglas, Townsville, and the Whitsundays.

magnificent fringing or inner shelf reefs much nearer than the main Outer Reef. Many people stay in Cairns simply because of its easy international airport access.

If you are a nonswimmer, choose a Reef cruise that visits a coral cay, because a cay slopes gradually into shallow water and the surrounding coral. The **Low Isles** at Port Douglas; **Green Island, Michaelmas Cay,** or **Upolu Cay** off Cairns; and **Heron Island,** off Gladstone, are all good locations. Swimmer supports are available so nonswimmers can snorkel, too.

Diving Reminders

Don't forget your "C" certification card. Bringing along your dive log is also a good idea. Remember not to fly for 24 hours after diving.

The major launching points for day trips to the Reef are Port Douglas, Cairns, Townsville, and the Whitsundays. Day-trip options for each are outlined in their dedicated sections of this chapter.

CAIRNS ★★

346km (215 miles) N of Townsville; 1,807km (1,120 miles) N of Brisbane

Cairns is the only place on earth where two World Heritage-listed sites—the Wet Tropics Rainforest and Great Barrier Reef—are side by side. Explore the reef and offshore islands and slip into the distinctive pace, heat, and style of a truly tropical city.

This is the departure point for the large-scale Reef boats that take hundreds of people out every day. Many smaller operators offer a more intimate experience, some on sailing boats. Offshore, **Michaelmas Cay** and **Upolu Cay** are two pretty coral sand blips in the ocean, 30km (19 miles) and 25km (16 miles) off Cairns, surrounded by reefs. Michaelmas is vegetated and is home to 27,000 seabirds; you may spot dugongs (cousins of manatees) off Upolu. Michaelmas and Upolu are great for snorkelers and introductory divers.

Cairns Esplanade offers top-to-bottom-dollar shopping plus an array of food halls, but its sparkling jewel is the manmade **lagoon** on the Esplanade, where you can cool off from the heat. There's plenty to do on days when the Reef's not on your radar.

Essentials

ARRIVING

BY PLANE **Qantas** (www.qantas.com.au; ✆ **131 313** in Australia) has direct flights to Cairns from Sydney, Brisbane, Townsville, Hamilton Island, and Melbourne, and to Uluru and Alice Springs. **Virgin Australia** (www.virginaustralia.com.au; ✆ **136 789** in Australia) flies to Cairns direct from Brisbane, Sydney, and Melbourne. **Jetstar** (www.jetstar.com.au; ✆ **131 538** in Australia) flies from the Gold Coast, Perth, and Adelaide. **Scoot** (www.flyscoot.com; ✆ **02/9009 0860** in Australia) flies to Cairns from Brisbane, Melbourne, and Sydney. **Regional Express**, also known as Rex (www.rex.com.au; ✆ **131 713** in Australia or 02/6393 5550) flies between Cairns and Townsville. Some international carriers serve Cairns from various Asian cities and New Zealand.

Cairns Airport (www.cairnsairport.com.au; ✆ **07/4080 6703**) is 8km (5 miles) north of downtown. A 5-minute walk along a covered walkway connects the international terminal with the domestic terminal.

Sun Palm Transport (www.sunpalmtransport.com.au; ✆ **07/4099 1191**) provides transfers from the airport to the city and northern beaches. The one-way fare is A$15 adults to Cairns and A$18 adults to Palm Cove and other beaches. Kids travel free with an adult (extra children A$7.50). Sun Palm also offers a **free Airport Connect** bus service from the airport to connect you to the Sun Bus public transport network on Sheridan Street in the city center.

Cairns

From there, you can jump on a Sun Bus service to the northern beaches for just a couple of dollars. To catch Airport Connect back to the airport, wait at the C9 bus stop on Sheridan Street (opposite the Tobruk Pool) and hail the driver of the Sun Palm Transport bus. Pre-bookings can be made 24 hours ahead.

A taxi from the airport costs around A$30 to the city, A$55 to Trinity Beach, and A$70 to Palm Cove. There is a set fee of A$190 to Port Douglas. Call **Cairns Taxis** (✆ **131 008** in Australia). An airport fee of A$4 is added to all pickups at the domestic and international terminals.

Avis (✆ **07/4033 9555**), **Budget** (✆ **07/4033 9777, Europcar** (✆ **131 390** in Australia or 07/4034 9088), **Hertz** (✆ **07/4035 9299**), **Thrifty** (✆ **1300/367 227** in Australia or 07/4033 9800), and **Redspot** (✆ **07/4034 9052**) all have car-rental offices at the domestic and international terminals (see "Getting Around By Car," p. 192).

BY TRAIN Long-distance trains operated by **Queensland Rail** (www.queenslandrailtravel.com.au; ✆ **1300/131 722** in Australia or 07/3606 6630) run from Brisbane several times a week. The 160kmph (100-mph) **Spirit of Queensland** takes about 24 hours to make the trip between Brisbane and Cairns. Trains leave Brisbane at 3:45pm on Monday, Tuesday, Wednesday, Friday, and Saturday; southbound runs depart Cairns at 9am on Monday, Wednesday, Thursday, Friday, and Sunday. The trains feature luxury business-class seating (A$369), with an entertainment system for each seat, including movie and audio channels, as well as lie-flat airline-style "railbeds" (A$519).

BY BUS **Greyhound Australia** (www.greyhound.com.au; ✆ **1300/473 946** in Australia, or 07/4033 4811 in Cairns) buses pull into Trinity Wharf Centre in the center of town. Buses travel from the south via all towns and cities on the Bruce Highway; they also run from the west, from Alice Springs and Darwin, via Tennant Creek on the Stuart Highway, and the Outback mining town of Mount Isa to Townsville, where they join the Bruce Highway and head north. The 48-hour Sydney-Cairns trip costs about A$500; the 29-hour trip from Brisbane is around A$350.

BY CAR From Brisbane and all major towns in the south, you'll approach Cairns on the Bruce Highway. To reach the northern beaches or Port Douglas, take Sheridan Street in the city center, which becomes the Captain Cook Highway.

VISITOR INFORMATION

Tourism Tropical North Queensland's **Cairns & Tropical North Visitor Information Centre,** 51 The Esplanade (www.cairnsgreatbarrierreef.org.au; ✆ **1800/093 300** in Australia or 07/4051 3588), has information on Cairns and the surrounding area. It's open Monday to Friday from 8:30am to 6pm and 10am to 6pm on Saturday, Sunday, and public holidays. Closed Christmas Day, New Year's Day, and Good Friday. The center also has a small stall of secondhand books for a couple of dollars each and claims to sell the cheapest bottled water in town!

CITY LAYOUT

The focal point of the city is the **Esplanade,** which has a 4,000-sq.-m (43,000-sq.-ft.) man-made saltwater swimming lagoon, with a wide sandy beach, and surrounding parkland with public artworks and picnic areas. Suspended over the mud flats and providing a platform for birding, a boardwalk runs 600m (1,968 ft.) along the waterfront and is lit at night. A walkway links the Esplanade to the Reef Fleet Terminal, the departure point for Great Barrier Reef boats.

> **Croc Alert!**
>
> Dangerous crocodiles inhabit Cairns' waterways. Do not swim in or stand on the bank of any river or stream.

Downtown Cairns is on a grid 5 blocks deep, bounded in the east by the Esplanade and in the west by McLeod Street, where the train station and the Cairns Central shopping mall are situated.

Heading 15 minutes north from the city along the Captain Cook Highway, you come to the **northern beaches:** Holloway's Beach, Yorkey's Knob, Trinity Beach, Kewarra Beach, Clifton Beach, Palm Cove, and Ellis Beach.

GETTING AROUND

BY BUS **Sunbus** (www.sunbus.com.au; © **07/4057 7411**) buses depart Cairns City Mall at the intersection of Lake and Shields streets. Buy all tickets and passes on board, and try to have correct change. Bus nos. 110 and 111 travel to Trinity Beach and Palm Cove. Routes and timetables change, so check with the driver. Most buses run from around 7am until almost midnight.

BY CAR **Avis** (© **07/4048 0522**), **Budget** (© **07/4048 8166**), **Europcar** (© **131 390** in Australia or 07/4033 4800), and **Thrifty** (© **1300/367 227** in Australia or 07/4051 8099) have offices in Cairns city as well as at the airport. One long-established local outfit, **Sugarland Car Rentals** (© **07/4052 1300**), has reasonable rates. **Britz Campervan Rentals** (© **1800/331 454** in Australia or 07/4032 2611) and **Maui Rentals** (© **1800/827 821** in Australia or 07/4032 2065) rent motor homes.

BY TAXI Call Cairns Taxis (© **131 008**).

Cairns & Northern Beaches Hotels

High season in Cairns includes 2 weeks at Easter, the period from early July to early October, and the Christmas holiday through January. Book ahead in those periods. In low season (Nov–June), many hotels offer discounts or negotiate fees. Cairns has a good supply of affordable accommodations, both in the heart of the city and along the northern beaches. You don't have to stay in Cairns city if you don't have a car—most tour and cruise operators provide transfers.

EXPENSIVE

Pullman Reef Hotel Casino ★★ This stylish seven-story hotel is a block from the water, with Trinity Inlet views from some rooms, and city/hinterland outlooks from others. All the rooms have lots of natural light, high-quality amenities, robes, and small balconies with smart timber furniture. The **Cairns Wildlife Dome** (p. 198) and **Reef Casino** are attached to the hotel. Be aware that there are two Pullman hotels in Cairns (the other is in the next street), which can be confusing (even to your taxi driver!). The **Tamarind** restaurant is one of Cairns' best dining spots, for breakfast *or* dinner.

35–41 Wharf St. www.pullmanhotels.com/2901. © **07/4030 8888.** 128 units. A$302–A$375 double; A$1,058–A$1,175 suite. Rates include breakfast. Valet parking A$15, free self-parking. **Amenities:** 4 restaurants; 4 bars; babysitting; concierge; health club; Jacuzzi; small outdoor rooftop pool; room service; sauna; free Wi-Fi.

The Reef House Palm Cove – MGallery by Sofitel ★★★ The old colonial-style Reef House has a romantic feel about it—the white walls are swathed in bougainvillea, the beds are draped in mosquito netting, and rooms have white wicker chairs. Verandah Spa rooms have a Jacuzzi on the balcony;

overlook the pool, waterfalls, and lush gardens; and have extra touches, such as bathrobes, and balconies within earshot of the ocean. One-, two-, and four-bedroom apartments are also available. Every night at sunset, all the candles throughout the resort are lit, and Brigadier's Punch is served to guests in an old tradition. The beachfront restaurant, on a covered wooden deck beneath towering Paperbarks, is a favorite for locals and tourists alike for its ocean views and gentle breezes.

99 Williams Esplanade, Palm Cove. www.reefhouse.com.au. ✆ **07/4080 2600.** 69 units. A$239–A$451 double; A$605 2-bedroom apt. Limited free parking; ample street parking. Bus: no. 110. **Amenities:** 2 restaurants; bar; babysitting; concierge; 3 small heated outdoor pools; room service; spa; free Wi-Fi.

MODERATE

Cairns Plaza Hotel ★★ The harbor views at this five-story complex are better than those at most of the more luxurious hotels in Cairns. Two blocks from town, the accommodations are a good size, with fresh, appealing furnishings and modern bathrooms. Suites and studios have kitchenettes. If your balcony does not have a water vista, you overlook a nice aspect of the city or mountains instead. This is a great place for families, because most rooms sleep three or four, and if you need more space and privacy, you can book a connecting suite and standard room. A children's playground is located just across the street.

145 The Esplanade (at Minnie St.). www.cairnsplaza.com.au. ✆ **07/4051 4688.** 60 units. A$180–A$210 double; A$280 suite. Limited free parking. **Amenities:** Restaurant (breakfast only); bar; babysitting; Jacuzzi; small outdoor pool; room service; free Wi-Fi (restaurant/lobby and 6th floor only).

Novotel Cairns Oasis Resort ★ The large pool, complete with swim-up bar and a little sandy beach, is the focus of this attractive six-story resort. All the contemporary-style rooms have balconies with views over the tropical gardens, the mountains, or the pool. The suites, with a large Jacuzzi bathtub, could well be the best-value suites in town.

122 Lake St. www.novotelcairnsresort.com.au. ✆ **07/4080 1888.** 314 units. A$199–A$239 double; A$399 suite. Parking A$9. **Amenities:** Restaurant; 2 bars; babysitting; concierge; gym; lagoon pool; kids pool; room service; spa; Internet (A$12/hr.; A$25/24 hr.).

The Reef Retreat ★★ Tucked back one row of buildings from the beach is this little gem—a collection of contemporary studios and suites built around a swimming pool in a grove of palms and silver Paperbarks. All the rooms have cool tile floors and smart teak and cane furniture. The studios are a terrific value and much larger than the average hotel room. Some suites have two rooms; others have a Jacuzzi and a kitchenette outside on the balcony. Rooms also have iPod docks. There's a barbecue and a Jacuzzi on the grounds, but no elevator.

10–14 Harpa St., Palm Cove. www.reefretreat.com.au. ✆ **07/4059 1744.** 36 units. A$169–A$210 double; A$229–A$349 suite. Free parking. Bus: no. 110. **Amenities:** Jacuzzi; heated saltwater pool; free Wi-Fi.

Rydges Esplanade Cairns Resort ★★ Despite its lack of glitz, this 14-story hotel has been the lodging of choice for a number of movie stars on location in Cairns. A 20-minute waterfront walk from downtown, the hotel offers a range of units, from hotel rooms to penthouse apartments. The one- and two-bedroom apartments face the sea; hotel rooms have sea or mountain views. Kitchenettes are in studios and apartments only. Rooms are spacious, but bathrooms are not. Out back are cheaper studios and apartments, with upgraded furnishings; in front is a pool and sun deck. Family rooms include a queen bed and separate "kids zone" with bunk beds, each featuring a personal 15-inch TV linked to an XBox. On-site are a masseuse and a tour desk.

207–209 Abbott St. (at Kerwin St.). www.rydges.com. ✆ **07/4044 9000.** 240 units. A$139–A$169 double; A$159 family room; A$179–A$379 1-bedroom apt; A$279–A$379 2-bedroom apt. Free covered parking. Bus stop about 100m (328 ft.) from the hotel. **Amenities:** 2 restaurants; 3 bars; airport transfers; babysitting; bikes; concierge; health club; Jacuzzi; 3 outdoor pools; room service; sauna; 2 lit tennis courts; free Wi-Fi.

INEXPENSIVE

Coral Tree Inn ★ The focal point of this airy, modern resort-style motel—a 5-minute walk from the city center—is the friendly communal kitchen that overlooks the palm-lined saltwater pool and paved sun deck. It's a great spot to cook a steak or reef fish on the free barbecue and join other guests at the big shared tables. The smallish, basic-but-neat motel rooms have painted brick walls, terra cotta tile or carpeted floors, and new bathrooms with marble-look laminate countertops. In contrast, the eight suites, which have kitchenettes, are huge and stylish—and some of the best-value rooms in town. All rooms have a balcony or patio; some overlook the commercial buildings next door, but most face the pool. Ask about packages that include cruises and other tours.

166–172 Grafton St. www.coraltreeinn.com.au. ✆ **07/4031 3744.** 58 units. A$145 double; A$169 family room; A$169 suite. Limited free parking; ample street parking. **Amenities:** Restaurant; bar; airport shuttle; babysitting; bike rental; outdoor saltwater pool; free Wi-Fi.

Ellis Beach Oceanfront Bungalows ★★ Set on what is arguably the loveliest of the northern beaches, about 30 minutes from Cairns, these bungalows and cabins sit under palm trees between the Coral Sea and a backdrop of mountainous rainforest. Lifeguards patrol the beach, and there are stinger nets in season as well as a shady pool and a toddlers' wading pool. You'll have plenty of privacy, and rooms are basic but pleasant. As you sit on your veranda and gaze at the ocean, keep an eye out for dolphins. Each bungalow and cabin sleeps two or four and has kitchen facilities (with microwave, fridge, and freezer), but cabins have no en suite bathrooms (they have use of the communal facilities at the campground in the same complex). Beachfront bungalows are the priciest; those behind them are slightly cheaper. The property has a laundry, coin-operated barbecues, and phone and fax facilities (but no phone in your room). No Wi-Fi.

Captain Cook Hwy., Ellis Beach. www.ellisbeach.com. ✆ **1800/637 036** in Australia or 07/4055 3538. 15 units. A$95–A$115 double cabin; A$150–A$190 double bungalow.

Overnighting on the Reef

The **Spirit of Freedom** (www.spiritoffreedom.com.au; ✆ **07/4047 9150**) in Cairns offers a chance to "sleep on the Reef" aboard the 36m (120-ft.) *Spirit of Freedom,* a sleek, modern motor yacht with electronic stabilizers, a widescreen TV with DVD player, comfortable lounge areas, sun decks, and 11 luxury double or quad shared cabins, each with an en suite bathroom. You will visit the popular Cod Hole and Ribbon Reef and on longer trips venture into the Coral Sea. A 3-day, 3-night trip will cost A$1,720 to A$2,520 depending on your choice of cabin and ends with a 193km (120-mile) one-way, 1-hour, low-level flight from Lizard Island back to Cairns. You will fit in up to 11 dives. Prices include meals and pickup from your Cairns accommodations. Allow A$120 extra for equipment rental. Additional 4- and 7-day cruises are offered, the latter a combination of both shorter trips.

2-night minimum stay; 3-night minimum June–Sept. **Amenities:** Restaurant; 2 outdoor pools.

Where to Eat

For cheap eats, head to the Esplanade along the seafront; it's lined with cafes, pizzerias, fish-and-chips shops, food courts, and ice-cream parlors. The northern beaches—particularly Palm Cove—also have some great restaurants (sometimes with prices to match!).

Creative cuisine and a beachfront setting at NuNu.

EXPENSIVE

NuNu ★★★ CONTEMPORARY With an absolute-beachfront location under the palm trees, this Palm Cove favorite offers the kind of food that makes you drag your eyes from the view to your plate! Dining fare includes some bold choices, such as spiced duck with pineapple and raw vegetable salad, a 1 kg (2.2 lb.) Black Angus rib-eye steak, the pricey Queensland mud crab with a chili tamarind sauce, or on the less expensive side, a curry dish. The menu changes seasonally, and you can always count on some surprises. You could easily settle in here for hours.

1 Veivers Rd., Palm Cove (in the Alamanda Resort). www.nunu.com.au. ✆ **07/4059 1880.** Main courses A$17–A$180. Daily 6:15–11am, 11am–4pm, and 5pm–late. Bus: no. 110.

MODERATE

L'Unico ★★ ITALIAN Ask for a table on the veranda, overlooking Trinity Beach's esplanade and the sea. This smart but relaxed Italian place has a great vibe and terrific staff. A wood-fired oven produces pizzas with unexpected toppings (such as lamb with caramelized onion, tomato, and spinach), and the kitchen makes good use of local ingredients in all dishes (angel-hair pasta with Moreton Bay bugs—that would be seafood—is one of my favorite dishes here). The cocktail bar offers a bar menu throughout the day—and there's a kids' menu, too.

75 Vasey Esplanade, Trinity Beach. www.lunico.com.au. ✆ **07/4057 8855.** Main courses A$18–A$46. Daily noon–3:30pm and 5:30–9:30pm. Bus: no. 110.

Ochre Restaurant ★★ GOURMET BUSH TUCKER With a new waterfront location, this Cairns institution is the place to visit if you want a taste of crocodile or kangaroo. You could accuse this restaurant/bar of using weird and wonderful Aussie ingredients as a gimmick, but the diners who have flocked to Ochre for more than a decade know good food when they taste it. Daily specials are big on fresh local seafood, and the regular menu changes often. There may be ingredients you've never heard of—but this is a place to be adventurous! Try salt-and-native-pepper crocodile and prawns with Vietnamese pickles and lemon aspen sambal, chargrilled kangaroo sirloin with a quandong chili glaze, sweet potato fritter and bok choy, or wallaby with lemon aspen cous cous and pea puree. It can be very busy, and you may have to wait for a table, but the food is very good.

1 Marlin Parade, Cairns. www.ochrerestaurant.com.au. ✆ **07/4051 0100.** Main courses A$19–A$42. Australian game platter A$54 per person; seafood platter A$76 per person; 4-course set menu A$70 per person (minimum 2 people). Mon–Fri noon–2:30pm, Sat–Sun and public holidays 11am–2:30pm; daily 5:30pm–midnight. Closed Christmas Day.

Vivo Bar and Grill ★★★ CONTEMPORARY White-painted colonial style, complete with wooden shutters and a wide veranda, this is an inviting choice, looking through the palm trees to the water. Choose from some tempting pasta dishes (such as spanner crab linguine) or something more exotic like a mild red duck curry. A fixed-price dinner menu—two courses ($39) or three courses ($49), including a glass of wine—changes every week, with a choice of dishes for entree, main, and dessert. There's a seafood platter for two for A$95. The restaurant is also open for breakfast. Cocktails and tapas are served daily from 3 to 5pm. A children's menu is available.

49 Williams Esplanade, Palm Cove. www.vivo.com.au. © **07/4059 0944.** Main courses A$30–A$48. Daily 7am–10pm. Bus: nos. 110 or 111.

INEXPENSIVE

Caffiend ★★ CAFE Tucked away between an alley full of street art and an arcade, this atmospheric little cafe is easy to miss. Tipped off by a friend, I headed here for what I'd been told was the best coffee in Cairns (it's roasted in house)—and ended up staying for lunch! Terrines, salads, soups, a big BLT, coffee-infused beef tacos, and other delicious eats are on a menu that changes monthly, but don't forget to check the specials board. Order and pay for your meals at the counter. There's live music at lunchtimes on Sundays.

Shop 5, 78 Grafton St., Cairns. www.caffiend.com.au. © **07/4051 5522.** Main courses A$16–A$24. Daily 7am–3pm.

Candy ★★ CAFE Huge murals and dangling chandeliers give this quirky little cafe/bar an offbeat but sophisticated feel. A tip from a local—and yes, the coffee here is good—led me to this standout on the Grafton Street cafe strip. Candy is a popular breakfast spot, offering the usual range of eggs, avocado on toast with feta cheese, sweet corn fritters, and pancakes. For lunch, you might go for something like the Candy Burger or a Southern Fried Chicken Burger, or a healthy Garden of Eden salad with beetroot, pumpkin, asparagus, and more.

70 Grafton St., Cairns. © **07/4031 8816.** Main courses A$9–A$20. Mon–Fri 7am–3pm; Sat 7am–2pm; Sun 8am–1pm.

Perrotta's at the Gallery ★★ CONTEMPORARY Locals flock here for brunch and lunch, particularly on weekends, and you can team a meal here with a visit to the Cairns Regional Art Gallery next door. Breakfast differs from the usual, offering delights such as blueberry ricotta pancakes with pistachios and lemon syrup. The all-day menu includes bruschetta, burgers, salads, and pasta, or mains such as fish tacos (Spanish mackerel with avocado and Italian-style coleslaw), or spaghetti with prawns—and perhaps a vanilla-bean *panna cotta* with mango for dessert.

Abbott and Shields sts., Cairns. www.perrottasatg.com. © **07/4031 5899.** Breakfast A$6–A$22; lunch A$7–A$28; main courses A$17–A$28. Daily 6:30am–10pm.

Exploring Cairns

Many of the Cairns region's attractions lie outside the city center. Apart from the Reef, there is a string of white sandy beaches just 15 minutes north of the city center. **Trinity Beach,** 15 minutes from the airport or 25 minutes from the city center, is secluded, elegant, and scenic. The most upscale is **Palm Cove,** 20 minutes from the airport or 30 minutes from the city. If you're staying in

Cairns, also check out activities in and around Port Douglas (p. 209). Many tour operators in Port Douglas offer transfers from Cairns. Ask about packages that include discounted entry when you visit several of Cairns' attractions, such as Tjapukai Aboriginal Cultural Park, Cairns Tropical Zoo, Skyrail, and Kuranda Scenic Rail.

Cairns ZOOM and Wildlife Dome ★★ Here, 200 animals—including a large saltwater crocodile named Goliath—are housed in a 20m-high (66-ft.) glass dome on the rooftop of the Pullman Reef Hotel Casino (p. 192). Birds soar overhead, and you can get up close with koalas, lizards, frogs, pademelons, turtles, and snakes. There are wildlife presentations and free, guided tours throughout the day. For A$16 (pay when you buy your entry ticket), you can have a photo taken with a koala or baby croc. Thrill-seekers can zipline through the dome, "climb" around its exterior, or do other adrenaline-charged activities (for an extra cost).

35–41 Wharf St. www.cairnsdome.com.au. ✆ **07/4031 7250.** A$24 adults, A$12 children 4–14, A$60 family. Tickets are valid for reentry for up to 4 days. Daily 9am–6:15pm (last entry 4pm). Closed Christmas Day.

Skyrail Rainforest Cableway ★★★ This magnificent feat of engineering is one of Australia's top tourist attractions. Six-person gondolas leave every few seconds for the 7.5km (4½-mile) journey to the rainforest village of

The Cairns Wildlife Dome tops the Pullman Reef Hotel Casino.

Kuranda (p. 206). The view of the coast as you ascend is so breathtaking that even those afraid of heights should find it worthwhile. As you rise over the foothills of the coastal range, watch the lush green of the rainforest take over beneath you. Looking back, you have spectacular views over Cairns and north toward Trinity Bay. On a clear day, you can see . . . if not forever, then at least to Green Island. For even better views—looking down, between your feet through the glass floor, take a Diamond View gondola. This slightly more expensive option (A$15 extra per adult, A$7.50 per child one-way) also gives you a dedicated boarding queue—and shorter wait—at all stations. If you're really fearless, the Canopy Glider is an open-air option, where for A$100 extra per person (one-way) four passengers and a ranger guide travel in an open gondola. There are two stops during the 90-minute trip, at Red Peak and Barron Falls. After about 10 minutes, you reach Red Peak. You are now 545m (1,788 ft.) above sea level, and massive kauri pines dominate the view. You must change gondolas at each station, so take the time to stroll around the boardwalks for the ground view of the rainforest. Free, guided walks are run regularly through the day.

On board again, you continue to Barron Falls station, built on the site of an old construction camp for workers on the first hydroelectric power station on the Barron River in the 1930s. A rainforest information center is here, as well as boardwalks to the lookouts for wonderful views of the Barron Gorge and Falls. From Barron Falls station, the gondola travels over the thick rainforest of the range. As you reach the end of the trip, the gondola passes over the Barron River and across the Kuranda railway line into the station. Don't worry if it rains on the day you go—one of the best trips of several I've made on Skyrail was in a misty rain, which added a new dimension to the rainforest.

For a wonderful day trip from Cairns I strongly recommend that you combine Skyrail with a trip on the Kuranda Scenic Rail (p. 207). The best way is to take the train from Cairns in the morning and return on Skyrail in the afternoon—for the views going down the range.

Cairns Western Arterial Rd. and Captain Cook Hwy., Smithfield. www.skyrail.com.au. ✆ **07/4038 5555.** Round-trip ticket A$100 adults, A$50 children, A$250 families, including transfers from Cairns or northern beaches hotels. Daily 9am–5:15pm. Closed Christmas Day. You must make a reservation to travel within a 15-minute time frame. Last boardings at 2:45pm for a round-trip or 3:30pm for a one-way journey. Bus: no. 123.

Tjapukai ★★ After a A$12-million revamp, completed in 2015, Tjapukai (pronounced Jab-oo-guy) offers new indigenous cultural experiences in an all-weather venue. This Aboriginal cultural park uses cutting-edge theater technology and an open-plan glass design to showcase the park's rainforest. Two state-of-the-art theater spaces—History and Hero's Walk—and a new restaurant and outdoor bar complement the interactive cultural village, where you can try fire-making, didgeridoo playing, and boomerang and spear throwing, and learn about bush foods, medicines, and hunting techniques. In addition to Aboriginal culture, Torres Strait Islander dance is part of the Tjapukai

Packaging Your Day Trip

Several options exist for a 1-day Cairns adventure. A package combining one-way travel on Skyrail and a trip back on the Kuranda Scenic Railway is A$124 for adults, A$62 for children 4 to 14, and A$310 for families of four with round-trip transfers from Cairns or the northern beaches. A package including the Skyrail, the Scenic Railway, and entry to the Tjapukai Aboriginal cultural park is A$239 for adults, A$128 for kids, and A$644 for families of four, including transfers. An option including the Skyrail, Scenic Railway, and Rainforestation Nature Park (p. 208) is A$185 for adults, A$93 for kids, and A$463 for families of four, including transfers. In most cases, these packages represent convenience rather than savings. Book them through Skyrail, Queensland Rail, or Tjapukai.

experience. Allow 2 to 3 hours to see everything (although you could spend longer here). Start in the Creation Theatre, where performers use the latest in illusion, theatrics, and technology to tell the story of the creation of the world according to the spiritual beliefs of Tjapukai people. Move on through the Magic Space museum and gallery section of the complex to the History Theatre, where a 20-minute film relates the history of the Tjapukai people since the arrival of white settlers 120 years ago.

Art of My People is a performance that explains the varying styles of Australian Indigenous art, including the role of totems, body painting traditions, and differing types of artistic expression used to identify tribes, languages, dialects, and geographical landscapes. A gallery stocks the work of Aboriginal artists and crafts workers.

Night Fire by Tjapukai tours include interactive time in the Magic Space museum, a Creation Show performance, and an outdoor Serpent Circle—a show featuring tap sticks for each guest to use, a join-in *corroboree* (an Aboriginal nighttime dance), and a ceremony involving fire and water. A buffet dinner and dance show follow, where you get the chance to meet the dancers.

Captain Cook Hwy. (beside the Skyrail terminal), Smithfield. www.tjapukai.com.au. © **07/4042 9999.** A$62 adults, A$42 children 5–14, A$166 families. Daily 9am–4:30pm. Night Fire tours run daily from 7–9:30pm and cost A$150 adults, A$90 children, or A$390 family of 4, including transfers to/from Cairns. Closed Christmas Day. Bus: no. 123. Tjapukai shuttle: A$21 adults, A$12 children, and A$24 families.

Outlying Attractions

Hartley's Crocodile Adventures ★★★ Hartley's is the original Australian croc show and quite possibly the best. Its fantastic natural setting is a 2-hectare (5-acre) lagoon surrounded by melaleuca (Paperbark) and bloodwood trees that is home to 23 estuarine crocs. The best time to visit is for the 3pm "croc attack" show, when you can witness the saltwater crocodile "death roll" during the 45-minute performance. At 11am you can see these monsters being hand-fed or hear an eye-opening talk on the less-aggressive freshwater crocs.

You can also have a **"Big Croc Experience,"** where you get to pole-feed a large crocodile yourself—and believe me, this is the way to feel the sheer power of these creatures as they tug the chicken off the pole. Available twice a day at 10:30am and 1pm (bookings essential), you'll be one of six adults (16 and over) to take part in each group (but your friends and family can come along to watch). The cost is A$130 per person. There are tours of the croc farm at 10am and 1:30pm; at 2pm there is a snake show; 4:30pm is koala-feeding time. Cassowaries are fed at 9:30am and 4:15pm. There are also croc- and snake-handling opportunities and heaps of other interesting things to see and do.

Captain Cook Hwy. (40km/24 miles north of Cairns; about 100m off the highway). www.crocodileadventures.com. © **07/4055 3576.** A$39 adults, A$20 children 4–15, A$98 families of 4 (admission good for 3 days). Daily 8:30am–5pm. Closed Christmas Day.

Day Trips to the Reef ★★★

For an introduction to the Great Barrier Reef, most visitors take one of the large-scale tour boats. These motorized catamarans can carry up to 300 passengers each and tie up at their own private permanent pontoons anchored to a platform reef. The boats are air-conditioned and have a bar, videos, and educational material, as well as a marine biologist who gives a talk on the Reef's ecology en route. The pontoons have glass-bottom boats for passengers who don't want to get wet, dry underwater viewing chambers, sun decks, shaded seats, and often showers. But be aware that you will be in a crowded environment. And if you are prone to seasickness, make sure you take some preventive measures before you set out!

An alternative is to go on one of the many smaller boats. These typically visit two or three Reef sites rather than just one. There are usually no more than 20 passengers on board, so you get more personal attention. Another advantage is that you will have the coral pretty much all to yourself. The drawbacks of a small boat are that you have only the cramped deck to sit on

Wildlife Passes

Wildlife enthusiasts who plan to visit several of the attractions in the Cairns region can save a few dollars by buying a **Four Park Pass,** which gives entry to the Cairns Wildlife Dome, The Wildlife Habitat at Port Douglas, and two Kuranda attractions (see "Day Trip to Kuranda," later in this chapter): the Rainforestation Nature Park and the Australian Butterfly Sanctuary (all owned by the same local family). The discounted price of A$90 adults, A$45 children, and A$225 for a family of four is a savings of A$38 per adult or A$95 per family. The pass is valid for 6 months and doesn't have to be used on consecutive days. Buy it at any of the participating parks. A **Kuranda Wildlife Experience pass** offers discounted admission to Birdworld, the Kuranda Koala Gardens, and the Australian Butterfly Sanctuary (p. 207). It can be bought on arrival at any of the three sanctuaries for A$50 adults, A$25 for children.

when you get out of the water, and your traveling time to the Reef may be longer. If you're a nervous snorkeler, you may feel safer on a boat where you will be swimming with 300 other people.

Most day-trip fares include snorkel gear—fins, mask, and snorkel (plus wetsuits in winter, if you want one)—free use of the underwater viewing chambers and glass-bottom-boat rides, a plentiful buffet or barbecue lunch, and morning and afternoon refreshments. Diving is an optional activity for which you pay extra. The big boats post snorkeling scouts to keep a lookout for anyone in trouble and count heads periodically. If you wear glasses, ask whether your boat offers prescription masks—this will make a big difference to the quality of your experience! Don't forget that you can travel as a snorkel-only passenger on most dive boats, too.

Great Adventures ★ (www.greatadventures.com.au; ✆ **07/4044 9944**) does daily cruises from Cairns on fast, air-conditioned catamarans that take you to a three-level pontoon on the Outer Reef. The pontoon has a kids' swimming area, a semisubmersible, and an underwater observatory. The cost for the day is A$239 for adults, A$128 for children 4 to 14, and A$611 for families. You spend at least 3 hours on the Reef. Hotel transfers are available from Cairns, the northern beaches, and Port Douglas for an extra cost. The boat departs the Reef Fleet Terminal at 10:30am.

You can also depart Cairns with Great Adventures at 8:30am and spend 2 hours on Green Island en route. This gives you time to walk nature trails, rent

Great Adventures offers day trips from Cairns to the Great Barrier Reef.

snorkel gear and watersports equipment, or laze on the beach before continuing to the Outer Reef. This cruise costs an extra A$20 per adult and A$12 per child, or A$52 per family.

Ocean Freedom ★★★ (www.oceanfreedom.com.au; ✆ **07/4052 1111**) offers a more intimate experience, giving you the option of a motor cruise or a sailing tour—in both cases with limited numbers to ensure you don't feel crowded. *Ocean Freedom* is a high-speed launch that gives you 6 hours on the reef with no more than 75 passengers and takes you to two Reef sites including Upolu Cay. The day starts at 7:30am at the Reef Fleet Terminal, returning about 4:30pm. The cost is A$205 adults, A$120 children, and A$589 for a family of four and includes glass-bottom-boat rides, all snorkeling gear, and lunch. You can do an introductory dive for A$105 (and a second one for A$50); if you are certified you can dive for A$70 (and a second one for A$35). This is a great way to see the Reef. On the sailing trip aboard *Ocean Free* (www.oceanfree.com.au) you'll be one of only 25 passengers. *Ocean Free* sails at 7:30am, bound for Pinnacle Reef, an exclusive mooring on the eastern lee of Green Island. Prices are the same as *Ocean Freedom.*

Ocean Spirit Cruises ★★ (www.oceanspirit.com.au; ✆ **07/4044 9944**) operates a 32m (105-ft.) luxury sailing catamaran that takes no more than 150 passengers to Michaelmas Cay, a lovely white-sand cay on the Outer Reef surrounded by rich reefs. This trip includes a 2-hour sail to the cay, snorkeling gear, and a guided beach walk—plus the usual reef ecology talks, semisubmersible rides, lunch, and morning and afternoon tea. You get about 4 hours on the Reef and spend your out-of-water time on a beautiful beach, not on a boat. The cost is A$209 for adults, A$108 for children 4 to 14, and A$531 for families of four. If you'd like a guided snorkeling safari rather than going it alone, add A$62 adults, A$32 children, or A$156 family. Introductory dives cost A$126 with all gear included. The trip departs Reef Fleet Terminal at 8:30am daily and returns around 5pm. Transfers from Cairns hotels are A$26 adults and A$17 kids; from the northern beaches it's A$32 adults, A$17 kids.

You can also take a coach transfer from Cairns or Palm Cove to join the **Quicksilver *Wavepiercer*** (www.quicksilver-cruises.com; ✆ **07/4087 2100**), based in Port Douglas, for a day trip to the Outer Reef (p. 215). Transfers cost A$30 per adult or A$16 per child, A$76 for families of four.

Great Adventures, Quicksilver, and Sunlover (see below) all offer helicopter flights over the Reef from their pontoons—a spectacular experience! There are fly-and-cruise trips as well.

Sunlover Cruises ★ (www.sunlover.com.au; ✆ **1800/810 512** in Australia or 07/4050 1333) motors large, fast catamarans to Moore Reef on the Outer Reef. The trip costs A$234 for adults, A$128 for children 4 to 15, and A$618 for families of four, including 4 hours on the Reef, a glass-bottom-boat ride, semisubmersible viewing, and transfers from city hotels. Introductory dives cost A$145 for one dive or A$224 for two. Certified divers pay A$95 for one dive or A$149 for two, including all gear. The cruise includes lunch and leaves from the Reef Fleet Terminal in Cairns at 10am daily.

Diving the Reef.

FOR DIVERS

Tusa Dive ★★ (www.tusadive.com; ✆ **07/4047 9100**) runs a custom-built 24m (72-ft.) dive boat daily to two dive sites from a choice of 15 locations on the Outer Reef. The day costs A$285 for certified divers (two dives included) or A$315 for three dives, and introductory divers pay A$280 for one dive or A$335 for two. Snorkelers pay A$210 adults and A$135 children aged 4 to 14, with wetsuits, guided snorkel tours, and lunch provided. If you want to be shown the best spots, you can take a guided dive for an extra A$10. Transfers from your Cairns or northern beaches hotel cost A$15 or A$20, respectively.

Diving Made Easy

Can't swim? Don't want to get your hair wet? Don't worry—you can still get underwater and see the wonders of the Reef. Several companies offer travelers the chance to don a dive helmet and "walk" underwater. Similar to old-style diving helmets, which allow you to breathe underwater, the helmet has air pumped into it by a hose. You walk into the water to a depth of about 4m (13 ft.), accompanied by instructors, and the Reef is right before you. **Quicksilver Cruises** calls it "Ocean Walker"; with **Sunlover Cruises** and at **Green Island Resort** it's called "Sea Walker." You must be at least 12 years old to walk (A$155–A$168/20 minutes).

The boat takes a maximum of 60 people, with a staff-to-passenger ratio of one to five, so you get a good level of personal attention.

Day Trips to the Islands

Cairns has several coral cays and reef-fringed islands within the **Great Barrier Reef Marine Park.** Less than an hour from the city wharf, **Fitzroy Island** is a rainforest-covered national park, with a coral beach and great snorkeling right off the shore. **Green Island** is a coral cay with snorkeling equal to that of most other places on the Great Barrier Reef. It is also a popular diving spot. You can visit it in half a day if time is short.

Fitzroy Island ★★★ Scenic Fitzroy Island (www.fitzroyislandcairns.com) is 45 minutes from Cairns by boat. There is a small resort on the island, and day-trippers visit for snorkeling and diving, glass-bottom-boat rides, watersports, rainforest walks, or hikes to the lighthouse at the top of the hill. Three ferry operators offer daily services to the island, costing around A$78 adults, A$39 for kids 4 to 13, or A$205 for a family round-trip; for a little extra you can add glass-bottom-boat rides or snorkel-gear to the package. A kiosk on the beach hires snorkeling gear, coral viewing boards, paddle skis, and stand-up paddling boards, or you can book a glass-bottom-boat tour. There is also a turtle rehabilitation center on the island that is worth visiting. **Raging Thunder Adventures** (www.ragingthunder.com.au; ✆ **07/4030 7990**) runs activities including daily guided sea-kayak expeditions around the island. These include snorkeling gear, lunch, and stinger suits (Nov–May), the return ferry trip, 3 hours of kayaking, and then you can stay on the island for the rest of the day. Tours cost A$149, but you must be at least 14 years old.

Green Island ★★ This 15-hectare (37-acre) coral cay is just 27km (17 miles) east of Cairns. You can rent snorkel gear, windsurfers, and paddle skis; take glass-bottom-boat trips; go parasailing; take an introductory or certified dive; walk vine-forest trails; or laze on the beach. The beach is coral sand, so it's a little rough underfoot. Day visitors have access to one of the Green Island Resort pools, its main bar, casual or upscale restaurants, and lockers and showers. Ask the beach staff to recommend the best snorkeling spots. The island is home to **Marineland Crocodile Park** (www.greenislandcrocs.com.au; ✆ **07/4051 4032**), where you can see old nautical artifacts, a Melanesian artifacts collection, a turtle and reef aquarium, and live crocodiles, including Cassius, who—at almost 5.5 meters (18 feet) in length—is listed by Guinness World Records as the largest croc in captivity in the world. Admission is A$19 adults, A$9 kids 5 to 14; croc shows are at 10:30am and 1:30pm.

Great Adventures (www.greatadventures.com.au; ✆ **07/4044 9944**) and **Big Cat Green Island Reef Cruises** (www.greenisland.com.au; ✆ **07/4051 0444**) run to Green Island from Cairns. Both offer a range of half-day and full-day trips with lots of options. Half-day trips with snorkel gear or a glass-bottom-boat cruise cost around A$95 adults, A$47 children 4 to 14, or A$235 for a family of four. Both tours offer pickup from hotels in Cairns, the northern beaches, and Port Douglas for a fee.

Day Trip to Kuranda ★★

34km (21 miles) NW of Cairns

Few travelers visit Cairns without making a trip to the mountain village of **Kuranda,** near the Barron Gorge National Park. Although it's undeniably touristy, the cool mountain air and mist-wrapped rainforest refuse to be spoiled, no matter how many tourists clutter the streets. The shopping in Kuranda—for leather goods, Australian-wool sweaters, opals, crafts, and more—is more unusual than in Cairns, and the handful of cafes and restaurants is much more atmospheric. The town is easy to negotiate on foot; pick up a visitors' guide and map at the Skyrail gondola station or train station. Aside from the village, you can explore the rainforest, the river esplanade, or Barron Falls along a number of easy walking trails.

ESSENTIALS

Getting There

Getting to Kuranda is part of the fun. Some people drive up the winding 25km (16-mile) mountain road, but the most popular approaches are to chuff up the mountainside in a scenic train, or to glide silently over the rainforest canopy in the world's longest gondola cableway, the Skyrail Rainforest Cableway. The most popular round-trip is one-way on the Skyrail and the other way on the train. Mornings are best for photography on Skyrail, but the view is

Kuranda mountain village is known for its local crafts markets.

spectacular coming down in the afternoon. Make up your own mind; both are wonderful!

BY SKYRAIL The **Skyrail Rainforest Cableway** (p. 198) takes you up the Kuranda Range in a six-person gondola suspended over the rainforest.

BY TRAIN The 34km (21-mile) **Kuranda Scenic Railway** (www.ksr.com.au; ✆ **1800/577 245** in Australia or 07/4036 9333) is one of the most scenic rail journeys in the world. The train snakes through the magnificent vistas of the Barron Gorge National Park, past gorges and waterfalls on the 90-minute trip from Cairns to Kuranda. It rises 328m (1,076 ft.) and goes through 15 tunnels before emerging at the pretty Kuranda station, which is smothered in ferns. Built by hand over 5 years in the late 1880s, the railway track is today a monument to the 1,500 men who toiled to link the two towns. The train departs Cairns Central at 8:30 and 9:30am daily (except Christmas Day) and leaves Kuranda at 2 and 3:30pm. The one-way fare is A$50 for adults, A$25 for children 4 to 14, and A$125 for families of four. An upgrade to "Royale" class (A$73 adults, A$48 children, A$217 for a family) adds snacks, drinks, and waiter service.

BY BUS **Trans North Bus & Coach Service** (www.transnorthbus.com; ✆ **07/4095 8644**) operates a bus to Kuranda from Cairns five times a day. The fare is A$6.70 one-way. ***Tip:*** Buying a return ticket will give you priority if the bus is full at the end of the day. Catch it at Orchid Plaza shopping center (79 Abbott St.), at the railway station, or at the Cairns Central Shopping Centre on Spence Street.

Visitor Information

The **Kuranda Visitor Information Centre** (www.kuranda.org; ✆ **07/4093 9311**) is in Centenary Park, at the top end of Coondoo Street. It is open 10am to 4pm daily, except Christmas Day.

EXPLORING KURANDA

Kuranda is known for its markets. The **Kuranda Original Rainforest Markets,** at 7 Therwine St. (enter through the Kuranda Market Mall; (✆ **07/4093 9440;** daily 9:30am–3pm), are devoted exclusively to local artisans who vend fashion, jewelry, leather work, and indigenous art, as well as local produce including honey, coffee, fruit, sugarcane juice, coconuts, and macadamias.

The 90-stall **Heritage Market** (www.kurandamarkets.com.au; ✆ **07/4093 8060**) is open daily from 9:30am to 3:30pm on Rob Veivers Drive, with a range of souvenirs, food, produce, and crafts.

A group of about 50 local artisans sell their work in the **Kuranda Arts Co-Operative** gallery on Coondoo Street, opposite the church (www.artskuranda.asn.au; ✆ **07/4093 9026**). It's open from 10am to 4pm daily. The gallery sells furniture crafted from recycled Australian hardwoods, jewelry, photography, glasswork, and more.

Australian Butterfly Sanctuary ★★ The fluttering array of 1,500 colorful tropical butterflies—including the electric-blue Ulysses and Australia's largest species, the Cairns bird wing—occupies a lush walk-through enclosure here. They may keep you entranced for hours (I was!). Take the free 30-minute guided tour and learn about the butterfly's fascinating life cycle. The butterflies will land on you if you wear pink, red, and other bright colors.

8 Rob Veivers Dr. www.australianbutterflies.com. ✆ **07/4093 7575.** A$20 adults, A$10 children 4–15, A$49 families of 4. Daily 9:45am–4pm. Closed Christmas Day.

Birdworld ★ Behind the markets off Rob Veivers Drive, Birdworld has eye-catching macaws, a pair of cassowaries, and Australia's largest collection of free-flying birds—about 500 of them, representing 75 worldwide species. Two lakes are home to water birds including stilts, herons, and Australia's Black Swan.

Rob Veivers Dr. www.birdworldkuranda.com. ✆ **07/4093 9188.** A$18 adults, A$9 children 4–15. Daily 9am–4pm. Closed Christmas Day.

Kuranda Koala Gardens ★ You can cuddle a koala and have your photo taken at this small wildlife park next to the Heritage Markets. Other animals include freshwater crocodiles, wombats, lizards, and wallabies. Or take a stroll through the walk-through snake enclosure while they slither at your feet—not for the fainthearted.

Rob Veivers Dr. www.koalagardens.com. ✆ **07/4093 9953.** A$19 adults, A$9.50 kids 4–15. Daily 9am–4pm. Closed Christmas Day.

Kuranda Riverboat Tours ★★ If you want to learn about the rainforest, take one of these informative 45-minute river cruises. The cruises depart hourly from 10:45am to 2:30pm from the riverside landing across the footbridge, near the train station, and are the only ones with rights to operate on the Barron River. A team of local naturalists will answer your questions and point out some of the rainforest secrets. Buy your tickets online or pay onboard (cash only). The last cruise of the day returns in time for the 3:30pm train to Cairns.

Rob Veivers Dr. www.kurandariverboat.com.au. ✆ **07/4093 0082** or 0412/159 212 (mobile). A$18 adults, A$9 children 5–15, A$45 family of 4.

Rainforestation Nature Park ★★ At this 40-hectare (99-acre) nature and cultural complex, you can take a 45-minute ride into the rainforest in a World War II amphibious Army Duck. You'll hear commentary on orchids and other rainforest wildlife along the way. You can also see a performance by Aboriginal dancers; learn about Aboriginal legends and throw a boomerang on the Dreamtime Walk; or have your photo taken cuddling a koala or holding a small freshwater crocodile in the wildlife park (photos extra, from A$20). The Army Duck runs on the hour, beginning at 10am; the Aboriginal dancers perform at 10:30am, noon, and 2pm; and the 30-minute Dreamtime Walk leaves at 10, 11, and 11:30am, and 12:30, 1:30, and 2:30pm.

Kennedy Hwy., a 5-min. drive from the center of Kuranda. www.rainforest.com.au. ✆ **07/4085 5008.** A$49 adults, A$25 kids 4–14, A$123 families of 4. Daily 9am–4pm. Closed Christmas Day. Shuttle from the Butterfly Sanctuary, Rob Veivers Dr., every 30 min. 10:45am–2:45pm for A$12 adults, A$6 children, A$30 families, round-trip.

WHERE TO EAT IN KURANDA

Frogs Restaurant ★★ CAFE This is a good place to stop for lunch, tucked into the wildlife attractions and Heritage Markets just off the main street. Simple offerings like wraps, pizzas, and salads dominate, but you can also get a hearty steak, seafood, or a bush tasting platter (kangaroo, emu, crocodile, prawns, and wild barramundi) if you want something bigger. Or try the Curry of the Day, a bargain at only A$8. Be on the lookout for the water dragons (they're harmless) on the deck overlooking the rainforest. It also has free Wi-Fi. 2/4 Rob Veivers Dr. www.frogsrestaurant.com.au. ✆ **07/4093 8952.** Main courses A$8–A$28. Daily 9:30am–4pm. Closed Christmas Day.

PORT DOUGLAS ★★★

Port Douglas: 67km (42 miles) N of Cairns; Mossman: 19km (12 miles) N of Port Douglas

The fishing village of Port Douglas is where the rainforest meets the Reef. Just over an hour's drive from Cairns, through rainforest and along a winding (sometimes treacherously so) road beside the sea, Port Douglas may be small, but stylish shops and seriously trendy restaurants line the main street, and beautiful Four Mile Beach is not to be missed. This is a favorite spot with celebrities big and small. Travelers often base themselves in "Port," as the locals call it, because they like the rural surroundings, the uncrowded beach, and the absence of tacky development (so far, anyway). Many Reef tours originate in Port, and many of the tours in the Cairns section pick up here.

The waters off Port Douglas boast just as many wonderful reefs and marine life forms as those around Cairns; the reefs are equally close to shore and equally colorful and varied. The closest Reef site off Port Douglas, the **Low Isles,** is only 15km (9 miles) northeast. Coral sand and 22 hectares (55 acres) of coral surround these two cays; the smaller is a sand cay covered in rich vegetation and the larger is a shingle/rubble cay covered in mangroves, home to thousands of nesting Torresian Imperial pigeons. If you visit the Low Isles, wear shoes that you can get wet, because the coral sand can be rough underfoot.

The coral is not quite as dazzling as the Outer Reef's—which is where you should head if you have only one day to spend on the Great Barrier Reef—but the fish life here is rich, and you may spot sea turtles. Because you can wade out to the coral right from the beach, the Low Isles are a good choice for nervous snorkelers. A half-day or day trip to the Low Isles makes for a more relaxing day than a visit to Outer Reef sites, because in addition to exploring the coral, you can sunbathe on the sand or laze under palm-thatched beach umbrellas.

Essentials

GETTING THERE

There is no train to Port Douglas, and no scheduled air service. A small airport handles light aircraft and helicopter charters.

BY CAR Port Douglas is a scenic 65-minute drive from Cairns, in part along a narrow winding road that skirts the coast. Take Sheridan Street north out of the city as it becomes the Captain Cook Highway; follow the signs to Mossman and Mareeba until you reach the Port Douglas turnoff on your right. A **taxi** fare from Cairns to Port Douglas will set you back around A$200; call **Cairns Taxis** (✆ **131 008** in Cairns).

BY BUS A one-way ticket with **Sun Palm Transport** (www.sunpalmtransport.com.au; ✆ **07/4099 1191**) to Port Douglas hotels from Cairns airport is A$36 for adults. One child rides free with a paying adult; additional children pay half price.

VISITOR INFORMATION

The biggest and most central information center in town is the privately run **Port Douglas Tourist Information Centre,** 38 Wharf St. (www.tourismportdouglas.com.au; ✆ **07/4099 4540**), open from 7:30am to 6pm daily. There is no official visitor information office in Port Douglas, but the tourism information website of **Tourism Port Douglas and Daintree** (www.visitportdouglasdaintree.com.au; ✆ **07/4099 4588**) is a good source.

GETTING AROUND

Avis (✆ **07/4099 4331**), **Budget** (✆ **07/4099 5702**), and **Thrifty** (✆ **07/4099 5555**) have offices in Port Douglas. All rent regular vehicles as well as four-wheel-drives, which you need if you plan to drive to Cape Tribulation. For a taxi, call **Port Douglas Taxis** (✆ **131 008**).

There is no bus service in Port Douglas, but several companies operate shuttles between the town center and major resorts. Ask your hotel or resort which one services them.

A good way to get around the town's flat streets is by bike. **Port Douglas Bicycle Centre,** 3 Warner St. (www.portdouglasbikehire.com; ✆ **07/4099 5799**), rents bikes from A$16 for 4 hours, A$20 for a full day (or A$16/day for multi-day rental).

Where to Stay

Port Douglas Accommodation Holiday Rentals (www.portdouglasaccom.com.au; ✆ **07/4098 5222**) rents a wide range of apartments and homes.

EXPENSIVE

QT Resort ★★ One of the quirkier resorts in Port Douglas, the QT is a magnet for the hip crowd that jams the bar on weekends, dying to be seen. The rooms are hip and colorful too, with a slightly retro feel (and in case you fall in love with any of the *objets* scattered around, there is—rather strangely, I thought—a price list for everything from the coat hangers to the armchairs). There are also one- and two-bedroom villas to rent. It's too far to walk to town, but you can borrow a bike or take the shuttle (A$6 one-way adults, A$3 kids). From June to October, the QT Moonlight Cinema shows classic and new release films.

87–109 Port Douglas Rd. www.qthotelsandresorts.com/port-douglas. ✆ **07/4099 8900.** 170 units. A$289–A$309 double; A$339–A$359 1-bedroom villa; A$429–A$449 2-bedroom villa. Free parking. Shuttle bus to town every 15 minutes from 7:30am–11:30pm daily (A$6 one-way adults, A$3 kids). **Amenities:** Restaurant; bar; babysitting; free use of bikes; concierge; health club; 2 outdoor pools; room service; spa; 2 tennis courts; free Wi-Fi.

Thala Beach Nature Reserve ★★ Open to the elements—and the odd curious wallaby—the reception area of this stunning rainforest hideaway makes a striking first impression. From the restaurant upstairs, the impact is even greater, with sweeping views of the coastline and rainforest. Thala (pronounced *Ta*-la) Beach is 16km (10 miles) outside Port Douglas, set on a 58-hectare (145-acre) private peninsula, bordered on three sides by private beaches and coves. Owners Rob and Oonagh Prettejohn took their inspiration from the flora and fauna of the World Heritage area that surrounds it to create secluded treehouse bungalows. I've stayed here twice, and all the rooms are spacious and comfortable, with timber-paneled walls and king-size or twin beds. The Coral Sea bungalows overlook the ocean; the rest have forest and mountain views. Some of the bungalows are a bit of a hike from the public areas, but it's a small price to pay for the privacy and the rainforest setting (and you can call for a golf-buggy pick-up).

Private Rd., Oaks Beach. www.thalabeach.com.au. ✆ **07/4098 5700.** 85 units. A$359–A$899 double. Free parking. Hotel shuttle to Port Douglas. **Amenities:** Restaurant; bar; 2 outdoor pools; spa; free Wi-Fi (in main lodge only).

MODERATE

By the Sea ★ You won't find a friendlier or more convenient place to stay in Port Douglas than these apartments, 10 seconds from the beach and less than 10 minutes' walk from town. There are also heaps of "extras" such as bikes, iPads, laptops, and beach towels on loan. Some of the apartments are on the small side (most suit only three people), but all are well cared for. You can opt for a tiny Garden apartment with a patio; Balcony and Seaview apartments are a bit larger and have private balconies. Seaview apartments are quite roomy and have side views of Four Mile Beach. Towels are changed daily and linen weekly, and rooms are serviced every 4 days (or you can pay A$15 per day extra for daily service). It has no elevator and no porter, so be prepared to carry your luggage upstairs.

72 Macrossan St. www.bytheseaportdouglas.com.au. ✆ **07/4099 5387.** 21 units. A$245–A$285 double studio; A$315–A$355 1-bedroom apt; A$415–A$475 2-bedroom apt. Free parking. **Amenities:** Jacuzzi; outdoor heated pool; bikes; free Wi-Fi.

Marae ★★ John and Pam Burden's architecturally stunning timber home, on a hillside 15km (9½ miles) north of Port Douglas, is a glamorous and restful bush retreat. The contemporary bedrooms have mosquito nets and smart linens on king-size beds, not to mention elegant bathrooms. The garden room overlooks the valley and the pool. Wallabies and bandicoots (small marsupials) feed in the garden, kingfishers and honeyeaters use the birdbaths, and butterflies are everywhere. A delicious tropical breakfast is served on the deck in the company of a flock of red-browed finches and peaceful doves. Mossman Gorge is just a few minutes' drive. You need a car to stay here.

Ponzo Rd., Shannonvale. www.marae.com.au. ✆ **07/4098 4900.** 2 units. A$235 double. 2-night minimum. Rates include full breakfast. Children 16 and under not accepted. **Amenities:** Outdoor pool; free Wi-Fi.

INEXPENSIVE

Coral Beach Lodge ★★ This modest lodge, popular with backpackers, families, and budget travelers, is on a suburban street that's just a 10-minute walk from town. All rooms were renovated in 2016, building on the Lodge's reputation as an award-wining hostel-style accommodation. You can swap stories with other guests as you cook and eat in the communal kitchen and dining room. The rooms have small patios and are air-conditioned at night. Dorm-style rooms (male and female) have shared bathrooms.

7 Craven Close. www.coralbeachlodge.com.au. ✆ **07/4099 5422.** 28 units. A$84–A$124 double; four- or five-share rooms A$25–A$40 per person. Free parking. Bus: no. 110 (stop at front door). **Amenities:** Outdoor pool; free use of bikes; free Wi-Fi.

Port Douglas Retreat ★ This well-kept two-story studio apartment complex on a quiet street, featuring white-battened balconies in the Queenslander architectural style, is a good value. Even some of the ritzier places in town can't boast its lagoon-like saltwater pool, surrounded by dense jungle and wrapped by an ample, shady sun deck that cries out to be lounged on with a good book and a cool drink. The apartments are not enormous, but they're fashionably furnished with terra cotta tile floors, wrought-iron beds, cane seating, and colorful bedcovers. All have large furnished balconies or patios looking onto tropical gardens; some on the ground floor open onto the common-area boardwalk, so you might want to ask for a first-floor (second-story) unit. The town and beach are a 5-minute walk away.

31–33 Mowbray St., at Mudlo St. www.portdouglasretreat.com.au. ✆ **07/4099 5053.** 36 units. A$129–A$179 double. Minimum 3-night stay. Secure covered parking. **Amenities:** Free airport transfers; outdoor saltwater pool; free Wi-Fi.

Where to Eat

EXPENSIVE

Sassi Cucina e Bar ★★ ITALIAN Presided over by gregarious Italian owner/chef Tony Sassi—who's something of a local celebrity—this traditional Italian *cucina* offers fresh seasonal flavors done simply and well. Start with some *spuntini* (small plates) of delicacies such as crispy fried small local prawns with garlic and chili, and then move on to a pasta or risotto. There are always specials, depending on what's fresh . . . but make sure you try Tony's special meatballs, or chili mud crab if it's on offer! Sit inside in the air-conditioning, on the pavement outside, or in the garden out the back. Prices are lower at lunch.

4 Macrossan St. (at Wharf St.), Port Douglas. www.sassi.com.au. ✆ **07/4099 6744.** Main courses A$20–A$49. Daily 11am–9:30pm.

MODERATE

Salsa Bar & Grill ★★★ CONTEMPORARY This trendy restaurant, in a timber Queenslander with wraparound verandas, has seriously good food, great prices, and lively, fun service. Little wonder you need to book well ahead—sometimes up to 2 weeks in advance—and it's the restaurant of choice for everyone from presidents to pop stars! Choose simple fare such as gnocchi or Caesar salad or such mouthwatering delights as a jambalaya with tiger prawns, squid, yabbie, smoked chicken, and crocodile sausage; or Paperbark-smoked kangaroo loin with guava pulp and goat-cheese marshmallow. There's a kids' menu too.

26 Wharf St. (at Warner St.), Port Douglas. www.salsaportdouglas.com.au. ✆ **07/4099 4922.** Main courses A$29–A$41. Daily noon–midnight.

Zinc ★★ CONTEMPORARY If you're like me, you may find yourself coming back more than once to this casual but very smart restaurant during your Port Douglas stay. The food is very good (think crispy-skinned barramundi with a sweet paprika and dill-scented cucumber and Greek yogurt salad with chili oil, rocket pesto, and lime-thyme dressing, or a simple eye fillet steak with mushroom pâté, green beans, and garlic-sage potatoes). Zinc offers service with a smile, and kids are welcomed with a children's menu (and eat free if you order between 5–5:30pm). Make sure you check out the restrooms, which have floor-to-ceiling aquariums. Reservations are recommended for dinner.

Macrossan St. (at Davidson St.), Port Douglas. www.zincportdouglas.com. ✆ **07/4099 6260.** Main courses A$26–A$39. Daily 8am–midnight.

Exploring Port Douglas

Some companies in Cairns that offer outdoor activities will pick up from Port Douglas hotels. The best outdoor activity in Port Douglas, however, is to do absolutely nothing on spectacular **Four Mile Beach** ★★★. From May through September, the water is stinger-free. From October through April, swim in the stinger safety net.

> **The Secret of the Seasons**
>
> High season in Port Douglas is roughly June 1 through October 31. Low-season holiday periods run from approximately November to May (excluding Christmas and New Year's).

Every Sunday from 7:30am to 1pm, a colorful **handicrafts and food market** is held on the lawn under the mango trees by Dickson Inlet, at the end of Macrossan Street. Stalls offer everything from foot massages to fresh coconut milk.

Kuku Yalanji Cultural Habitat Tours ★★★ Brothers Linc and Brandon Walker will take you on the walk of a lifetime, on the beach opposite their parents' house. This is the traditional fishing ground of the Kubirri Warra people, when the mudflats and mangroves are exposed at low tide and the place where you will spend 2½ hours learning to throw a spear, hunt and stalk, and use coastal resources wisely. If you are lucky, you may spear a crab (not so lucky for the crab!), and when enough has been foraged to make a small meal, you'll take it back to the house where Linc and Brandon's mother will cook it up for you to eat on the veranda. It's an authentic and unforgettable experience. Don't forget to take insect repellent (just in case), and wear shoes you don't mind getting wet (though bare feet are best!).

Bougainvillea St., Cooya Beach (north of Port Douglas; take Bonnie Doon Rd., off the Captain Cook Highway). www.kycht.com.au. ✆ **07/4098 3437.** A$75 adults, A$45 kids 5–14, A$240 family of 4. Daily at 9:30am and 1:30pm.

Kuku Yalanji Cultural Habitat Tours.

Mossman Gorge Centre ★★★ This is the gateway to wonderful Mossman Gorge, where the gushing Mossman River tumbles over massive boulders through the rainforest. You can visit the gorge on your own and take the short boardwalks along the river, but I highly recommend joining one of the guided **Ngadiku Dreamtime Walks,** with a member of the local Kuku-Yalanji tribe. You will learn about Aboriginal bush medicines and food, Dreamtime legends, and the sacred sites their families have called home for thousands of years. There are two tours to choose from, starting from A$62 adults, A$31 children 5 to 15, or A$155 for a family of four. The center has a gift shop, art gallery, and cafe. You can only access the gorge by taking the shuttle bus, which leaves the visitor center every 15 minutes between 8am and 5:45pm daily. The cost is A$9.10 for adults, A$4.55 for children, or A$23 for a family of four. Most tour companies from Cairns and Port Douglas will get you here.

Mossman Gorge Rd., Mossman (20km N of Port Douglas). www.mossmangorge.com.au. ✆ **07/4099 7000.** Daily 8am–6pm. Closed Christmas Day.

Wildlife Habitat ★★★ This is a great place to see animals that are too shy to be spotted in the wild. Here, 180 animal species from the Wet Tropics are in one place for you to see up close. You can see saltwater and freshwater crocodiles, hand-feed kangaroos, and have your photo taken with a koala. The highlight is the walk-through aviary that houses more than 100 Wet Tropics bird species, including cassowaries. Between 9 and 10:30am, the park serves "breakfast with the birds," and between noon and 2pm "lunch with the lorikeets." Breakfast costs A$54 for adults, A$27 for kids, and A$135 families, and includes Habitat admission; lunch costs a few dollars more. Don't miss one of the excellent free, guided tours that run regularly from 9:30am to 4pm. You can also do a "wildnight" tour for A$42 adults, A$31 children, or A$115 families, to see some of Australia's amazing nocturnal creatures. Allow at least 2 hours here.

Port Douglas Rd. (corner Captain Cook Hwy). www.wildlifehabitat.com.au. © **07/4099 3235.** A$35 adults, A$18 kids 4–14, A$88 families of 4. Daily 8am–5pm. Closed Christmas Day.

Day Trips to the Reef

The waters off Port Douglas are home to dramatic coral spires and swim-throughs at the Cathedrals; giant clams at Barracuda Pass; a village of parrot fish, anemone fish, unicorn fish, and two moray eels at the pinnacle of Nursery Bommie; fan corals at Split-Bommie; and many other wonderful sites.

Without a doubt, the most popular large vessels visiting the Outer Reef are the **Quicksilver Wavepiercers** (www.quicksilver-cruises.com; © **07/4087 2100**), based out of Port Douglas. These ultrasleek, high-speed, air-conditioned 37m (121-ft.) and 46m (151-ft.) catamarans carry 300 or 440 passengers to Agincourt Reef, a ribbon reef 39 nautical miles (72km/45 miles) from shore on the outer edge of the Reef. After the 90-minute trip to the Reef, you tie up at a two-story pontoon, where you spend 3½ hours.

Quicksilver departs Marina Mirage at 10am daily except on December 25. The cost for the day is A$253 for adults, A$131 for kids 4 to 14, and A$642 for families of four. Guided snorkel safaris cost A$62 per adult, A$32 for kids, A$156 for families; introductory dives cost A$168 per person. Qualified divers can take a dive-tender boat to make one dive for A$120 or two dives for A$170 per person, all gear included. Booking in advance is a good idea.

The dive boat ***Poseidon*** (www.poseidon-cruises.com.au; © **07/4087 2100**) welcomes snorkelers. It presents a Reef ecology talk and takes you on a guided snorkel safari. The *Poseidon* is a fast 24m (79-ft.) vessel that visits three Outer Reef sites. The day-trip price of A$243 for adults, and A$173 for kids 4 to 14, includes snorkel gear, a marine-biology talk, snorkel safaris, lunch, and pickups from Port Douglas hotels. Certified divers pay an extra A$48 for one dive, A$68 for two dives, or A$84 for three, including all gear. Guides will accompany you, free of charge, to show you great locations. The boat departs the Reef Marina daily at 8:30am, taking about 2 hours to get to the first of three reef sites you will visit during the day at Agincourt Reef. Among the 25-plus dive sites visited by Poseidon's cruises are **Turtle Bay,** where you may meet a friendly Maori wrasse; the **Cathedrals,** a collection of coral pinnacles and swim-throughs; and **Barracuda Pass,** home to coral gardens, giant clams, and schooling barracuda.

The snorkeling specialist boat ***Wavelength*** (www.wavelength.com.au; © **07/4099 5031**) does a full-day trip to the Outer Reef for A$240 for adults, A$190 for children 8 to 14. ***Note:*** This trip is not suitable for children under 8 years old. The trip visits three different snorkel sites each day and incorporates a guided snorkel tour and a reef presentation by a marine biologist. It carries only 30 passengers and includes snorkel gear, sunsuits, lunch, and transfers from your Port Douglas hotel. Both beginners and experienced snorkelers will like this trip, which departs daily at 8:30am.

Another way to spend a pleasant day—closer to shore—on the Great Barrier Reef is to visit the **Low Isles,** 15km (9½ miles) northeast of Port Douglas. The isles are 1.5-hectare (3¾-acre) coral-cay specks of lush vegetation surrounded by white sand and 22 hectares (54 acres) of coral—which is what makes them so appealing. The coral is not quite as good as the Outer Reef's, but the fish life is rich, and the proximity makes for a relaxing day.

The trip aboard the 30m (98-ft.) luxury sailing catamaran ***Wavedancer,*** operated by Quicksilver (www.wavedancerlowisles.com; ✆ **07/4087 2100**), is A$201 for adults, A$103 for kids 4 to 14, and A$510 for families. You'll leave Port Douglas at 10am, and once there, you can snorkel, take a glass-bottom-boat ride, or do a guided beach walk with a marine biologist. Coach transfers are available through Quicksilver from your Port Douglas accommodations for A$12 adults, A$6 kids, or A$30 for a family.

TOWNSVILLE & MAGNETIC ISLAND ★★

346km (215 miles) S of Cairns; 1,371km (850 miles) N of Brisbane

With a population of 140,000, Townsville is Australia's largest tropical city. With an economy based on mining, manufacturing, education, and tourism, it is sometimes—rather unjustly, I think—overlooked as a holiday destination. The people are friendly, the city is pleasant, and there's plenty to do. The town nestles by the sea below the pink face of Castle Rock, which looms 300m (about 1,000 ft.) directly above. Townsville's popular waterfront parkland, The Strand (p. 220), is complemented by the **Jezzine Barracks,** a A$40-million redevelopment of unused land which is now home to a stunning collection of outdoor sculptures and memorials honoring the city's wartime history (with more than a passing nod to the American forces who served here in World War II). It is a wonderful parkland that's well worth exploring.

Cruises depart from the harbor for the Great Barrier Reef, about 2½ hours away, and just 8km (5 miles) offshore is Magnetic Island—"Maggie" to the locals—a popular place for watersports, hiking, and spotting koalas in the wild.

Townsville's waters boast hundreds of large patch reefs, some miles long, with excellent coral and marine life, including mantas, rays, turtles, and sharks, and sometimes canyons and swim-throughs in generally good visibility. One of the best reef complexes is **Flinders Reef,** which is actually in the Coral Sea, beyond the Great Barrier Reef Marine Park boundaries. At 240km (149 miles) offshore, it has 30m (100-ft.) visibility, plenty of coral, and big walls and pinnacles with big fish to match, such as whaler shark and barracuda.

What draws most divers to Townsville, though, is one of Australia's best wreck dives, the **SS *Yongala.*** Still largely intact, the sunken remains of this steamer lie in 15m to 30m (50–98 ft.) of water, with visibility of 9m to 18m (approximately 30–60 ft.). Diving the *Yongala* is not for beginners—most dive companies require their customers to have advanced certification or to have logged a minimum of 15 dives with open-water certification. The boat is usually visited on a live-aboard trip of at least 2 days, but some companies run day trips.

Although Townsville can be hot and humid in the summer—and sometimes in the path of cyclones—it is generally spared the worst of the wet-season rains and boasts 300 days of sunshine a year.

Essentials

GETTING THERE

BY CAR Townsville is on the Bruce Highway, a 3-hour drive north of Airlie Beach and 4½ hours south of Cairns. The Bruce Highway breaks temporarily in the city. From the south, take Bruce Highway Alt. 1 route into the city. From the north, the highway leads into the city. The drive from Cairns to Townsville through sugar-cane fields, cloud-topped hills, and lush bushland is a pretty one—one of the most picturesque stretches in Queensland.

BY PLANE **Qantas** (www.qantas.com.au; ✆ **131 313** in Australia) flies direct from Brisbane and Cairns. **Jetstar** (www.jetstar.com.au; ✆ **131 538** in Australia) flies direct from Sydney and Melbourne's Tullamarine airport; and **Virgin Australia** (www.virginaustralia.com.au; ✆ **136 789** in Australia) flies direct from Brisbane, Melbourne, and Sydney daily. **Regional Express** (www.rex.com.au; ✆ **131 713** in Australia or 02/6393 5550) flies from Cairns. **Townsville City Shuttle** (www.shuttletsv.com.au; ✆ **0478/160 036** mobile) operates an airport shuttle service to the city for A$10 adults, A$15 for two or three passengers, and A$20 for a group of four. Bookings essential. A **taxi** from the airport to most central hotels costs about A$25.

BY TRAIN **Queensland Rail** (www.queenslandrailtravel.com.au; ✆ **1300/131 722** in Queensland or 07/3606 6630) long-distance trains stop at Townsville on the Brisbane-Cairns route. The 17-hour Spirit of Queensland journey from Brisbane costs A$315 for a premium economy seat.

BY BUS **Greyhound Australia** (www.greyhound.com.au; ✆ **1300/473 946** in Australia or 07/4799 3715 in Townsville) coaches stop at Townsville several times a day on their Cairns-Brisbane-Cairns routes. The fare from Cairns is A$65; trip time is around 5 to 6 hours. The fare from Brisbane is around A$282; trip time is 24 hours (sometimes longer).

VISITOR INFORMATION

There are two official information centers in town. One is in the heart of the city on Townsville Bulletin Square, just off Flinders St. (www.townsvillenorthqueensland.com.au; ✆ **1800/801 902** in Australia or 07/4721 3660); it's open Monday through Friday, 9am to 5pm, and weekends from 9am to 1pm. It is closed Good Friday, Christmas Day, and until 1pm on Anzac Day (Apr 25). The **Bruce Highway Visitor Information Centre** (✆ **07/4780 4397**) is at Billabong Sanctuary (p. 220); it's open Monday to Saturday 9am to 4pm and Sunday 10am to 2pm.

GETTING AROUND

Local **Sunbus** (www.sunbus.com.au; ✆ 07/4771 9800) buses depart from Flinders Street. Car-rental chains include **Avis** (✆ 07/4799 2022), **Budget** (✆ 07/4762 7433), **Europcar** (✆ 07/4760 1380), **Hertz** (✆ 07/4728 9530), and **Thrifty** (✆ 07/4725 4600).

For a taxi, call ✆ **131 008.**

Where to Stay

Grand Hotel and Apartments Townsville ★★ Just off the bustle of the Palmer Street restaurant strip, all the rooms at this smart hotel, opened in 2014, have private balconies. There's no restaurant—but no need of one. The hotel offers a charge-back service from six nearby restaurants (and room service as well). As well as standard hotel rooms, you have the choice of one- or two-bedroom apartments, which have open-plan kitchen and living space, separate bedroom(s) and bathroom, and a washing machine and dryer.

8–10 Palmer St. www.grandhoteltownsville.com.au. ✆ **07/4753 2800.** 230 units. A$143–A$315 double or 1-bedroom apt; A$278–A$378 2-bedroom apt. Free parking. **Amenities:** Gym; Jacuzzi; outdoor pool; room service; Wi-Fi (A$5.50/1 hr.; A$24/24 hr.), free Wi-Fi if you book direct.

Hotel Grand Chancellor Townsville ★ Just a stroll from all the city's major attractions and the Magnetic Island ferries, this 20-story hotel is fairly standard but a good choice for its heart-of-the-city location. The locals call it the "Sugar Shaker" because of its distinctive circular shape (which gives every room a view of the city, the bay, or Castle Hill). Suites have kitchenettes. The star attractions are the rooftop pool and sun deck with barbecues. Parking is in a separate building, which can be inconvenient at times.

334 Flinders St. www.grandchancellorhotels.com. ✆ **1800/753 379** in Australia or 07/4729 2000. 200 units. A$122–A$140 double; A$160–A$170 suite. Parking A$13 per day. **Amenities:** Restaurant; 2 bars; babysitting; bikes; concierge; gym; rooftop pool; room service; free Wi-Fi.

Mercure Townsville ★★ Set in tropical gardens on the shores of a large lake, this resort-style hotel is a pleasant surprise. It's a bit out of town (on the main road north), right next to a big shopping center, but once you're there you may not want to travel far. The free-form swimming pool is Townsville's largest (it also has a Jacuzzi); take a dip or go for a stroll around the lake and watch the birds. Rooms are a good size, and family suites sleep four and have kitchenettes.

Woolcock and Attlee sts. www.mercuretownsville.com.au. ✆ **07/4759 4900.** 162 units. A$149–A$189 double; A$189 family room. Free parking. **Amenities:** Restaurant; bar; babysitting; pool; room service; 2 lit tennis courts; free Wi-Fi.

Seagulls Seafront Resort ★★ This popular, low-key resort, a 5-minute drive from the city, is built around an inviting free-form saltwater pool in 1.2

hectares (3 acres) of tropical gardens. Despite the Esplanade location, the motel-style rooms do not boast waterfront views, but they are comfortable and a good size. The larger deluxe rooms have painted brick walls, sofas, dining furniture, and kitchen sinks. Studios and family rooms have kitchenettes; executive suites have Jacuzzis. Apartments have a main bedroom and a bunk bedroom (sleeps three), a kitchenette, dining area, and a roomy balcony. The resort is wheelchair-friendly, with some ground-floor rooms specially adapted for guests with disabilities. The accommodations wings surround the pool and its pretty open-sided restaurant, which is popular with locals. It's a 10-minute walk to the Strand, and most tour companies pick up at the door.

74 The Esplanade, Belgian Gardens. www.seagulls.com.au. © **07/4721 3111.** 70 units. A$120–A$165 double; A$180–A$206 family rooms; A$208–A$228 2-bedroom apt; A$205 suite. Free parking. Bus: no. 7. **Amenities:** Restaurant; bar; children's playground; 2 large outdoor saltwater pools and children's wading pool; room service; small tennis court; free Wi-Fi.

Where to Eat

There are many restaurants and cafes on **Palmer Street,** an easy stroll across the river from Flinders Street, and on the Strand.

C Bar ★★ CONTEMPORARY Right on the waterfront, C Bar is a great place for casual seaside dining any time of day, offering good, healthy choices for breakfast and an interesting all-day menu (from 11:30am). It's a lovely spot for sundowners or dinner, too. At lunch or dinner, try a prawn and coconut laksa with rice noodles and Asian greens, a simple fish 'n' chips, or maybe a roasted beetroot and haloumi salad. The service is patchy and sometimes slow, but for my money the view is one of the best in town. Kids' menu available.

Gregory Street Headland, The Strand. www.cbar.com.au. © **07/4724 0333.** Main courses A$17–A$30. Daily 6am–10pm.

Jam Corner ★★★ CONTEMPORARY Dishes that will make you groan with pleasure, with flavors designed to delight . . . that's what you will find at this smart, friendly restaurant. On my last visit to Townsville I ate here three times in 2 days—it was that good. At breakfast, try the Asian chicken omelet with snow peas, bean shoots, fried shallots, and chili jam (or the most popular item on the menu, the Queensland avocado on wholegrain sourdough with whipped Danish feta and poached eggs). For dinner, you might find dishes like Townsville bugs (a crustacean), prawn, clam, and calamari in orange curry with kai-lan, yam dumpling, and noodles, or a pork cutlet wrapped in pancetta and served with pumpkin and apple risotto. The menu changes regularly, but you can be assured that the quality won't. Really, don't miss this restaurant. It's no wonder the awards are rolling in.

Palmer St. www.jamcorner.com.au. © **07/4721 4900.** Main courses A$35–A$42; 6-course tasting menu A$70 (or A$100 with wine). Tues–Fri 6:30am–2:30pm and 5:30pm–late; Sat 7am–2:30pm and 5:30pm–late; Sun 7:30am–2pm.

Exploring Townsville

Don't miss the views of the city, Cleveland Bay, and Magnetic Island from **Castle Hill;** it's a 2.5km (1½-mile) drive or a shorter, steep walk up from town (make sure to do it in the cool part of the day). To drive to the top, follow Stanley Street west from Flinders Street to Castle Hill Drive; the walking trails up are posted en route.

The Strand is a 2.5km (1½-mile) strip with safe swimming beaches, a fitness circuit, a great free water park for the kids, and plenty of covered picnic areas and free gas barbecues. Stroll along the promenade or relax at one of the many cafes, restaurants, and bars while you gaze across the Coral Sea to Magnetic Island. For the more active, there are areas to in-line skate, cycle, walk, fish, or play half-court basketball. Four rocky headlands and a picturesque jetty adjacent to Strand Park provide good fishing spots, and two surf lifesaving clubs service the three swimming areas along the Strand. Cool off in the Olympic-size Tobruk Pool (A$5 adults, A$3 kids 2–12) or the seawater Rockpool or at the beach itself. During summer (Nov–Mar), three swimming enclosures operate to keep swimmers safe from marine stingers. If watersports are on your agenda, try jet-skiing, hire a canoe, or take to the latest in pedal skis. A state-of-the-art water park has waterfalls, water slides, and water cannons, plus a huge bucket of water that continually fills until it overturns and drenches laughing children.

Billabong Sanctuary ★★★ You could easily spend 2 or 3 hours here, seeing Aussie wildlife in a natural setting and hand-feeding kangaroos and emus. You can also be photographed (starting at A$24) holding a koala, a (baby) crocodile, a python, or a wombat. Engaging interactive talks and shows run continuously starting at 9:15am; among the most popular are the saltwater-crocodile feeding at 1 and 3:15pm (for an extra A$99, you can also personally feed the croc from a large pole dangled over the fence). The sanctuary also has gas barbecues, a cafe, and a pool.

Bruce Hwy. (17km/11 miles S of Townsville). www.billabongsanctuary.com.au. ✆ **07/4778 8344.** A$36 adults, A$23 children 4–16, A$105 families of 5. Daily 9am–5pm. Closed Christmas Day.

Museum of Tropical Queensland ★★ If you're lucky enough to be here on the second Tuesday of the month, you'll have the chance to hear a museum expert give an hour-long lunchtime talk as part of the museum's "Discover More" lecture series. Subjects cover everything from underwater robotic research to frogs to the history of Townsville. With its curved roof, shaped like a ship under sail, this interesting museum holds the treasures salvaged from the wreck of the HMS *Pandora,* which sank in 1792 and lies 33m (108 ft.) underwater on the edge of the Great Barrier Reef. This is the highlight of the museum; the exhibit's centerpiece is a full-scale replica of a section of the ship's bow and its 17m-high (56-ft.) foremast, crafted by local shipwrights. The exhibition traces the ship's voyage and the retrieval of the sunken treasure—make sure you watch the film about the salvage. The museum has five other galleries, including a hands-on science center; a natural history display; one dedicated to north Queensland's indigenous heritage, with items from Torres Strait and the South Sea Islands; and stories from people of different cultures about the settlement of north Queensland. Another is devoted to touring exhibitions, which change every 3 months. Allow 2 to 3 hours.

70–102 Flinders St. (next to Reef HQ). www.mtq.qm.qld.gov.au. ✆ **07/4726 0600.** A$15 adults, A$8.80 children 4–16, A$38 families of 5. Daily 9:30am–5pm. Closed Good Friday, Christmas Day, Boxing Day (Dec 26), and Anzac Day (Apr 25).

Reef HQ Aquarium ★★★ Reef HQ is the education center for the Great Barrier Reef Marine Park Authority's headquarters and the largest living-coral-reef aquarium in the world. The highlight is walking through a 20m-long (66-ft.) transparent acrylic tunnel, gazing into a giant predator tank where sharks cruise silently. A replica of the wreck of the SS *Yongala* provides an eerie backdrop for blacktip and whitetip reef sharks, leopard sharks, and nurse sharks, sharing their 750,000-liter (195,000-gal.) home with stingrays, giant trevally, and a green turtle. Watching them feed is quite a spectacle. The tunnel also reveals the 2.5-million-liter (650,000-gal.) coral-reef exhibit, with its hard and soft corals providing a home for thousands of fish, giant clams, sea cucumbers, sea stars, and other creatures. During the scuba show, the divers speak to you over an intercom while they swim with the sharks and feed the fish. Other highlights include a touch tank and a wild-sea-turtle rehabilitation center, plus interactive activities for children. Reef HQ is an easy walk from the city center.

2–68 Flinders St. www.reefhq.com.au. ✆ **07/4750 0800.** A$28 adults, A$22 students, A$14 children 5–16, A$42–A$70 families. Daily 9:30am–5pm. Closed Christmas Day. All buses from the City Mall stop nearby.

Day Trips to the Reef

Most boats visiting the Reef from Townsville are live-aboard vessels that make trips of 2 or more days, designed for serious divers. **Adrenalin Dive** (www.adrenalindive.com.au; ✆ **07/4724 0600**) operates day trips on which you can make introductory dives for A$80 for the first one and A$120 for two; certified divers also dive for A$80, all gear included. The cruise costs A$239 for adults and A$189 for children 6 to 12. The price includes lunch, morning and afternoon tea, and snorkel gear. Cruises depart Townsville at 7am, with a pickup at Magnetic Island en route at 7:50am, on Tuesday, Thursday, Friday, and Sunday. They also run day trips to the ***Yongala*** wreck, in which you will do two dives on the *Yongala*. The cost is A$319, including all gear, and A$10 per dive for a guide, if you have logged fewer than 15 dives.

Day Trip to Magnetic Island ★★

Magnetic Island—or just "Maggie"—is a delightful 51-sq.-km (20-sq.-mile) national-park island 20 minutes from Townsville by ferry. About 2,500 people live here, and it's popular with Aussies, who love its holiday atmosphere.

Small settlements dot the coastline, and there's a good range of restaurants and laid-back cafes. Most people come for the 20 or so pristine and uncrowded bays and white beaches, but hikers, botanists, and birders may want to explore the eucalyptus woods, patches of gully rainforest, and granite tors. The island got its name when Captain Cook thought its "magnetic" rocks were interfering with his compass readings. It is famous for koalas, easily spotted in roadside gum trees; ask a local to point you to the nearest colony. Rock wallabies are often seen in the early morning.

The island is not on the Great Barrier Reef, but surrounding waters are part of the Great Barrier Reef Marine Park. There is good reef snorkeling at Florence Bay on the southern edge; Arthur Bay on the northern edge; and Geoffrey Bay, where you can even reef-walk at low tide. (Wear sturdy shoes and do not walk directly on coral to avoid damaging it.) First-time snorkelers will have an easy time of it in Maggie's weak currents and softly sloping beaches. Outside the stinger season, there is good swimming at any number of bays all around the island. Reef-free Alma Bay, with its shady lawns and playground, is a good choice for families; Rocky Bay is a small, secluded cove.

ESSENTIALS

GETTING THERE **Sealink** (www.sealinkqld.com.au; © **07/4726 0800**) runs 19 round-trip ferry services a day from the Breakwater terminal on Sir Leslie Thiess Drive. Round-trip tickets are A$34 for adults, A$17 for children 5 to 14, and A$76 for families of five. The trip takes about 20 minutes.

VISITOR INFORMATION There is no information center on Magnetic Island, but you can check **www.magneticinformer.com.au** online. Also, stop off at the **Townsville Bulletin Square Visitor Information Centre** (© **1800/801 902** in Australia or 07/4721 3660) before you cross to the island. It's open daily (Mon–Fri 9am–5pm, weekends 9am–1pm).

GETTING AROUND You can take your car on the ferry, but most people get around by renting an open-sided minimoke (similar to a golf cart) from the many rental outfits on the island. Minimokes are unlikely to go much over 60kmph (36 mph). **MI Wheels** (www.miwheels.com.au; © **07/4758 1111**) rents them—and other vehicles—from around A$65 to A$80 a day. **Magnetic Island Bus Services** (www.sunbus.com.au; © **07/4778 5130**) will get you anywhere on the island for A$3.50 adults and A$1.80 kids aged 5 to 15 (or less, depending on where you want to go).

EXPLORING MAGNETIC ISLAND

There is no end to the things you can do on Maggie—snorkeling, swimming in one of a dozen or more bays, catamaran sailing, waterskiing, paraflying, horseback riding on the beach, biking, tennis or golf, scuba diving, sea kayaking, sailing or cruising around the island, taking a Harley-Davidson tour, fishing, and more. Equipment for all these activities is for rent on the island.

One of the best, and most popular, of the island's 20km (13 miles) of hiking trails is the **Nelly Bay–Arcadia trail,** a one-way journey of 5km (3 miles) that takes 2½ hours. The first 45 minutes, starting in rainforest and climbing to a saddle between Nelly Bay and Horseshoe, are the most interesting. Another excellent walk is the 2km (1¼-mile) trail to the **Forts,** remnants of World War II defenses, which, not surprisingly, have great 360-degree sea views. The best koala spotting is on the track up to the Forts off Horseshoe Bay Road. Carry water when walking—some bays and hiking trails are not near shops.

If you feel like splurging, consider a jet-ski circumnavigation of the island with **Magnetic Jet Ski Tours** (www.facebook.com/MagneticJet; ✆ **07/4778 5533**). The 3-hour tour on a two-seat jet ski costs A$395 per ski rental, and a 2-hour tour of the northern side of the island costs A$200 per ski. They'll kit you out with wetsuits, life jackets, and tinted goggles for the ride. Keep your eyes peeled for dolphins, dugongs (manatees), sea turtles, and humpback whales in season. Tours depart from "the Red Shed" on Pacific Drive, Horseshoe Bay. Minimum age is 6 years.

Bungalow Bay Koala Village (www.bungalowbay.com.au; ✆ **07/4778 5577**), on Horseshoe Bay Road, Horseshoe Bay, is a backpacker hostel that has a wildlife sanctuary on its 6.5 hectares (16 acres) of bushland, home to rock wallabies, curlews, lorikeets, and koalas. Two-hour tours of the koala park run at 10am, noon, and 2:30pm, and begin at the reception desk. The first hour is within the wildlife park, where you can wrap yourself in a python, pet a lizard, hold a small saltwater crocodile, and get up close with a koala. The second hour is a guided bush walk to explore nearby habitats of eucalyptus forest, wetlands, mangroves, or coastal dunes, and to learn about the history of the traditional owners, the Wulgurukaba people. Entry to the park costs A$29 adults, A$25 backpackers or students, A$13 children 4 to 16, or A$80 for families of five. Koala holding costs A$18 including a souvenir photo, with proceeds supporting Magnetic Island wildlife care groups.

THE WHITSUNDAYS ★★★

Airlie Beach: 640km (397 miles) S of Cairns; 1,146km (711 miles) N of Brisbane

A day's drive or a 1-hour flight south of Cairns brings you to the dazzling collection of 74 islands known as the Whitsundays. No more than 3 nautical miles (3.4km/2 miles) separate most of the islands, and altogether they represent countless bays, beaches, dazzling coral reefs, and fishing spots that make up one fabulous Great Barrier Reef playground. Sharing the same latitude as Rio de Janeiro and Hawaii, the water is at least 72°F (22°C) year-round, the sun shines most of the year, and in winter you'll require only a light jacket at night.

Most of the islands consist of densely rainforested national park land. The surrounding waters belong to the Great Barrier Reef Marine Park. But don't expect palm trees and coconuts—these islands are covered with dry-looking pine and eucalyptus forests full of dense undergrowth, and rocky coral coves far outnumber the few sandy beaches. Only a few islands have resorts, but all offer just about every activity you could ever want—snorkeling, scuba diving, sailing, reef fishing, water-skiing, jet-skiing, parasailing, sea kayaking, hiking, rides over the coral in semisubmersibles, fish feeding, putt-putting around in dinghies to secluded beaches, tennis, and more! Accommodations range from small, low-key wilderness retreats to midrange family havens to some of Australia's most luxurious resorts.

The village of **Airlie Beach ★★** is the center of the action on the mainland. But the islands themselves are just as good a stepping stone to the outer Great Barrier Reef as Cairns, and some people consider them better, because you don't have to make the 90-minute trip to the Reef before you hit coral. Just about any Whitsunday island has fringing reef around its shores, and there are good snorkeling reefs between the islands, a quick boat ride away from your island or mainland accommodations. In early 2017, the Whitsunday region took a direct hit from Cyclone Debbie, which caused extensive damage to some islands and to Airlie Beach. While much of this was quickly rectified, resorts on Daydream and Hayman islands have closed until mid-2018 for renovations.

The reef here is just as good as off Cairns, with many drop-offs and drift dives, a dazzling range of corals, and a rich array of marine life, including whales, mantas, shark, reef fish, morays, turtles, and pelagics. Visibility is usually around 15 to 23m (49–75 ft.).

A popular reef for both snorkeling and diving is **Blue Pearl Bay ★★** off Hayman Island, which has loads of corals and some gorgonian fans in its gullies, and heaps of reef fish, including Maori wrasse and sometimes manta rays. It's a good place to make an introductory dive, walking right in off the beach. A little island commonly called **Bali Hai Island ★★**, between Hayman and Hook islands, is a great place to be left to your own devices. You'll see soft-shelf and wall coral, tame Maori wrasse, octopus, turtles, reef shark, various kinds of rays including mantas, eagles and cow-tails, plus loads of fish.

Essentials

GETTING THERE

BY CAR The Bruce Highway leads south from Cairns or north from Brisbane to Proserpine, 26km (16 miles) inland from Airlie Beach. Take the Whitsunday turnoff to reach Airlie Beach and Shute Harbour. Allow a good 8 hours to drive from Cairns. There are several car-storage facilities at Shute Harbour when you want to go to the islands.

BY PLANE There are two air routes into the Whitsundays: Great Barrier Reef Airport on Hamilton Island and Whitsunday Coast Airport at Proserpine on the mainland. **Qantas** (www.qantas.com.au; ✆ **131 313** in Australia) flies direct to Hamilton Island from Cairns, Brisbane, and Sydney. **Virgin Australia** (www.virginaustralia.com; ✆ **136 789** in Australia) flies to Proserpine direct from Brisbane, with connections from other capitals, and direct from Brisbane, Melbourne, and Sydney to Hamilton Island. **Jetstar** (www.jetstar.com.au; ✆ **131 538** in Australia) flies from Brisbane to Proserpine, and from Melbourne to Hamilton Island. If you stay on an island, the resort may book your launch transfers automatically. These may appear on your airline ticket, in which case your luggage will be checked through to the island. **Whitsunday Transit** (www.whitsundaytransit.com.au; ✆ **07/4946 1800**) provides airport transfers from Proserpine to Airlie Beach for A$20 adults, A$10 children 4 to 14 one-way, or A$34 adults and A$18 children round-trip.

BY TRAIN Several **Queensland Rail** (www.queenslandrailtravel.com.au; ✆ **1300/131 722** in Australia) long-distance trains stop at Proserpine every week. The one-way fare from Brisbane on the Spirit of Queensland is A$289 for a premium economy seat. There is a bus link to Airlie Beach; book through Queensland Rail when booking the train.

BY BUS **Greyhound Australia** (www.greyhound.com.au; ✆ **1300/473 946** in Australia) operates plentiful daily services to Airlie Beach from Brisbane (trip time: around 18 hr.) and Cairns (trip time: 11 hr.). The fare is around A$250 from Brisbane, A$110 from Cairns.

VISITOR INFORMATION

The **Whitsunday Region Information Centre** (www.tourismwhitsundays.com.au; ✆ **07/4945 3967**) is at 192 Main St., Proserpine (on the Bruce Highway in the town's south). It's run by Tourism Whitsundays and is open daily from 10am to 4pm; closed Christmas Day, Boxing Day (Dec 26), Good Friday, Anzac Day (Apr 25), and Queensland Labour Day (May 7 in 2018). It's also easy to pick up information from the private booking agents lining the main street of Airlie Beach. All stock a vast range of cruise, tour, and hotel information, and make bookings free of charge. All have similar material, but because some represent certain boats exclusively, and because prices can vary a little from one to the next, it pays to shop around.

GETTING AROUND

BY BOAT **Cruise Whitsundays** (www.cruisewhitsundays.com.au; ✆ **07/4846 7000**) operates Resort Connections, providing transfer services between its maritime terminal at Port of Airlie and Hamilton Island Airport, Whitsunday Coast Airport at Proserpine, and Shute Harbour (as well as Daydream Island when the resort re-opens).

Island ferries and Great Barrier Reef cruises leave from the Port of Airlie, on The Cove Road, on the edge of Airlie Beach's shopping strip and an easy walk from most hotels in the town center. Some tour-boat operators and bareboat charters anchor at Abell Point Marina, a 15-minute walk west from Airlie Beach. Most tour-boat operators pick up guests free from Airlie Beach hotels and at some or all island resorts.

BY BUS **Whitsunday Transit** (www.whitsundaytransit.com.au; ✆ **07/4946 1800**) meets all flights at Proserpine and provides door-to-door transfers to Proserpine, Airlie Beach, and Shute Harbour (p. 229). It also runs buses regularly between Proserpine, Airlie Beach, and Shute Harbour.

BY CAR **Avis** (✆ **07/4967 7188**) and **Hertz** (✆ **07/4946 4687**) have outlets in Airlie Beach and Proserpine Airport (telephone numbers serve both locations). **Budget** (✆ **07/4945 1024**) has an office at Proserpine Airport and **Europcar** (✆ **07/4946 4133**) has an office at Airlie Beach.

Whitsunday Hotels & Resorts

The advantages of staying on the mainland are cheaper accommodations, a choice of restaurants, the freedom to visit a different island each day, and a bevy of activities such as jet skiing, kayaking, parasailing, catamaran sailing, and windsurfing.

But if you are here it would be a shame not to spend at least a couple of days soaking up the island life. By staying on an island you get swimming, snorkeling, bushwalking, and a huge range of watersports, many of them free, right outside your door. You won't be isolated if you stay on an island, because most Great Barrier Reef cruise boats, sail-and-snorkel yacht excursions, Whitehaven Beach cruises, dive boats, fishing tour vessels, and so on stop at the island resorts every day or on a frequent basis. Be warned, however, that once you're "captive" on an island, you may be slugged with high food and drink prices. And although most island resorts offer non-motorized watersports (such as windsurfing and sailing) free of charge, you will pay for activities that use fuel, such as parasailing, water-skiing, and dinghy rental.

AIRLIE BEACH

Coral Sea Resort ★★★ In Airlie Beach's best location, on the edge of Paradise Point, this resort is one of the best places to stay on the Whitsunday mainland. It suits everyone from honeymooners to families, and although it's relatively sprawling, the design is such that you can easily feel you're alone. The Coral Sea suites are divine, complete with a Jacuzzi and double hammock on the balcony. There are four styles of suites, plus apartments and family units. Bayview suites have a Jacuzzi inside. It's a 3-minute walk along the waterfront to Airlie Beach village.

25 Oceanview Ave. www.coralsearesort.com. ✆ **1800/075 061** in Australia or 07/4964 1300. 78 units. A$195–A$235 double; A$255–A$285 suite; A$338 family room; A$365 1-bedroom apt; A$465 2-bedroom apt; A$620 3-bedroom apt; A$455–A$585 penthouse. Free parking. **Amenities:** Restaurant; bar; babysitting; bikes; exercise room; 25m (82-ft.) outdoor pool; room service; spa; watersports rental; free Wi-Fi.

Mantra Boathouse Apartments ★★ Right on the waterfront in the Port of Airlie development that opened in 2015, these smart and spacious two- and three-bedroom apartments have everything you need. Large balconies open out to views over the marina and the Coral Sea. There is no restaurant, but downstairs in the Port of Airlie development are three dining options (at last count) and you are only a 5 minutes' walk from Airlie Beach town center. But you're also not far from nature; I woke to find a row of half a dozen sulphur-crested cockatoos lined up on my balcony rail!

33 Port Drive, Port of Airlie. www.mantra.com.au. ✆ **131 517** in Australia or 07/4841 4100. 56 units. A$319 2-bedroom apt (sleeps 4); A$439 3-bedroom apt (sleeps 6). Free secure parking. **Amenities:** Outdoor pool; tennis court; kids' playground; Wi-Fi A$23/24 hr.

ISLAND RESORTS

Daydream Island Resort ★★ One of the Whitsundays' oldest and most popular resorts was badly damaged when Cyclone Debbie hit the island in early 2017. A planned major renovation project under new owners was brought forward, and is scheduled for completion in mid-2018, when the resort will reopen. Features such as the outdoor cinema and the kids' club have always made it popular with families, while pleasure-seekers head to the 16 therapy rooms at the **Rejuvenation Spa.** Rooms are large, with uninterrupted ocean views. The "village" at the southern end of the island, a short stroll along the boardwalk from the resort, has shops, cafes, a pool and bar, and a tavern. A rainforest walk stretches almost the entire length of the kilometer-long (just over half a mile) island. Check the website for updates.

Daydream Island (40km/25 miles northeast of Shute Harbour). www.daydreamisland.com. ✆ **1800/075 040** in Australia or 07/3259 2350. 296 units. Closed through mid-2018; rates for reopening not available at press time. **Amenities:** 3 restaurants, 3 bars; gym; 3 Jacuzzis; kids' club; 3 freshwater outdoor pools (1 heated); sauna; spa; 2 lit tennis courts; watersports; free Wi-Fi.

Hamilton Island ★★ More a vacation village than a single resort, Hamilton has the widest range of activities, accommodations styles, and restaurants of any Great Barrier Reef island resort and it's ideal for families.

Accommodations options include extra-large rooms and suites in the high-rise hotel; high-rise one-bedroom apartments; Polynesian-style bungalows in tropical gardens (ask for one away from the road for real privacy); and glamorous rooms in the two-story, adults-only **Beach Club** (with a personal "host" to cater to your every whim, plus a private restaurant, lounge, and pool for exclusive use of Beach Club guests); as well as one-, two-, three-, and four-bedroom apartments and villas, including villas at the waterfront Yacht Club. The best sea views are from the second-floor Beach Club rooms, from floors 5 to 18 of the **Reef View Hotel,** and from most apartments and villas. If your budget is huge, the poshest part of the resort is the ultraluxe **qualia,** an exclusive, adults-only retreat on the northern part of the island. It has 60 one-bedroom pavilions, each with a private swimming pool and a guest pavilion. There's a spa and two restaurants reserved just for qualia guests.

Snorkeling off Hamilton Island.

A marina village with cafes, restaurants, shops, and a yacht club is set apart from the accommodations, most of which are set around a large free-form pool and swim-up bar and the curve of Catseye Beach. Hamilton offers a huge range of watersports, fishing trips, cruises, speedboat rides, go-karts, a "wire flyer" flying-fox hang glider, a shooting range, mini-golf, an aquatic driving range, beach barbecue safaris, hiking trails, a wildlife sanctuary (you may have seen Oprah here, cuddling a koala), and an extensive daily activities program.

There are no cars on the island, and because a steep hill splits the resort, the best way to get around is on the free bus service, which operates on three loops around the island from 7am to 11pm, or by rented golf buggy (A$46/1 hr.; A$87/24 hr.). The biggest drawback is that just about every activity costs extra, so you are constantly adding to your bill. To get away from the main resort area, hit the beach or the hiking trails—most of the 750-hectare (1,853-acre) island is virgin bushland.

Hamilton Island (16km/10 miles SE of Shute Harbour). www.hamiltonisland.com.au or www.qualia.com.au. ✆ **137 333** in Australia, 02/9007 0009 (Sydney reservations office), or 866/209 0891 toll-free or 424/206 5274 for North American inquiries. 880 units. A$410 Palm Bungalow; A$390–A$470 double; A$710–A$1,295 suite; A$740 Beach Club double; A$1,200–A$1,800 qualia; A$4,115–A$4,800 qualia house. **Amenities:** 12 restaurants, 7 bars; babysitting; child-care center for kids 6 weeks to 14 years (in three groups); mini-golf and driving range; health club; 7 outdoor pools; room service; lit tennis courts; free Wi-Fi.

Where to Eat

Hemingway's ★★ CONTEMPORARY In homage to the literary great Ernest Hemingway, this new waterfront dining spot has references to his life and work throughout the decor and the menu. Oysters and seafood feature heavily, and there are Cuban and South African influences as well. For dessert, try the "edible cigar," a pastry filled with maple Chantilly cream, pistachios, hazelnut chocolate, and cocoa and coconut "ash." And, of course, the cocktail list has a Hemingway.

60 Shingley Drive (at Abell Point Marina), Airlie Beach. www.hemingwaysairliebeach.com.au. ✆ **07/4946 4277.** Main courses A$24–A$42. Daily noon–10pm.

Mangrove Jacks Café/Bar ★★ PIZZA/CAFE FARE Bareboat sailors, local sugar farmers, Sydney yuppies, and European backpackers all flock to this big, open-fronted sports bar and restaurant. The mood is upbeat and pleasantly casual, the surroundings are spick-and-span, and the food passes muster. Wood-fired pizzas with trendy toppings are the specialty. There is no table service; place your order at the bar and collect your food when your number is called.

In the Airlie Beach Hotel, 16 The Esplanade (enter from Shute Harbour Rd.), Airlie Beach. ✆ **07/4964 1888.** Main courses A$17–A$30. Mon–Fri 11:30am–2:30pm and 5:30–9:30pm (to 10pm on Fri); Sat 11:30am–10pm; Sun 11:30am–9:30pm.

> **Safety in the Water**
>
> Deadly **marine stingers** may frequent the shorelines of the Whitsundays from October through April. The best place to swim is in the beachfront Airlie Beach lagoon. The rivers in these parts are home to dangerous **saltwater crocodiles** (which mostly live in fresh water, contrary to their name), so don't swim in streams, rivers, or water holes.

Whitsunday Sailing Club ★★ CONTEMPORARY This casual club is a popular hangout for locals, with one of the best views in the Whitsundays, overlooking Pioneer Bay and the islands. The menu includes light meals such as burgers or a Caesar salad; for something heartier go for "reef & beef" (a steak topped with local seafood) or fish 'n' chips. Great for drinks at sunset.

Airlie Point (enter from The Esplanade), Airlie Beach. www.whitsundaysailingclub.com.au. © **07/4946 6138.** Main courses A$16–A$29. Mon–Fri 11:30am–2.30pm and 5:30pm–late; Sat–Sun 11:30am–late.

Exploring the Whitsundays

The little town of Airlie Beach, perched on the edge of the Coral Sea with views across Pioneer Bay and the Whitsunday Passage, is the focal point of activity on the Whitsunday mainland. Cruises and yachts depart from the Port of Airlie, from Shute Harbour, a 10-minute drive south on Shute Harbour Road. For a bird's-eye view of it all, head to the Lions Lookout.

Airlie Beach has a massive beachfront artificial lagoon, with sandy beaches and landscaped parkland, which solves the problem of where to swim in stinger season. The lagoon is the size of about six full-size Olympic swimming pools, set in 4 hectares (10 acres) of botanic gardens, with a children's pool, plenty of shade, barbecues, picnic shelters, toilets, showers, and parking.

Getting out on the water is the most important thing here. Countless opportunities are offered, with the focus firmly on sailing, snorkeling, and diving.

REEF CRUISES

Cruise Whitsundays (www.cruisewhitsundays.com.au; © **07/4946 4662**) makes daily trips to Hardy Reef in a high-speed, air-conditioned catamaran. The boat has a bar, and a biologist gives a marine ecology talk en route. You anchor at the massive Reefworld pontoon, which was built to hold up to 600 people, and spend up to 3½ hours on the Reef. The day trip costs A$245 for adults, A$120 for children 4 to 14. Guided snorkel safaris cost A$55 extra for adults and A$30 for children. You can book dives on board for A$139 for first-time divers and A$99 for certified divers (A$59 for a second dive). Cruises depart at 8am from the Port of Airlie, picking up at Hamilton Island at 9am. Passengers from other islands take the ferry to Hamilton to board there.

A unique experience is Cruise Whitsundays' **ReefSleep,** during which you spend the night on the pontoon. You travel with the day-trippers, but when they leave at 3pm you will be with a maximum of nine people. This gives you a fabulous chance to snorkel at night when the coral is luminescent in the moonlight and nocturnal sea creatures get busy. The trip includes 2 full days

OUTRIGGER sailing

For a different look at the Whitsunday Coast, take a 90-minute tour with **Whitsunday Sailing Outrigger** (www.whitsundaysailingoutrigger.com; ✆ **0402/473 059** mobile) to skim along the water aboard Stephen and Michelle Lynes's lovely craft *Ohana.* With only four guests on board, this is a terrific, personal experience. Tours depart daily at 9am, 11am, and 1pm and cost A$50 per person (ages 7 and older). A 2-hour tour to Pigeon Island costs A$100 and sunset champagne tours cost A$80. Bookings are essential.

on the Reef, all meals, and the chance to sleep on the upper deck under the stars in a swag (a type of outdoor sleeping bag). The cost is A$489 for a double swag or A$649 for a single. This is an experience only for those over 12 years old.

In and around the Whitsunday islands, you can visit and explore the many excellent dive sites close to shore. **Mantaray Charters** (www.mantaraycharters.com; ✆ **07/4948 1117**), based at Abell Point Marina, runs day tours to Whitehaven Beach and gives you the chance to dive near Hayman Island or Hook Island. Tours are limited to 36 passengers and leave at 8am, returning around 4:30pm. The cost is A$197 adults, A$98 kids ages 4 to 12, and A$555 for a family of four. The cost includes lunch, snacks, and all equipment, whether you are diving or snorkeling. You'll pay A$100 for an introductory dive or A$80 if you're certified. Second dives cost A$60.

SAILING & SNORKELING TRIPS

A journey on one of the many yachts offering 3-day, 2-night sailing adventures is a great way to see the islands. You can learn to sail or get involved with sailing the boat as much or as little as you want, snorkel to your heart's content over one dazzling reef after another, beachcomb, explore national park trails, stop at secluded bays, swim, sunbathe, and generally have a laid-back good time. A few companies offer introductory and qualified scuba diving for an extra cost per dive. Most boats carry a maximum of 12 passengers, so the atmosphere is always friendly and fun. The food is generally good, the showers are usually hot, and you sleep in comfortable but small berths off the galley. Some have small private twin or double cabins.

Prices usually include all meals, Marine Park entrance fees, snorkel gear, and transfers to the departure point (Abell Point Marina or Shute Harbour). In the off season, the boats compete fiercely for passengers; you'll see signboards on the main street in Airlie Beach advertising standby deals.

Prosail (www.prosail.com.au; ✆ **1800/810 116** in Australia or 07/4946 7533) runs sailing trips through the Great Barrier Reef Marine Park. All trips include sailing, snorkeling, scuba diving, and bushwalking, and you can sail on mega-yachts such as the *Condor, Broomstick,* and *Hammer.* A 2-day overnight trip costs A$359 per person or A$429 per person for a private double cabin.

These kinds of trips are a cheaper alternative to "bareboating" (skippering your own yacht)—which is a hugely popular thing to do, despite the cost. If you are confident about sailing yourself—and most yacht-charter companies in the islands will want one person on the boat to have a little experience—you do not need a license, and sailing is surprisingly easy in these uncrowded waters, where the channels are deep and the seas are protected from big swells by the Great Barrier Reef. The 74 islands are so close to one another that one is always in sight, and safe anchorages are everywhere. But for extra reassurance, the company may require you to take a skipper along at an extra cost of around A$400 per day (plus meals) if you want them to stay with you. Before departure, the company provides a thorough 2- to 3-hour briefing and easy-to-read maps marking channels, anchorage points, and the very few dangerous reefs. Your charter company will radio in once or twice a day to check that you're still afloat, and you can contact them anytime for advice.

You can buy your own provisions or have the charter company stock the boat at an extra cost of about A$30 per person per day. Most operators will load a windsurfer, fishing tackle, and scuba-diving equipment on request, for an extra fee if they are not standard.

In peak season, you may have to charter the boat for a week. At other times, most companies impose a minimum of 5 days, but many will rent for 3 nights if you ask, rather than let a vessel sit idle. In peak season, expect to pay A$750 to A$985 per night for a standard four- to six-berth yacht, more if you want something luxurious. Rates in the off season, and even in the Whitsundays' busiest time, June through August, will be anywhere from A$100 to A$200 less. If you are prepared to book within 14 days of when you want to sail, the deals can be even better; you should be able to find a boat that late in the off-season. You may be asked to post a credit card bond of up to A$2,000. Fuel and park fees are extra, and mooring fees apply if you want to stop at one of the island resorts overnight. A number of bareboat-charter companies offer "sail-'n'-stay" packages that combine a few days of sailing with a few days at an island resort.

Most bareboat charter companies will make complete holiday arrangements for you in the islands, including accommodations, transfers, tours, and sporting activities. Most companies operate out of Airlie Beach, Hamilton Island, or both. Well-known operators include **Whitsunday Rent-A-Yacht**

The Secret of the Seasons

High season in the Whitsundays coincides with school vacations, which occur in January, in mid-April, from late June to early July, from late September to early October, and in late December. The Aussie winter, June through August, is popular, too. You have to book months ahead to get high-season accommodations, but any other time you can indeed find some good deals: Specials on accommodations, sailing trips, day cruises, and diving excursions fairly leap off the blackboards outside the tour-booking agents in Airlie Beach.

Hitting the Sand at Whitehaven Beach

The 6km (3¾-mile) stretch of pure-white silica sand on **Whitehaven Beach ★★** will leave you in rapture. The beach, on uninhabited Whitsunday Island, does not boast a lot of coral, but the swimming is good and the forested shore is beautiful. Take a book and chill out. Some sailboat day trips visit it, as do some motorized vessels. A half-day trip with **Cruise Whitsundays** (www.cruisewhitsundays.com; ✆ **07/4946 4662**) costs A$99 for adults and A$52 for children ages 4 to 14 and gives you around 2 hours on the beach. You can travel in the morning (leaving the Port of Airlie at 7am) or in the afternoon (departing at noon), with pick-ups at Hamilton Island and Daydream Island on the way. Full-day trips combine Whitehaven Beach with other islands on some tours. **Air Whitsunday** (www.airwhitsunday.com.au; ✆ **07/4946 9111**) offers seaplane flights to Whitehaven Beach for A$295 adults or A$250 children, with a glass of bubbles when you land.

(www.rentayacht.com.au; ✆ **1800/075 000** in Australia or 07/4946 9232); **Queensland Yacht Charters** (www.yachtcharters.com.au; ✆ **1800/075 013** in Australia or 07/4946 7400); and **Sunsail** (www.sunsail.com.au; ✆ **1800/803 988** in Australia or 02/8912 7040).

ISLAND HOPPING

Day-trippers to the resorts on Hamilton and Daydream islands can rent water-sports equipment, laze by the beaches and pools, scuba dive, join the resorts' activities programs, hike their trails, and eat at some or all of their restaurants. **Cruise Whitsundays** (www.cruisewhitsundays.com; ✆ **07/4946 4662**) has an Island Hopper Pass that allows you to hop-on, hop-off at Hamilton and Daydream islands for A$135 adults or A$79 children 4 to 14. They also offer day-trip packages (including lunch) to the islands.

SOUTHERN GREAT BARRIER REEF REGION ★★

Off this stretch of the Queensland coast is the southernmost part of the Great Barrier Reef, where you will find the spectacular **Heron Island,** whose reefs are a source of enchantment for divers and snorkelers. Its waters boast 21 dive sites, and in summer, large turtles lumber ashore to nest on its beaches.

Off the small town of Bundaberg is another tiny coral cay, **Lady Elliot Island ★★**, a nesting site for tens of thousands of seabirds and home to a first-rate fringing reef. Bundaberg's major attraction is a mainland loggerhead turtle rookery that draws large crowds in summer.

About 50km (31½ miles) from Gladstone, on the coast, are the lovely coastal hamlets of **Agnes Water ★★** and **1770 ★** (so named by British explorer Captain James Cook the year he mapped the coastline of Australia). These tiny places are well worth the detour. Stop in at the **Agnes Water/1770 Visitor Information Centre,** 71 Springs Rd., Agnes Water (✆ **07/4902 1533**),

Heart Reef

The iconic image of the Great Barrier Reef is the stunning heart-shaped reef called—yes, **Heart Reef.** But Heart Reef is not a place you can visit; it is protected by law and you can neither swim nor snorkel there. In any case, the best way to see this tiny reef's perfect shape is from the air. There are many helicopter or seaplane options available for that perfect photographic opportunity (or, of course, if you are planning a mid-air proposal). A 1-hour seaplane flight over the Great Barrier Reef costs A$330 adults and A$290 children with **Air Whitsunday** (www.airwhitsunday.com.au; ✆ **07/4946 9111**), which offers a large range of tours, including seaplane flights to a Reef pontoon to snorkel for a couple of hours.

to get the low-down on things to do in the region. The info center is open Monday through Friday 9am to 5pm and weekends from 10am to 2pm; it's closed Christmas Day and Good Friday.

I highly recommend two tours in this area. The **1770 LARC! Tours** (www.1770larctours.com.au; ✆ **07/4974 9422**) will see you ride high on a bright pink amphibious craft that gives access to land and sea to explore the waterways and coast of 1770. Owner Neil Mergard and his team provide fascinating and entertaining commentary about the land and environment and you'll come away with a new appreciation of this part of Australia. One-hour afternoon tours cost A$38 adults, A$17 kids 5 to 16; a full-day tour costs A$156 adults, A$96 children. Another way of getting out on the water is on a kayak tour with Simon and Janina of **1770 Liquid Adventures** (www.1770liquidadventures.com.au; ✆ **0428/956 630** mobile). A 2-hour tour costs A$50 per person; 2½-hour sunset tours cost A$55. You might spot dolphins, and may also have the company of Bailey, their golden Labrador, who rides in the lead kayak!

Gladstone: Gateway to Heron Island

Gladstone: 550km (341 miles) N of Brisbane; 1,162km (720 miles) S of Cairns

The industrial port town of Gladstone is the departure point for beautiful Heron Island. Gladstone is on the coast 21km (13 miles) off the Bruce Highway. Most flights to Gladstone arrive in time to connect with the ferry to Heron Island, but if you need to stay overnight, a couple of good, centrally located options are **Mercure Gladstone** (www.accorhotels.com.au; ✆ **07/4979 8200**) and **Rydges Gladstone** (www.rydges.com; ✆ **07/4970 0000**).

ESSENTIALS

Getting There

BY PLANE **Qantaslink** (book through Qantas [www.qantas.com.au; ✆ **131 313** in Australia]) and **Virgin Australia** (www.virginaustalia.com.au; ✆ **136 789** in Australia) both have daily flights from Brisbane.

BY TRAIN **Queensland Rail** (www.queenslandrailtravel.com.au; ✆ **1800/872 467** in Queensland) operates trains to Gladstone from Brisbane and

Cairns most days. The economy fare from Brisbane is A$119 on the high-speed Tilt Train (trip time: 6 hr.).

BY BUS **Greyhound Australia** (www.greyhound.com.au; ✆ **1300/473 946** in Australia) operates daily coaches to Gladstone on the Brisbane-Cairns run. The fare is A$153 from Brisbane (trip time: 11½ hr.), around A$200 from Cairns (trip time: 20 hr.).

GETTING AROUND **Avis** (✆ **07/4978 2633**), **Budget** (✆ **07/4972 8488**), **Europcar** (✆ **07/4978 7787**), and **Hertz** (✆ **07/4978 6899**) have offices in Gladstone.

VISITOR INFORMATION The **Gladstone Visitor Information Centre** is in the ferry terminal at Gladstone Marina, 72 Bryan Jordan Dr., Gladstone (www.gladstoneregion.info; ✆ **07/4972 9000**). It's open 8:30am to 4:30pm Monday through Friday and 9am to 1pm Saturday and Sunday. Closed Christmas Day.

Heron Island ★★★

72km (45 miles) NE of Gladstone

Heron Island is often referred to as "the jewel of the Reef." And rightly so. The difference between Heron and other islands is that once there, you are right on the Reef. Step off the beach and you enter magnificent fields of coral that seem to stretch for miles. And the myriad life forms that abound here are accessible to everyone through diving, snorkeling, or reef walks at low tide.

There has been a resort on Heron since 1932, and in 1943 the island became a national park. It is a haven for wildlife and people, and an experience of a lifetime is almost guaranteed at any time of year, particularly if you love turtles—Heron is a haven for giant green and loggerhead turtles. Resort guests gather on the beach from late November to February to watch the female turtles lay eggs, and from February to mid-April to see the hatched babies scuttle down the sand to the water. Every night during the season, volunteer guides from the island's University of Queensland research station tag and measure the turtles before they return to the water. Only 1 in 5,000 hatchlings will live to return in about 50 years to lay its own eggs. Humpback whales also pass through from June through September.

Three days on Heron will give you plenty of time. The island is so small that you can walk around it at a leisurely pace in about half an hour. One of the first things to do is to take advantage of the organized activities that operate several times a day and are designed so guests can plan their own days. Snorkeling and reef walking are major occupations for visitors—if they're not diving, that is. The island is home to 21 of the world's most stunning dive sites.

Guided walks provide another way to explore the island. Walks include a visit to the island's research station. As for the reef walk, just borrow a pair of sand shoes, a balance pole, and a viewing bucket, and head off with a guide at low tide. The walk can take up to 90 minutes.

Heron is also home to colonies of mutton birds; be warned, they can be particularly noisy during their breeding and mating season, from November to January. They also create a fairly . . . shall I say . . . distinctive smell (you get used to it, but some people find it highly offensive). That's nature for you.

GETTING THERE

A **170-seater launch** departs Gladstone Marina, Bryan Jordan Drive, at 2pm, 5 days a week (Mon, Wed, Fri, Sat, and Sun). Transfers cost A$62 one-way for adults, half-price for kids 2 to 12. Trip time is around 2 hours. Seaplane transfers can also be arranged for A$349 per person.

Heron Island Resort ★★★ This is a lovely, low-key resort, with no day-trippers and a focus very much on the outdoors. The colors of the island's surrounding water and Reef are reflected in the interiors, and everything is light-filled and breezy. Heron's central complex is equal parts grand Queenslander home and sophisticated beach house, with bar and lounge areas open to ocean views and sunsets. Duplex-style Turtle rooms are designed for couples or families, or you can go for greater luxury in the Wistari or Point suites or the private Beach House (the only rooms with air-conditioning). Rooms are TV-free, but there is a lounge with TVs and public phones (only the four Point suites and the Beach House have private phones). There is no mobile phone coverage, but you can get Wi-Fi in the bar. The **Aqua Soul Spa** offers double treatment rooms and all the usual spa treatments and pampering.

Heron Island, off Gladstone. www.heronisland.com. ✆ **1300/731 551** in Australia or 844/887 6724 in the U.S., or 07/4972 9055 (resort). 109 units. A$330 Turtle Room double or A$346 for families; A$428 Reef Room double or A$459 families; A$572–A$788 suites; A$840 Beach House. Rates include breakfast and some activities. **Amenities:** Restaurant; bar; children's program (ages 7–12) during Australian school vacations; Jacuzzi; outdoor pool; spa; 2 lit tennis courts; limited watersports equipment rental.

Bundaberg ★: Gateway to Lady Elliot Island

384km (238 miles) N of Brisbane; 1,439km (892 miles) S of Cairns

The small sugar town of Bundaberg is the closest to the southernmost point of the Great Barrier Reef. If you visit the area between November and March, allow an evening to visit the Mon Repos Turtle Rookery. Divers may want to take in some of Australia's best shore diving right off Bundaberg's beaches. The southern reefs of the Great Barrier Reef are just as prolific, varied, and colorful as the reefs farther north off Cairns. However, because this part of the coast is less accessible by visitors and the reefs farther offshore, fewer snorkel and dive boats visit them.

There are two islands to be visited in this area, both part of the **Bunker Group,** which are around 80km (50 miles) due north of Bundaberg. The islands are due east of Gladstone and closer to that town, but only live-aboard boats visit them from there. The only one visited by snorkelers and divers on a daily basis is pretty **Lady Musgrave Island,** a vegetated 14-hectare (35-acre) national-park coral cay, 52 nautical miles off the coast. It is surrounded by a lagoon 8km (5 miles) in circumference, filled with hundreds of corals and some 1,200 of the 1,500 species of fish and other marine creatures found on the Great Barrier Reef. The other is **Lady Elliot Island,** which is accessed by air and has a resort on it.

ESSENTIALS

Getting There

BY CAR Bundaberg is on the Isis Highway, about 50km (31 miles) off the Bruce Highway from Gin Gin in the north and 53km (33 miles) off the Bruce Highway from just north of Childers in the south.

BY PLANE **Qantas** (www.qantas.com.au; ✆ **131 313** in Australia) and **Virgin Australia** (www.virginaustralia.com.au; ✆ **136 789** in Australia) both fly from Brisbane daily.

BY TRAIN **Queensland Rail** (www.queenslandrail.com.au; ✆ **1800/872 467** in Queensland) trains stop in Bundaberg every day en route between Brisbane and Cairns. The fare is A$89 from Brisbane in economy class or A$115 business class on the Tilt Train; the trip takes about 4½ hours.

BY BUS **Greyhound Australia** (www.greyhound.com.au; ✆ **1300/473 946** in Australia) stops here many times a day on runs between Brisbane and Cairns. The 8-hour trip from Brisbane costs A$94.

Getting Around

BY CAR **Avis** (✆ **07/4131 4533**), **Budget** (✆ **07/4155 0095**), **Hertz** (✆ **07/4154 1030**), and **Thrifty** (✆ **07/4151 6222**) all have offices in Bundaberg.

BY BUS **Duffy's City Buses** (www.duffysbuses.com.au; ✆ **1300/383 397** or 07/4151 4226) operates the town bus service. There are no public buses on Sundays.

VISITOR INFORMATION The **Bundaberg Visitor Information Centre** (www.bundabergregion.org; ✆ **1300/722 099** in Australia or 07/4143 8888), at 271 Bourbong St., Bundaberg (next to the hospital), is open daily 9am to 5pm, public holidays 9am to 2pm. Closed Good Friday, Anzac Day (Apr 25), and Christmas Day.

EXPLORING BUNDABERG

By far the most popular attraction in Bundaberg is the annual turtle nesting season on Mon Repos Beach, about 14km (8¾ miles) from the city center. **Mon Repos Regional Park** is one of the two largest loggerhead-turtle rookeries in the South Pacific. The visitor center by the beach has a great display on the turtle life cycle and shows films at 7:30pm daily in summer. There is a strict booking system for turtle-watching tours, to help cope with the crowds. Access to the beach is by ticket only, and you must book your visit to Mon Repos during the turtle season. Tickets are sold through the **Bundaberg Visitor Information Centre** at 271 Bourbong St., Bundaberg (✆ **1300/722 099** in Australia or 07/4143 8888), or online at www.bundabergregion.org/turtles. The website has a lot of very useful information on how to get to the rookery

Turtle nesting at Mon Repos Regional Park.

and what to expect from your turtle-watching experience. Tours start at 7pm, but you may have to wait up to 2 hours or more, depending on when the turtles appear. Nesting happens around high tide; hatching usually occurs between 8pm and midnight. Take a sweater, as it can get quite cool.

The **Mon Repos Turtle Centre** (www.nprsr.qld.gov.au/parks/mon-repos; ✆ **07/4159 1652**) is at 141 Mon Repos Rd. and is well signposted. During turtle-nesting season (Nov to late Mar), the park and information center are open 24 hours a day. Public access to the beach is closed from 6pm to 6am, unless you are on a tour. Turtle-viewing tours run from 7pm until midnight daily (except for Dec 24, 25, and 31). From April to early November (when no turtles are around), the information center is open Monday to Friday (except public holidays) from 8am to 3:30pm, but the park is still open 24 hours. Admission to the visitor center is free from April through November; but when the turtles start nesting, you pay A$12 for adults, A$6.25 for children ages 5 to 14 and seniors, and A$29 for families of four, including your tour. It's the best value anywhere!

WHERE TO STAY

Zen Beach Retreat ★★★ Hosts Shane and Pascaline Emms transformed an old beachfront motel into some of the best accommodations in the Bundaberg region. Four themed two-story villas sit behind the main building (no sea views, unfortunately), opening out onto a Balinese-style pavilion and the pool. The exotic and colorful Oriental villa is my favorite, with design touches from Morocco, Turkey, and the Middle East, but you might prefer the French villa, adorned with some of Pascaline's personal treasures. The Asian villa and a more subdued Executive villa round out the villa options. You can also book the main house, which has three bedrooms, plus entertaining areas, as well as access to the expansive upstairs open-plan living area and gourmet kitchen.

54 Miller St., Bargara. www.zenbeachretreat.com. ✆ **07/4154 7757.** 5 units. A$350 double; A$1,500 whole house (sleeps 6). Free parking. **Amenities:** Outdoor pool; spa; free Wi-Fi.

WHERE TO EAT

Café 1928 ★ CAFE Set in the leafy surrounds of the Bundaberg Botanic Gardens, this casual cafe is a nice spot for brunch or lunch. Apart from good coffee, it offers quite an extensive menu, everything from muffins and sandwiches to home-cooked lasagna, quiche, salads, chicken schnitzel, and a range of burgers and pizzas. There's also a A$7 kids' menu.

Bundaberg Botanic Gardens, Young St. www.bundabergcafe.com.au. ✆ **07/4153 1928.** Main courses A$8–A$18. Daily 9am–4pm (kitchen closes at 2:30pm); public holidays 10am–3pm.

Lady Elliot Island ★★

80km (50 miles) NE of Bundaberg

Lady Elliot is a 42-hectare (104-acre) coral cay ringed by a wide, shallow lagoon filled with dazzling coral life. Reef walking, snorkeling, and diving are the main reasons people come to this coral cay, which is so small you can walk across it in 15 minutes. You may snorkel and reef walk only during the 2 to 3 hours before and after high tide, so plan your day accordingly. You will see dazzling corals and brilliantly colored fish, clams, sponges, urchins, and anemones. Divers will see a good range of marine life, including green and loggerhead turtles (which nest on the beach Nov–Mar). Whales pass by from June through September.

Lady Elliot is a sparse, grassy island rookery, not a sandy tropical paradise. Some find it too spartan; others relish chilling out in a beautiful, peaceful spot with reef all around. Just be prepared for the smell and constant noise of the birds.

GETTING THERE

The 30-minute flight with **Seair** (www.seairpacific.com.au; ✆ **07/5599 4509**) from Bundaberg runs twice daily. You can also do a day-trip flight from Brisbane (p. 180). From Bundaberg, it costs A$310 adults, A$175 kids 3 to 12, round-trip. The flight leaves Bundaberg at 8:40am and leaves the island for the return trip at 4pm. Day trips include a welcome drink and orientation tour, glass-bottom-boat ride or guided snorkel tour, lunch, and use of the resort facilities (including towels, reef-walking shoes, sunscreen, and snorkel equipment). If you plan to stay longer than a day, book your flights with your accommodation, and remember there is a 10-kilogram (22-lb.) luggage limit.

WHERE TO STAY

Lady Elliot Island Eco Resort ★★★ Accommodations here are fairly basic, but visitors come for the Reef, not the room. The top-of-the-range rooms are Island suites (and the only rooms with air-conditioning), which have one or two separate bedrooms and great sea views from the deck. Most Reef rooms sleep four and have decks with views through the trees to the sea. The cool, spacious safari-tent "eco-cabins" have four bunks, electric lighting, fans, and timber floors, but share the toilets and showers. The limited facilities include a boutique, an education center, and a dive shop, which runs shore and boat dives, introductory dives, and rents equipment. There are no TVs, radio, mobile phone reception, or phones in the rooms (but there is a public telephone). A program of mostly free activities includes glass-bottom-boat rides, table tennis, guided walks, and beach volleyball.

Great Barrier Reef, off Bundaberg, Runaway Bay. www.ladyelliot.com.au. ✆ **1800/072 200** in Australia or 07/4156 4444. 40 units. A$350–A$380 eco-cabin double; A$558–A$648 double; A$738–A$768 suite. A$80–A$95 children 3–12 years. 3-night minimum Christmas/New Year; 2-night minimum for suites. Rates include breakfast, dinner, and some guided tours. **Amenities:** Restaurant; bar; children's program (ages 5–12) during school holidays; saltwater pool; Wi-Fi hotspot available with fee.

8

ULURU & THE RED CENTRE

The Red Centre is the landscape most closely associated with Australia's Outback—endless horizons, vast deserts of red sand, a mysterious monolith, and cloudless blue skies. If there is a soundtrack, it is the rhythmic, haunting tones of the didgeridoo. At its heart is the magnificent monolith called Uluru—the "Rock"—that is the reason every visitor is drawn to this arid land.

The Centre is home to sprawling cattle ranches, ancient mountain ranges, "living fossil" palm trees that survived the Ice Age, cockatoos and kangaroos, ochre gorges, lush water holes, and intriguing tracks leading to heart-stopping landscapes.

Aboriginal people have lived here for tens of thousands of years, but the Centre is still largely unexplored by non-Aboriginal Australians. One highway cuts from Adelaide in the south to Darwin in the north, and a few roads and four-wheel-drive tracks make a lonely spider web across it; in many other areas, non-Aborigines have never set foot.

Alice Springs is the only big town in Central Australia, which together with the Top End makes up the Northern Territory. And let's get one thing straight from the start: Alice Springs and Uluru are *not* side by side. Uluru is 462km (286 miles) away. You can get there and see it in a day from Alice Springs but it's an effort, and in doing so you will miss much of what is on offer, because visiting Uluru is much more than just a quick photo opportunity. It may well be the most meaningful and memorable part of your trip to Australia.

"The Alice" is a gateway to Uluru, but you can also fly there direct to Ayers Rock Airport, which takes its name from the European name given to Uluru by early explorers but seldom used today.

Give yourself a few days to experience all there is in the Centre—visiting the magnificent domes of Kata Tjuta ("the Olgas") near Uluru, walking the rim of Kings Canyon, riding a camel down a dry riverbed, exploring the intricacies of Aboriginal paintings (either on rock or canvas), swimming in water holes, or staying at an Outback homestead. A few days in Alice will give you the chance to see beautiful surrounding attractions such as Palm Valley, Ormiston Gorge, and Trephina Gorge Nature Park; each is an easy day trip. Too many visitors jet in, snap a photo of Uluru, and head home, only to miss the essence of the desert.

RED CENTRE ESSENTIALS

Visitor Information

The **Central Australian Tourism Industry Association** (see "Visitor Information" under "Alice Springs," p. 245) is your best one-stop source of information.

Most of the Red Centre lies within the Northern Territory. **Tourism NT** has a great website (www.northernterritory.com) with special sections tailored for international travelers (choose your country). It details many hotels, tour operators, car-rental companies, and attractions, and offers information on local Aboriginal culture and Aboriginal tours. Tourism NT's **Territory Discoveries division** (www.territorydiscoveries.com; ✆ **1300/738 111** in Australia or 08/8968 3200) offers package deals.

When to Go

April, May, September, and October have sunny days (coolish in May, hot in Oct). Winter (June–Aug) means mild temperatures with cold nights. Summer (Nov–Mar) is ferociously hot and best avoided. In summer, limit exertions to early morning and late afternoon, and choose air-conditioned accommodations. Rain is rare but can come at any time of year.

DRIVING TIPS

The **Automobile Association of the Northern Territory,** 14 Knuckey St., Darwin, NT 0800 (www.aant.com.au; ✆ **08/8925 5901**), offers emergency-breakdown service (✆ **131 111**) to members of affiliated overseas automobile associations and dispenses maps and advice. It has no office in the Red Centre. For **road condition reports,** call ✆ **1800/246 199** in Australia or check out www.roadreport.nt.gov.au.

Only a handful of highways and arterial roads in the Northern Territory are sealed (paved) roads. A conventional two-wheel-drive car will get you to most of what you want to see, but consider renting a four-wheel-drive (4WD) for complete freedom. All the big car-rental chains have them. Some attractions are on unpaved roads good enough for a two-wheel-drive car, but your car-rental company will not insure a two-wheel-drive for driving on them.

Normal restricted speed limits apply in all urban areas, but speed limits on Northern Territory highways (introduced in 2006) are considerably higher than in other states. The speed limit is set at 130kmph (81 mph) on the Stuart, Arnhem, Barkly, and Victoria highways, while rural roads are designated 110kmph (68 mph) speed limits unless otherwise signposted. The road fatality toll in the Northern Territory is high: an average of 21 fatalities per 100,000 people each year, compared with the Australian average of 5 per 100,000.

Another considerable risk while driving is that of hitting wildlife: camels, kangaroos, and other protected native species. Avoid driving at night, early

Buzz Off!

Uluru is notorious for plagues of flies in summer. Don't be embarrassed to cover your head with the fly nets sold in souvenir stores—there will be "no flies on you, mate," an Aussie way of saying you are clever.

morning, and late afternoon, when 'roos are more active; beware of cattle lying down on the warm bitumen at night.

Road trains (trucks hauling more than one container) and fatigue caused by driving long distances are two other major threats. For details on safe driving, review the tips in the "By Car" section of "Getting Around" in chapter 10.

OTHER TRAVEL TIPS

Always carry drinking water. When hiking, carry 4 liters (about a gallon) per person per day in winter and a liter (1 quart) per person per hour in summer. Wear a broad-brimmed hat, high-factor sunscreen, and insect repellant.

Bring warm clothing for chilly winter evenings. Make sure you have a full tank of gas before setting out and check distances between places you can fill up.

TOUR OPERATORS

Numerous coach, minicoach, and 4WD tour operators run tours that take in Alice Springs, Kings Canyon, and Uluru. These depart from Alice Springs or Uluru, offering accommodations ranging from spiffy resorts, comfortable motels, and basic cabins to shared bunkhouses, tents, or swags (sleeping bags) under the stars. Most pack the highlights into a 2- or 3-day trip, though leisurely trips of 6 days or more are available. Many offer one-way itineraries between Alice and the Rock (via Kings Canyon if you like), or vice versa, which will allow you to avoid backtracking.

Among the reputable companies are **AAT Kings** (www.aatkings.com; ✆ **1300/228 546** in Australia), which specializes in coach tours but also has 4WD camping itineraries, and **Intrepid** (www.intrepidtravel.com; ✆ **1300/797 010** in Australia), which conducts camping safaris (or if you prefer, hotel, motel, or lodge accommodation) in small groups for all ages. **Tailormade Tours** (www.tailormadetours.com.au; ✆ **08/8952 1731**) offers public tours as well as customized luxury charters.

ALICE SPRINGS ★

462km (286 miles) NE of Uluru; 1,491km (924 miles) S of Darwin; 1,544km (957 miles) N of Adelaide; 2,954km (1,831 miles) NW of Sydney

"Alice" or "the Alice," as Australians fondly call it, is the unofficial capital of the Red Centre and a gateway to Uluru.

Many tourists visit Alice only to get to Uluru, but you might like to spend a few days here exploring its indigenous culture and outlying natural attractions. Home to about 28,500 people, it's a rambling, unsophisticated place that is the heart of the Aboriginal Arrernte people's country. Alice is a rich source

Alice Springs

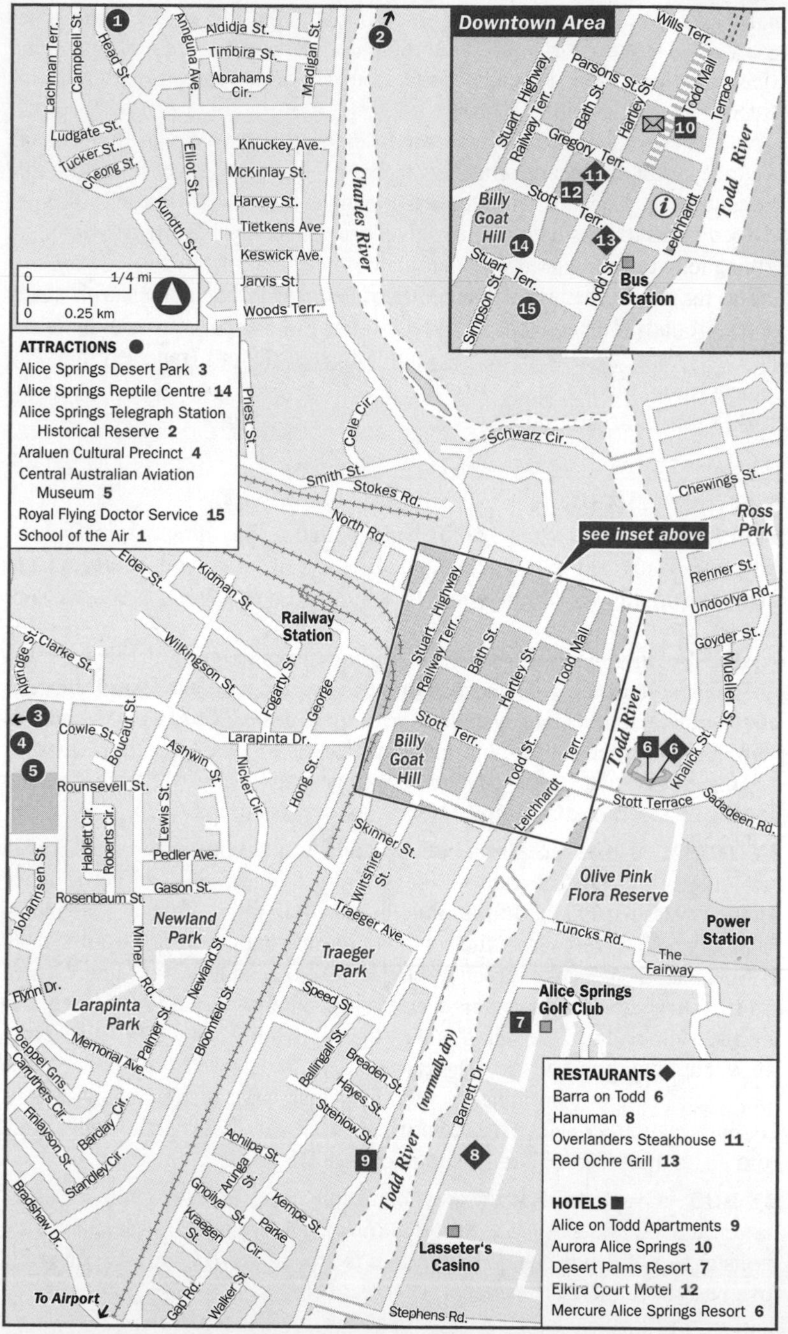

of tours, shops, and galleries for those interested in Aboriginal culture, art, or souvenirs. However, parts of this region are also evidence that ancient Aboriginal civilization has not always meshed well with the 21st century, which has resulted in fractured riverbed communities plagued by alcohol and other social problems. And it is likely that you will see evidence of this on the streets.

No matter what direction you come from to get here, you will fly for hours over a vast, flat landscape. On arrival, you will see that in fact it is close to a low, dramatic range of rippling red mountains, the **MacDonnell Ranges.** Many visitors excitedly expect to see Uluru, but that marvel is about 462km (286 miles) down the road.

The red folds of the MacDonnell Ranges hide lovely gorges with shady picnic grounds. The area has an old gold-rush town to poke around in, quirky little museums, wildlife parks, a couple of cattle stations (ranches) that welcome visitors, hiking trails to put red dust on your boots, and one of the world's top 10 desert golf courses.

Essentials

GETTING THERE

BY PLANE **Qantas** (✆ **131 313** in Australia) flies direct from Sydney, Adelaide, Darwin, Perth, Melbourne, Brisbane, Cairns, and Uluru. **Virgin Australia** (✆ **136 789** in Australia) flies direct from Adelaide, Brisbane, Melbourne, and Darwin.

Alice Springs Airport (www.alicespringsairport.com.au) is about 15km (9⅓ miles) out of town. The airport shuttle operated by **Alice Wanderer Airport Transfers** (www.alicewanderer.com.au; ✆ **1800/722 111** in Australia or 08/8952 2111) meets all flights and transfers you to your Alice hotel door for A$16 per passenger for the first two passengers and then A$11 for each additional passenger. A taxi from the airport to town is around A$35.

BY TRAIN If you are a train buff, you may want to plan a trip that takes in two of Australia's great train journeys. From Sydney, you can get to Alice Springs by train using the **Indian Pacific** and **Ghan** trains. First take the Indian Pacific (which travels across the continent from Sydney to Perth) from Sydney to Adelaide, then change direction (and trains) to head north to Alice. Named after Afghan camel-train drivers who carried supplies in the Red Centre during the 19th century, the Ghan makes the trip from Adelaide to Alice every week, continuing to Darwin. The twice-weekly Adelaide-Alice service takes roughly 24 hours. It promises to be a very long—but memorable—journey. For information, contact **Great Southern Railway** (www.greatsouthernrail.com.au; ✆ **1800/703 357** in Australia or 08/8213 4401).

BY BUS **Greyhound** (www.greyhound.com.au; ✆ **1300/473 946** in Australia or 08/8952 7888 in Alice Springs) runs from Sydney via Adelaide. It's a monster trip of 3 full days, and the fare is around A$702. Unless you really love bus travel, there are better ways to get here!

Who was Alice?

Alice Springs was named after Alice Todd, wife of astronomer and engineer Charles Todd, who won the tender to construct the Overland Telegraph line. In 1871, surveyor William Mills was charged with finding a suitable location for a repeater station as part of the Overland Telegraph line, and discovered a massive inland river system. He named it for his boss, Charles Todd—not knowing that the Todd River would almost always be dry. He found what he believed to be a natural spring in the river system, and named it for Mrs. Todd. In fact, there was no spring, just a water hole left when the rest of the river had dried up. Alice Todd died in Adelaide in 1898, aged 52.

BY CAR Alice Springs is on the Stuart Highway linking Adelaide and Darwin. Allow a very long 2 days or a more comfortable 3 days to drive from Adelaide, the same from Darwin. From Sydney, connect to the Stuart Highway via Broken Hill and Port Augusta north of Adelaide; from Cairns, head south to Townsville, then west via the town of Mount Isa to join the Stuart Highway at Tennant Creek. Both routes are long and dull. From Perth, it is even longer; drive across the Nullarbor Plain to connect with the Stuart Highway at Port Augusta. If you fancy a driving holiday of the area, check out **www.northernterritory.com** for advice on routes, accommodations, and other important details, such as locations of fuel stops.

VISITOR INFORMATION

The **Alice Springs Visitor Information Centre,** Todd Mall (www.discovercentralaustralia.com; ✆ **1800/645 199** in Australia or 08/8952 5800), is the official one-stop shop for bookings and touring information for the Red Centre, including Alice Springs, Kings Canyon, and Uluru–Kata Tjuta National Park. It also acts as the visitor center for the Parks & Wildlife Commission of the Northern Territory. It's open Monday through Friday from 8:30am to 5pm and weekends and public holidays (except Christmas Day, New Year's Day, and Good Friday) from 9:30am to 4pm.

GETTING AROUND

Virtually all tours pick you up at your hotel. If your itinerary traverses unpaved roads, as it may in outlying areas, you will need to rent a 4WD vehicle, because regular cars will not be insured on an unpaved surface. However, a regular car will get you to most attractions. **Budget,** 113 Todd Mall (✆ **08/8952 8899**); **Hertz,** 34 Stott Terrace (✆ **08/8953 6257**); and **Thrifty,** 71 Hartley St. (✆ 08/8952 9999), all rent conventional and 4WD vehicles. **Avis** (✆ **08/8952 3694**) and **Europcar** (✆ **08/8953 3799**) have desks at the airport, as do all the other companies.

Many rental outfits for motor homes (camper vans) have Alice offices. They include **Apollo Campers,** 40 Stuart Highway (✆ **08/8955 5305** or 1800/777 779 in Australia), and **Britz Campervan Rental,** corner of Stuart Highway and Power Street (✆ **08/8952 8814**). Renting a camper van can be significantly cheaper than staying in hotels and going on tours, but do the math first.

Behold the Bizarre

Alice Springs hosts a couple of bizarre events. The **Camel Cup** camel race (www.camelcup.com.au) takes place on the second Saturday in July. On the third Saturday in August, people from hundreds of miles around come out to cheer the **Henley-on-Todd Regatta** (www.henleyontodd.com.au), during which gaudily decorated, homemade bottomless "boats" race down the dry Todd River bed. Well, what else do you do on a river that rarely flows? See "Australia Calendar of Events" in chapter 2 for more details.

The best way to get around town without your own transport is aboard the **Alice Wanderer** bus (see "Organized Tours," p. 252). **Public buses** (✆ **08/8924 7666**) run around town; the main bus stop is at the corner of Gregory Terrace and Railway Terrace. The A$3 fare gives you unlimited bus travel for 3 hours. A daily ticket costs A$7 and provides unlimited bus travel on that day. For A$20 you can buy a weekly ticket, valid for 7 days from the date of purchase, or a 10-trip flexi-trip ticket (each valid for 3 hours). Both A$20 tickets are electronic "tap-and-ride" cards. Tickets can be bought on the bus. There are no public bus services on Sundays or public holidays.

For a taxi, call **Alice Springs Taxis** (✆ **131 008** or 08/8952 1877) or find one at the rank (stand) on the corner of Todd Street and Gregory Terrace. Taxi fares here are high.

The Henley-on-Todd Regatta of bottomless boats racing on the dry Todd River bed.

CITY LAYOUT

Todd Mall is the heart of town. Most shops, businesses, and restaurants are here or within a few blocks' walk. Most hotels, the casino, the golf course, and many of the town's attractions are a few kilometers outside of town. The dry Todd River "flows" through the city east of Todd Mall.

Where to Stay

Alice's hotel stock is not grand. Many properties have dated rooms and modest facilities; they're no match for the gleaming **Ayers Rock Resort** (described later in this chapter). You may pay lower rates than those listed in the summer off-season (Dec–Mar) and even as late as June. Peak season typically runs from July through October or November.

If you've rented a camper van, the **Alice Springs Tourist Park,** Larapinta Drive, Alice Springs (www.alicespringstouristpark.com.au; © **1300/823 404** in Australia or 08/8952 2547), has powered sites costing A$40 a night. Cabins here cost between A$85 and A$175 per night, depending on the cabin and the season.

Alice on Todd Apartments ★★ This contemporary complex has nice studios and one- and two-bedroom apartments. The one-bedroom "deluxe" apartments are a good option, particularly if you have kids. The apartments are very large, and some have two bathrooms. The hotel overlooks the Todd River and is a short stroll from town. All but the studios have balconies, and some two-bedroom apartments have sofa beds. There is a washing machine in each unit and other amenities such as free storage lockers.

Strehlow St. and South. www.aliceontodd.com.au. © **08/8953 8033.** 57 units. A$135 studio apt; A$158–A$180 1-bedroom apt; A$210–A$245 2-bedroom apt. Covered parking. **Amenities:** Babysitting; bikes; children's playground; Jacuzzi; pool; free Wi-Fi.

Aurora Alice Springs ★★ This pleasant hotel is smack in the center of town. Rooms all have a fresh, contemporary decor. Executive rooms have a king-size bed and private balconies facing the Todd River. Deluxe and standard rooms have either a double or queen bed and one single bed. Family rooms have a queen-size bed and two single beds. The small pool and Jacuzzi are tucked away in a corner, so this is not the place for chilling out poolside; stay here to be within walking distance of shops and restaurants. The hotel's Red Ochre Grill (p. 249) is recommended for gourmet "bush tucker" dining.

11 Leichhardt Terrace (backing onto Todd Mall). www.auroraresorts.com.au. © **1800/089 644** in Australia or 08/8950 6666. 109 units. A$149–A$229 double; A$159 family room. **Amenities:** Restaurant; barbecue in courtyard; airport shuttle; babysitting; Jacuzzi; small outdoor pool; room service; free Wi-Fi.

Desert Palms Resort ★★ A large swimming pool with its own palm-studded island is the focal point at this complex of bright cabins, where privacy from your neighbors is ensured by trailing pink bougainvillea and palm trees. Don't be deterred by the prefab appearance; inside the cabins is surprisingly large, well kept, and inviting, with pine-pitched ceilings, kitchenettes, a tiny bathroom, and furnished front decks. Four rooms are suitable for travelers with disabilities. The pleasant staff at the front desk sells basic grocery and liquor supplies and books tours. You are also right next door to Lasseter's Casino (a debatable advantage) and the Alice Springs Golf Club. This is one of the nicest places to stay in Alice.

74 Barrett Dr. www.desertpalms.com.au. ✆ **1800/678 037** in Australia or 08/8952 5977. 80 units. A$145 double; A$185 family. **Amenities:** Pool; half-size tennis court; free Wi-Fi.

Elkira Court Motel ★ The cheapest rooms in the heart of town—decent ones, that is—are at this clean, comfortable, unpretentious motel. The rooms are basic, but you won't get better value and all are air-conditioned. Deluxe rooms have kitchenettes, and some have king-size beds. Deluxe Spa rooms have two-person Jacuzzis. Ask for a room away from the road; the traffic is noisy during the day.

65 Bath St. (opposite Kmart). www.elkiracourtmotel.com.au. ✆ **08/8952 1222.** 58 units. A$110–A$180. **Amenities:** Restaurant; airport shuttle; nearby golf course; Jacuzzi; outdoor pool; free Wi-Fi.

Mercure Alice Springs Resort ★★ This low-rise property, a 3-minute walk from town over the Todd River, underwent a A$2-million upgrade in mid-2017, with all new fittings in the standard bedrooms and bathrooms, along with the installation of floor-to-ceiling artworks that reflect the history of the Alice Springs region in all rooms. Deluxe rooms have bathtubs and bathrobes, a coffee machine, and a balcony or veranda overlooking the Todd River or the gardens. In summer, it's nice to repair to the pool under a couple of desert palms for a drink at the poolside bar, which also received an upgrade during renovations. Still to come is an outdoor amphitheatre, which will be a hub for Aboriginal workshops and cultural sessions.

34 Stott Terrace. www.accorhotels.com. ✆ **08/8951 4545.** 139 units. A$130–A$159 double. **Amenities:** Restaurant; 2 bars; free airport shuttle; babysitting; bikes; concierge; solar-heated outdoor pool; room service; free Wi-Fi.

Where to Eat

Barra on Todd ★★ CONTEMPORARY Part of the Mercure Alice Springs Resort, this restaurant serves up barramundi 10 ways! You can try this freshwater fish simply chargrilled with lemon and dill risotto, topped with

Taking Care at Night

Incidents of violence and crime in Alice Springs, including attacks on tourists by groups of young people—fueled by alcohol and substance abuse—have made headlines in Australia in recent years. Much of the trouble is centered around the dry bed of the Todd River and Aboriginal "town camps." Visitors are advised not to wander the streets at night.

asparagus, green beans, beurre blanc, and king prawns, or served in a variety of ways with nods to Chinese, Indian, Thai, and Greek tastes. If you're not a fan of fish, the menu offers plenty of other dishes including chicken, steaks, lamb, and duck. Barra on Todd does a buffet breakfast and has all-day (well, 11:30am–9pm) dining by the pool. It's popular for dinner, so book ahead.

In the Mercure Alice Springs Resort, 34 Stott Terrace. www.accorhotels.com. ✆ **08/8951 4545.** Main courses A$29–A$42. Daily 6–10am breakfast; 11:30am–5:30pm lunch; 6–11pm dinner.

Hanuman ★★★ CONTEMPORARY ASIAN This is one of the most exotic restaurants in Alice Springs. The cuisine is a fusion of Thai and Indian cooking, and the decor is created with use of Asian artifacts and moody lighting. You are very unlikely to be disappointed by dishes such as red duck curry with coconut, lychees, kaffir lime, Thai basil, and fresh pineapple; or black pepper prawns with garlic, onion, and fresh curry leaf. There are plenty of vegetarian options too.

In the Double Tree by Hilton, 82 Barrett Dr. www.hanuman.com.au. ✆ **08/8953 7188.** Main courses A$15–A$38. Mon–Fri noon–2:30pm (except public holidays); daily 6–10:30pm. Closed Christmas Day, Boxing Day (Dec 26), and New Year's Day.

Overlanders Steakhouse ★ STEAK/BUSH TUCKER This landmark on the Alice dining scene is famous for its "Drover's Blowout" menu, which assaults the mega-hungry with soup and *damper* (a traditional Australian campfire bread), then a tasting platter of crocodile, camel, kangaroo filets, and wild buffalo—these are just the appetizers—followed by rump steak or barramundi and dessert (apple pie or Pavlova). There's a regular menu with a 500-gram (1.1-lb.) steak, plus some lighter fare. The barnlike interior is Outback throughout, from the rustic bar to the saddlebags hanging from the roof beams. Vegetarians, take heart: There's actually a reasonable menu for you too.

72 Hartley St. www.overlanders.com.au. ✆ **08/8952 2159.** Reservations required in peak season. Main courses A$22–A$43. Daily 6–10pm.

Red Ochre Grill ★★ GOURMET BUSH TUCKER The chef at this upscale restaurant fuses native Aussie ingredients with dishes from around the world. If you've never tried crocodile ribs (served with a charred red pepper and yam fritter) or chargrilled kangaroo filet with a pepper-berry glaze, then this is your chance. A grazing platter of smoked 'roo, buffalo mozzarella, crocodile ribs, and some bush tomato relish will offer a variety of tastes. Although it might seem a touristy formula, the food is delicious. Dine in the contemporary interior fronting Todd Mall or outside in the attractive courtyard. Reservations recommended at dinner, when the menu offers the best "bush tucker" options.

Todd Mall. www.redochrealice.com.au. ✆ **08/8952 9614.** Main courses A$15 lunch, A$19–A$39 dinner. Daily noon–2:30pm and 6–9pm (closed Christmas Day).

Exploring Alice Springs

All the major attractions in Alice Springs are within easy reach of the city center.

Alice Springs Desert Park ★★★ By means of an easy 1.6km (1-mile) trail through three reconstructed natural habitats, this impressive wildlife and flora park shows you 120 or so of the animal species that live in the desert around Alice but that you won't spot too easily in the wild (including kangaroos you can walk among). Most of the creatures are small mammals (like the rare bilby), reptiles (cute thorny devil lizards), and birds. Don't miss the excellent free-flying bird presentation at 10am and 3:30pm daily. For a close-up meeting with Australia's largest bird of prey, the wedge-tailed eagle, another A$30 will give entry (and a photo session) to the **Eagle Encounter** show at 1:30pm weekdays. There's a cafe on premises. Allow 2 to 3 hours to see it all.

Larapinta Dr., 6km (3¾ miles) west of town. www.alicespringsdesertpark.com.au. ✆ **08/8951 8788.** A$32 adults, A$16 children 5–15, A$55–A$87 families. Daily 7:30am–6pm (last suggested entry 4:30pm). Closed Christmas Day. **Tailormade Tours** (www.tailormadetours.com.au; ✆ **08/8952 1731**) and **Alice Wanderer** (www.alicewanderer.com.au; ✆ **1800/722 111** in Australia or 08/8952 2111) both offer transfers from accommodations several times a day in each direction.

Alice Springs Reptile Centre ★★ Kids love this place, where they can drape a python around their neck or have a bearded dragon (lizard) perch on their shoulder. Rex, the easygoing proprietor, helps you get the best photos and lets kids hand-feed bugs to the animals at feeding time. More than 50 species are on display, including the world's deadliest land snake (the taipan) and big goannas. Also here are brown snakes, death adders, and mulga, otherwise known as king brown snakes. Don't miss the saltwater croc exhibit, with underwater viewing. The best time to visit is between 11am and 3pm, when the reptiles are at their most active. There are talks at 11am, 1pm, and 3:30pm. Allow an hour or so.

9 Stuart Terrace (opposite the Royal Flying Doctor Service). www.reptilecentre.com.au. ✆ **08/8952 8900.** A$17 adults, A$9 children 4–16, A$44 families of 4. Daily 9:30am–5pm. Closed Christmas Day and New Year's Day.

Alice Springs Telegraph Station Historical Reserve ★★ This oasis marks the first European settlement of Alice Springs, which takes its name from the water hole nearby. Alice Springs began life here in 1872 as a telegraph repeater station, against a backdrop of red hills and sprawling gum trees. Arm yourself with the free map or join a free 45-minute tour at 9:30am, 11:30am, 1:30pm, and 3:30pm. You can wander around the old stationmaster's residence; the telegraph office, with its Morse-code machine tap-tapping away; the shoeing yard, packed with blacksmithing equipment; and the stables, housing vintage buggies and saddlery. From the on-site computer, you can "telegraph" e-mail messages to your friends or be really old-fashioned and send mail through the Telegraph/Post Office, which will be stamped with a special franking stamp. It's a charming and much-underrated place. Allow an hour—more to walk one of the several hiking trails—or bring a picnic and stay longer. You are also likely to see kangaroos and rock wallabies. It has a gift shop and a kiosk where you can buy coffee and snacks, hire bikes, or take a guided mountain bike tour (from A$155 for 3 hours).

Stuart Hwy., 4km (2½ miles) north of town (past the School of the Air turnoff). www.alicespringstelegraphstation.com.au. ✆ **08/8952 3993.** Free admission to picnic grounds and trails; station A$14 adults, A$8.50 children 12–16, A$5 children 6–11, A$32 families of 4. Daily 9am–5pm (picnic grounds and trails 8am–9pm). Station closed Christmas Day. To get there, take a cab or Alice Wanderer bus (see "Organized Tours," p. 252) or the 4km (2½-mile) riverside pedestrian/bike track that starts near the corner of Wills Terrace and Undoolya Rd.

Araluen Cultural Precinct ★★ Take several hours to explore the many facets of this interesting grouping of attractions. Some impressive Aboriginal and contemporary Aussie art is on display at the **Araluen Arts Centre** (www.araluenartscentre.nt.gov.au; ✆ **08/8951 1122**), the town's performing-arts hub, which incorporates the **Araluen Art Collection,** which focuses on works by Aboriginal artists from Central Australia from the early 1930s onwards, including Albert Namatjira and artists from the Papunya community in the early 1970s. Check out the "Honey Ant Dreaming" stained-glass window in the foyer. You can buy stylish crafts, and sometimes catch artists at work, in the **Central Craft** gallery. You may also want to amble among the fabulous outdoor sculptures, including the 15m (49-ft.) Yeperenye caterpillar, or among the gravestones in the cemetery next door, where "Afghani" camel herders (from what is now Pakistan) are buried facing Mecca. The **Museum of Central Australia** mostly shows local fossils, natural history displays, and meteorites, and the **Central Australian Aviation Museum** has a collection of old radios, aircraft, and wreckage that preserves the territory's aerial history. The museum is on the site of the 1939 Alice Springs "aerodrome" and includes the original hangar. Among its highlights are a Beech 18 and a Wackett Trainer aircraft.

The gigantic Yeperenye caterpillar is among the outdoor sculptures featured in the Araluen Cultural Precinct.

61 Larapinta Dr., at Memorial Ave., 2km (1¼ miles) west of town. www.dtc.nt.gov.au/arts-and-museums/araluen-cultural-precinct. ✆ **08/8951 1120.** A$15 adults, A$10 children 5–16, A$40 families of 4. Daily 10am–4pm. Closed Good Friday and 2 weeks from Christmas Day.

Royal Flying Doctor Service Tourist Facility ★★ Alice is a major base for this airborne medical service that treats people living and traveling in the vast Outback. The visitor center provides a great insight into the work the RFDS does. Guided tours run every half-hour from 9am (last tour at 4pm); allow another 30 minutes or so to browse the museum and listen to some of the recorded conversations between doctors and patients. You can explore a replica fuselage of a Pilatus PC12, test your hand at the throttle in a flight simulator, and "meet" the life-size hologram of RFDS founder Reverend John Flynn. It also has a cafe, gift shop, and art gallery.

8–10 Stuart Terrace (at end of Hartley St.). www.rfdsalicesprings.com.au. © **08/8958 8412.** A$16 adults, A$11 ages 11–18, A$9 kids 6–10, A$42 families of 4. Mon–Sat 9am–5pm; Sun and public holidays 1–5pm. Closed New Year's Day and Christmas Day.

School of the Air ★★★ Sitting in on school lessons may not be your idea of a vacation, but this school is different—it broadcasts by radio to a 1.3-million-sq.-km (502,000-sq.-mile) "schoolroom" of 141 children on Outback stations. That area is as big as Germany, Great Britain, Ireland, New Zealand, and Japan combined—or twice the size of Texas. Visitors watch and listen in when classes are in session; outside class hours, you may hear taped classes. You can browse the kids' artwork, photos, video, and other displays in the well-organized visitor center. Allow about an hour.

80 Head St. (2.5km/1½ miles from town). www.assoa.nt.edu.au. © **08/8951 6834.** A$11 adults, A$8.50 children 5–16, A$25–A$30 families. Mon–Sat 8:30am–4:30pm; Sun and public holidays 1:30–4:30pm. Closed Good Friday and Dec 21–Jan 5. Bus: nos. 100 or 101 (except Sun and public holidays) or Alice Wanderer (see "Organized Tours," below).

Organized Tours

AROUND TOWN & OUT IN THE DESERT **Alice Wanderer Centre Sightseeing** (www.alicewanderer.com.au; © **1800/722 111** in Australia or 08/8952 2111) offers a large range of half- and full-day tours. It's well worth checking out their website to help you plan your time before you visit. The company also runs full- and half-day tours to outlying areas, including to Palm Valley in the West MacDonnell Ranges, costing A$152 for adults and A$81 for kids (p. 255).

Many Alice-based companies offer minicoach or 4WD day trips and extended tours of Alice and of outlying areas including the East and West Macs, Hermannsburg, and Finke Gorge National Park. **Mulga's Adventures** (www.mulgasadventures.com.au; © **1800/359 089** in Australia or 08/8952 1545), operates a 3-day backpackers' tour of the area, including Uluru (A$390).

CAMEL SAFARIS The camel's ability to get by without water was key to opening the arid inland parts of Australia to European settlement in the 1800s. With the advent of cars, they were released into the wild, and today more than 200,000 roam Central Australia. Australia even exports them to the Middle East! **Pyndan Camel Tracks** (www.cameltracks.com; © **0416/170 164**) runs

Outback Ballooning offers dawn flights over the desert.

camel rides daily, with pickup from your hotel. A 1-hour tour, at noon, 2:30pm, or sunset, costs A$70 adults and A$40 for kids 14 and under. Kids 2 and under must ride with an adult. Make sure you wear comfortable, casual clothes, and sensible shoes—you are likely to get a bit dirty.

HOT-AIR BALLOON FLIGHTS Dawn balloon flights above the desert are popular in Central Australia. You have to get up 90 minutes before dawn, though. **Outback Ballooning** (www.outbackballooning.com.au; ✆ **1800/809 790** in Australia or 08/8952 8723) offers a 1-hour flight followed by champagne breakfast in the bush for A$390 adults, A$318 for kids 6 to 16. A 30-minute breakfast flight costs A$295 adults, A$242 for children. Kids 5 and under are discouraged from participating because they cannot see over the basket. Don't make any other morning plans—you probably won't get back to your hotel until close to noon.

Outdoor Activities

BUSHWALKING The 223km (138-mile) **Larapinta Trail** winds west from Alice through the sparse red ranges, picturesque semi-desert scenery, and rich bird life of the **Tjoritja/West MacDonnell National Park** (p. 255). This long-distance walking track is divided into 12 sections, each a 1- to 2-day walk. Sections range from easy to hard. The shortest is 8km (5 miles), and they go up to 29km (18 miles). The trail begins at the old Alice Springs Telegraph Station and meanders through many gaps and sheltered gorges and climbs steeply over rugged ranges. Each section is accessible to vehicles (some by high-clearance 4WD only), so you can join or leave the trail at any of the trail heads. Camping out under a sea of stars in the Outback is a highlight of the experience. Although they vary, most campsites offer picnic tables and hardened tent sites—all trail heads have a water supply and some have free gas barbecues. The Parks & Wildlife Commission of the Northern Territory strongly recommends any individual or group walking the Larapinta Trail to carry a satellite phone or a location device such as a PLB/EPIRBS or Spot-Messenger. Trail maps and information can be obtained from the **Visitor**

Information Centre (see "Visitor Information," earlier in this chapter). For details on the trail, visit www.nt.gov.au/leisure/recreation/bushwalking-hiking/larapinta-trail. The website also lists companies that provide transfers to access points along the way, food drops, camping equipment, or fully guided and supported treks. ***Warning:*** *Always* carry drinking water. The trail may close in extremely hot summer periods.

GOLF The **Alice Springs Golf Club,** 1km (.6 mile) from town on Cromwell Drive (www.alicespringsgolfclub.com.au; ✆ **08/8952 1921**), boasts a Thomson-Wolveridge course rated among the world's top desert courses by touring pros. The course is open from sunup to sundown. Nine holes cost A$27; 18 holes, A$48. Club rental is A$29, and a motorized cart, which many locals don't bother with, goes for A$35 for 18 holes. There's also a driving range (A$9 for a small bucket of balls). If lawn bowling is more your style, the golf club completed a new bowling green in late 2016.

Shopping for Aboriginal Art

Alice Springs is one of the best places in Australia to buy Aboriginal art and crafts. You will find no shortage of paintings, didgeridoos, spears, clapping sticks, *coolamons* (dishes used by women to carry anything from water to babies), animal carvings, baskets, and jewelry, as well as books, CDs, and all kinds of merchandise printed with Aboriginal designs. Prices can soar to many thousands for large canvases by world-renowned painters, but you'll also find plenty of smaller, more affordable works. Most galleries arrange shipment. Store hours can vary with the seasons and the crowds, so it pays to check ahead.

Mbantua Fine Art Gallery and Cultural Museum, 64 Todd Mall (www.mbantua.com.au; ✆ **08/8952 5571**), is a highly respected and reliable source of authentic Aboriginal art, with a dazzling selection to choose from. The art comes from a harsh desert region called Utopia, home to several Aboriginal communities. Mbantua owner Tim Jennings began supplying locals with paints and canvas in the late 1980s during food deliveries to Utopia, first as sheriff, then as the general-store owner. Some of the 200 Utopia residents who paint have been recognized internationally, including Barbara Weir, Gloria Petyarre, the late Emily Kame Kngwarreye, and Minnie Pwerle. Jennings authenticates every piece of art; he and his team photograph the artist with the work and record the traditional meaning behind it. Works by established artists can be priced up to tens of thousands of dollars, but a much smaller investment can get you work by lesser-known but talented painters. Mbantua Gallery is a member of Art Trade, an organization that promotes the ethical trade of indigenous art. The gallery is open Monday to Friday 9am to 5pm, Saturday 9am to 3pm, and (May–Oct only) Sunday 10am to 2pm.

Papunya Tula Artists, 63 Todd Mall (www.papunyatula.com.au; ✆ **08/8952 4731**), sells paintings on canvas and linen from Papunya, a settlement 240km (150 miles) northwest of Alice Springs, and work by other artists living in the Western Desert, as far as 700km (434 miles) from Alice Springs.

Day Trips to the MacDonnell Ranges ★★★

The key attraction of a day trip to the MacDonnell Ranges is unspoiled natural scenery and few crowds. Many companies run coach or 4WD tours—half- or full-day, sometimes overnight—to the West and East Macs. Some options appear in "Organized Tours" in the "Alice Springs" section, earlier in this chapter.

GETTING THERE

If you are not driving yourself, you can arrange to be dropped off by **Larapinta Transfers** (www.larapintatransfers.com.au; ✆ **1800/722 111** in Australia, or 08/8952 2111) at several stops in the Ranges. It costs A$90 per person (minimum of two) for the return trip to Simpson's Gap or Standley Chasm; A$155 to Serpentine Gorge, Ormiston Gorge, or Glen Helen Gorge. The Alice Wanderer (p. 252) also does group tours.

THE WEST MACDONNELL RANGES

TJORITJA/WEST MACDONNELL NATIONAL PARK The 300km (186-mile) round-trip drive west from Alice Springs into Tjoritja/West MacDonnell National Park (www.nt.gov.au/leisure/parks-reserves/find-a-park-to-visit/tjoritja-west-macdonell-national-park) is a stark but picturesque expedition to a series of red gorges, semi-desert country, and the occasional peaceful swimming hole. The 12-stage, 223km (138-mile) **Larapinta Walking Trail** takes you along the backbone of the West MacDonnell Ranges through some of the most unique and isolated country in the world. The hills, colors, birds, water holes, gorges, and the never-ending diversity of this trail will leave you spellbound by the beauty of Central Australia. The track stretches from the Telegraph Station in Alice Springs to Mount Sonder, past Glen Helen Gorge. Detailed track notes are at the Visitor Information Center in Alice Springs and online at www.nt.gov.au/leisure/recreation/bushwalking-hiking/larapinta-trail. Don't attempt the walk in the height of summer unless you are very well prepared. For great tips and other information, look up the **Alice Wanderer** website (www.alicewanderer.com.au).

From Alice, take Larapinta Drive west for 18km (11 miles) to the 8km (5-mile) turnoff to **Simpson's Gap,** a water hole lined with ghost gums. Black-footed rock wallabies hop out on the cliffs in the late afternoon (so you may want to time a visit here on your way back to Alice). There are a couple of short trails here, including a .5km (.3-mile) Ghost Gum circuit and a 17km (11-mile) round-trip trail to Bond Gap. Swimming is not permitted. The place has an information center/ranger station and free use of barbecues.

Twenty-three kilometers (14 miles) farther down Larapinta Road, 9km (5½ miles) down a turnoff, is **Standley Chasm** (www.standleychasm.com.au; ✆ **08/8956 7440**). This rock cleft is only a few meters wide but 80m (262 ft.) high, reached by a 10-minute creekside trail. Aim to be here at midday, when the walls glow orange in the overhead sun. A kiosk sells snacks and drinks. Admission is A$12 for adults, A$7 for children 5 to 14, and A$30 for a family of 4. The chasm is open daily from 8am to 5pm (last entry at 4:30pm; closed

Christmas Day). This is a private reserve, owned by local Aboriginal people. Half-day indigenous tours are offered daily at 9am (bookings required) for A$85 adults and A$60 children.

Six kilometers (3¾ miles) past Standley Chasm, you can branch right onto Namatjira Drive or continue to Hermannsburg Historic Precinct (see below). If you take Namatjira Drive, you'll go 42km (26 miles) to picturesque **Ellery Creek Big Hole.** ***Be warned:*** The spring-fed water is icy cold. A 3km (2-mile) walking trail explains the area's geological history.

Eleven kilometers (7 miles) farther along Namatjira Drive is **Serpentine Gorge,** where a trail leads up to a lookout for a lovely view of the ranges through the gorge walls. Another 12km (7½ miles) on are **ochre pits,** which Aboriginal people quarried for body paint and for decorating objects used in ceremonial performances. Twenty-six kilometers (16 miles) farther west, 8km (5 miles) from the main road, is **Ormiston Gorge and Pound** (**© 08/8956 7799** for the ranger station/visitor center). This is a good spot to picnic, swim in the wide, deep pool below red cliffs, and walk a choice of trails, such as the 30-minute Ghost Gum Lookout trail or the easy 7km (4⅓-mile) scenic loop (allow 3–4 hr.). The water is warm enough for swimming in the summer.

Farther on is **Glen Helen Gorge,** where the Finke River cuts through the ranges, with more gorge swimming, a walking trail, guided hikes, and helicopter flights. **Glen Helen Homestead Lodge** (www.glenhelen.com.au; **© 08/8956 7489**) has a restaurant and offers 4WD tours from A$190 per person for a half day and scenic helicopter flights from March through November (two-person minimum) from A$70 per person (call to schedule).

ROAD trips TO THE EAST & WEST MACS

Facilities are scarce outside Alice, so bring food, drinking water, and a full gas tank. Leaded, unleaded, and diesel fuel are for sale at Glen Helen Resort and Hermannsburg. Wear walking shoes.

Many of the water holes dry up too much to be good for swimming—those at Ellery Creek, Ormiston Gorge, and Glen Helen are the most permanent. They can be intensely cold, so take only short dips to avoid cramping and hypothermia, don't swim alone, and be careful of underwater snags. Don't wear sunscreen, because it pollutes drinking water for native animals.

Two-wheel-drive rental cars will not be insured on unsealed (unpaved) roads, which includes the last few miles into Trephina Gorge Nature Park and the 11km (7-mile) road into N'Dhala Gorge Nature Park, both in the East Macs. If you are prepared to risk it, you can probably get into Trephina in a two-wheel-drive car, but you will definitely need a 4WD vehicle for N'Dhala and Arltunga. The West MacDonnell road is paved to Glen Helen Gorge; a few points of interest may require driving for short lengths on unpaved road. Before setting off, drop into the Tourism Central Australia **Visitor Information Centre** (see "Visitor Information," earlier in this chapter) for tips on road conditions and details on the free ranger talks, walks, and slideshows that take place in the West and East Macs from April through October. Entry to all sights, parks, and reserves (except Standley Chasm) is free.

HERMANNSBURG HISTORIC PRECINCT An alternative to visiting the West Mac gorges is to stay on Larapinta Drive all 128km (79 miles) from Alice Springs to the old **Lutheran Mission** at the **Hermannsburg Historic Precinct** (www.hermannsburg.com.au; ✆ **08/8956 7402**). Some maps show this route as an unpaved road, but it is paved. Settled by German missionaries in the 1870s, this is a cluster of 16 National Trust–listed farmhouse-style mission buildings and a historic cemetery. There is a museum, a gallery housing landscapes by Aboriginal artist Albert Namatjira, and tearooms serving light snacks and apple strudel from an old German recipe. The precinct is open daily 9am to 5pm; closed Good Friday and Christmas Day. Admission to the precinct is A$11 for adults, free for children.

FINKE GORGE NATIONAL PARK Just west of Hermannsburg is the turnoff to the 46,000-hectare (113,620-acre) **Finke Gorge National Park,** 16km (10 miles) to the south on an unpaved road (or about a 2-hr. drive west of Alice Springs). Turn south off Larapinta Drive just west of Hermannsburg. Access along the last 16km (10 miles) of road, which follows the sandy bed of the Finke River, is limited to four-wheel-drive vehicles only. Heavy rains may cause this section of the road to be impassable. The park is most famous for **Palm Valley,** where groves of rare *Livistona mariae* cabbage palms have survived since Central Australia was a jungle millions of years ago. You will need to have a four-wheel-drive vehicle or take a tour to explore this park. Four walking trails between 1.5km (1 mile) and 5km (3 miles) take you among the palms or up to a lookout over cliffs; one is a sign-posted trail exploring Aboriginal culture. For information, call the Visitor Information Centre in Alice Springs before you leave; there is no visitor center in the park.

THE EAST MACDONNELL RANGES

Not as many tourists tread the path on the Ross Highway into the East Macs, but if you do, you'll be rewarded with lush walking trails, fewer crowds, traces of Aboriginal history, and possibly even the sight of wild camels.

The first points of interest are **Emily Gap,** 10km (6 miles) from Alice, and **Jessie Gap,** an additional 7km (4⅓ miles), a pretty picnic spot. You can cool off in the Emily Gap swimming hole if there is any water. Don't miss the *Caterpillar Dreaming* Aboriginal painting art on the wall, on your right as you walk through.

At **Corroboree Rock,** 37km (23 miles) farther, you can make a short climb up the outcrop, which was important to local Aborigines. The polished rock "seat" high up in the hole means Aboriginal people must have used this rock for eons.

Twenty-two kilometers (14 miles) farther is the turnoff to **Trephina Gorge Nature Park,** an 18-sq.-km (7-sq.-mile) beauty spot with peaceful walking trails that can take from 45 minutes to 4½ hours. The last 5km (3 miles) of the 9km (5½-mile) road into the park are unpaved, but you can make it in a two-wheel drive car.

N'Dhala Gorge Nature Park, 10km (6 miles) past Trephina Gorge Nature Park, houses an "open-air art gallery" of rock carvings, or petroglyphs, left by

Caterpillar Dreaming Aboriginal painting at Emily Gap swimming hole.

the Eastern Arrernte Aboriginal people. An interesting 1.5km (1-mile) signposted trail explains the Dreamtime meanings of a few of the 6,000 rock carvings, hundreds or thousands of years old, that are thought to be in this eerily quiet gorge. A 4WD vehicle is a must to traverse the 11km (7-mile) access road.

The Ross Highway is paved all the way to Ross River Resort, 86km (53 miles) from Alice Springs.

ULURU–KATA TJUTA NATIONAL PARK ★★★

462km (286 miles) SW of Alice Springs; 1,934km (1,199 miles) S of Darwin; 1,571km (974 miles) N of Adelaide; 2,841km (1,761 miles) NW of Sydney

Why travel so far to look at a large red rock? Because it will send a shiver up your spine. Because it may move you to tears. Because there is something indefinable and indescribable but definitely spiritual about this place. Up close, Uluru is more magnificent than you can imagine. It is immense and overwhelming and mysterious. Photographs never do it justice. There is what is described as a "spirit of place" here. It is unforgettable and irresistible (and you may well want to come back again, just for another look). It will not disappoint you. On my first visit—yes, I am one who will keep coming back—a stranger whispered to me: "Even when you are not looking at it, it is always just *there,* waiting to tap you on the shoulder." A rock with a presence.

"The Rock" has a circumference of 10.6km (6½ miles), and two-thirds of it is thought to be underground. In photos, it looks smooth and even, but the reality is much more interesting—dappled with holes and overhangs, with curtains of stone draping its sides, creating little coves that hide water holes and Aboriginal rock art. It also changes color from pink to a deep wine red depending on the angle and intensity of the sun. And if you are lucky enough to be visiting when it rains, you will see a sight like no other. Here, rain brings everyone outside to see the spectacle of the waterfalls created off the massive rock, which was formed by sediments laid down 600 to 700 million years ago in an inland sea and thrust up aboveground 348m (1,141 ft.) by geological forces.

In 1985, **Uluru–Kata Tjuta National Park** was returned to its Aboriginal owners, the Pitjantjatjara and Yankunytjatjara people, known as the Anangu, who manage the property jointly with the Australian government. A visit to Uluru isn't just about snapping a few photos and going home. There are many ways of exploring it, and one of the best is to join Aboriginal people on guided walks. You can walk around the Rock, climb it (we'll talk about *that* later), fly over it, ride a camel to it, circle it on a Harley-Davidson or a bicycle, trek through the nearby Olgas, and dine under the stars while you learn about them.

Just do yourself one favor: Plan to spend at least 2 days here, if not 3.

Isolation (and a lack of competition) makes such things as accommodations, meals, and transfers relatively expensive. A coach tour or 4WD camping safari is often the cheapest way to see the place. See "Red Centre Essentials," at the beginning of this chapter, for recommended tour companies.

The massive monolith known as Uluru.

Essentials

GETTING THERE

BY PLANE **Qantas** (© **131 313** in Australia) flies to Ayers Rock (Connellan) Airport direct from Alice Springs and Cairns. Flights from other airports go via Alice Springs. **Jetstar** (© **131 538** in Australia) flies from Sydney and Melbourne, and **Virgin Australia** (© **136 789** in Australia) from Sydney. The airport is 6km (3¾ miles) from Ayers Rock Resort. A free shuttle ferries all resort guests, including campers, to their door.

BY CAR Take the Stuart Highway south from Alice Springs 199km (123 miles), turn right onto the Lasseter Highway, and go 244km (151 miles) to Ayers Rock Resort. The Rock is 18km (11 miles) farther on. It is about a 4½-hour drive in total.

If you are renting a car in Alice Springs and want to drop it at Uluru and fly out from there, be prepared for a one-way penalty. Only Avis, Hertz, and Thrifty have Uluru depots ("Getting Around, p. 245).

VISITOR INFORMATION

For online information before you arrive, check out the Uluru–Kata Tjuta National Park website, www.parksaustralia.gov.au/uluru. Tourism Central Australia has a **Visitor Information Centre** at the corner of Todd Mall and Parsons St., Alice Springs (www.discovercentralaustralia.com; © **1800/645 199** in Australia or 08/8952 5800). Another good source of online information is Ayers Rock Resort's site (www.ayersrockresort.com.au).

One kilometer (.6 mile) from the base of the Rock is the **Uluru–Kata Tjuta Cultural Centre** (www.parksaustralia.gov.au/uluru/do/cultural-centre.html; © **08/8956 1128**), owned and run by the Anangu, the Aboriginal owners of Uluru. It uses eye-catching wall displays, frescoes, interactive recordings, and videos to tell about Aboriginal Dreamtime myths and laws. It's worth spending some time here to understand a little about Aboriginal culture. A National Park desk has information on ranger-guided activities and animal, plant, and bird-watching checklists. The center also has a cafe, a souvenir shop, and two Aboriginal arts and crafts galleries. It's open daily 7am to 6pm.

You can book tours at the **tour desk** in every hotel at Ayers Rock Resort, or visit the **Ayers Rock Resort Tour & Information Centre** (© **08/8957 7324**) in the resort's Town Square. It's open daily 8am to 7pm.

The Rock in a Day?

It's a *loooong* day to visit Uluru in a day from Alice by road. Many organized coach tours pack a lot—perhaps a Rock-base walk or climb, Kata Tjuta (the Olgas), the Uluru–Kata Tjuta Cultural Centre, and a champagne sunset at the Rock—into a busy trip that leaves Alice around 5:30 or 6am and gets you back late at night. You should consider a day trip only between May and September. At other times, it's too hot to do much from early morning to late afternoon.

PARK ENTRANCE FEES

Entry to the Uluru–Kata Tjuta National Park is A$25 per adult, A$13 for children 5 to 15, and valid for 3 days. Some tours include this fee but others do not, so it pays to check. National Park tickets can only be purchased from the National Park Entry Station. The park opens somewhere between 5 and 6:30am (depending on the time of year) and closes between 7:30 and 9pm.

GETTING AROUND

Ayers Rock Resort runs a **free shuttle** every 20 minutes or so around the resort complex from 10:30am to after midnight, but to get to the Rock or Kata Tjuta (the Olgas), you will need to take transfers, join a tour, or have your own wheels. The shuttle also meets all flights. There are no taxis at Yulara.

BY SHUTTLE **Uluru Hop On Hop Off** (www.uluruhoponhopoff.com.au; ✆ **08/8956 2019**) provides a shuttle from Ayers Rock Resort to and from the Rock several times a day from before sunrise to sundown, and twice a day to Kata Tjuta. The basic round-trip fare is A$49 for adults and A$15 for kids 1 to 14. To Kata Tjuta, it costs A$95 for adults and A$40 for children. A 2-day pass that enables you to explore Uluru and Kata Tjuta costs A$160 adults and A$60 children; a 3-day pass costs A$210 for adults and A$100 for kids. A National Park entry pass, if you don't already have one, is A$25 extra.

> **Cultural Etiquette**
>
> The Anangu ask you not to photograph sacred sites or Aboriginal people without permission and to approach quietly and respectfully. For discussion on climbing Uluru, see p. 266.

BY CAR If there are two of you, the easiest and cheapest way to get around is likely to be a rental car. All roads in the area are paved, so 4WD is unnecessary. Expect to pay around A$120 to A$140 per day for a medium-size car. Rates drop a little in low season. Most car-rental companies give you unlimited kilometers on all vehicles, but take the cost of your fuel into account because the round-trip from the resort to the Olgas is just over 100km (63 miles), and it's about 20km (13 miles) to the Rock and back. Hire periods of less than 3 days incur a one-way fee up to about A$385. **Avis** (✆ **08/8956 2266**), **Hertz** (✆ **08/8956 2244**), and **Thrifty** (✆ **08/8956 2556**) all rent regular cars and four-wheel-drives.

BY ORGANIZED TOUR Several tour companies run a range of daily sunrise and sunset viewings, circumnavigations of the Rock by coach or on foot, guided walks at the Rock or the Olgas, camel rides, observatory evenings, visits to the Uluru–Kata Tjuta Cultural Centre, and innumerable combinations of all of these. Some offer "passes" containing the most popular activities. Virtually every company picks you up at your hotel. Among the most reputable are AAT Kings and Tailormade Tours (see "Red Centre Essentials" on p. 241).

WHERE TO STAY & EAT

Ayers Rock Resort is not only in the township of Yulara—it *is* the township. Located about 30km (19 miles) from Uluru, outside the national park boundary, it is the only place to stay. It is an impressive contemporary complex, built to a high standard, efficiently run, and attractive—all things (along with its remoteness) that don't come cheaply. Because everyone either is a tourist, or lives and works here, it has a village atmosphere—with a supermarket, bank, post office, newsstand, medical center, beauty salon, gas station, and several gift, clothing, and souvenir shops.

You have a choice of six places to stay, from luxury hotel rooms and apartments to campsites. No matter where you stay, even in the campground, you are free to use all the pools, restaurants, and other facilities of every hostelry, except the exclusive Sails in the Desert pool, which is reserved for Sails guests, and Longitude 131°.

> **Water, Water . . .**
>
> Water taps are scarce and kiosks nonexistent in Uluru–Kata Tjuta National Park. Always carry plenty of your own drinking water when sightseeing.

You can book any of the accommodations through a central reservations office in Sydney (www.ayersrockresort.com.au; ✆ **1300/134 044** in Australia or 02/8296 8010). High season is July through November. Book well ahead, and shop around for special deals on the Internet and with travel agencies. Ask about special packages for 2- or 3-night stays. All stays include a free indigenous activities program, including guided walks, dance shows, and access to the Mani Mani Indigenous Cultural Theatre.

In addition to the resort dining options, the small shopping center has the pleasant **Gecko's Café,** which offers gourmet pizzas, pastas, and burgers (as well as take-out); **Kulata Academy Cafe,** where the staff are part of an indigenous trainee program; and the **Ayers Wok Noodle Bar** (yes, really!). Several of the resort restaurants offer kids' menus.

Ayers Rock Campground ★ Instead of red dust, you get green lawns at this campground, which has barbecues, a playground, swimming pool, a small general store, and clean communal bathrooms and kitchen. If you don't want to camp but want to travel cheap, consider the modern two-bedroom cabins. They're a great value; each has air-conditioning, a TV, a kitchenette, dining furniture, a double bed, and four bunks (but no phone). They book up quickly in winter. Bookings must be made directly through the campground.

Yulara Dr. www.ayersrockresort.com.au/accommodation/ayers-rock-campground. ✆ **08/8957 7001.** 220 tent sites, 198 powered sites, 14 cabins with shared bathroom. A$169–A$179 cabin for up to 6; A$37–A$50 tent site; A$44–A$50 motor-home site. **Amenities:** Free airport shuttle; children's playground; outdoor pool; Wi-Fi kiosk.

Desert Gardens Hotel ★★ This is the only hotel with views of Uluru (albeit rather distant ones) from some of the rooms. It is set amid wonderful ghost gum trees and the flowering native shrubs that give it its name. The accommodations are not as lavish as Sails in the Desert (below), but they're equally comfortable and were completely refurbished in mid-2016. The **Arnguli Grill** serves a la carte flame-grilled meals at dinner.

Yulara Dr. www.ayersrockresort.com.au/accommodation/desert-gardens-hotel. ✆ **08/8957 7714.** 218 units. A$350–A$400 double; A$440 deluxe Rock-view. 2-night minimum. **Amenities:** Restaurant, bar; free airport shuttle; outdoor pool; room service; free Wi-Fi.

Emu Walk Apartments ★★ Completely renovated and refurbished in 2015, these bright, contemporary apartments have full kitchens, separate bedrooms, and roomy living areas. They have daily maid service, and sleep four or six people, so they're great for families or groups of friends. There's no restaurant or pool, but the Town Square cafes and supermarket are close, and you can cool off in the Desert Gardens Hotel pool.

Yulara Dr. www.ayersrockresort.com.au/accommodation/emu-walk-apartments. ✆ **08/8957 7799.** 63 apts. A$380 double 1-bedroom apt; A$470 double 2-bedroom apt. 2-night minimum. **Amenities:** Free airport shuttle; free Wi-Fi.

Longitude 131° ★★★ When you wake in your luxury "tent" here, you can reach out from your king-size bed and press a button to raise the blinds on your window for a view unmatched anywhere in the world: Uluru as dawn strikes its ochre walls. Your bed, under a softly draped romantic white canopy, is in one of 15 five-star eco-sensitive "tents" set among isolated sand dunes a mile or two from the main resort complex. Each room is decorated in tribute to the European explorers and pioneers of this region. There's a CD player and MP3 docking station but no TV (and who needs one?). The central area, the

DINNER IN THE desert

Why sit in a restaurant when you can eat outside and soak up the desert air? Ayers Rock Resort offers two fine-dining-under-the-stars experiences in the dunes outside the resort. The **Sounds of Silence** dinner is hugely popular (so book well ahead, even up to three months ahead in peak season). In an outdoor clearing, you sip champagne and nibble canapés as the sun sets over the Rock to the strains of a didgeridoo. Then head to communal white-clothed, candlelit tables and a buffet meal that will include kangaroo, emu, crocodile, and barramundi. The food is not exceptional, but you're really here for the atmosphere. After dinner, the lanterns fade and you're left with stillness. For some city folk, it's the first time they have ever heard complete silence. Look up into the usually clear skies, and (if it's a clear night) an astronomer will point out the constellations of the Southern Hemisphere. You can also look at the stars through telescopes. Sounds of Silence is held nightly, weather permitting, and costs A$199 adults and A$100 children, including transfers from Ayers Rock Resort. Surcharges apply for Christmas Day. A more intimate desert dinner is **Tali Wiru,** limited to only 20 people, where you can sit at a table for two or your own party of up to six people. This is a more upmarket experience, offering four courses, French champagne, and waiter service. It costs A$345 per person, and runs April to October only. Book through the Ayers Rock Resort office in Sydney (✆ **1300/134 044** in Australia or 02/0296 0010) or online (www.ayersrockresort.com.au).

Dune House, has a restaurant with superb food, a 24-hour bar, and a library. Settle in for some after-dinner chess or chat. For a special dining experience, book your place at **Table 131°,** where dinner is set up in style under the stars among gently rolling sand dunes. No children under 10.

Yulara Dr. www.longitude131.com.au. ✆ **08/8957 7131** (lodge) or 02/9918 4355 (bookings). 15 units. From A$2,700 double. Rates include walking and bus tours, entry to the national park, meals, selected drinks. 2-night minimum. **Amenities:** Restaurant; bar; free airport shuttle; outdoor pool; no Wi-Fi or mobile phone access.

Outback Pioneer Hotel and Lodge ★ An all-ages crowd congregates at this midrange collection of hotel rooms, budget rooms, shared bunkrooms, and dorms. Standard hotel rooms offer clean, simple accommodations with private bathrooms, a queen-size bed, and a single; these have TVs with pay movies, a fridge, a minibar, and a phone. Budget rooms have access to a common room with a TV and Internet access, as well as a communal kitchen and laundry. Quad bunkrooms are coed and share bathrooms. The single-sex dorms sleep 20. Plenty of lounge chairs sit by the pool. The **Bough House Restaurant** offers a la carte meals, or settle in at the **Outback Pioneer Bar,** where what seems like the entire resort gathers nightly. This barn with big tables, lots of beer, and live music is the place to join the throngs throwing a steak or sausage on the cook-it-yourself barbie (buy your meat at the bar).

Yulara Dr. www.ayersrockresort.com.au/accommodation. ✆ **08/8957 7605.** 125 units. A$260 double with bathroom; A$210 budget room without bathroom; A$46 bed in coed quad; A$38 dorm bed; A$184 budget quad room. **Amenities:** 2 restaurants; bar; free airport shuttle; outdoor pool; free Wi-Fi in most units.

Sails in the Desert ★★★ This top-of-the-range hotel offers expensive, contemporary-style rooms with private balconies, many overlooking the pool, and some with Jacuzzis. You can't see the Rock from your room, but most guests are too busy sipping cocktails by the pool to care. The pool area is shaded by white shade "sails" and surrounded by sun lounges. The lobby art gallery has artists in residence. **Ilkari** is a smart brasserie with an international menu and some dishes incorporating bush-tucker ingredients. The hotel's **Red Ochre Spa** is the only day spa at Yulara. It has four therapy rooms, with two rooms offering "dry" massage therapies and two "wet" rooms with tubs on the veranda.

Yulara Dr. www.ayersrockresort.com.au/accommodation/sails-in-the-desert. ✆ **08/8957 7888.** 228 units. A$420–A$500 double; A$940 suite. **Amenities:** Restaurant, 2 bars; free airport shuttle; heated outdoor pool; room service; 2 lighted tennis courts; free Wi-Fi.

Exploring Uluru

AT SUNRISE & SUNSET The peak time to catch the Rock's beauty is sunset, when oranges, peaches, pinks, reds, and then indigo and deep violet creep across its face. Some days it's fiery; on others, the colors are muted. A sunset-viewing car park is on the Rock's western side. Plenty of sunset and sunrise tours operate from the resort, and many throw in a glass of wine to toast the end of the day as you watch. At sunrise, the colors are less dramatic,

FIELD OF light

The incredible Field of Light art installation, created by internationally acclaimed artist Bruce Munro, will run at Uluru until March 31, 2018. As darkness falls in the desert, a field of more than 50,000 stems of light, covering an area the size of seven football fields, comes to life. The exhibition, aptly named **Tili Wiru Tjuta Nyakutjaku** or "looking at lots of beautiful lights" in local Pitjantjatja language, was created in 2016 and has drawn thousands of visitors. Pathways allow visitors to walk into the field. Entry passes cost from A$39 adults and A$28 children, including transfers from all hotels. You can also take a camel ride or helicopter tour there or spend the whole evening. Field of Light is also packaged with the Sounds of Silence dinner, at A$199 adults and A$100 children, including transfers from Ayers Rock Resort. Sunrise tours cost from A$69 adults and A$35 children. Book through the Ayers Rock Resort office in Sydney (© **1300/134 044** in Australia or 02/8296 8010) or online at www.ayersrockresort.com.au.

but the bonus is seeing Uluru unveiled by the dawn to birdsong. It's an early start—most tours leave about 90 minutes before sunup. A typical sunrise tour is offered by **AAT Kings** (www.aatkings.com; © **08/8956 2171**). It includes morning tea and costs A$69 for adults, A$35 for children 5 to 15. AAT Kings offers several other tours around the area, so if large-group touring is what you want, check out its website.

WALKING, DRIVING, OR BUSING AROUND IT A paved road runs around the Rock. The easy 10.6km (6½-mile) **Base Walk** circumnavigating Uluru takes about 2 hours (the best time is early morning), but allow extra time to linger around the water holes, caves, folds, and overhangs that make up its walls. A shorter walk is the easy 1km (.6-mile) round-trip trail from the

The Base Walk around Uluru reveals water holes, caves, folds, and overhangs.

TO climb OR NOT TO CLIMB?

The Pitjantjatjara people refer to tourists as *minga*—little ants—because that's what they look like crawling up Uluru. Climbing this sacred rock is a fraught subject, one into which Australians fall into two camps: those who have climbed or want to and those who never will. I fall into the latter category. Climbing Uluru is against the wishes of the traditional owners, the Anangu ("the people," a term used by Aboriginal people from the Western Desert to refer to themselves), because of its deep spiritual significance to them. The climb follows the trail the ancestral Dreamtime Mala (rufous hare-wallaby) men took when they first came to Uluru, something you will hear about when you visit. While tourists are still allowed to climb, the traditional owners strongly prefer that they don't, and you will see signs and information to this effect.

Apart from respecting Uluru as a sacred place, there are several good practical reasons for not undertaking the 348m (1,142-ft.) hike. "The Rock" is dangerously steep and rutted with ravines about 2.5m (8¼ ft.) deep; and 36 people have died while climbing—either from heart attacks or falls—in the past 5 decades. In 2016, three men who went off the regular path to the top got stuck and it took 11 hours of work for the rescue team to get them safely down. The Anangu feel a duty to safeguard visitors to their land, and feel great sorrow and responsibility when visitors are killed or injured. The climb, by all accounts, is tough. There are sometimes strong winds, the walls are almost vertical in places (you have to hold onto a chain), and it can be freezing cold or maddeningly hot. Heat stress is a real danger. If you're unfit, have breathing difficulties, heart trouble, high or low blood pressure, or are fearful of heights, don't do it. The climb takes at least 1 hour up for the fit, and 1 hour down. The less sure-footed should allow 3 to 4 hours. The Rock is closed to climbers during bad weather; when the forecasted temperature is expected to exceed 97°F (36°C), which it often does from November to March; and when wind speed exceeds 25 knots. It is always closed overnight, and at 8am daily in December, January, and February because of the extreme heat.

The Australian government recognized the existence of the traditional Aboriginal owners in 1979 and created a national park to protect Uluru and Kata Tjuta. In 1983, the traditional owners were granted ownership of the land and the park was leased to the Australian National Parks and Wildlife Service for 99 years, with the agreement that the public could continue to climb it. The Australian government's 10-year management plan for Uluru decrees that the climb will close permanently if climber numbers drop below 20% of all visitors to Uluru. That target is close to being met, but visitors will be given 18 months' warning of closure.

Mutitjulu parking lot to the pretty water hole near the Rock's base, where there is some rock art. The **Liru Track** is another easy trail; it runs 2km (1.2 miles) from the Cultural Centre to Uluru, where it links with the Base Walk.

Before setting off, it's a good idea to pick up the self-guided walking notes available from the Cultural Centre (see "Visitor Information," p. 260).

CYCLING AROUND IT Hire a bike and cycle the flat and easy paths around the base of the Rock. **Outback Cycling** (www.outbackcycling.com;

© **0437/917 018** mobile) has a trailer based at the Cultural Centre, where you can hire a basic bike (and a helmet) for 3 hours, beginning at 7:30am, 10:30am, and 1:30pm. The cost is A$45 adults, A$30 kids aged 7 and up. Toddler seats to attach to your bike are A$20. This is a really fun and easy way to see the Rock.

FLYING OVER IT Several companies do scenic flights by light aircraft or helicopter over Uluru, Kata Tjuta (the Olgas), nearby Mount Conner, the vast white saltpan of Lake Amadeus, and as far as Kings Canyon. **Professional Helicopter Services** (www.phs.com.au; © **08/8956 2003**), for example, does a 15-minute flight over Uluru for A$150 per person, and a 30-minute flight, which includes Kata Tjuta, for A$285, among others. Helicopters don't land on top of the Rock.

MOTORCYCLING AROUND IT Harley-Davidson tours are available as sunrise or sunset rides, laps of the Rock, and various other Uluru and Kata Tjuta tours with time for walks. A blast out to the Rock at sunset with **Uluru Motorcycle Tours** (www.ulurucycles.com; © **08/8956 2019**) will set you back A$229; it includes a glass of champagne. The guide drives the bike, and you sit behind and hang on.

VIEWING IT ON CAMELBACK Legend has it that a soul travels at the same pace as a camel; it's certainly a peaceful way to see the Rock. **Uluru Camel Tours** (www.ulurucameltours.com.au; © **08/8956 3333**) makes daily forays aboard "ships of the desert" to view Uluru. Amble through red-sand dunes with great views of the Rock, dismount to watch the sun rise or sink over

A camelback tour is a peaceful way to see Uluru.

Timing Your Trip

Most tourists visit Uluru in the mornings and Kata Tjuta (the Olgas) in the afternoon. Reverse the order (do the Valley of the Winds walk in the morning and Uluru in the afternoon), and you'll likely find both spots a little more silent and spiritual.

it, and ride back to the depot for billy tea and beer bread in the morning, or champagne in the evening. The 1-hour rides depart Ayers Rock Resort 1 hour before sunrise or 1½ hours before sunset and cost A$129 per person, including transfers from your hotel. All tours leave from the Camel Depot at the Ayers Rock Resort. Shorter rides are available.

Exploring Kata Tjuta

While it would be worth coming all the way to Central Australia just to see Uluru, there is a second unique natural wonder to see, just a 50km (31-mile) drive away. Kata Tjuta, or the Olgas, consists of 36 immense ochre rock domes rising from the desert, rivaling Uluru for spectacular beauty. Some visitors find it lovelier and more mysterious than Uluru. With its tallest dome 200m (656 ft.) higher than Uluru, Kata Tjuta ("many heads") figures more prominently in Aboriginal legend than Uluru.

English explorers first came upon this part of Australia's red heart in the 1870s. Ernest Giles named part of Kata Tjuta "Mount Olga" after the reigning Queen Olga of Wurttemberg, while William Gosse gave Uluru the name "Ayers Rock" after Sir Henry Ayers, the Chief Secretary of South Australia.

Two walking trails wind among the domes: the 7.4km (4.6-mile) **Valley of the Winds ★★** walk, which is fairly challenging and takes 3 to 5 hours, and the easy 1-hour, 2.6km (1.6-mile) **Gorge** walk. The Valley of the Winds trail is the more rewarding in terms of scenery. Both have lookout points and shady stretches. The trail closes when temperatures hit 97°F (36°C).

TASMANIA & HOBART

A place of wild beauty colored by a tragic past, the Australian island of Tasmania—of which Hobart is the capital and largest city—stands separated from the rest of Australia by Bass Strait. For centuries, this island state has forged its own, not always smooth, path. While geographical isolation has preserved much of its unique wilderness, it has still had to contend with the worst efforts of man to spoil it at times.

9

Tasmanians have always been at the forefront of Australia's environmental movement, and some of Australia's fiercest battles over development have been waged in Tasmania. Among the issues Tasmania is grappling with right now are the possible extinction of Tasmanian devils due to a spreading facial-tumor disease (p. 285), reports that foxes have been introduced to this predator-free environment, and ongoing vigilance against proposals for pulp mills that may hasten destruction of forestlands. You will not, despite local legend, run into any Tasmanian tigers here (the last known one died in 1936 despite more recent "sightings").

Tasmania's history has been a violent one. Tasmania made its mark as a dumping ground for convicts from Great Britain, often transported for petty crimes. The brutal system of control, still evident in the ruins at Port Arthur and elsewhere, spilled over into persecution of the native population. The last full-blooded Tasmanian Aborigine died in 1876, 15 years after the last convict transportation.

Despite its dark history, Tasmania is a tranquil and largely unspoiled place to visit—more than 20% of it has been declared a World Heritage area, and nearly a third of the island is protected by national parks. The locals are friendly and hospitable—and they have a reputation for producing some of Australia's best food. Remnants of the Aboriginal people who lived here for thousands of years are evident in rock paintings, engravings, and storytelling, as well as a pervasive aura of spirituality that still holds in places that modern civilization has not yet reached.

Hobart (pop. 226,500), set on the Derwent River, is Tasmania's capital. Europeans settled in Hobart in 1804, a year after

Tasmania's first colony was set up at Risdon (10km/6¼ miles up the Derwent), making it Australia's second-oldest city after Sydney.

The southernmost Australian state capital, Hobart is closer to the Antarctic coast than it is to Perth in Western Australia; navigators, whalers, and explorers have long regarded it as the gateway to the south. Hobart's main features are its wonderful harbor (the city's focal point) and the colonial cottages that line the narrow lanes of Battery Point. At the waterfront, picturesque Salamanca Place bursts with galleries, pubs, cafes, and an excellent market on Saturdays.

ESSENTIALS

Arriving

BY PLANE

Qantas (www.qantas.com.au; ✆ **131 313** in Australia) and **Jetstar** (www.jetstar.com.au; ✆ **131 538** in Australia) fly from Sydney, Brisbane, and Melbourne to Hobart. **Virgin Australia** (www.virginaustralia.com.au; ✆ **136 789** in Australia) flies to Hobart from Sydney, Melbourne, Brisbane, and Adelaide. **Scoot** (www.flyscoot.com; ✆ **02/9009 0860** in Australia) flies to Hobart from Melbourne.

The trip from the airport (www.hobartairport.com.au) to the city center takes about 20 minutes and costs about A$40 by taxi. The **Redline Airporter** shuttle bus (www.tasredline.com.au; ✆ **1300/385 511** in Australia) meets all flights and delivers passengers to hotels in the city for A$19 one-way or A$35 round-trip to the city center for adults, and A$15/A$25 for kids. Book 24 hours ahead for departures; note that the booking line operates from 8am to 6pm daily.

Car- and camper-rental offices at the airport include **Avis** (✆ **03/6248 5424**), **Budget** (✆ **1300/362 848** in Australia or 03/6248 5333), **Europcar** (✆ **131 390** in Australia or 03/6248 5849), **Hertz** (✆ **1300/030 222** in Australia), and **Thrifty** (✆ **136 139** in Australia or 03/6248 5678). You might find better bargains at some of the local rental companies such as **Redspot** (✆ **03/6248 4043**).

BY FERRY

Two high-speed ships, both fully refurbished in 2015, connect Melbourne and Tasmania. ***Spirit of Tasmania* I and II** can each carry up to 1,400 passengers and up to 500 vehicles. They make the crossing from Melbourne's Station Pier to Tasmania's Devonport (on the north coast) in 9 to 11 hours. The twin ships leave both Melbourne and Devonport at 7:30pm and arrive at around 6am the next day. During busy times, a day service is added leaving both ports at 9am and arriving at 6pm. Day tickets with no seat allocation start at A$89.

Accommodation on these ships ranges from reclining seats to comfortable air-conditioned cabins with queen-size beds and en suite bathrooms, and four-berth cabins suited to families. Reclining seats cost from A$99 adults, or you can upgrade to a twin cabin from A$180 per cabin. Fares for an inside four-berth cabin start from A$132 (or A$33 if you are willing to share a single-sex cabin, backpacker style). Top of the range is a deluxe cabin with queen-size bed, from A$460.

Tasmania

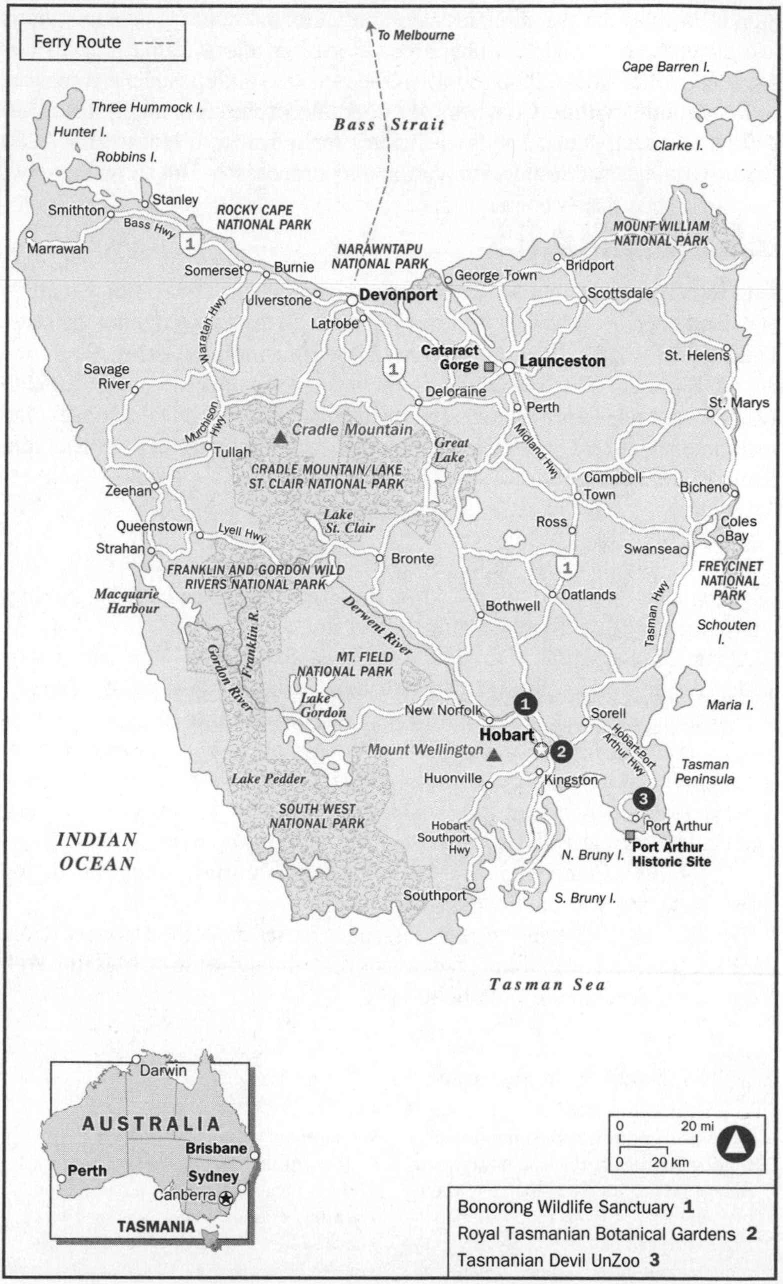
Ferry Route
To Melbourne
Bass Strait
Cape Barren I.
Clarke I.
Three Hummock I.
Hunter I.
Robbins I.
Stanley
Smithton
Marrawah
Bass Hwy
ROCKY CAPE NATIONAL PARK
NARAWNTAPU NATIONAL PARK
MOUNT WILLIAM NATIONAL PARK
Somerset
Burnie
George Town
Bridport
Scottsdale
Ulverstone
Devonport
Latrobe
Waratah Hwy
Cataract Gorge
Launceston
St. Helens
Savage River
Deloraine
Perth
St. Marys
Murchison Hwy
Cradle Mountain
Great Lake
Tullah
CRADLE MOUNTAIN/LAKE ST. CLAIR NATIONAL PARK
Midland Hwy
Campbell Town
Bicheno
Zeehan
Queenstown
Lyell Hwy
Lake St. Clair
Ross
Coles Bay
Strahan
Swansea
Bronte
FRANKLIN AND GORDON WILD RIVERS NATIONAL PARK
FREYCINET NATIONAL PARK
Macquarie Harbour
Oatlands
Derwent River
Bothwell
Tasman Hwy
Schouten I.
Franklin R.
Gordon River
MT. FIELD NATIONAL PARK
Lake Gordon
New Norfolk
Sorell
Maria I.
Hobart
Hobart-Port Arthur Hwy
Mount Wellington
Tasman Peninsula
Lake Pedder
Huonville
Kingston
SOUTH WEST NATIONAL PARK
Port Arthur
Hobart-Southport Hwy
INDIAN OCEAN
N. Bruny I.
Port Arthur Historic Site
Southport
S. Bruny I.
Tasman Sea
Darwin
AUSTRALIA
Brisbane
Perth
Sydney
Canberra
TASMANIA
0 20 mi
0 20 km
Bonorong Wildlife Sanctuary 1
Royal Tasmanian Botanical Gardens 2
Tasmanian Devil UnZoo 3

Prices vary depending on demand and availability, but specials and discounts are regularly available. Transporting a standard car costs A$89 year-round. Facilities on the ships include a la carte and buffet restaurants, bars, two cinemas, and children's play areas. For reservations, call © **132 010** in Australia or 03/6421 7209 or book online at www.spiritoftasmania.com.au.

Tasmanian Redline Coaches (www.redlinecoaches.com.au; © **1300/360 000** in Australia) connect with each ferry for transfers to Hobart, for A$60 adults. Driving a car from Devonport on the north coast to Hobart on the south coast takes less than 4 hours.

Visitor Information

Tourism Tasmania (www.discovertasmania.com.au) is the official tourism body and operates visitor centers in more than 20 towns throughout the state. The city of Hobart's **Tasmanian Travel and Information Centre,** 20 Davey St. (at Elizabeth St.), Hobart (www.hobarttravelcentre.com.au; © **03/6238 4222**), can arrange travel passes, ferry and bus tickets, car rentals, cruises, and accommodations. It is open daily 9am to 5pm and public holidays 9am to 2pm (closed Christmas Day).

City Layout

Hobart straddles the Derwent River on the south coast of Tasmania. The open ocean is about 50km (31 miles) down the river, though the Derwent empties into Storm Bay just 20km (12 miles) downstream.

Along the waterfront, the popular areas of Salamanca Place and nearby Battery Point overlook **Sullivan's Cove,** home to hundreds of yachts. The row of sandstone warehouses that dominates **Salamanca Place** dates to the city's heyday as a whaling base in the 1830s. Behind Princes Wharf, **Battery Point** is the city's historic district, which in colonial times was the home of sailors, fishermen, whalers, coopers, merchants, shipwrights, and master mariners. The **central business district** is on the west side of the water, with the main thoroughfares—Campbell, Argyle, Elizabeth, Murray, and Harrington streets—sloping down to the busy harbor.

The Tasman Bridge and regular passenger ferries cross the Derwent River. Set back from and overlooking the city is 1,270m-tall (4,166-ft.) **Mount Wellington,** a popular day-trip destination.

Tasmania's Tricky Roads

Driving in Tasmania can be dangerous; there are more accidents involving tourists on Tasmania's roads than anywhere else in Australia. Many roads are narrow and bends can be tight, especially in the mountainous inland regions, where you may also come across black ice early in the morning or any time in winter.

Marsupials are common around dusk, and swerving to avoid them has caused countless crashes. In fact, you may be shocked by the amount of roadkill you will see here.

Hobart, viewed from the top of Mount Wellington.

Getting Around

Central Hobart is very small, and most of the attractions are in easy walking distance. **Metro Tasmania** (www.metrotas.com.au; ✆ **132 201** in Australia) operates public buses throughout the city and suburbs. The buses operate on an electronic Green Card system, or you can just buy a ticket on board. Single tickets cost from A$3.30, and the most you'll pay is A$6.90.

WHERE TO STAY

Expensive

The Henry Jones Art Hotel ★★★ One of Australia's most unique and interesting hotels, the Henry Jones takes its name from one of Hobart's most successful pioneering entrepreneurs. Henry Jones's name, and that of his IXL brand of jam, is still on the factory building that became Australia's first dedicated art hotel. The walls of this luxurious hotel are hung with more than 400 works, in changing exhibitions, often by young, emerging Tasmanian artists, many from the Tasmanian School of Arts (next door). Guest rooms are works of art in themselves, reflecting Australia's early trade with China and India in an eclectic mix of modern and historic. Sandstone walls abut ultra-modern glass and stainless steel bathrooms. (All but standard rooms have double spa tubs.) Every room has a view, either of the harbor or the hotel's magnificent glass atrium. I've stayed here several times, and so far my favorite is the spacious Art Installation Suite, which has a small balcony.

22 Hunter St., Hobart. www.thehenryjones.com. ✆ **03/6210 7700.** 56 units. A$280–A$450 double; A$560–A$950 suite. Free parking. **Amenities:** Restaurant; bar; room service; free Wi-Fi.

The Islington ★★★ This luxury boutique hotel, just 10 minutes' walk from the city center, may make you feel as if you are staying in someone's home. Someone wealthy. The Islington is lavishly but tastefully decorated with fine artworks and antiques, its contemporary extension (with soaring glass walls and ceilings, and views of Mount Wellington) blending beautifully with the original 1847 Regency-style building (one of the first in Hobart's "dress circle" area). At the end of a busy day's sightseeing there's nothing better than a long soak in the generous bathtub, and sinking into an "Islington Angel," a king-size bed custom-made in Tasmania, for a fabulous night's sleep. No kids 14 and under.

321 Davey St., Hobart. www.islingtonhotel.com. ✆ **03/6220 2123.** 11 units. A$475–A$625 double. Rates include breakfast. **Amenities:** Restaurant; bar; free Wi-Fi.

The MONA Pavilions ★★★ Eight state-of-the-art pavilions (all equipped with wireless touch panels to control temperature, audiovisual components, lighting, blinds, and more) are named for either noted architects or Australian modernist painters (these pavilions are decorated with the artists' works). All sit high above the banks of the Derwent Estuary, with large balconies overlooking the water. Antiquities and artworks from owner David Walsh's private collection are included in the decor of each pavilion. Each of the one- or two-bedroom pavilions also has a private cellar stocked with Moorilla wines and Moo Brew beer from the estate. Guests can arrive by private boat or on the fast catamaran from Hobart. MONA is about a 15 minutes' drive from the city center, but the river is an even more appealing way to get there. See also Museum of Old and New Art (p. 282).

655 Main Rd., Berriedale. www.mona.net.au/stay/mona-pavilions. ✆ **03/6277 9900.** 8 units. A$700–A$1,100 double. Rates include breakfast. **Amenities:** Restaurant; bar; gym; heated indoor pool; room service; sauna; free Wi-Fi.

Zero Davey ★ With a great waterfront location, and fresh, contemporary studios and apartments, Zero Davey is a good choice for those who want a bit of space. The three-bedroom Zero Penthouse, with its pink, orange, and red decor, will fulfill those rock-star fantasies; the Davey Penthouse has harbor views, and some studios have balconies and Jacuzzis. All are very functional as well as being bright, fun, and a little bit funky.

15 Hunter St., Hobart. www.zerodavey.com.au. ✆ **1300/733 422** in Australia or 03/6270 1444. 31 units. A$280–A$340 studio double; A$450–A$600 apt. **Amenities:** Restaurant; exercise room; sauna; free Wi-Fi.

Hobart

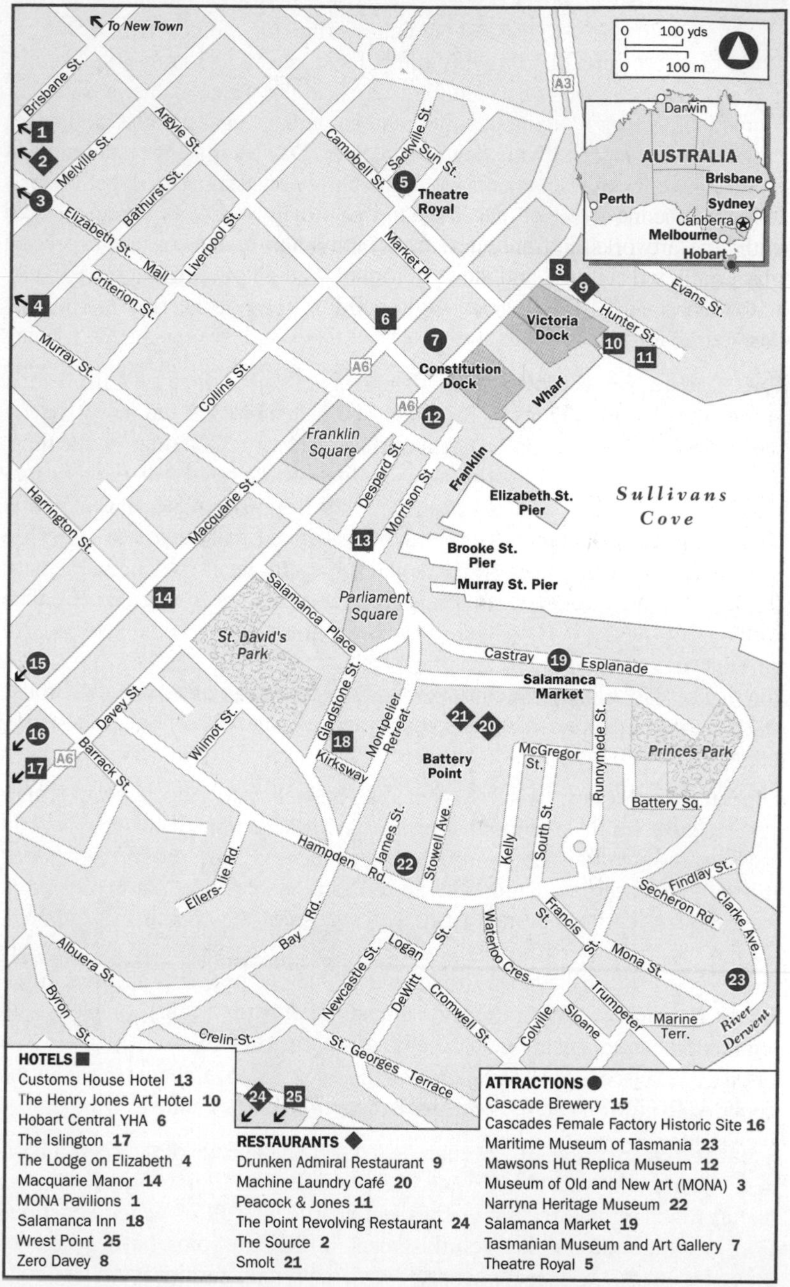
To New Town
0 100 yds
0 100 m
AUSTRALIA
Darwin
Perth
Brisbane
Sydney
Canberra
Melbourne
Hobart
Brisbane St.
Melville St.
Argyle St.
Bathurst St.
Elizabeth St. Mall
Liverpool St.
Criterion St.
Campbell St.
Sackville St.
Sun St.
Theatre Royal
Market Pl.
Murray St.
Collins St.
Victoria Dock
Constitution Dock
Evans St.
Hunter St.
Wharf
Franklin Square
Despard St.
Morrison St.
Franklin
Elizabeth St. Pier
Sullivans Cove
Harrington St.
Macquarie St.
Brooke St. Pier
Murray St. Pier
Salamanca Place
Parliament Square
St. David's Park
Castray Esplanade
Salamanca Market
Davey St.
Wilmot St.
Gladstone St.
Montpelier Retreat
Kirksway
Battery Point
McGregor St.
Runnymede St.
Princes Park
Battery Sq.
Barrack St.
Hampden Rd.
James St.
Stowell Ave.
Kelly
South St.
Ellers- lie Rd.
Bay Rd.
Francis St.
Secheron Rd.
Findlay St.
Clarke Ave.
Albuera St.
Logan
Newcastle St.
Waterloo Cres.
Mona St.
Byron St.
DeWitt
Cromwell St.
Colville
Sloane
Trumpeter
Marine Terr.
River Derwent
Crelin St.
St. Georges Terrace
A3
A6
HOTELS
Customs House Hotel 13
The Henry Jones Art Hotel 10
Hobart Central YHA 6
The Islington 17
The Lodge on Elizabeth 4
Macquarie Manor 14
MONA Pavilions 1
Salamanca Inn 18
Wrest Point 25
Zero Davey 8
RESTAURANTS
Drunken Admiral Restaurant 9
Machine Laundry Café 20
Peacock & Jones 11
The Point Revolving Restaurant 24
The Source 2
Smolt 21
ATTRACTIONS
Cascade Brewery 15
Cascades Female Factory Historic Site 16
Maritime Museum of Tasmania 23
Mawsons Hut Replica Museum 12
Museum of Old and New Art (MONA) 3
Narryna Heritage Museum 22
Salamanca Market 19
Tasmanian Museum and Art Gallery 7
Theatre Royal 5

Moderate

Customs House Hotel ★★ You won't find a better value than the rooms above this historic sandstone pub overlooking the waterfront. Built in 1846, the Heritage-listed property offers large, clean, and comfortable colonial-style rooms, seven of which look across at the water. Some of the other rooms look across Parliament House and its gardens, and the rest are toward the back of the hotel with no views to speak of. Downstairs, the restaurant and public bar overlook the water. Live music plays downstairs (Wed–Sat nights). During the summer period, when the Sydney-to-Hobart Yacht Race comes to town, it can get noisy but is central to all the action.

1 Murray St., Hobart. www.customshousehotel.com. ✆ **03/6234 6645.** 22 units. A$110–A$240 double; A$280 family room (sleeps 5). Rates include breakfast. **Amenities:** Restaurant; bar; free Wi-Fi.

The Lodge on Elizabeth ★ The convict-built Lodge on Elizabeth is among the oldest buildings in Tasmania, completed in 1829 and now listed by the National Trust. Originally a gentleman's residence (including, at one time, a Tasmanian premier), it later became the first private boys' school in Tasmania. It's well situated, just a 12-minute walk from Salamanca Place, and is surrounded by restaurants. All rooms are decorated with antiques; many are quite romantic, with four-poster beds and some with Jacuzzis. Complimentary drinks are served in the communal living room in the evening. The Convict Cottage is a cute, self-contained spa cottage, just for two, on the grounds. No children 13 and under.

249 Elizabeth St., Hobart. www.thelodge.com.au. ✆ **03/6231 3830.** 13 units. A$185–A$210 double; A$270 convict cottage (2-night minimum). Rates include breakfast. **Amenities:** Bar; free Wi-Fi.

Macquarie Manor ★★ As soon as you walk into this classic colonial-style manor, you'll know you want to stay. Macquarie Manor was built in 1875 as a surgeon's operating office and residence. Extra rooms were added in 1950. Thick carpets and double-glazed windows keep the place very quiet, even though it's on the main road, 2 blocks from the central bus terminal. Rooms, which vary enormously and include single rooms, are comfortable and elegantly furnished. One room is suitable for people with disabilities. Check out the delightful dining room and the drawing room, complete with old couches and a grand piano. Smoking is not permitted.

172 Macquarie St., Hobart. www.macmanor.com.au. ✆ **03/6224 4999.** 16 units. A$190 single; A$320–A$420 double; A$350–A$380 suite. **Amenities:** Free Wi-Fi.

Salamanca Inn ★★ Conveniently located on the edge of the central business district and toward the waterfront near Battery Point, Salamanca Inn features modern and pleasant suites and apartments, all of which benefitted from a multimillion-dollar refurbishment in 2015. Rooms have queen- or king-size beds, leather couches, Tasmanian oak furniture, galley-style kitchens, and spacious living areas. The pricier suites are a bit plusher. There's also a heated indoor pool on the rooftop.

10 Gladstone St., Hobart. www.salamancainn.com.au. ✆ **1800/030 944** in Australia or 03/6223 3300. 60 units. A$172–A$335 double; A$266–A$480 2-bedroom apt; A$285–A$390 family apts. Bus: no. 54B. **Amenities:** Restaurant; bar; babysitting; Jacuzzi; indoor pool; room service; free Wi-Fi.

Wrest Point ★ This Hobart landmark, built in 1973, launched Australia's annual A$2-billion casino industry. Beside the Derwent River, 3km (almost 2 miles) from the city center, the casino-hotel complex looks out across the harbor and the city and up to nearby Mount Wellington. All rooms feature Tasmanian oak furniture and plush carpets, and more expensive units have exceptional views. While it may be a little out of the city center (though it's certainly a walkable distance from downtown), the views make it a worthwhile choice. The hotel's signature restaurant, the **Point Revolving Restaurant,** is another city icon. It's open for dinner from 6:30pm Tuesday to Saturday, and on Fridays for lunch from noon and for high tea from 2:30 to 4:30pm.

410 Sandy Bay Rd., Sandy Bay. www.wrestpoint.com.au. ✆ **1800/420 155** in Australia or 03/6225 7016. 197 units. A$129–A$249 double; A$279–A$399 suite. Bus: nos. 54 or 55 from Franklin Square, Macquarie St., to stop 15. **Amenities:** 5 restaurants; 4 bars; babysitting; concierge; 9-hole putting course; health club; indoor pool; room service; tennis court; free Wi-Fi.

Inexpensive

Hobart Central YHA ★ With a great location just 2 blocks from the waterfront and close to both the city center and Salamanca precinct, this is a great value-for-money location. Rooms are clean, comfortable, and basic. Double rooms (some with en suite bathrooms) and family rooms are available, along with dorms, and there is a small, plainly furnished lounge area, as well as a laundry and small kitchen.

9 Argyle St., Hobart. www.yha.org.au. ✆ **03/6231 2660.** 22 units. A$87–A$99 double; A$28–A$32 dorms; A$128–A$145 family room (sleeps 4). **Amenities:** Bar; free Wi-Fi.

WHERE TO EAT

Tasmania is known for its fresh seafood, including oysters, crab, crayfish, salmon, and trout. Although the seafood here was once cheap, in recent years prices have crept up to match or even surpass those on the mainland. Generally, the food in Tasmania is of very good quality.

Expensive

The Source ★★★ TASMANIAN/AUSTRALIAN As you climb the stairs to this amazing restaurant, your eyes will be drawn to the painting from which it takes its name: *The Source,* by Australian artist John Olsen, is a stunning 6m (20-ft.) work set into the ceiling directly above the central staircase. It will take your breath away. So too will the entire experience of dining here, which promises delivery "with a MONA twist" (the restaurant is part of the

Museum of Old and New Art; see p. 282). The menu changes daily, but you can be assured that seasonal and local produce (with an eye toward "food miles") is important here. Choose from share plates (oysters, rabbit terrine, seared scallops, baked figs) or the a la carte menu which might include dishes such as seared wallaby with smoked eggplant, orange, and carrot puree and chermoula with pine nuts, or an eye filet with roasted beets, black quinoa, lentils, and red wine vinaigrette. Huge windows afford stunning views of the Derwent River.

Moorilla Estate, 655 Main Rd., Berriedale. www.mona.net.au/eat-drink. ✆ **03/6277 9904.** Main courses A$22–A$38. Wed–Mon 7:30–10am and noon–3pm; Fri–Sat 6pm–late. Free parking.

Moderate

Drunken Admiral Restaurant ★ SEAFOOD The Drunken Admiral, on the waterfront, is an extremely popular spot with tourists and can get raucous on busy evenings. The main attraction to start the meal is the famous seafood chowder, swimming with anything that was on sale at the docks that morning. The seafood platter for two (A$67 per person; minimum 2) is a huge plate of squid, oysters, fish, mussels, and prawns, but there are plenty of simpler dishes on the menu, too. Try the crunchy fried prawns or the steamed mussels in a tomato, garlic, and white wine sauce.

17–19 Hunter St., Hobart. www.drunkenadmiral.com.au. ✆ **03/6234 1903.** Main courses A$16–A$45. Daily 6–10:30pm.

Peacock & Jones ★★ CONTEMPORARY A fireplace in the atrium of the Henry Jones factory building might lure you in to this smart and buzzing addition to the Hobart dining scene, but it's the cozy atmosphere and fine food inside that will keep you here. The open kitchen produces unique combinations, with a focus on local produce. The snack menu—charcuterie, beef tartare, and other tapas-style dishes—is available from 4 to 6pm. Heartier fare such as steaks, twice-cooked pork neck, or duck breast are on the dinner menu, starting at 6pm.

33 Hunter St., Hobart. www.peacockandjones.com.au. ✆ **1800/375 692.** Snacks A$12–A$25; main courses A$35–A$38. Mon–Sat 4–10pm. Closed Sun and public holidays.

Peppermint Bay ★★ CONTEMPORARY You'd be hard pressed to find a lovelier setting for lunch. A 150-year-old oak tree dominates the gardens, and the relaxed Terrace Bar has water's-edge views of Bruny Island and the D'Entrecasteaux Channel. The menu includes Tasmanian oysters and smoked trout, locally grazed beef, and more. There are some interesting vegetarian dishes too, such as buckwheat and broccoli salad or roasted mushroom risotto. For something special, try the slow-cooked lamb shoulder (A$69 for two). Hobart Cruises (✆ **1300/137 919** in Australia) runs 90-minute scenic cruises, priced from A$118 adults and A$88 children, which include a three-course lunch at Peppermint Bay.

Channel Hwy., Woodbridge (35km/22 miles from Hobart). www.peppermintbay.com.au. ✆ **03/6267 4088.** Main courses A$12–A$34. Daily noon–3pm; Thurs–Sat 5:30–8:30pm.

Hello, Sailor!

The annual **Sydney Hobart Yacht Race,** which launches from Sydney Harbour on December 26, fills Hobart's Constitution Dock Marina and harbor area close to overflowing with spectators and party-goers when the yachts finally turn up in Tasmania. This world-class sailing event takes anywhere from 2 to 4 days, making it very handy for sailors and fans to stay on in Hobart to celebrate New Year's Eve.

Conveniently, food and wine lovers can also indulge themselves after the race at the **Hobart Summer Festival,** which starts on December 28.

Smolt ★★ CONTEMPORARY This chic and stylish place is a great spot for people watching, with windows opening onto busy Salamanca Square. Great for breakfast, a midday caffeine hit, lunch, or dinner, Smolt offers modern cuisine with Italian (pizza, risotto) and Spanish (tapas) influences. The food is simple but still imaginative, not to mention delicious and presented with flair. There's also a good wine list featuring selections from around Australia (heavily weighted toward local Tassie wines) and some from New Zealand, Spain, and Italy.

2 Salamanca Square, Hobart. www.smolt.com.au. ✆ **03/6224 2554.** Main courses A$23–A$39. Mon–Fri 11:30am–10pm; Sat–Sun 8am–10pm.

Inexpensive

Machine Laundry Cafe ★★ CAFE Here's a colorful and cute retro-style cafe that's popular with all demographics. There are bright tables and chairs outside on Salamanca Square if you prefer, or a cozy interior that is separated by the line of washing machines in the laundromat by a large window. Yes, wash your clothes while you eat! Great for breakfast or brunch, with offerings such as scrambled eggs in roti, eggs Benedict, or ricotta hotcakes.

12 Salamanca Square, Hobart. ✆ **03/6224 9922.** Main courses A$15–A$20. Mon–Sat 7:30am–5pm; Sun 8:30am–5pm.

EXPLORING HOBART

Simply strolling around the harbor and popping into the shops at Salamanca Place can keep you nicely occupied, but don't miss the lovely colonial stone cottages of Battery Point. This area got its name from a battery of guns set up on the promontory in 1818 to defend the town against potential invaders (particularly the French). Today, there are tearooms, antiques shops, restaurants, and atmospheric pubs interspersed between grand dwellings.

For magnificent views over Hobart and across a fair-size chunk of Tasmania, drive to the **Pinnacle** on top of Mount Wellington, about a 40-minute drive from the city center. Take a warm coat; the wind in this alpine area can really bite. An extensive network of walking trails offers good hiking. You can order a copy of the *Wellington Park Recreation Map and Notes,* as well as other day-walk maps, for A$12 online from **Tasmap** (www.tasmap.tas.gov.au). The website also has other free maps for download, including street maps of Hobart and Launceston.

Bonorong Wildlife Sanctuary ★★★ Tasmanian devils and wallabies are the main attractions at Bonorong (it means "native companion"). Most of the animals have been rescued after injury, and owner Greg Irons is passionate about saving and conserving indigenous creatures. You'll also find snakes, koalas, echidnas, kangaroos, and wombats here. Everyone gets a free bag of kangaroo food on entry. Koala cuddling isn't allowed in Tasmania, but you may get to stroke one. Tour times are 11:30am, 2pm, and 3:30pm daily, with a special Tasmanian devil tour at 10am. Night tours (A$157 adults, A$83 children 3–15) allow you to see the animals when they are most active, and are highly recommended. Feeding Frenzy tours (A$157 adults, A$83 children) and 10-minute Animal Encounters (with sugar gliders, wombats, tawny frogmouth owls, or brushtail possums; A$15 per person) are also on offer.

593 Briggs Rd., Brighton. www.bonorong.com.au. ✆ **03/6268 1184.** A$28 adults, A$14 children 3–15, A$77 families of 4. Daily 9am–5pm. Drive north on Rte. 1 to Brighton; it's about 25 min. north of Hobart and is well signposted.

Cascade Brewery ★ Cascade Premium is one of Australia's most popular beers. To see how this heady amber nectar is produced, head to Australia's oldest brewery and tag along on a 90-minute tour, which includes a stroll through the grand old Woodstock Gardens behind the factory. Three days a week (Mon, Fri, and Sat) there is also a historical play (no tastings served) performed based on the founders of the brewery. Wear flat shoes and long trousers.

140 Cascade Rd., South Hobart. www.cascadebreweryco.com.au. ✆ **03/6224 1117.** Tours (which include tastings for participants aged 18 and over) A$30 adults, A$15 students and seniors. No children 15 and under. Tours daily at 11am, 12:30pm, and 2:15pm. Closed Christmas Day and Good Friday. Reservations required. Bus: nos. 44, 46, or 49 (stop 18).

Cascades Female Factory Historic Site ★ Unless you are really into convict history, you may wish to save yourself for Port Arthur. All that is left here are the stone walls of this prison and a memorial garden, but recent improvements to the interpretation of the site—including the stories of 57 women incarcerated here—help tell its important history. The "factory" prison, where women worked at spinning, washing, and sewing, operated from 1828 to 1856, housing up to 1,200 women and children. After it ceased operation as a female factory, the institution continued as a jail until 1877. Taking a guided tour ensures you get the most from your visit. Another option besides a tour is "Her Story," a 45-minute dramatized tour by two actors, performed daily at noon. It costs A$20 adults, A$13 children, or A$60 families.

16 Degraves St., South Hobart. www.femalefactory.org.au. ✆ **03/6233 6656.** A$5 adults and children 7–17, A$15 families of eight. Tours A$15 adults, A$10 children, A$40 families. Daily 9:30am–4pm. Tours daily 10 and 11am, 1, 2, and 3pm. Closed Christmas Day. Bus: nos. 44, 46, 47, or 49 from Franklin Square in the city to South Hobart (stop 13).

Maritime Museum of Tasmania ★★★ Renowned as one of the best of its type in Australia, this museum explores the influence of the sea on the lives of Tasmanians and the island's strong maritime heritage. It has displays about Aboriginal watercraft, early European explorers and whalers, and how ships helped develop Tasmania's industries. Collections include ship models, artifacts, paintings, boat builder's tools, historic dinghies, and navigation instruments. There's also a section on shipwrecks. Free 1-hour talks are held on the first Tuesday of each month (except Jan) at noon.

16 Argyle St. (at Davey St.), Hobart. www.maritimetas.org. ✆ **03/6234 1427.** A$10 adults, A$5 children 13–18, free for children 12 and under, A$20 for families. Daily 9am–5pm. Closed Good Friday and Christmas Day.

Mawson's Hut Replica Museum ★★ Designed to raise funds for the conservation and maintenance of the originals, these wooden huts on the Hobart waterfront, just opposite Mawson Place, are exact replicas of the shelter afforded to the explorer Douglas Mawson and his expedition team in 1912 to 1914. One of Hobart's newest attractions, they are also fast becoming one of the city's most popular. Inside, there are tributes to the men and 50 huskie dogs that traveled with them to the frozen south.

Corner Argyle and Morrison sts. www.mawsons-huts-replica.org.au. ✆ **03/6231 1518** or 1300/551 422. A$12 adults, A$4 kids 15 and under, A$28 family. Daily 9am–6pm (Oct–Apr), 10am–5pm (May–Sept). Closed Good Friday, Anzac Day (Apr 25), and Christmas Day.

The Maritime Museum explores the island's strong maritime heritage.

Museum of Old and New Art (MONA) ★★★ Australia's largest privately owned art gallery promises to "shock and offend." Owner David Walsh wants his art museum to be daring and provocative—and so it is. But more often, it delights and amazes. This museum of old and new art challenges, informs, and entertains, with a collection that ranges from antiquities from Egypt, Greece, Italy, Africa, and Mesoamerica to contemporary art, including Australian modernism and contemporary Australian, British, European, and American art. For the sensitive (or those bringing children with them), there's a map that shows how to avoid works that are sexually explicit or "potentially confronting." The museum is part of Walsh's Moorilla Estate, which is also home to a winery, a microbrewery, a restaurant (**The Source ★★★**; see p. 277), and stunning accommodations (**The MONA Pavilions ★★★**; see p. 274). It's almost worth going to Tasmania just for this.

655 Main Rd., Berriedale. www.mona.net.au. ✆ **03/6277 9900.** A$28, kids 17 and under free. Wed–Mon 10am–5pm; daily (same hours) in Jan. Closed Christmas Day. Bus: nos. 510, 520, 521, 522, or X20.

Narryna Heritage Museum ★ One of the houses worth looking into at Battery Point is Narryna, which depicts the life of upper-class pioneers. Built by Captain Andrew Haig in 1837 to 1840, it was later the home of several Hobart businessmen and women, lawyers, politicians, and bankers.

103 Hampden Rd. www.tmag.tas.gov.au/visitor_information/house_museums/narryna_heritage_museum. ✆ **03/6234 2791.** A$10 adults, A$8 students, A$4 children 5 and under. Tues–Sat 10am–4:30pm; Sun noon–4:30pm. Closed 12:30–1pm Mon–Fri, and all day Good Friday, Hobart Show Day (late Oct), Christmas Day, Boxing Day (Dec 26), New Year's Day. Open 12:30–5pm on Anzac Day (Apr 25).

Royal Tasmanian Botanical Gardens ★ Established in 1818, these gardens are known for English-style plant and tree layouts—including a great conifer collection—a superb Japanese garden, and seasonal blooming plants. A restaurant serves lunch and teas. To walk here from the city center, partly along a pleasant country lane known as Soldier's Walk, takes around 40 minutes, or you can use the cycle track or arrive by ferry. There are maps of the gardens at each entrance, or visitor guides and self-guided tour brochures are available at the Visitor Centre, which is near the entrance on Lower Domain Road.

Queens Domain, near Government House. www.rtbg.tas.gov.au. ✆ **03/6236 3075.** Free. Oct–Mar daily 8am–6:30pm; May–Aug daily 8am–5pm; Apr and Sept daily 8am–5:30pm. Bus: no. 17 from the GPO.

Salamanca Market ★★ If you are in Hobart on a Saturday, don't miss this market—it's one of the best markets in Australia. Some 300 stalls offer everything from fruit and vegetables to crafts made from pottery, glass, and native woods. Salamanca Place has plenty of crafts shops that are worth exploring, though the prices sometimes reflect the fashionable area.

Salamanca Place, Hobart. www.salamanca.com.au. Sat 8:30am–3pm.

Hobart's famed Salamanca Market offers everything from produce to crafts.

Tasmanian Museum and Art Gallery ★ Come here to find out more about Tasmania's Aboriginal heritage, its history since settlement, and the island's wildlife. This wonderful museum has undergone a major redevelopment—with more to come—to open up new areas and transform it, while still telling Tasmania's story. Traveling exhibitions are mounted from time to time, but always on display are colonial-era paintings, including an impressive collection of works by Tom Roberts and several convict artists. The pride of the collection is the historically significant *The Conciliation,* by Benjamin Duterreau. You can also find out about the fate of the Tasmanian tiger and see archival film of this lost treasure. Free 40-minute guided tours are run Wednesday to Sunday at 11am, 1 and 2pm. One-hour theatrical tours called "Settlement Secrets" run through the museum buildings at 11:30am and 2pm and cost A$20 adults, A$15 children 15 and under, or A$60 families of six (visit www.antipodeanentertainment.com.au for details).

Dunn Place (via Macquarie and Davey sts.). www.tmag.tas.gov.au. ✆ **03/6165 7000.** Free. Tues–Sun 10am–4pm. Closed Good Friday, Christmas Day, and Anzac Day (Apr 25).

Theatre Royal ★ Built in 1837, this 747-seat venue is the oldest live theater in Australia. It's known for its excellent acoustics and its classical Victorian decor, and is Hobart's major stage venue. Learn about the theater's fascinating history on a 1-hour tour by Friends of the Theatre Royal. Tours are lead Monday, Wednesday, and Friday at 11am (A$15 adults, A$10 kids). Otherwise, check out what's on and have a night out in this grand old theater. 29 Campbell St. www.theatreroyal.com.au. ✆ **1800/650 277** in Australia or 03/6233 2299.

ORGANIZED TOURS

Cruises

Pennicott Wilderness Journeys (www.pennicottjourneys.com.au; ✆ **03/6234 4270**) offers a range of tours including a full-day jaunt from Hobart to Bruny Island, leaving Franklin Wharf at 8am and returning around 5:30pm daily. A bus and ferry take you to Bruny Island, where (after morning tea) you take a 3-hour boat trip along the coastline to a seal colony and a memorable (but sometimes wet; warm shower-proof coats are provided) foray onto the wild Southern Ocean. On returning, lunch includes a much-needed hot soup to warm you up, before you get back on the bus for the trip back to Hobart. It's a pleasant day out, although considering the hours spent, serious wildlife fans might be disappointed. The trip costs A$225 adults, A$165 children ages 3 to 16.

Navigators, Brooke Street Pier, Sullivans Cove (www.navigators.net.au; ✆ **03/6223 1914**), offers cruises to Port Arthur (see below) on Sundays and Fridays. The cruise leaves at 8:15am and costs A$189 adults, A$149 children 5 to 18, or A$588 for a family of four. The boat cruises down the harbor giving a good chance to see the coastline and cliffs at Cape Raoul, and returns by coach. It includes morning tea, lunch, entry to the Port Arthur Historic Site, and a walking tour of the site. A premium package, for A$229 adults and A$189 children 5 to 18, also includes a guided tour of Port Arthur's Isle of the Dead, which is well worth doing.

Bus Tours

Grayline (www.grayline.com.au; ✆ **1300/858 687** in Australia) offers a range of sightseeing tours of Hobart and Mount Wellington by coach. A 3-hour tour costs A$49 for adults, half price for kids. Grayline also runs tours to other Tasmanian destinations including Russell Falls, Bruny Island, Port Arthur, Cradle Mountain, Launceston, and the Bay of Fires.

Walking Tours

Hobart Historic Tours (www.hobarthistorictours.com.au; ✆ **03/6234 5550**) runs fascinating 90-minute walking tours of Hobart. The Historic Walk departs from outside the **Hobart Travel Centre** (p. 272) at 2pm Wednesday to Sunday. The Old Hobart Pub Tour (not recommended for children), departing at 5pm runs on Thursdays, Fridays, and Saturdays, takes you to two waterfront pubs and will enthrall you with stories of alcohol-fueled shenanigans. Tours cost A$30 per person. A 3-hour Grand Hobart Walk costs A$45 per person and runs Wednesday to Sunday at 2pm.

TASMANIAN DEVIL disaster

Tasmania's unique carnivorous mammal, the handsomely sleek Tasmanian devil, is much more interesting than his namesake, the manic character from Bugs Bunny cartoons. Whereas dingoes wiped out the devil's cousin on the Australian mainland, dingoes never crossed Bass Strait, and so Tasmania's devils flourished, becoming one of the island's iconic mascots. But now, the Tasmanian devil population is in desperate trouble.

Since 1996, the animals have been afflicted by a deadly cancer known as Devil Facial Tumour Disease (DFTD). This malady has decimated the wild population—in some areas by an estimated 90%—and the disease is spreading rapidly. It's believed that around half of the state's approximately 150,000 Tasmanian devils have already died, and some scientists fear that it may soon wipe out the wild population entirely. Healthy specimens are being captured and relocated in an urgent campaign to try to preserve the species from extinction.

There are several places where you can see captive Tasmanian devils and learn more about this one-of-a-kind animal. About 88km (55 miles) from Hobart, on the Port Arthur Highway, Taranna, is the **Tasmanian Devil UnZoo** (www.tasmaniandevilunzoo.com.au; ✆ **1800/641 641** in Australia or 03/6250 3230), which is currently working to breed devils with genes that could make them resistant to the disease. The park is open daily from 9am to 5pm. Devil feeding is at 10 and 11am, 12:15, 1:30, 3, and 5pm (4:30pm May–Sept) daily. Entry is A$35 adults, A$20 children 4 to 16, and A$85 for a family of six.

Another great place to see devils near Hobart is **Bonorong Wildlife Sanctuary** (p. 280).

For more information on devil conservation efforts, visit www.tassiedevil.com.au.

Cute yet fierce, Tasmanian devils are an endangered species found only on the island.

A DAY TRIP TO PORT ARTHUR ★★★

Port Arthur, on the Tasman Peninsula, is an incredibly picturesque yet haunting place. Set on one of Australia's prettiest harbors, it shelters the remains of Tasmania's largest penal colony. It's the state's number-one tourist destination, and you really should plan to spend at least a day here.

From 1830 to 1877, Port Arthur was one of the harshest institutions of its type anywhere in the world. It was built to house the most notorious prisoners transported from Great Britain, many of whom had escaped from lesser institutions elsewhere in Australia. Nearly 13,000 convicts found their way here, and nearly 2,000 died while incarcerated.

A strip of land called Eaglehawk Neck connects Port Arthur to the rest of Tasmania. Guards and dogs kept watch over this narrow path, while the authorities perpetuated rumors that the waters around the peninsula were shark-infested. Only a few convicts ever managed to escape, and most of them either eventually perished in the bush or were tracked down and hanged. As you pass through Eaglehawk Neck, look out for the blowhole and other weird coastal formations, including Tasman's Arch, Devil's Kitchen, and the Tesselated Pavement.

The **Port Arthur Historic Site ★★** (www.portarthur.org.au; ✆ **1800/659 101** in Australia or 03/6251 2310) is large and scattered, with around 30 19th-century buildings. You can tour the remains of the church, the guard tower, a prison, and several other buildings. Don't miss the fascinating museum in the old lunatic asylum, which has a scale model of the prison complex, as well as leg irons and chains.

Port Arthur's tragic history did not finish at the end of the convict era. In 1996, the Port Arthur Historic Site became the scene of one of Australia's worst mass murders, when a lone gunman killed 35 people and injured dozens more, including tourists and staff. The devastating events of that day led to new gun-control laws for Australia that are among the strictest in the world. The gunman was sentenced to life imprisonment with no eligibility for parole. Many of the staff at Port Arthur lost friends, colleagues, and family members, and they still find it difficult and painful to talk about that tragic day. Visitors are requested not to question their guide about these events, but to instead read the plaque at the Memorial Garden.

The site is open daily from 8:30am to dusk; admission is A$39 for adults, A$17 for children 4 to 17, and A$99 for families of two adults and up to six children. The admission price includes a guided walking tour and a boat cruise around the harbor, which leaves eight times daily in summer.

Passes that combine different experiences and tours are also available. You can get off the harbor cruise for a 45-minute guided walk on the **Isle of the Dead,** where 1,769 convicts and 180 free settlers were buried, mostly in mass graves with no headstones, or at Point Puer, which was once home to 800 boys shipped to Tasmania for a "better life" or for petty crimes. The tour costs an extra A$20 for adults, A$10 for kids, and A$45 for families. Lantern-lit **Ghost Tours** of Port Arthur leave nightly at 6 and 8pm and cost A$27 for adults, A$15 for kids, or A$75 for a family. Reservations are essential. Tours last about 90 minutes. There are various other passes and tours available; check the website.

The main feature of the visitor center is an interesting **Interpretive Gallery,** which takes visitors through the process of sentencing in England to transportation to Van Diemen's Land (Tasmania's original name). The gallery contains a courtroom, a section of a transport ship's hull, a blacksmith's shop, a lunatic asylum, and more.

A DAY TRIP TO MOUNT FIELD NATIONAL PARK ★★

Mount Field National Park, about 80km (50 miles) northwest of Hobart, is one of the prettiest landscapes in Tasmania. It was proclaimed a national park in 1916 to protect a plateau dominated by dolerite-capped mountains (**Mount Field West** is the highest point at 1,417m/4,647 ft.) and dramatic glaciated valleys (some of the lakes and tarns were formed as much as 30,000 years ago). Since 2013, it has been included as part of the Tasmanian Wilderness World Heritage Area.

The most mountainous regions support alpine moorlands of cushion plants, pineapple and sword grass, waratahs, and giant pandani. You can get a look at these various ecosystems on a 16km (10-mile) drive from the park entrance to Lake Dobson. Note that this drive is along an unpaved and often badly rutted road, which is not suitable for conventional vehicles in winter or after heavy rains. As you follow the drive, you'll notice that wallabies, wombats, bandicoots, Tasmanian devils, and quolls are prolific, as is the birdlife: You may

A DAY TRIP TO bothwell ★★

A charming little town an hour's drive north of Hobart, Bothwell has several claims to fame. Set on the picturesque Clyde River at the foothills of the central Tasmanian highlands, the town was settled by Scottish colonists in 1822, with convict labor building many of the sandstone establishments still lining the streets today.

Bothwell's major claim to fame is as the home of **Ratho,** Australia's oldest golf course (www.rathofarm.com; ✆ **03/6259 5553**), which was also established in 1822, as soon as the Scottish settlers arrived. **Ratho Farm**, on which the 18-hole course sits, is also home to new luxury accommodations in the form of 16 converted convict cottages and stables, priced from A$175 double. Ratho is a public course, and greens fees are only A$40.

After a round of golf, drop into the **Australasian Golf Museum** (www.ausgolfmuseum.com; ✆ **03/6259 4033**), which doubles as the local information center, on Market Place. It's open daily 10am to 4pm September to May and 11am to 3pm June to August. While you're there, pick up a brochure that gives you a self-guided tour of Bothwell's many historic buildings.

And then there's the lure of a whisky distillery at nearby **Nant Estate** (www.nant.com.au; ✆ **1800/746 453** in Australia or 03/6128 3105), built in 1821. (Clearly the Scottish settlers were determined to bring with them all the most important amenities of home.) Today, it offers whisky tours, tastings, dinners, and the option to buy a 100-liter barrel of whisky with bespoke bottling and labeling. The distillery, at 254 Nant Lane, is open Wednesday to Sunday from 10am to 4pm; tours run daily at 11am, 1:30, and 3pm (from A$15; bookings essential).

Another spot worth ducking into is the historic **Castle Hotel** (✆ **03/6259 5502**), in Bothwell's main street. The sandstone pub, built in 1829, is one of Australia's oldest and like much of town is heritage-listed. There are three guest rooms upstairs, but the action is mostly in the bar, where locals gather to swap stories of trout fishing.

spot such bird species as black cockatoos, green rosellas, honeyeaters, currawongs, wedge-tailed eagles, and lyrebirds.

There are many walking trails running through the park, including one to the spectacular 45m (148-ft.) **Russell Falls,** near the park's entrance. The walk to the falls along a paved, wheelchair-accessible track takes 15 minutes and passes ferns and forests, with some of Tasmania's tallest trees, swamp gums that stand up to 85m (279 ft.) high.

Mount Field National Park is just over an hour's drive from Hobart via the town of New Norfolk. From Hobart, take the Brooker Highway (A10) northwest to New Norfolk. After New Norfolk, you can follow the road on either side of the Derwent River (the A10 or B62) until you reach Westerway. From there, it is a short drive to the clearly marked entrance to Mount Field National Park. There is an entrance fee of A$12 per person or A$24 per car (up to eight people).

Grayline (www.grayline.com.au; ✆ **1300/858 687** in Australia) offers a day tour from Hobart on Sundays (and Tues from Nov–Apr), costing A$135 for adults, A$68 for kids ages 4 to 14; it includes entrance fees to the national park.

The park's visitor center (www.parks.tas.gov.au; ✆ **03/6288 1149**) on Lake Dobson Road has a cafe and information on walks. It's open daily from 8:30am to 5pm between November and April and 9am to 4pm in winter.

PLANNING YOUR TRIP TO AUSTRALIA

10

A little preparation is essential before you start your journey to Australia, especially if you plan to do any special-interest activities, such as diving the Great Barrier Reef or visiting the Aboriginal landmarks in the Red Centre. This chapter provides a variety of planning tools, including information on how to get there and on-the-ground resources.

GETTING THERE

By Plane

Australia is a very long haul from just about anywhere except New Zealand. Sydney is a nearly 15-hour nonstop flight from Los Angeles, and even longer if you come via Honolulu, Hawaii. If you're flying from the East Coast of the United States, add 5½ hours. If you're coming from the U.S. via Auckland, add transit time in New Zealand plus 3 hours for the Auckland-Sydney leg.

If you are coming from the United Kingdom, brace yourself for a flight of 12 hours, more or less, from London to Asia, followed possibly by a long day in transit, because flights to Australia have a habit of arriving in Asia early in the morning and then not departing until around midnight, after which you still have an 8- to 9-hour flight to Australia.

Sydney (SYD), Cairns (CNS), Melbourne (MEL), and Brisbane (BNE) are all international gateways. Sydney is the major entry point into Australia, but you may also fly through another port first, depending on your departure point.

By Boat

Sydney Harbour is Australia's main port for cruise ships and the only port in Australia with two dedicated cruise-passenger terminals—the Overseas Passenger Terminal at Circular Quay (in the heart of the city, close to major tourist attractions) and the White Bay Cruise Terminal in the suburb of Rozelle, about 5km (3 miles) from the city center. Melbourne and Brisbane are also major ports.

GETTING AROUND

By Plane

Australia is a big country with a small population to support its air routes, so airfares may be higher than you are used to paying. Don't assume there is a direct flight to your chosen destination, or that there is a flight every hour or even every day.

Most domestic air travel is operated by **Qantas** (www.qantas.com.au; ✆ **800/227-4500** in the U.S. and Canada, 131 313 in Australia, 0800/964 432 in the U.K., 09/357 8900 in Auckland, 0800/808 767 in New Zealand), **Virgin Australia** (www.virginaustralia.com; ✆ **1855/253-8021** in the U.S., 136 789 or 07/3295 2296 in Australia, 0800/051 1281 in the U.K.), or Qantas-owned **Jetstar** (www.jetstar.com.au; ✆ **1866/397-8170** in the U.S.; 131 538 in Australia or 03/9645 5999; 0800/800 995 in New Zealand). **Regional Express** (www.rex.com.au; ✆ **131 713** in Australia) serves some regional ports in New South Wales, Victoria, South Australia, Tasmania, southern Western Australia, and Queensland.

Between them, Virgin Australia and Qantas and its subsidiaries, QantasLink and Jetstar, service every capital city, as well as most major regional towns on the east coast. Melbourne has two airports: the main international and domestic terminals at Tullamarine, and Avalon Airport, about 50km (31 miles) from the city, which is used by some Jetstar flights. Make sure you check which one your flight leaves from before you book.

Low-cost carrier **Scoot** (www.flyscoot.com; ✆ **02/9009 0860** in Australia) flies to all capital cities as well as the Queensland ports of Cairns, Townsville, Whitsunday Coast (Proserpine), and Gold Coast.

Competition is hot, so it's likely that all airlines will have added to their route networks by the time you read this.

DISCOUNTED FARES FOR INTERNATIONAL TRAVELERS

Qantas offers international travelers discounts off the full fares that Australians pay for domestic flights bought within Australia. To qualify, quote your passport number and international ticket number when reserving. Don't assume the fare for international travelers is the best deal, though—the latest deal in the market that day (or even better, perhaps, a package deal with accommodations thrown in) may be cheaper still.

AIR PASSES

If you are visiting from the U.S. and plan on visiting more than one city, purchasing a **Qantas Explorer pass** is much cheaper than buying regular fares. The pass is for economy-class travel only and must be purchased along with your Qantas or American Airlines fare from the U.S. to Australia. Prices vary according to which "zone" you are traveling to, and there are more than 60 domestic Australia city pairs to choose from, but the deals will get you to all major destinations covered in this book.

By Car

Australia's roads sometimes leave a bit to be desired. The taxes of 24 million people get spread pretty thin when it comes to maintaining roads across a continent. Some "highways" are two-lane affairs with the occasional rut and pothole, often no outside line markings, and sometimes no shoulders to speak of. You will strike these if you plan to drive in the Red Centre.

If you plan long-distance driving, get a road map (see "Maps" below for sources) that marks paved and unpaved roads.

You can use your current driver's license or an international driver's permit in every state of Australia. By law, you must carry your license with you when driving. The minimum driving age is 16 or 17, depending on which state you visit, but some car-rental companies require you to be 21, or sometimes 26, if you want to rent a four-wheel-drive (4WD) vehicle.

CAR RENTALS

Think twice about renting a car in tourist hot spots such as Cairns. In these areas most tour operators pick you up and drop you back at your hotel door, so having a car may not be worth the expense.

The "big four" car-rental companies—Avis, Budget, Hertz, and Thrifty—all have networks across Australia. Other major car-rental companies are Europcar, which has the third largest fleet in Australia, and Red Spot Car Rentals, which has depots in all state capital cities as well as other major centers such as Cairns, Townsville, and Rockhampton.

A small sedan for zipping around a city will cost about A$45 to A$80 a day. A feistier vehicle with enough grunt to get you from state to state will cost around A$70 to A$100 a day. Rentals of a week or longer usually reduce the price by A$5 a day or so.

A regular car will get you to most places in this book, except for some parts of the Red Centre, where you will need a 4WD vehicle. All the major car-rental companies rent them. Four-wheel-drives are more expensive than a regular car, but you can get them for as little as A$75 per day if you shop around (cheaper for rentals of a week or longer).

The rates quoted here are only a guide. Many smaller local companies—and the big guys, too—offer competitive specials, especially in tourist areas with distinct off-seasons. Advance purchase rates, usually 7 to 21 days ahead, can offer significant savings.

If you are concerned about reducing your carbon emissions, consider hiring a **hybrid car.** In Australia, the major car-hire companies have the hybrid Toyota Prius available. Ask when making your bookings.

INSURANCE

Insurance for loss of or damage to the car and third-party property insurance are usually included, but read the agreement carefully because the fine print contains information the front-desk staff may not tell you. For example, damage to the car body may be covered, but not damage to the windshield or tires, or damage caused by water or driving too close to a bushfire.

Insurance Alert

Damage to a rental car caused by an animal (hitting a kangaroo, for instance) may not be covered by your car-rental company's insurance policies. Different car-rental companies have very different rules and restrictions, so make sure you check each one's coverage. For example, some will not cover animal damage incurred at night, while others don't have such limits. The same applies to the rules about driving on unpaved roads, of which Australia has many. Avis and Budget say you may only drive on roads "properly formed and constructed as a sealed, metalled, or gravel road," while the others limit you largely to sealed roads. Check the fine print.

The deductible, known as "excess" in Australia, on insurance may be as high as A$2,000 for regular cars and up to A$5,500 on 4WDs and motor homes. You can reduce it, or avoid it altogether, by paying a premium of between about A$20 to A$50 per day on a car or four-wheel-drive, and around A$25 to A$50 per day on a motor home. The amount of the excess reduction premium depends on the vehicle type and the extent of reduction you choose. Your rental company may bundle personal accident insurance and baggage insurance into this premium. And again, check the conditions; some excess reduction payments do not reduce excesses on single-vehicle accidents, for example.

ONE-WAY RENTALS

Australia's long distances often make one-way rentals a necessity, for which car-rental companies can charge a hefty penalty amounting to hundreds of dollars. A one-way fee usually applies to motor-home rentals, too—usually around A$260 to A$360. An extra A$650 remote-location fee can apply for Outback areas such as Alice Springs. And there are minimum rental periods of between 7 and 21 days.

MOTOR HOMES

Motor homes (Aussies call them camper vans) are popular in Australia. Generally smaller than the RVs in the United States, they come in two- to six-berth versions and usually have everything you need, such as a minifridge and/or freezer (icebox in the smaller versions), microwave, gas stove, cooking and cleaning utensils, linens, and touring information, including maps and campground guides. All have showers and toilets, except some two-berthers.

Most of these camper vans have air-conditioned driver's cabins, but note that not all have air-conditioned living quarters, which is more or less a necessity to have in most parts of the country from November through March. Ask to make sure that the vehicle you're renting is fully air-conditioned if you're traveling this time of year. Four-wheel-drive campers are available, but while they offer an advantage in traversing wilderness roads, they tend to be small, and some lack hot water, toilet, and shower, not to mention air-conditioning.

Australia's biggest national motor-home-rental companies are **Apollo Motorhome Holidays** (www.apollocamper.com; ✆ **1800/777 779** in Australia, or 07/3265 9200), **Britz Campervan Rentals** (www.britz.com; ✆ **1800/331 454** in Australia or 800/2008 0801 from outside Australia), and **Maui** (www.maui.com.au; ✆ **800/2008 0801** from anywhere in the world, or 1800/827 821 within Australia or 03/8398 8829).

Rates vary with the seasons and your choice of vehicle. May and June are the slowest months; December and January are the busiest. It's sometimes possible to get better rates by booking in your home country before departure. Renting for longer than 3 weeks knocks a few dollars off the daily rate. Most companies will require a minimum 4- or 5-day rental. Give the company your itinerary before booking, because some routes may need the company's permission. Note that the minimum driver age for renting motor homes is usually 21.

Most local councils take a dim view of "free camping," the practice of pulling over by the roadside to camp for the night. Instead, in most places you will have to stay in a campground—and pay for it.

ON THE ROAD

GAS The price of petrol (gasoline) will probably elicit a cry of dismay from Americans and a whoop of delight from Brits. Prices go up and down, but at press time you were looking at around A$1.24 a liter (about ¼ gallon) for unleaded petrol in Sydney, and slightly more in the Outback. Most rental cars take unleaded gas, and motor homes run on diesel.

DRIVING RULES Australians drive on the left, which means you give way to the right. Left turns on a red light are not permitted unless a sign says so.

Roundabouts (traffic circles) are common at intersections; approach these slowly enough to stop if you have to, and give way to all traffic on the roundabout. Flash your indicator as you leave the roundabout (even if you're going straight, because technically that's a left turn).

The only strange driving rule is Melbourne's requirement that drivers turn right from the left lane at certain intersections in the city center and in South Melbourne. This allows the city's trams to carry on uninterrupted in the right lane. Pull into the left lane opposite the street you are turning into, and make the turn when the traffic light in the street you are turning into becomes green. These intersections are signposted.

The maximum permitted blood alcohol level when driving is .05%, which equals approximately two 200-milliliter (6.6-oz.) drinks in the first hour for men, one for women, and one drink per hour for both sexes after that. The police set up random breath-testing units (RBTs) in cunningly disguised and unlikely places all the time, so getting caught is easy. You will face a court appearance if you do.

The speed limit is 50kmph (31 mph) or 60kmph (37 mph) in urban areas, 100kmph (62 mph) in most country areas, and sometimes 110kmph (68 mph) on freeways. In the Northern Territory, the speed limit is set at 130kmph (81 mph) on the Stuart, Arnhem, Barkly, and Victoria highways, while rural roads are designated 110kmph (68 mph) unless otherwise signposted. ***Be warned:*** The Territory has a high death toll. Speed-limit signs show black numbers circled in red on a white background.

Drivers and passengers, including taxi passengers, must wear a seatbelt at all times when the vehicle is moving forward, if the car is equipped with a belt. Young children are required to sit in the rear seat in a child-safety seat or harness; car-rental companies will rent these to you, but be sure to book them. Tell the taxi company you have a child when you book a cab so that it can send a car with the right restraints.

MAPS The maps published by the state automobile clubs listed below in "Auto Clubs" will likely be free if you are a member of an affiliated auto club in your home country. None will mail them to you overseas; pick them up on arrival. Remember to bring your auto-club membership card to qualify for discounts or free maps.

Two of the biggest map publishers in Australia are **HEMA Maps** (www.hemamaps.com) and **UBD Gregory's** (www.hardigrant.com.au/explore; ✆ **02/9857 3700**). Both publish an extensive range of national (including road atlases), state, regional, and city maps. HEMA has a strong list of regional maps, while UBD Gregory's produces a complete range of street directories by city, region, or state. HEMA produces 4WD and motorbike road atlases and many regional 4WD maps—good if you plan to go off the trails. Many of its maps are also available as apps.

TOLL ROADS Electronic "beeper" or e-tags are used on all major Australian toll roads, including Melbourne's City Link motorways, Brisbane's tunnels and Logan and Gateway motorways, the Sydney Harbour Bridge and tunnel, and all Sydney's major tunnels and motorways. The tag is a small device attached to the front windscreen of the vehicle, which transmits signals to the toll points on the road. This deducts the toll amount from your toll account. The same e-tag can be used on all Australian toll roads. While some toll roads still have physical collection points at which you can pay the toll, others—such as Melbourne's freeways—don't. If you are likely to need an e-tag, your car-rental company can arrange one for you.

ROAD SIGNS Australians navigate by road name, not road number. The easiest way to get where you're going is to familiarize yourself with the major towns along your route and follow the signs toward them.

AUTO CLUBS Every state and territory in Australia has its own auto club. Your auto association back home probably has a reciprocal agreement with Australian clubs, which may entitle you to free maps, accommodations guides, and roadside assistance. Don't forget to bring your membership card.

Even if you're not a member, the clubs are a good source of advice on local traffic regulations, touring advice, road conditions, traveling in remote areas, and any other motoring questions you may have. The clubs sell maps, accommodations guides, and camping guides to nonmembers at reasonable prices. They even share a website: **www.aaa.asn.au**, which lists numerous regional offices.

ROAD CONDITIONS & SAFETY

Here are some common motoring dangers and ways to avoid them:

FATIGUE Fatigue is a killer on Australia's roads. The rule is to take a 20-minute break every 2 hours, even if you don't feel tired. In some states, "driver reviver" stations operate on major roads during holiday periods. They serve free tea, coffee, and cookies and are often found at roadside picnic areas that have restrooms.

KANGAROOS & OTHER WILDLIFE It's a sad fact, but kangaroos are a road hazard. Avoid driving in country areas between dusk and dawn, when 'roos are most active. If you hit one, always stop and check its pouch for live joeys (baby kangaroos), because females usually have one in the pouch. Wrap the joey tightly in a towel or old sweater, don't feed or over-handle it, and take it to a vet in the nearest town or call one of the following wildlife care groups: **Wildlife Information & Rescue Service (WIRES)** in New South Wales (✆ **1300/094 737**); **Wildlife Victoria** (✆ **1300/094 535**); or **Wildcare Australia** in Queensland (✆ **07/5527 2444**). In Tasmania, **Bonorong Wildlife Sanctuary** (✆ **03/6268 1184**) has the state's only 24-hour wildlife rescue service. Most vets will treat native wildlife for free.

Some highways run through unfenced stations (ranches), where sheep and cattle pose a threat. Cattle like to rest on the warm bitumen road at night, so put your lights on high to spot them. If an animal does loom up, slow down—but never swerve, or you may roll. If you have to, hit it. Tell farmers within 24 hours if you have hit their livestock.

Car-rental companies will not insure for animal damage to the car, which should give you an inkling of how common an occurrence this is.

ROAD TRAINS Road trains consist of as many as three big truck carriages linked together to make a "train" up to 54m (177 ft.) long. If you're in front of one, give the driver plenty of warning when you brake, because the trains need a lot of distance to slow down. Allow at least 1 clear kilometer (.6 miles) before you pass one, but don't expect the driver to make it easy—"truckies" are notorious for their lack of concern for motorists.

UNPAVED ROADS Many country roads are unsealed (unpaved). They are usually bone-dry, which makes them more slippery than they look, so travel at a moderate speed—35kmph (22 mph) is not too cautious, and anything over 60kmph (37 mph) is dangerous. That said, when you are on a heavily corrugated or rutted road (which many are), you may need to keep to a higher speed (60kmph/37 mph) just to stay on top of them. Don't overcorrect if you veer to one side. Keep well behind any vehicles, because the dust they throw up can block your vision.

FLOODS Floods are common north of Cairns from November or December through March or April (the "Wet" season). Never cross a flooded road unless you are sure of its depth. Crocodiles may be in the water, so do not wade in to test it! Fast-flowing water is dangerous, even if it's very shallow. When in doubt, stay where you are and wait for the water to drop; most flash floods subside in 24 hours. Check the road conditions ahead at least once a day in the Wet season.

RUNNING OUT OF GAS Gas stations (also called "roadhouses" in rural areas) can be few and far between in the Outback, so fill up at every opportunity.

WHAT IF YOUR VEHICLE BREAKS DOWN?

Warning: If you break down or get lost, never leave your vehicle. Many a motorist—often an Aussie who should have known better—has died wandering off on a crazy quest for help or water, knowing full well that neither is to be found for maybe hundreds of miles. Most people who get lost do so in Outback spots; if that happens to you, conserve your body moisture by doing as little as possible and staying in the shade of your car.

EMERGENCY ASSISTANCE

The emergency breakdown assistance telephone number for every Australian auto club is ✆ **131 111** from anywhere in Australia. It is billed as a local call. If you are not a member of an auto club at home that has a reciprocal agreement with the Australian clubs, you'll have to join the Australian club on the spot before the club will tow or repair your car. This usually costs around A$80, not a big price to pay when you're stranded—although in the Outback, the charge may be considerably higher. Most car-rental companies also have emergency assistance numbers.

TIPS FOR FOUR-WHEEL DRIVERS

Always keep to the four-wheel-drive track. Going off-road causes soil erosion, a significant environmental problem in Australia. Leave gates as you found them. Obtain permission from the owners before venturing onto private station (ranch) roads. On an extended trip or in remote areas, carry 5 liters (1⅓ gallons) of drinking water per person per day (dehydration occurs fast in the Australian heat); enough food to last 3 or 4 days more than you think you will need; a first-aid kit; spare fuel; a jack and two spare tires; spare fan belts, radiator hoses, and air-conditioner hoses; a tow rope; and a good map that marks all gas stations. In seriously remote areas outside the scope of this book, carry a high-frequency and a CB radio. (A mobile phone may not work in the Outback.) Advise a friend, your hotel manager, the local tourist bureau, or a police station of your route and your expected time of return or arrival at your destination.

By Train

Australia's trains are clean, comfortable, and safe, and for the most part service standards and facilities are perfectly adequate. The rail network in Australia links Perth to Adelaide and on to Melbourne and north to Sydney, Brisbane, and Cairns. There's also a line into the interior from Adelaide to Alice Springs and Darwin. Trains generally cost more than buses but are still reasonably priced.

Most long-distance trains have sleepers with big windows, air-conditioning, electric outlets, wardrobes, sinks, and fresh sheets and blankets. First-class sleepers have en suite bathrooms, and fares often include meals. Second-class sleepers use shared shower facilities, and meals are not included. Some second-class sleepers are private cabins; on other trains, you share with strangers. Single cabins are usually of broom-closet dimensions but surprisingly comfy, with their own toilet and basin. The onboard food ranges from mediocre to pretty good. Note that smoking is banned on all Australian rail networks.

Different entities manage Australia's rail routes. They include the government-owned **Queensland Rail** (www.queenslandrailtravel.com.au; ✆ **1300/131 722** in Australia or 07/3606 6630), which handles rail within that state, and **NSW TrainLink** (www.nswtrainlink.info; ✆ **132 232** in Australia or 02/4907 7501), which manages travel within New South Wales and from Sydney south to Melbourne and north to Brisbane. **Great Southern Rail** (www.greatsouthernrail.com.au; ✆ **1800/703 357** in Australia or 08/8213 4401) has a range of other fabulous Outback train journeys, including ***The Ghan***, which links Adelaide, Alice Springs, and Darwin, ***The Indian Pacific***, which travels between Sydney and Perth, and ***The Overland***, between Melbourne and Adelaide.

Queensland Rail operates the high-speed ***Spirit of Queensland*** five times a week on the Brisbane-Cairns route with business-class-style seating and "railbeds" (similar to Business Class lie-flat airline beds). The trip takes around 24 hours. The ***Tilt Train*** runs between Brisbane and the coastal towns of Bundaberg and Rockhampton. All Queensland and New South Wales long-distance trains stop at most towns en route, so they're useful for exploring the eastern states.

RAIL PASSES NSW TrainLink's **Discovery Pass** gives you unlimited economy-class trips anywhere on its network, including to Melbourne and Brisbane, for up to 6 months. A 14-day pass costs A$232, a 1-month pass A$275, a 3-month pass A$298, and a 6-month pass A$420.

The **Queensland Explorer** pass offers unlimited economy seat travel for 1 or 2 months across the Queensland Rail network, from Cairns in the north to Brisbane in the south, and in the Queensland outback. It costs A$299 for 1 month or A$389 for 2 months. If you only fancy the coast, the **Queensland Coastal Pass** allows travel between Brisbane and Cairns for A$209 for 1 month, A$289 for 2 months. These passes are only available to international travelers.

By Bus

Bus travel in Australia is as comfortable as it can be, given the nature of long-distance coach travel. Terminals are centrally located and well lit, the buses—called "coaches" Down Under—are clean and air-conditioned, you sit in adjustable seats, videos play onboard, and drivers are polite and sometimes even point out places of interest along the way. Buses are all nonsmoking and some have restrooms. The country's extensive bus network will take you almost everywhere.

Australia has one national coach operator: **Greyhound Australia** (www.greyhound.com.au; ✆ **1300/473 946** in Australia or 07/4690 9850; no relation to Greyhound in the U.S.). In addition to point-to-point services, Greyhound Australia offers a limited range of tours at popular locations on its networks, including Uluru and the Great Ocean Road in Victoria.

Fares and some passes are considerably cheaper for students, backpacker cardholders, and Hostelling International/YHA members.

BUS PASSES Bus passes are a great value. There are several kinds: short hop, hop-on-hop-off passes, and kilometer passes. Note that even with a pass, you may still need to book the next leg of your trip 12 or 24 hours ahead as a condition of the pass; during school vacation periods, which are always busy, booking as much as a week ahead is smart.

Greyhound Australia's **Short Hop Passes** let you travel between two destinations, with limited stops over 30 days, as long as you don't backtrack. **Hop-on-hop-off Passes** are valid for 90 days and link most of the popular destinations. Travel from Melbourne to Cairns costs A$529. These passes can be bought for a range of destinations around Australia.

The **KM (Kilometre) Pass,** which is valid for 12 months, allows unlimited stops in any direction within the mileage you buy. Passes are available for 1,000km (620 miles) for A$189, and then in increasing mileage increments. A 2,500km (1,553-miles) pass—enough to get you from Brisbane to Cairns—will cost A$415, and from there you can go up to A$2,675 for a whopping 25,000km (15,535 miles).

[FastFACTS] AUSTRALIA

ATMs/Banks The easiest and best way to get cash away from home is from an **ATM (automated teller machine),** sometimes referred to as a "cash machine" or "cashpoint."

The **Cirrus** (www.mastercard.com) and **PLUS** (www.visa.com) networks span the globe. Go to your bank card's website to find ATM locations at your destination. Be sure you know your daily withdrawal limit before you depart.

Note that Australian ATMs use a four-digit code, so check with your bank and make sure you change yours before you leave. ***Note:*** Many banks impose a fee every time you use a card at another bank's ATM, and that fee can be higher for international transactions (A$5 or more) than for domestic ones (usually A$2 or A$2.50). In addition, the bank from which you withdraw cash may charge its own fee. For international withdrawal fees, ask your bank.

Customs The duty-free allowance in Australia is A$900 or, for those under 18, A$450. Anyone over 18 can bring in up to 50 cigarettes or 50 grams of cigars or other tobacco products, 2.25 liters (41 fluid oz.) of alcohol, and "dutiable goods" to the value of A$900 or A$450 if you are under 18. "Dutiable goods" are luxury items such as perfume, watches, jewelry, furs, plus gifts of any kind. Keep this in mind if you intend to bring presents for family and friends in Australia; gifts given to you also count toward the dutiable limit.

Personal goods that you're taking with you are usually exempt from duty, but if you are returning with valuable goods that you already own, file form B263. Customs officers do not collect duty—less than A$50—as long as you declared the goods in the first place.

A helpful brochure, available from Australian consulates or Customs offices, as well as online, is *Know Before You Go*. For more information, contact the **Department of Immigration and Border Protection** (✆ **131 881** in Australia), or check out **www.border.gov.au**.

You need not declare cash in any currency, and other currency instruments, such as traveler's checks, under a value of A$10,000.

Australia is a signatory to the **Convention on International Trade in Endangered Species (CITES),** which restricts or bans the import of products made from protected wildlife. Banned items include ivory, tortoise (marine turtle) shell, rhinoceros, or tiger products, and sturgeon caviar. Bear this in mind if you stop in other countries en route to Australia, where souvenirs made from items like these may be sold. Australian authorities may seize these items.

Because Australia is an island, it is free of many agricultural and livestock diseases. To keep it that way, ***strict* quarantine** applies to importing plants, animals, and their products, including food. "Sniffer" dogs at airports detect these products (as well as drugs). Some items may be confiscated, and others may be held over for you to take with you when you leave the country. Heavy fines apply to breaches of the laws. Amnesty trash bins are available before you reach the immigration counters in airport arrivals halls for items such as fruit. Don't be alarmed if, just before landing, the flight attendants spray the aircraft cabin (with products approved by the World Health Organization) to kill potentially disease-bearing insects. For more information on what is and is not allowed, contact the nearest Australian embassy or consulate, or Australia's Department of Agriculture and Water Resources (www.agriculture.gov.au/travelling; ✆ **1800/900 090** in Australia).

For information on what you're allowed to bring home, contact one of the following agencies:

U.S. Citizens: U.S. Customs & Border Protection (CBP), 1300 Pennsylvania Ave. NW, Washington, DC 20229 (www.cbp.gov; ✆ **877/CBP-5511** [227-5511]).

Canadian Citizens: Canada Border Services Agency, Ottawa, Ontario, K1A 0L8 (www.cbsa-asfc.gc.ca).

U.K. Citizens: Check with HM Revenue & Customs (www.gov.uk/duty-free-goods).

New Zealand Citizens: Auckland City Customhouse, 50 Anzac Ave., Auckland, (www.customs.govt.nz; ✆ **09/927-8036** or 0800/428-786 in New Zealand).

Doctors & Hospitals Doctors are listed under "M," for "Medical Practitioners," in the Yellow Pages in Australia, and most large towns and cities have 24-hour clinics. Your hotel may be able to help you find a local doctor. Failing that, go to the local emergency room. See "Fast Facts" in other chapters of this book for local details.

Drinking Laws Hours vary from pub to pub, but most are open daily from 10am or noon to 10pm or midnight. The minimum drinking age is 18.

Random breath tests to catch drunk drivers are common, and drunk-driving laws are strictly enforced. Getting caught drunk behind the wheel will mean a court appearance, not just a fine. The maximum permitted blood-alcohol level is .05%.

Alcohol is sold in liquor stores, in the "bottle shops" attached to every pub, and in some states in supermarkets.

Electricity The current is 240 volts AC, 50 hertz. Sockets take two or three flat, not rounded, prongs. Bring a connection kit of the right power and phone adapters, a spare phone cord, and a spare Ethernet network cable—or find out whether your hotel supplies them to guests. North Americans and Europeans will need to buy a converter before they leave home. (Don't wait until you get to Australia, because Australian stores are likely to stock only converters for Aussie appliances to fit American and European outlets.)

Some large hotels have 110V outlets for electric shavers (or dual voltage), and some will lend converters, but don't count on it in smaller, less expensive hotels, motels, or B&Bs. Power does not start automatically when you plug in an appliance; you need to flick the switch beside the socket to the "on" position.

Embassies & Consulates Most diplomatic posts are in Canberra. **United States:** United States Embassy, 21 Moonah Place, Yarralumla, ACT 2600 (www.canberra.usembassy.gov; ✆ **02/6214 5600**), the United States Consulate General, 553 St Kilda Rd., Melbourne (✆ **03/9526 5900**); or the United States Consulate General in Sydney, Level 10, 19-29 Martin Place (✆ **1300/139 399**).

Canada: High Commission of Canada, Commonwealth Avenue, Yarralumla, ACT 2600 (www.canada international.gc.ca/australia-australie; ✆ **02/6270 4000**).

Ireland: Consulate General of Ireland, Level 26, 1 Market St., Sydney, NSW 2000 (www.irishconsulatesydney.net; ✆ **02/9264 9635**).

New Zealand: New Zealand High Commission, Level 2, 65 Canberra Avenue, Canberra, ACT 2600 (www.mfat.govt.nz; ✆ **02/6270 4211**).

United Kingdom: British High Commission, Commonwealth Avenue, Yarralumla, ACT 2600 (www.british-consulate.org; ✆ **02/6270 6666**).

Emergencies Dial ✆ **000** anywhere in Australia for police, ambulance, or the fire department. This is a free call from public and private telephones and needs no coins. The TTY emergency number is ✆ **106.**

Family Travel Australians travel widely with their own kids, so facilities for families, including family passes to attractions, are common.

Many hotels will offer connecting units or "family rooms." Ask when booking. Most Australian hotels will arrange babysitting when given a day's notice.

Many Australian resorts have "kids' clubs" with extensive programs designed for children 11 and under and, in some cases, teenagers. Other resorts have "kids stay, eat, and play free" offers, particularly during holiday periods.

A great accommodations option for families is Australia's huge stock of serviced or unserviced apartments (with or without daily maid service). Often less expensive than a hotel room, they offer a living room, a kitchen, a bathroom or two, and the privacy of a separate bedroom for adults.

International airlines and domestic airlines in Australia charge 75% of the adult fare for kids 11 and under. Most charge 10% for infants under 2 years not occupying a seat. Australian transport companies, attractions, and tour operators typically charge half-price for kids under 12 or 14 years.

Don't forget that children entering Australia on their parent's passport still need their own visa.

Resources for Family Travel: Rascals in Paradise (www.rascalsinparadise.com; ✆ **415/273-2224**) is a San Francisco–based company specializing in family vacation packages to Australia. The Australian travel magazine ***Holidays with Kids*** has a comprehensive website listing great options for family travel in Australia (www.holidayswithkids.com.au). **Family Travel Forum** is also a good resource; see **www.myfamilytravels.com** for destinations, ideas, and more.

Health No vaccinations are needed to enter Australia unless you have been in a yellow fever danger zone—that is, South America or Africa—in the 6 days prior to entering.

Australian pharmacists may only fill prescriptions written by Australian doctors, so carry enough medication with you for your trip. Doctors are listed under "M," for "Medical Practitioners," in the Yellow Pages, and most large towns and cities have 24-hour clinics. Failing that, go to the local hospital emergency room.

Generally, you don't have to worry much about health issues on a trip to Australia. Hygiene standards are high, hospitals are modern, and doctors and dentists are well qualified. Because of the continent's size, however, you can sometimes be a long way from a hospital or a doctor. Remote areas are served by the Royal Flying Doctor Service. But it may be advisable to purchase standard medical travel insurance.

- **Tropical Illnesses** Some parts of tropical far-north Queensland have sporadic outbreaks of the mosquito-borne dengue fever. The areas affected include Cairns, Port Douglas, and Townsville. But as dengue-fever mosquitoes breed in urban environments, tourist activities in north Queensland such as reef and rainforest trips carry a modest risk. The risk can be further minimized by staying in screened or air-conditioned accommodations, using insect repellent at all times, and wearing long, loose, light-colored clothing that covers arms and legs.
- **Bugs, Bites & Other Wildlife Concerns** Snake and spider bites may not be as common as the hair-raising stories you will hear would suggest, but it pays to be wary. Your other concerns should be marine life, including jellyfish, and saltwater crocodiles. For more information and background on the fauna of Australia, and how to avoid dangerous encounters with them, see p. 29.
- **Sun/Elements** Australians have the world's highest death rate from skin cancer because of the country's intense sunlight. Limit your exposure to the sun, especially during the first few days of your trip, and from 11am to 3pm in summer and 10am to 2pm in winter.

  Remember that UV rays reflected off walls, water, and the ground can burn you even when you're not in direct sunlight. Use a broad-spectrum sunscreen with a high protection factor (SPF 30 or higher). Wear a broad-brimmed hat that covers the back of your neck, ears, and face (a baseball cap won't do it), and a long-sleeved shirt.

  Remember that children need more protection than adults do. Don't even think about traveling without sunglasses, or you'll spend your entire vacation squinting against Australia's "diamond light."
- **Extreme Weather Exposure** Cyclones sometimes affect tropical areas, such as Queensland's coastal regions, from about Gladstone north, during January and February. Serious damage is normally rare.

Insurance Standard medical and travel insurance is advisable for travel to Australia. Divers should also ensure they have the appropriate insurance. For information on traveler's insurance, trip cancelation insurance, and medical insurance while traveling, please visit www.frommers.com/tips.

Internet Access Most hotels throughout Australia offer dataports for laptop modems, high-speed Internet access, and free Wi-Fi. Check the list of hotel amenities in each hotel listing to see what kind of Internet service your hotel offers, and at what cost.

Most **youth hostels** and **public libraries** have Internet access. Avoid **hotel business centers** unless you're willing to pay exorbitant rates. Cybercafes (called **Internet cafes** in Australia) can be found almost everywhere.

Most major cities also have free Wi-Fi hubs that you can hook into in public places. Most major airports have **Internet kiosks** that provide basic Web access for a per-minute fee that's usually higher than cybercafe prices.

For help locating cybercafes and other establishments where you can go for Internet access, please see the "Fast Facts" sections of other chapters in this book.

Legal Aid If you find yourself in trouble with the long arm of the law while visiting Australia, the first thing you should do is contact your country's embassy or nearest consulate in Australia. See contact details for Canberra diplomatic posts under "Embassies & Consulates" above.

Embassies or consulates with posts in state capitals are listed in "Fast Facts," in the relevant state chapters of this book.

The U.S. Embassy considers an "emergency" to be either your arrest or the loss of your passport. If arrested in Australia, you will have to go through the Australian legal process for being charged, prosecuted, possibly convicted and sentenced, and for any appeals process. However, U.S. consular officers (and those of other countries) provide a wide variety of services to their citizens arrested abroad and to their families. These may include providing a list of local attorneys, providing info about judicial procedures, and notifying your family and/or friends, if you wish. However, they cannot demand your release, represent you at your trial, give you legal advice, or pay your fees or fines.

LGBTQ Travelers Sydney is one of the most gay-friendly cities in the world, and across most of Australia the gay community has a high profile and lots of support services. There are plenty of gay and lesbian bars, and most Saturday nights see a privately operated gay dance party taking place in an inner-city warehouse somewhere.

The cafes and pubs of Oxford Street in Darlinghurst, a short cab ride or long stroll from Sydney's downtown area, are the liveliest gay spots in that city. The annual **Sydney Gay & Lesbian Mardi Gras,** culminating in a huge street parade and party in late February or early March, is a high point on the city's calendar.

In rural areas of Australia, you may still encounter a little conservative resistance to gays and lesbians, but Australians everywhere are generally open-minded. Noosa, on Queensland's Sunshine Coast, is a favored destination for gay revelers after Mardi Gras, and a couple of resorts in north Queensland cater to gay and lesbian travelers. One of the best known is **Turtle Cove Beach Resort** (www.turtlecove.com; ✆ **1300/727 979** in Australia or 07/4059 1800), located on a private beach between Cairns and Port Douglas.

LGBTQ Resources: A service you may find useful is **Twenty10** (incorporating the Gay & Lesbian Counselling Service of NSW), which runs a national hotline (✆ **1800/184 527** in Australia) from 3pm to midnight daily. Its website, **www.twenty10.org.au**, has lots of useful information.

In Sydney, the **Albion Street Centre** (www.thealbioncentre.org.au; ✆ **1800/451 600** in Australia or 02/9332 9700 for the information line) is an HIV clinic and information service for gay men's health.

The International Gay and Lesbian Travel Association (IGLTA; www.iglta.org; ✆ **954/630-1637** in the U.S.) is the trade association for the gay and lesbian travel industry and offers an online directory of gay- and lesbian-friendly travel businesses and tour operators. **Gay and Lesbian Tourism Australia** (www.galta.com.au) has listings of businesses in each state.

Mail & Postage A postcard or letter (up to 250g/8.8 oz. in weight) will cost A$1.95 to send from Australia to New Zealand, or A$2.95 from Australia to the U.S., Canada, or U.K. Mail will take up to 6 business days to reach North America or Europe from Australia.

A parcel of up to 500 grams (17.6 oz.) will cost A$15.85 to send to the United States by airmail.

Mobile Phones The three letters that define much of the world's wireless capabilities are **GSM** (Global System for Mobile Communications), a big, seamless network that makes for easy cross-border cellphone use throughout Europe and dozens of other countries worldwide.

In the U.S., T-Mobile and AT&T Wireless use this quasi-universal system; in Canada, Microcell, and some Rogers customers are GSM; and all Europeans and most Australians use GSM.

GSM phones function with a removable plastic SIM card, encoded with your phone number and account information. If your cellphone is on a GSM system, and you have a world-capable multiband phone, you can make and receive calls around much of the globe.

Just call your wireless operator and ask for "international roaming" to be activated on your account. But be sure to check the cost of "data roaming" on smart phones, because the cost can be astronomical, and you do not want a nasty (and I mean *really* nasty!) surprise on your return home when you get the bill. Unless you turn off your data roaming, it will activate automatically.

For many, **renting** a phone is a good idea. While you can rent a phone from any number of overseas sites, including kiosks at airports and at car-rental agencies, we suggest renting the phone before you leave home. North Americans can rent one before leaving home from **RoadPost** (www.roadpost.com; ✆ **888/290-1616** or 416/253-4539) or **InTouch U.S.A.** (www.intouchglobal.com). InTouch will also give free advice on whether your existing phone will work overseas; simply call ✆ **703/222-7161** between 9am and 4pm EST, or go to **http://intouchglobal.com/travel.htm**.

In Australia—reputed to have one of the world's highest per-capita rates of ownership of "mobile" telephones, as they are known here—the cell network is digital, not analog. Calls to or from a mobile telephone are generally more expensive than calls to or from a fixed telephone. The price varies depending on the telephone company, the time of day, the distance between caller and recipient, and the telephone's pricing plan.

Buying a prepaid phone can be economically attractive. Once you arrive in Australia, stop by a local cellphone shop and get the cheapest package; you'll probably pay less than A$100 for a phone and a starter calling card with a significant amount of free credit.

In Australia, the mobile phone company **Vodafone** (www.vodafone.com.au; ✆ **1300/650 410** in Australia or +61/426 320 000) has outlets at Brisbane and Melbourne international airports and at both international and domestic terminals in Sydney selling SIMs, handsets, and mobile broadband. **Optus** (www.optus.com.au; ✆ **1800/780 219** in Australia) has stores at Sydney and Melbourne airports.

Charges vary depending on the kind of phone and coverage you want, but some of the benefits include one low call rate throughout Australia, free incoming calls, international direct-dialing access, text messaging, and voicemail. Alternatively, you should be able to rent a mobile phone or SIM card for your existing mobile phone to stay in touch while you're traveling.

Money & Costs The Australian dollar is divided into A100¢. Coins are A5¢, A10¢, A20¢, and A50¢ pieces (silver) and A$1 and A$2 pieces (gold).

Bank notes come in denominations of A$5, A$10, A$20, A$50, and A$100.

Note that Australian prices often end in a variant of A1¢ and A2¢ (for example, A78¢ or A$2.71), a relic from the days before 1-cent and 2-cent pieces were phased out. In these cases, prices are rounded to the nearest A5¢—so A77¢ rounds down to A75¢, and A78¢ rounds up to A80¢.

Frommer's lists exact prices in the local currency. However, exchange rates always fluctuate, so before departing consult a currency exchange website such as **www.oanda.com/currency/converter** to check up-to-the-minute rates.

You should consider changing a small amount of money into Australian currency before you leave (though don't expect the exchange rate to be ideal), so that you can avoid long lines at airport ATMs or exchange desks. You can exchange money at your local American Express or Thomas Cook office or your bank.

If you're using a **credit card,** note that Visa and MasterCard are universally accepted in Australia; American Express and Diners Club are less common; and Discover is not used. Always carry a little cash, because many merchants will not take credit cards for purchases under A$10 or so.

Beware of hidden credit-card **fees** while traveling.

Check with your credit-or debit-card issuer to see what fees, if any, will be charged for overseas transactions. Fees can amount to 3% or more of the purchase price. Check with your bank before your departure to avoid any surprise charges on your credit card statement.

For help with currency conversions, tip calculations, and more, download Frommer's convenient **Travel Tools app** for your mobile device. Go to www.frommers.com/go/mobile and click on the Travel Tools icon.

Newspapers & Magazines The national daily newspaper is ***The Australian,*** which publishes an expanded edition with a color magazine on Saturday. All capital cities also have their own daily papers. Newspapers and magazines can be bought at a wide range of retail outlets including newsagents, supermarkets, gas stations, and convenience stores.

Packing Tips Dressing in layers (and packing layers) is the best way of kitting yourself out for Australia.

Depending on where you are going in Australia—and the season—you will need different gear. For example, if you are visiting Queensland or central Australia in the summer, pack only light clothing (but always throw in a little something warm just in case!). But if you're heading for Victoria in winter you'll need full cold-weather outfits.

Wherever and whenever you go, take a light rain jacket: Summer in the tropics can often be quite wet!

Most restaurants in Australia accept "smart casual" dress; in the cities, you will need proper shoes (no thongs/flip-flops) and often (for men) a shirt with a collar to dine in most places.

For more helpful information on packing for your trip, download our convenient Travel Tools app for your mobile device. Go to www.frommers.com/go/mobile and click on the Travel Tools icon.

Police Dial ✆ **000** anywhere in Australia. This is a free call from public and private telephones and requires no coins.

Safety Travelers to Australia should follow the same precautions against petty theft and potential identity theft as they would at home or in any other country. Violent crime is, of course, not uncommon, but you are not likely to become a target in the normal course of your travels.

Driving probably poses one of the greatest safety risks to visitors to Australia. Australians drive on the left, something that North American and European visitors often have difficulty remembering. Drivers and passengers, including taxi passengers, must wear a seatbelt at all times, by law.

Avoid driving between dusk and dawn in country areas, because this is when kangaroos and other wildlife are most active, and a collision with a 'roo is something to be avoided at all costs, for both party's sakes. Road trains—as many as three big truck carriages linked together, which can be up to 54m (177 ft.) long—are another danger to look out for, particularly when you are in the Outback.

Warning: If you break down or get lost, *never* leave your vehicle. Most people who get lost do so in Outback spots, and those who wander off to look for help or water usually die in the attempt. If it happens to you, stay with your car. See "By Car" in the "Getting Around" section, p. 291.

Senior Travel Seniors—often called "pensioners" in Australia—from other countries don't always qualify for the discounted entry prices to tours, attractions, and events that Australian seniors enjoy, but it is always worth asking. Inquire about discounts when booking hotels, flights, and train or bus tickets. The best ID to bring is something that shows your date of birth or that marks you as an "official" senior, such as a membership card from AARP.

Senior Resources: Many reliable agencies and organizations target the 50-plus market. **Road Scholar** (formerly Elderhostel; www.roadscholar.org; ✆ **800/454-5768** in the U.S.) arranges worldwide study programs—including to Australia—for those ages 55 and over.

Smoking Smoking is banned in most indoor public places throughout the country, including government buildings, museums, cinemas, theaters, restaurants, and airports (and on all aircraft).

In Queensland, you are not allowed to smoke on a patrolled beach or near children's playgrounds; in Victoria, you may find that some pubs have outdoor (or rooftop) smoking areas. Laws vary from state to state, so the safest thing is to ask before you light up.

Student Travel Australia has agreements with many countries, including the U.S., Canada, and the U.K., that give students between 18 and 30 years old the right to apply for a "working holiday" visa to stay in Australia for up to 12 months. You must apply for your visa outside of Australia, show evidence of your student or recent graduate status, and hold a return ticket as well as sufficient funds for the first part of your stay. For more information, check the website **www.border.gov.au**.

Check out the **ISIC Association** (www.isic.org) website for comprehensive travel-services information and details on how to get an **International Student Identity Card (ISIC),** which qualifies students for substantial savings on rail passes, plane tickets, entrance fees, and more. It also provides students with basic health and life insurance and a 24-hour helpline. The card is valid for a maximum of 16 months. You can apply for the card online or in person at your university or a host of other outlets (check the website). If you're no longer a student but are still under 30, you can get an **International Youth Travel Card (IYTC),** which entitles you to some discounts. **Travel CUTS** (www.travelcuts.com; ✆ **800/667-2887**) offers similar services for Canadians and U.S. residents. Irish students may prefer to turn to **USIT** (www.usit.ie; ✆ **01/602-1906**), an Ireland-based specialist in student, youth, and independent travel.

Taxes Australia applies a 10% Goods and Services Tax (GST) on most products and services. Your international airline tickets to Australia are not taxed, nor are domestic airline tickets for travel within Australia *if you bought them outside Australia*. If you buy Australian airline tickets once you arrive in Australia, you will pay GST on them.

There are other exceptions. Items bought in duty-free stores will not be charged GST. Nor will items you export—such as an Aboriginal painting that you buy in a gallery in Alice Springs and have shipped straight to your home outside Australia. Basic groceries are not GST-taxed, although restaurant meals are.

Through the **Tourist Refund Scheme (TRS),** Australians and international visitors can claim a refund of the GST (and of a 14.5% wine tax called the Wine Equalisation Tax, or WET) paid on a purchase of more than A$300 from a single outlet, within the last 60 days before you leave. More than one item may be included in that A$300. For example, you can claim the GST you paid on 10 T-shirts, each worth A$30, as long as they were bought from a single store. Do this as you leave by presenting your receipt or "tax invoice" to the Australian Customs Service's TRS booths, in the International Terminal departure areas at most airports.

Items must be taken as carry-on baggage, because you must show them to Customs. You can use the goods before you leave Australia and still claim the refund, but you cannot claim a refund on things you have consumed (say, perfume or food). You cannot claim a refund on alcohol other than wine.

Claims at airports are available up to 30 minutes before your flight's scheduled departure.

You can also claim a refund if you leave Australia as a cruise passenger from Sydney, Melbourne, Brisbane, Cairns, Darwin, Hobart, or Fremantle (Perth). Claims at seaports should be made no later than 1 hour before the scheduled departure time of the ship. If your cruise departs from elsewhere in Australia, or if you are flying out from an airport other than Sydney, Melbourne, Brisbane, Adelaide, Cairns, Perth, Darwin, or the Gold Coast, telephone the **Department of Immigration and Border Protection** (✆ **131 881** in Australia) to see if you can still claim the refund.

Other taxes include a "reef tax," officially dubbed the **Environmental Management Charge,** of A$6.50 per day (or A$3.25 for a half day) for every person over the age of 4 every time he or she enters the Great Barrier Reef Marine Park on a commercial tour. This charge goes toward park upkeep, and is sometimes (but not always) included in the ticket price.

Most airlines and an increasing number of tour operators, such as cruise companies and long-distance trains, also impose a "fuel surcharge" to help them combat rising fuel costs. This is usually added to the price of your ticket.

Tipping Tipping is not expected in Australia, but it is always appreciated. It is usual to tip around 10% or round up to the nearest A$10 for a substantial meal in a family restaurant.

Some passengers round up to the nearest dollar in a taxicab, but it's quite okay to insist on every bit of change back. Tipping bellboys and porters is sometimes done, but no one tips bar staff, barbers, or hairdressers.

Toilets Public toilets are easy to find—and free—in most Australian cities and towns. If you are driving, most towns have "restrooms" on the main street (although the cleanliness may vary wildly).

In some remote areas, public toilets are "composting," meaning there is no flush, just a drop into a pit beneath you.

If you really want to plan ahead, consult the **National Public Toilet Map** (www.toiletmap.gov.au).

Travelers with Disabilities Most disabilities shouldn't stop anyone from traveling to Australia. There are more options and resources than ever before. Most hotels, major stores, attractions, and public restrooms in Australia have wheelchair access. Many smaller lodges and even B&Bs are starting to cater to guests with disabilities, and some diving companies cater to scuba divers with disabilities. National parks make an effort to include wheelchair-friendly pathways. Taxi companies in bigger cities can usually supply a cab equipped for wheelchairs.

TTY facilities are still limited largely to government services. For information on all kinds of facilities and services (not just travel-related organizations) for people with disabilities, contact **National Information Communication Awareness Network,** (www.nican.com.au; ✆ **1300/655 535** in Australia). This free service can put you in touch with accessible accommodations and attractions throughout Australia, as well as with travel agents and tour operators who understand your needs.

Index

See also Accommodations and Restaurant indexes, below.

General Index

D

E

F

G

Accommodations

Restaurants

Photo Credits

p. i: © Photodigitaal.nl; p. ii: ©travellight / Shutterstock.com; p. iii: ©Taras Vyshnya / Shutterstock.com; p. iv: ©ChameleonsEye / Shutterstock.com; p. v, top: ©GagliardiImages / Shutterstock.com; p. v, bottom left: Courtesy of Let's Go Surfing; p. v, bottom right: ©alfotokunst / Shutterstock.com; p. vi, top left: Courtesy of OTTO/ Nikki To; p. vi, top right: ©worldswildlifewonders / Shutterstock.com; p. vi, bottom: ©m. letschert / Shutterstock.com; p. vii, top: ©Sean Heatley / Shutterstock.com; p. vii, bottom left: ©CO Leong / Shutterstock.com; p. vii, bottom right: ©patjo / Shutterstock.com; p. viii, top: ©matiascausa; p. viii, middle: ©Neale Cousland / Shutterstock.com; p. viii, bottom: ©VarnaK; p. ix, top: ©Martin Valigursky / Shutterstock.com; p. ix, bottom: ©Martin Valigursky / Shutterstock.com; p. x, top left: Courtesy of Summit Restaurant & Kuta Cafe Pty Ltd; p. x, top right: ©Martin Valigursky / Shutterstock.com; p. x, bottom: Courtesy of Tjapukai; p. xi, top: Courtesy of Lady Elliot Island Eco Resort; p. xi, bottom: ©Martin Valigursky; p. xii, top: ©Alberto Loyo; p. xii, middle: ©Olga Kashubin / Shutterstock.com; p. xii, bottom: ©EpochCatcher; p. xiii, top: ©Prazis / Shutterstock.com; p. xiii, bottom: ©ingehogenbijl / Shutterstock.com; p. xiv, top: ©wargunner / Shutterstock.com; p. xiv, bottom left: ©edella / Shutterstock.com; p. xiv, bottom right: ©Albert Pego / Shutterstock.com; p. xv, top: ©Robyn Mackenzie / Shutterstock.com; p. xv, bottom: ©ingehogenbijl / Shutterstock.com; p. xvi, top: ©Cyrus_2000 / Shutterstock.com; p. xvi, middle: ©Olga Kashubin / Shutterstock.com; p. xvi, bottom: ©Jason Ho / Shutterstock.com; p. 4: ©Debra James / Shutterstock.com; p. 5: Courtesy of Skyrail Rainforest Cableway; p. 6: Courtesy of Donovans; p. 7: Courtesy of Longitude 131; p. 8: Courtesy of Australian Butterfly Sanctuary; p. 9: ©Meghan Lamb; p. 10: ©dinozzaver / Shutterstock.com; p. 11: ©surfing; p. 13: ©EcoPrint / Shutterstock.com; p. 15: ©Taras Vyshnya / Shutterstock.com; p. 20: ©fritz16 / Shutterstock.com; p. 23: ©Janelle Lugge; p. 26: ©Taras Vyshnya; p. 27: ©PomInOz / Shutterstock.com; p. 29: ©Tourism Australia / Maxime Coquard; p. 35: ©CoolR / Shutterstock.com; p. 38: Courtesy of Featherdale Wildlife Park; p. 39: ©Tjapukai; p. 41: ©Maurizio De Mattei / Shutterstock.com; p. 42: ©Marc Witte; p. 44: ©Johnny Jet; p. 45: ©Alan Samuel; p. 46: ©Michael Coghlan; p. 47: ©Vividrange | Dreamstime.com; p. 49: ©Meghan Lamb; p. 51: ©Dan Breckwoldt / Shutterstock.com; p. 53: ©Dan Breckwoldt | Dreamstime.com; p. 56: ©byvalet / Shutterstock.com; p. 57: ©PomInOz / Shutterstock.com; p. 63: ©tourpics_net; p. 74: Courtesy of OTTO/ Nikki To; p. 79: ©Anthony Ngo | Dreamstime.com; p. 82: Courtesy of Museum of Contemporary Art, Sydney; p. 84: ©Tourism Australia / Hugh Stewart; p. 97: ©CoolR / Shutterstock.com; p. 99: ©David May | Dreamstime.com; p. 105: ©PomInOz; p. 110: ©Tourism Australia; p. 125: Courtesy of MoVida Bar de Tapas; p. 131: Courtesy of Eureka Skydeck; p. 133: ©Hanafi Latif / Shutterstock.com; p. 134: ©MagSpace / Shutterstock.com; p. 136: Courtesy of Polly Woodside ; p. 137: ©TK Kurikawa / Shutterstock.com; p. 139: Courtesy of Puffing Billy Railway; p. 140: ©Sunflowerey / Shutterstock.com; p. 146: ©www.penguins.org.au; p. 154: ©FiledIMAGE / Shutterstock.com; p. 162: ©Gordon Bell / Shutterstock.com; p. 164: ©ChameleonsEye / Shutterstock.com; p. 174: ©Queensland Museum; p. 175: ©Martin Valigursky / Shutterstock.com; p. 177: ©David Bostock / Shutterstock.com; p. 178: ©Courtesy of Brisbane Whale Watching; p. 184: ©Tanya Puntti | Dreamstime.com; p. 195: Courtesy of NuNu, Cairns; p. 198: Courtesy of Cairns ZOOM & Wildlife Dome; p. 202: Courtesy of Great Adventure Tours; p. 204: Courtesy of Delaware North Companies; p. 206: ©ChameleonsEye / Shutterstock.com; p. 214: Courtesy of Adventure North Australia Pty Ltd and the Bama Way Aboriginal Journeys; p. 227: ©Tomas Sykora; p. 237: ©Amacphoto7 / Shutterstock.com; p. 246: ©Lauren Cameo / Shutterstock.com; p. 251: Courtesy of Araluen Cultural Precinct; p. 253: Courtesy of Outback Ballooning; p. 258: ©mark higgins / Shutterstock.com; p. 259: ©Wesley Walker / Shutterstock.com; p. 265: ©Marc Witte | Dreamstime.com; p. 267: ©wargunner / Shutterstock.com; p. 273: ©gnoparus / Shutterstock.com; p. 281: Courtesy of The Maritime Museum of Tasmania; p. 283: ©TK Kurikawa / Shutterstock.com; p. 285: ©Kummeleon / Shutterstock.com.

Map List

Frommer's EasyGuide to Australia 2018, 5th Edition

Published by
FROMMER MEDIA LLC

ISBN 978-1-62887-346-7 (paper), 978-1-62887-347-4 (e-book)

Editorial Director: Pauline Frommer
Developmental Editor: Lorraine Festa
Production Editor: Cheryl Lenser
Cartographer: Roberta Stockwell
Photo Editor: Meghan Lamb
Indexer: Cheryl Lenser
Cover Design: Howard Grossman

For information on our other products or services, see www.frommers.com.

Frommer Media LLC also publishes its books in a variety of electronic formats. Some content that appears in print may not be available in electronic formats.

Manufactured in the United States of America

5 4 3 2 1

ABOUT THE AUTHOR

Lee Mylne is an award-winning journalist who has specialized in travel writing for more than two decades. Based in Brisbane, Lee has traveled to almost every corner of Australia and is still enthralled by what she sees. She has written several Frommer's guidebooks, and her work appears regularly in a wide range of Australian consumer and travel trade publications. She is a Life Member and former president of the Australian Society of Travel Writers.

ABOUT THE FROMMER TRAVEL GUIDES

For most of the past 50 years, Frommer's has been the leading series of travel guides in North America, accounting for as many as 24% of all guidebooks sold. I think I know why.

Though we hope our books are entertaining, we nevertheless deal with travel in a serious fashion. Our guidebooks have never looked on such journeys as a mere recreation, but as a far more important human function, a time of learning and introspection, an essential part of a civilized life. We stress the culture, lifestyle, history, and beliefs of the destinations we cover, and urge our readers to seek out people and new ideas as the chief rewards of travel.

We have never shied from controversy. We have, from the beginning, encouraged our authors to be intensely judgmental, critical—both pro and con—in their comments, and wholly independent. Our only clients are our readers, and we have triggered the ire of countless prominent sorts, from a tourist newspaper we called "practically worthless" (it unsuccessfully sued us) to the many rip-offs we've condemned.

And because we believe that travel should be available to everyone regardless of their incomes, we have always been cost-conscious at every level of expenditure. Though we have broadened our recommendations beyond the budget category, we insist that every lodging we include be sensibly priced. We use every form of media to assist our readers, and are particularly proud of our feisty daily website, the award-winning Frommers.com.

I have high hopes for the future of Frommer's. May these guidebooks, in all the years ahead, continue to reflect the joy of travel and the freedom that travel represents. May they always pursue a cost-conscious path, so that people of all incomes can enjoy the rewards of travel. And may they create, for both the traveler and the persons among whom we travel, a community of friends, where all human beings live in harmony and peace.

Arthur Frommer